DATE DUE

Demco, Inc. 38-293

WORKERS OF ALL COUNTRIES, UNITE!

毛澤東

SELECTED WORKS

OF

MAO TSE-TUNG

Volume I

FOREIGN LANGUAGES PRESS
PEKING 1967

First Edition   1965
Second Printing   1967

The present volume is an English translation of the second Chinese edition of the first volume of the *Selected Works of Mao Tse-tung*, published by the People's Publishing House, Peking, in April 1960.

Printed in the People's Republic of China

PUBLICATION NOTE

This edition of the *Selected Works of Mao Tse-tung* includes important articles he wrote in the different periods of the Chinese revolution. A number of Chinese editions of his works have appeared in various places, but none of them had been gone over by the author; their arrangement was haphazard, there were errors in the text, and certain important writings were omitted. The contents of the present edition are arranged in chronological order and according to the main periods in the history of the Communist Party of China since its foundation in 1921. The present edition includes a number of important writings not included in the earlier editions. The author has read all the articles, made certain verbal changes and, in isolated cases, revised the text.

The following points need to be made clear in connection with the publication:

1. The present selection remains incomplete. As revolutionary records were destroyed by the Kuomintang reactionaries or dispersed and lost over the long years of war, we cannot collect all the writings of Comrade Mao Tse-tung, and particularly his numerous letters and telegrams which form a considerable part of his writings.

2. Some articles which have been widely circulated (*e.g.*, *Rural Surveys*) were omitted in compliance with the author's wishes, and for the same reason only Chapter 1 of *Economic and Financial Problems* ("A Basic Summing-Up of Our Past Work") was included.

3. Explanatory notes are added to this selection. Some explaining the titles are placed at the bottom of the first page of each article, while the rest, political or otherwise, come at the end of each article.

4. The present Chinese edition is available in a single volume or in a set of four volumes. The first volume of the set covers the periods of the First Revolutionary Civil War (1924-27) and of the

5

Second Revolutionary Civil War (1927-37); the second and third volumes cover the period of the War of Resistance Against Japan (1937-45); and the fourth volume covers that of the Third Revolutionary Civil War (1945-49).

Committee for the Publication of the Selected Works of Mao Tse-tung, Central Committee of the Communist Party of China

August 25, 1951

CONTENTS

THE FIRST REVOLUTIONARY CIVIL WAR PERIOD

THE SECOND REVOLUTIONARY CIVIL WAR PERIOD

THE FIRST
REVOLUTIONARY CIVIL WAR
PERIOD

ANALYSIS OF THE CLASSES
IN CHINESE SOCIETY

March 1926

Who are our enemies? Who are our friends? This is a question of the first importance for the revolution. The basic reason why all previous revolutionary struggles in China achieved so little was their failure to unite with real friends in order to attack real enemies. A revolutionary party is the guide of the masses, and no revolution ever succeeds when the revolutionary party leads them astray. To ensure that we will definitely achieve success in our revolution and will not lead the masses astray, we must pay attention to uniting with our real friends in order to attack our real enemies. To distinguish real friends from real enemies, we must make a general analysis of the economic status of the various classes in Chinese society and of their respective attitudes towards the revolution.

What is the condition of each of the classes in Chinese society?

The landlord class and the comprador class.[1] In economically backward and semi-colonial China the landlord class and the comprador class are wholly appendages of the international bourgeoisie, depending upon imperialism for their survival and growth. These classes represent the most backward and most reactionary relations of production in China and hinder the development of her productive forces. Their existence is utterly incompatible with the aims of the Chinese revolution. The big landlord and big comprador classes in particular always side with imperialism and constitute an extreme counter-

This article was written by Comrade Mao Tse-tung to combat two deviations then to be found in the Party. The exponents of the first deviation, represented by Chen Tu-hsiu, were concerned only with co-operation with the Kuomintang and forgot about the peasants; this was Right opportunism. The exponents of the second deviation, represented by Chang Kuo-tao, were concerned only with the labour movement, and likewise forgot about the peasants; this was "Left" opportunism. Both were aware that their own strength was inadequate, but

13

revolutionary group. Their political representatives are the *Étatistes*[2] and the right-wing of the Kuomintang.

The middle bourgeoisie. This class represents the capitalist relations of production in China in town and country. The middle bourgeoisie, by which is meant chiefly the national bourgeoisie,[3] is inconsistent in its attitude towards the Chinese revolution: they feel the need for revolution and favour the revolutionary movement against imperialism and the warlords when they are smarting under the blows of foreign capital and the oppression of the warlords, but they become suspicious of the revolution when they sense that, with the militant participation of the proletariat at home and the active support of the international proletariat abroad, the revolution is threatening the hope of their class to attain the status of a big bourgeoisie. Politically, they stand for the establishment of a state under the rule of a single class, the national bourgeoisie. A self-styled true disciple of Tai Chi-tao[4] wrote in the *Chen Pao*,[5] Peking, "Raise your left fist to knock down the imperialists and your right to knock down the Communists." These words depict the dilemma and anxiety of this class. It is against interpreting the Kuomintang's Principle of the People's Livelihood according to the theory of class struggle, and it opposes the Kuomintang's alliance with Russia and the admission of Communists[6] and left-wingers. But its attempt to establish a state under the rule of the national bourgeoisie is quite impracticable, because the present world situation is such that the two major forces, revolution and counter-revolution, are locked in final struggle. Each has hoisted a huge banner: one is the red banner of revolution held aloft by the Third International as the rallying point for all the oppressed classes of the world, the other is the white banner of counter-revolution held aloft by the League of Nations as the rallying point for all the counter-revolutionaries of the world. The intermediate classes are bound to disintegrate quickly, some sections turning left to join the revolution, others turning right to join the counter-revolution; there is no room for them to remain "independent". Therefore

neither of them knew where to seek reinforcements or where to obtain allies on a mass scale. Comrade Mao Tse-tung pointed out that the peasantry was the staunchest and numerically the largest ally of the Chinese proletariat, and thus solved the problem of who was the chief ally in the Chinese revolution. Moreover, he saw that the national bourgeoisie was a vacillating class and predicted that it would disintegrate during the upsurge of the revolution, with its right-wing going over to the side of imperialism. This was borne out by the events of 1927.

the idea cherished by China's middle bourgeoisie of an "independent" revolution in which it would play the primary role is a mere illusion.

The petty bourgeoisie. Included in this category are the owner-peasants,[7] the master handicraftsmen, the lower levels of the intellectuals — students, primary and secondary school teachers, lower government functionaries, office clerks, small lawyers — and the small traders. Both because of its size and class character, this class deserves very close attention. The owner-peasants and the master handicraftsmen are both engaged in small-scale production. Although all strata of this class have the same petty-bourgeois economic status, they fall into three different sections. The first section consists of those who have some surplus money or grain, that is, those who, by manual or mental labour, earn more each year than they consume for their own support. Such people very much want to get rich and are devout worshippers of Marshal Chao;[8] while they have no illusions about amassing great fortunes, they invariably desire to climb up into the middle bourgeoisie. Their mouths water copiously when they see the respect in which those small moneybags are held. People of this sort are timid, afraid of government officials, and also a little afraid of the revolution. Since they are quite close to the middle bourgeoisie in economic status, they have a lot of faith in its propaganda and are suspicious of the revolution. This section is a minority among the petty bourgeoisie and constitutes its right-wing. The second section consists of those who in the main are economically self-supporting. They are quite different from the people in the first section; they also want to get rich, but Marshal Chao never lets them. In recent years, moreover, suffering from the oppression and exploitation of the imperialists, the warlords, the feudal landlords and the big comprador-bourgeoisie, they have become aware that the world is no longer what it was. They feel they cannot earn enough to live on by just putting in as much work as before. To make both ends meet they have to work longer hours, get up earlier, leave off later, and be doubly careful at their work. They become rather abusive, denouncing the foreigners as "foreign devils", the warlords as "robber generals" and the local tyrants and evil gentry as "the heartless rich". As for the movement against the imperialists and the warlords, they merely doubt whether it can succeed (on the ground that the foreigners and the warlords seem so powerful), hesitate to join it and prefer to be neutral, but they never oppose the revolution. This section is very numerous, making up about one-half of the petty bourgeoisie.

The third section consists of those whose standard of living is falling. Many in this section, who originally belonged to better-off families, are undergoing a gradual change from a position of being barely able to manage to one of living in more and more reduced circumstances. When they come to settle their accounts at the end of each year, they are shocked, exclaiming, "What? Another deficit!" As such people have seen better days and are now going downhill with every passing year, their debts mounting and their life becoming more and more miserable, they "shudder at the thought of the future". They are in great mental distress because there is such a contrast between their past and their present. Such people are quite important for the revolutionary movement; they form a mass of no small proportions and are the left-wing of the petty bourgeoisie. In normal times these three sections of the petty bourgeoisie differ in their attitude to the revolution. But in times of war, that is, when the tide of the revolution runs high and the dawn of victory is in sight, not only will the left-wing of the petty bourgeoisie join the revolution, but the middle section too may join, and even right-wingers, swept forward by the great revolutionary tide of the proletariat and of the left-wing of the petty bourgeoisie, will have to go along with the revolution. We can see from the experience of the May 30th Movement[9] of 1925 and the peasant movement in various places that this conclusion is correct.

The semi-proletariat. What is here called the semi-proletariat consists of five categories: (1) the overwhelming majority of the semi-owner peasants,[10] (2) the poor peasants, (3) the small handicraftsmen, (4) the shop assistants,[11] and (5) the pedlars. The overwhelming majority of the semi-owner peasants together with the poor peasants constitute a very large part of the rural masses. The peasant problem is essentially their problem. The semi-owner peasants, the poor peasants and the small handicraftsmen are engaged in production on a still smaller scale than the owner-peasants and the master handicraftsmen. Although both the overwhelming majority of the semi-owner peasants and the poor peasants belong to the semi-proletariat, they may be further divided into three smaller categories, upper, middle and lower, according to their economic condition. The semi-owner peasants are worse off than the owner-peasants because every year they are short of about half the food they need, and have to make up this deficit by renting land from others, selling part of their labour power, or engaging in petty trading. In late spring and early summer when the crop is still in the blade and the old stock is consumed, they borrow at exorbitant rates of interest and buy grain at high prices; their plight is naturally harder than that of the owner-peasants who need no help from others, but they are better off than the poor peasants. For the poor peasants own no land, and receive only half the harvest or even less for their year's toil, while the semi-owner peasants, though receiving only half or less than half the harvest of land rented from others, can keep the entire crop from the land they own. The semi-owner peasants are therefore more revolutionary than the owner-peasants, but less revolutionary than the poor peasants. The poor peasants are tenant-peasants who are exploited by the land-lords. They may again be divided into two categories according to their economic status. One category has comparatively adequate farm implements and some funds. Such peasants may retain half the product of their year's toil. To make up their deficit they cultivate side-crops, catch fish or shrimps, raise poultry or pigs, or sell part of their labour power, and thus eke out a living, hoping in the midst of hardship and destitution to tide over the year. Thus their life is harder than that of the semi-owner peasants, but they are better off than the other category of poor peasants. They are more revolutionary than the semi-owner peasants, but less revolutionary than the other category of poor peasants. As for the latter, they have neither adequate farm implements nor funds nor enough manure, their crops are poor, and, with little left after paying rent, they have even greater need to sell part of their labour power. In hard times they piteously beg help from relatives and friends, borrowing a few *tou* or *sheng* of grain to last them a few days, and their debts pile up like loads on the backs of oxen. They are the worst off among the peasants and are highly receptive to revolutionary propaganda. The small handicraftsmen are called semi-proletarians because, though they own some simple means of production and moreover are self-employed, they too are often forced to sell part of their labour power and are somewhat similar to the poor peasants in economic status. They feel the constant pinch of poverty and dread of unemployment, because of heavy family burdens and the gap between their earnings and the cost of living; in this respect too they largely resemble the poor peasants. The shop assistants are employees of shops and stores, supporting their families on meagre pay and getting an increase perhaps only once in several years while prices rise every year. If by chance you get into intimate conversation with them, they invariably pour out their endless grievances. Roughly the same in status as the poor peasants and the small handicraftsmen, they are highly receptive to revolutionary propaganda. The pedlars, whether they carry their wares around on a pole or set up stalls along the street, have tiny funds and very small earnings, and do not make enough to feed and clothe themselves. Their status is roughly the same as that of the poor peasants, and like the poor peasants they need a revolution to change the existing state of affairs.

The proletariat. The modern industrial proletariat numbers about two million. It is not large because China is economically backward. These two million industrial workers are mainly employed in five industries — railways, mining, maritime transport, textiles and ship-building — and a great number are enslaved in enterprises owned by foreign capitalists. Though not very numerous, the industrial prole-tariat represents China's new productive forces, is the most progres-sive class in modern China and has become the leading force in the revolutionary movement. We can see the important position of the industrial proletariat in the Chinese revolution from the strength it has displayed in the strikes of the last four years, such as the seamen's strikes,[12] the railway strike,[13] the strikes in the Kailan and Tsiaotso coal mines,[14] the Shameen strike[15] and the general strikes in Shanghai and Hongkong[16] after the May 30th Incident. The first reason why the industrial workers hold this position is their concentration. No other section of the people is so concentrated. The second reason is their low economic status. They have been deprived of all means of production, have nothing left but their hands, have no hope of ever becoming rich and, moreover, are subjected to the most ruthless treat-ment by the imperialists, the warlords and the bourgeoisie. That is why they are particularly good fighters. The coolies in the cities are also a force meriting attention. They are mostly dockers and rick-shawmen, and among them, too, are sewage carters and street cleaners. Possessing nothing but their hands, they are similar in economic status to the industrial workers but are less concentrated and play a less important role in production. There is as yet little modern capitalist farming in China. By rural proletariat we mean farm labourers hired by the year, the month or the day. Having neither land, farm imple-ments nor funds, they can live only by selling their labour power. Of all the workers they work the longest hours, for the lowest wages, under the worst conditions, and with the least security of employment. They are the most hard-pressed people in the villages, and their position in the peasant movement is as important as that of the poor peasants.

Apart from all these, there is the fairly large *lumpen*-proletariat, made up of peasants who have lost their land and handicraftsmen who cannot get work. They lead the most precarious existence of all. In every part of the country they have their secret societies, which were originally their mutual-aid organizations for political and economic struggle, for instance, the Triad Society in Fukien and Kwangtung, the Society of Brothers in Hunan, Hupeh, Kweichow and Szechuan, the Big Sword Society in Anhwei, Honan and Shantung, the Rational Life Society in Chihli[17] and the three northeastern provinces, and the Green Band in Shanghai and elsewhere.[18] One of China's difficult problems is how to handle these people. Brave fighters but apt to be destructive, they can become a revolutionary force if given proper guidance.

To sum up, it can be seen that our enemies are all those in league with imperialism — the warlords, the bureaucrats, the comprador class, the big landlord class and the reactionary section of the intelligentsia attached to them. The leading force in our revolution is the industrial proletariat. Our closest friends are the entire semi-proletariat and petty bourgeoisie. As for the vacillating middle bourgeoisie, their right-wing may become our enemy and their left-wing may become our friend — but we must be constantly on our guard and not let them create confusion within our ranks.

NOTES

[1] A comprador, in the original sense of the word, was the Chinese manager or the senior Chinese employee in a foreign commercial establishment. The compradors served foreign economic interests and had close connection with imperialism and foreign capital.

[2] The *Étatistes* were a handful of shameless fascist politicians who at that time formed the Chinese *Étatiste* Youth League, later renamed the Chinese Youth Party. They made counter-revolutionary careers for themselves by opposing the Communist Party and the Soviet Union and received subsidies from the various groups of reactionaries in power and from the imperialists.

[3] For further discussion of the role of the national bourgeoisie, see "The Chinese Revolution and the Chinese Communist Party", Chapter 2, Section 4, *Selected Works of Mao Tse-tung*, Vol. II.

[4] Tai Chi-tao joined the Kuomintang in his youth and for a time was Chiang Kai-shek's partner in stock exchange speculation. After Sun Yat-sen's death in 1925 he carried on anti-Communist agitation and prepared the ground ideologically for

Chiang Kai-shek's counter-revolutionary coup d'état in 1927. For years he was a faithful running dog to Chiang Kai-shek in the counter-revolution. He committed suicide in February 1949, driven to despair by the imminent doom of Chiang Kai-shek's regime.

[5] The *Chen Pao* was the organ of the Association for the Study of Constitutional Government, a political group which supported the rule of the Northern warlords.

[6] In 1923 Sun Yat-sen, with the help of the Chinese Communist Party, decided to reorganize the Kuomintang, bring about Kuomintang-Communist co-operation and admit members of the Communist Party into the Kuomintang. In January 1924, he convened in Canton the Kuomintang's First National Congress at which he laid down the Three Great Policies — alliance with Russia, co-operation with the Communist Party and assistance to the peasants and workers. Mao Tse-tung, Li Ta-chao, Lin Po-chu, Chu Chiu-pai and other comrades attended the Congress and played an important part in helping the Kuomintang to take the road of revolution. Some of these comrades were elected members, and others alternate members, of the Central Executive Committee of the Kuomintang.

[7] By owner-peasants Comrade Mao Tse-tung means the middle peasants.

[8] Marshal Chao is Chao Kung-ming, God of Wealth in Chinese folklore.

[9] The May 30th Movement was the nation-wide anti-imperialist movement in protest against the massacre of the Chinese people by the British police in Shanghai on May 30, 1925. Earlier that month, major strikes had broken out in Japanese-owned textile mills in Tsingtao and Shanghai, which the Japanese imperialists and the Northern warlords who were their running dogs proceeded to suppress. On May 15 the Japanese textile mill-owners in Shanghai shot and killed the worker Ku Cheng-hung and wounded a dozen others. On May 28 eight workers were slaughtered by the reactionary government in Tsingtao. On May 30 more than two thousand students in Shanghai agitated in the foreign concessions in support of the workers and for the recovery of the foreign concessions. They rallied more than ten thousand people before the British police headquarters, shouting such slogans as "Down with imperialism!" and "People of China, unite!" The British imperialist police opened fire, killing and wounding many students. This became known as the May 30th Massacre. It immediately aroused country-wide indignation, and demonstrations and strikes of workers, students and shopkeepers were held everywhere, forming a tremendous anti-imperialist movement.

[10] By "the overwhelming majority of the semi-owner peasants", Comrade Mao Tse-tung is here referring to the impoverished peasants who worked partly on their own land and partly on land rented from others.

[11] There were several strata of shop assistants in old China. Here Comrade Mao Tse-tung is referring to the largest. There was also the lower stratum of shop assistants who led the life of proletarians.

[12] The seamen's strikes were staged by the seamen at Hongkong and by the crews of the Yangtse River steamers early in 1922. The Hongkong seamen held out for eight weeks. After a bitter and bloody struggle, the British imperialist authorities in Hongkong were finally forced to raise wages, lift the ban on the Seamen's Union, release the arrested workers and indemnify the families of the martyrs. The crews of the Yangtse steamers went on strike soon afterwards, carried on the struggle for two weeks and also won victory.

[13] Immediately after its founding in 1921, the Chinese Communist Party set about organizing the railway workers. In 1922-23 strikes took place under the Party's leadership on all the trunk lines. The best known was the general strike on the Peking-Hankow Railway which began on February 4, 1923. It was a fight for the freedom to organize a general trade union. On February 7 the Northern warlords Wu Pei-fu and Hsiao Yao-nan, who were backed by British imperialism, butchered the strikers. This became known as the February 7th Massacre.

[14] The Kailan Coal Mines was an inclusive name for the large contiguous Kaiping and Luanchow coalfields in Hopei Province, then employing over fifty thousand workers. During the Yi Ho Tuan Movement of 1900 the British imperialists seized the Kaiping mines. Subsequently the Chinese organized the Luanchow Coal Mining Company, which was later incorporated into the Kailan Mining Administration. Both coalfields thus came under the exclusive control of British imperialism. The Kailan strike took place in October 1922. The Tsiaotso Coal Mines, situated in Honan Province, are also well known in China. The Tsiaotso strike lasted from July 1 to August 9, 1925.

[15] Shameen, a section of the city of Canton, was held on lease by British imperialism. In July 1924 the British imperialists who ruled it issued a new police regulation requiring all Chinese to produce passes with photos on leaving or entering the area. But foreigners were exempt. On July 15 the workers in Shameen went on strike to protest against this preposterous measure, which the British imperialists were finally forced to cancel.

[16] Following the May 30th Incident in Shanghai, general strikes broke out on June 1, 1925 in Shanghai and on June 19 in Hongkong. More than 200,000 workers took part in Shanghai and 250,000 in Hongkong. The big Hongkong strike, with the support of the people throughout the country, lasted sixteen months. It was the longest strike in the history of the world labour movement.

[17] Chihli was the old name for Hopei Province.

[18] The Triad Society, the Society of Brothers, the Big Sword Society, the Rational Life Society and the Green Band were primitive secret organizations among the people. The members were mainly bankrupt peasants, unemployed handicraftsmen and other *lumpen*-proletarians. In feudal China these elements were often drawn together by some religion or superstition to form organizations of a patriarchal pattern and bearing different names, and some possessed arms. Through these organizations the *lumpen*-proletarians sought to help each other socially and economically, and sometimes fought the bureaucrats and landlords who oppressed them. Of course, such backward organizations could not provide a way out for the peasants and handicraftsmen. Furthermore, they could easily be controlled and utilized by the landlords and local tyrants and, because of this and of their blind destructiveness, some turned into reactionary forces. In his counter-revolutionary coup d'état of 1927, Chiang Kai-shek made use of them to disrupt the unity of the labouring people and destroy the revolution. As the modern industrial proletariat arose and grew from strength to strength, the peasants, under the leadership of the working class, gradually formed themselves into organizations of an entirely new type, and these primitive, backward societies lost their *raison d'être*.

REPORT ON AN INVESTIGATION OF THE PEASANT MOVEMENT IN HUNAN

March 1927

THE IMPORTANCE OF THE PEASANT PROBLEM

During my recent visit to Hunan[1] I made a first-hand investigation of conditions in the five counties of Hsiangtan, Hsianghsiang, Hengshan, Liling and Changsha. In the thirty-two days from January 4 to February 5, I called together fact-finding conferences in villages and county towns, which were attended by experienced peasants and by comrades working in the peasant movement, and I listened attentively to their reports and collected a great deal of material. Many of the hows and whys of the peasant movement were the exact opposite of what the gentry in Hankow and Changsha are saying. I saw and heard of many strange things of which I had hitherto been unaware. I believe the same is true of many other places, too. All talk directed against the peasant movement must be speedily set right. All the wrong measures taken by the revolutionary authorities concerning the peasant movement must be speedily changed. Only thus can the future of the revolution be benefited. For the present upsurge of the peasant movement is a colossal event. In a very short time, in China's central, southern and northern provinces, several hundred million peasants will rise like a mighty storm, like a hurricane, a force so swift and violent that no power, however great, will be able to hold it back. They will smash all the trammels that

This article was written as a reply to the carping criticisms both inside and outside the Party then being levelled at the peasants' revolutionary struggle. Comrade Mao Tse-tung spent thirty-two days in Hunan Province making an investigation and wrote this report in order to answer these criticisms. The Right opportunists in the Party, headed by Chen Tu-hsiu, would not accept his views and stuck to their own wrong ideas. Their chief error was that, frightened by the reactionary trend in the Kuomintang, they dared not support the great revolutionary struggles bind them and rush forward along the road to liberation. They will sweep all the imperialists, warlords, corrupt officials, local tyrants and evil gentry into their graves. Every revolutionary party and every revolutionary comrade will be put to the test, to be accepted or rejected as they decide. There are three alternatives. To march at their head and lead them? To trail behind them, gesticulating and criticizing? Or to stand in their way and oppose them? Every Chinese is free to choose, but events will force you to make the choice quickly.

GET ORGANIZED!

The development of the peasant movement in Hunan may be divided roughly into two periods with respect to the counties in the province's central and southern parts where the movement has already made much headway. The first, from January to September of last year, was one of organization. In this period, January to June was a time of underground activity, and July to September, when the revolutionary army was driving out Chao Heng-ti,[2] one of open activity. During this period, the membership of the peasant associations did not exceed 300,000-400,000, the masses directly under their leadership numbered little more than a million, there was as yet hardly any struggle in the rural areas, and consequently there was very little criticism of the associations in other circles. Since its members served as guides, scouts and carriers of the Northern Expeditionary Army, even some of the officers had a good word to say for the peasant associations. The second period, from last October to January of this year, was one of revolutionary action. The membership of the associations jumped to two million and the masses directly under their leadership increased to ten million. Since the peasants generally enter only one name for the whole family on joining a peasant association, a membership of two million means a mass following of about ten million. Almost half the peasants in Hunan are now organized. In counties like Hsiangtan, Hsianghsiang, Liuyang, Changsha, Liling,

of the peasants which had erupted or were erupting. To appease the Kuomintang, they preferred to desert the peasantry, the chief ally in the revolution, and thus left the working class and the Communist Party isolated and without help. It was mainly because it was able to exploit this weakness within the Communist Party that the Kuomintang dared to betray the revolution, launch its "party purge" and make war on the people in the summer of 1927.

Ninghsiang, Pingkiang, Hsiangyin, Hengshan, Hengyang, Leiyang, Chenhsien and Anhua, nearly all the peasants have combined in the peasant associations or have come under their leadership. It was on the strength of their extensive organization that the peasants went into action and within four months brought about a great revolution in the countryside, a revolution without parallel in history.

DOWN WITH THE LOCAL TYRANTS AND EVIL GENTRY! ALL POWER TO THE PEASANT ASSOCIATIONS!

The main targets of attack by the peasants are the local tyrants, the evil gentry and the lawless landlords, but in passing they also hit out against patriarchal ideas and institutions, against the corrupt officials in the cities and against bad practices and customs in the rural areas. In force and momentum the attack is tempestuous; those who bow before it survive and those who resist perish. As a result, the privileges which the feudal landlords enjoyed for thousands of years are being shattered to pieces. Every bit of the dignity and prestige built up by the landlords is being swept into the dust. With the collapse of the power of the landlords, the peasant associations have now become the sole organs of authority and the popular slogan "All power to the peasant associations" has become a reality. Even trifles such as a quarrel between husband and wife are brought to the peasant association. Nothing can be settled unless someone from the peasant association is present. The association actually dictates all rural affairs, and, quite literally, "whatever it says, goes". Those who are outside the associations can only speak well of them and cannot say anything against them. The local tyrants, evil gentry and lawless landlords have been deprived of all right to speak, and none of them dares even mutter dissent. In the face of the peasant associations' power and pressure, the top local tyrants and evil gentry have fled to Shanghai, those of the second rank to Hankow, those of the third to Changsha and those of the fourth to the county towns, while the fifth rank and the still lesser fry surrender to the peasant associations in the villages.

"Here's ten yuan. Please let me join the peasant association," one of the smaller of the evil gentry will say.

"Ugh! Who wants your filthy money?" the peasants reply.

Many middle and small landlords and rich peasants and even some middle peasants, who were all formerly opposed to the peasant associations, are now vainly seeking admission. Visiting various places, I often came across such people who pleaded with me, "Mr. Committeeman from the provincial capital, please be my sponsor!"

In the Ching Dynasty, the household census compiled by the local authorities consisted of a regular register and "the other" register, the former for honest people and the latter for burglars, bandits and similar undesirables. In some places the peasants now use this method to scare those who formerly opposed the associations. They say, "Put their names down in the other register!"

Afraid of being entered in the other register, such people try various devices to gain admission into the peasant associations, on which their minds are so set that they do not feel safe until their names are entered. But more often than not they are turned down flat, and so they are always on tenterhooks; with the doors of the association barred to them, they are like tramps without a home or, in rural parlance, "mere trash". In short, what was looked down upon four months ago as a "gang of peasants" has now become a most honourable institution. Those who formerly prostrated themselves before the power of the gentry now bow before the power of the peasants. No matter what their identity, all admit that the world since last October is a different one.

"IT'S TERRIBLE!" OR "IT'S FINE!"

The peasants' revolt disturbed the gentry's sweet dreams. When the news from the countryside reached the cities, it caused immediate uproar among the gentry. Soon after my arrival in Changsha, I met all sorts of people and picked up a good deal of gossip. From the middle social strata upwards to the Kuomintang right-wingers, there was not a single person who did not sum up the whole business in the phrase, "It's terrible!" Under the impact of the views of the "It's terrible!" school then flooding the city, even quite revolutionary-minded people became down-hearted as they pictured the events in the countryside in their mind's eye; and they were unable to deny the word "terrible". Even quite progressive people said, "Though terrible, it is inevitable in a revolution." In short, nobody could altogether deny the word "terrible". But, as already mentioned, the fact is that the great peasant masses have risen to fulfil their historic mission and that the forces of rural democracy have risen to overthrow the forces of rural feudalism. The patriarchal-feudal class of local tyrants, evil gentry and lawless landlords has formed the basis of autocratic government for thousands of years and is the cornerstone of imperialism, warlordism and corrupt officialdom. To overthrow these feudal forces is the real objective of the national revolution. In a few months the peasants have accomplished what Dr. Sun Yat-sen wanted, but failed, to accomplish in the forty years he devoted to the national revolution. This is a marvellous feat never before achieved, not just in forty, but in thousands of years. It's fine. It is not "terrible" at all. It is anything but "terrible". "It's terrible!" is obviously a theory for combating the rise of the peasants in the interests of the landlords; it is obviously a theory of the landlord class for preserving the old order of feudalism and obstructing the establishment of the new order of democracy, it is obviously a counter-revolutionary theory. No revolutionary comrade should echo this nonsense. If your revolutionary viewpoint is firmly established and if you have been to the villages and looked around, you will undoubtedly feel thrilled as never before. Countless thousands of the enslaved — the peasants — are striking down the enemies who battened on their flesh. What the peasants are doing is absolutely right; what they are doing is fine! "It's fine!" is the theory of the peasants and of all other revolutionaries. Every revolutionary comrade should know that the national revolution requires a great change in the countryside. The Revolution of 1911[3] did not bring about this change, hence its failure. This change is now taking place, and it is an important factor for the completion of the revolution. Every revolutionary comrade must support it, or he will be taking the stand of counter-revolution.

THE QUESTION OF "GOING TOO FAR"

Then there is another section of people who say, "Yes, peasant associations are necessary, but they are going rather too far." This is the opinion of the middle-of-the-roaders. But what is the actual situation? True, the peasants are in a sense "unruly" in the country-

side. Supreme in authority, the peasant association allows the landlord
no say and sweeps away his prestige. This amounts to striking the
landlord down to the dust and keeping him there. The peasants
threaten, "We will put you in the other register!" They fine the local
tyrants and evil gentry, they demand contributions from them, and
they smash their sedan-chairs. People swarm into the houses of local
tyrants and evil gentry who are against the peasant association,
slaughter their pigs and consume their grain. They even loll for a
minute or two on the ivory-inlaid beds belonging to the young ladies
in the households of the local tyrants and evil gentry. At the slightest
provocation they make arrests, crown the arrested with tall paper-
hats, and parade them through the villages, saying, "You dirty landlords, now you know who we are!" Doing whatever they like and
turning everything upside down, they have created a kind of terror
in the countryside. This is what some people call "going too far", or
"exceeding the proper limits in righting a wrong", or "really too
much". Such talk may seem plausible, but in fact it is wrong. First,
the local tyrants, evil gentry and lawless landlords have themselves
driven the peasants to this. For ages they have used their power to
tyrannize over the peasants and trample them underfoot; that is why
the peasants have reacted so strongly. The most violent revolts and
the most serious disorders have invariably occurred in places where
the local tyrants, evil gentry and lawless landlords perpetrated the
worst outrages. The peasants are clear-sighted. Who is bad and who
is not, who is the worst and who is not quite so vicious, who deserves
severe punishment and who deserves to be let off lightly — the
peasants keep clear accounts, and very seldom has the punishment
exceeded the crime. Secondly, a revolution is not a dinner party, or
writing an essay, or painting a picture, or doing embroidery; it cannot
be so refined, so leisurely and gentle, so temperate, kind, courteous,
restrained and magnanimous.[4] A revolution is an insurrection, an act
of violence by which one class overthrows another. A rural revolution
is a revolution by which the peasantry overthrows the power of the
feudal landlord class. Without using the greatest force, the peasants
cannot possibly overthrow the deep-rooted authority of the landlords
which has lasted for thousands of years. The rural areas need a mighty
revolutionary upsurge, for it alone can rouse the people in their millions
to become a powerful force. All the actions mentioned here which
have been labelled as "going too far" flow from the power of the
peasants, which has been called forth by the mighty revolutionary

upsurge in the countryside. It was highly necessary for such things to be done in the second period of the peasant movement, the period of revolutionary action. In this period it was necessary to establish the absolute authority of the peasants. It was necessary to forbid malicious criticism of the peasant associations. It was necessary to overthrow the whole authority of the gentry, to strike them to the ground and keep them there. There is revolutionary significance in all the actions which were labelled as "going too far" in this period. To put it bluntly, it is necessary to create terror for a while in every rural area, or otherwise it would be impossible to suppress the activities of the counter-revolutionaries in the countryside or overthrow the authority of the gentry. Proper limits have to be exceeded in order to right a wrong, or else the wrong cannot be righted.[5] Those who talk about the peasants "going too far" seem at first sight to be different from those who say "It's terrible!" as mentioned earlier, but in essence they proceed from the same standpoint and likewise voice a landlord theory that upholds the interests of the privileged classes. Since this theory impedes the rise of the peasant movement and so disrupts the revolution, we must firmly oppose it.

THE "MOVEMENT OF THE RIFFRAFF"

The right-wing of the Kuomintang says, "The peasant movement is a movement of the riffraff, of the lazy peasants." This view is current in Changsha. When I was in the countryside, I heard the gentry say, "It is all right to set up peasant associations, but the people now running them are no good. They ought to be replaced!" This opinion comes to the same thing as what the right-wingers are saying; according to both it is all right to have a peasant movement (the movement is already in being and no one dare say otherwise), but they say that the people running it are no good and they particularly hate those in charge of the associations at the lower levels, calling them "riffraff". In short, all those whom the gentry had despised, those whom they had trodden into the dirt, people with no place in society, people with no right to speak, have now audaciously lifted up their heads. They have not only lifted up their heads but taken power into their hands. They are now running the township peasant associations (at the lowest level), which they have turned into something fierce and formidable. They have raised their rough, work-soiled hands and laid them on the gentry. They tether the evil gentry with ropes, crown them with tall paper-hats and parade them through the villages. (In Hsiangtan and Hsianghsiang they call this "parading through the township" and in Liling "parading through the fields".) Not a day passes but they drum some harsh, pitiless words of denunciation into these gentry's ears. They are issuing orders and are running everything. Those who used to rank lowest now rank above everybody else; and so this is called "turning things upside down".

VANGUARDS OF THE REVOLUTION

Where there are two opposite approaches to things and people, two opposite views emerge. "It's terrible!" and "It's fine!", "riffraff" and "vanguards of the revolution" — here are apt examples.

We said above that the peasants have accomplished a revolutionary task which had been left unaccomplished for many years and have done an important job for the national revolution. But has this great revolutionary task, this important revolutionary work, been performed by all the peasants? No. There are three kinds of peasants, the rich, the middle and the poor peasants. The three live in different circumstances and so have different views about the revolution. In the first period, what appealed to the rich peasants was the talk about the Northern Expeditionary Army's sustaining a crushing defeat in Kiangsi, about Chiang Kai-shek's being wounded in the leg[6] and flying back to Kwangtung,[7] and about Wu Pei-fu's[8] recapturing Yuehchow. The peasant associations would certainly not last and the Three People's Principles[9] could never prevail, because they had never been heard of before. Thus an official of the township peasant association (generally one of the "riffraff" type) would walk into the house of a rich peasant, register in hand, and say, "Will you please join the peasant association?" How would the rich peasant answer? A tolerably well-behaved one would say, "Peasant association? I have lived here for decades, tilling my land. I never heard of such a thing before, yet I've managed to live all right. I advise you to give it up!" A really vicious rich peasant would say, "Peasant association! Nonsense! Association for getting your head chopped off! Don't get people into trouble!" Yet, surprisingly enough, the peasant associations have now been established several months, and have even dared to stand up to the gentry. The gentry of the neighbourhood who refused to surrender their opium pipes were arrested by the associations and paraded through the villages. In the county towns, moreover, some big landlords were put to death, like Yen Jung-chiu of Hsiangtan and Yang Chih-tse of Ninghsiang. On the anniversary of the October Revolution, at the time of the anti-British rally and of the great celebrations of the victory of the Northern Expedition, tens of thousands of peasants in every township, holding high their banners, big and small, along with their carrying-poles and hoes, demonstrated in massive, streaming columns. It was only then that the rich peasants began to get perplexed and alarmed. During the great victory celebrations of the Northern Expedition, they learned that Kiukiang had been taken, that Chiang Kai-shek had not been wounded in the leg and that Wu Pei-fu had been defeated after all. What is more, they saw such slogans as "Long live the Three People's Principles!" "Long live the peasant associations!" and "Long live the peasants!" clearly written on the "red and green proclamations". "What?" wondered the rich peasants, greatly perplexed and alarmed, " 'Long live the peasants!' Are these people now to be regarded as emperors[10]?" So the peasant associations are putting on grand airs. People from the associations say to the rich peasants, "We'll enter you in the other register," or, "In another month, the admission fee will be ten yuan a head!" Only under the impact of all this are the rich peasants tardily joining the associations,[11] some paying fifty cents or a yuan for admission (the regular fee being a mere ten coppers), some securing admission only after asking other people to put in a good word for them. But there are quite a number of die-hards who have not joined to this day. When the rich peasants join the associations, they generally enter the name of some sixty or seventy year-old member of the family, for they are in constant dread of "conscription". After joining, the rich peasants are not keen on doing any work for the associations. They remain inactive throughout.

How about the middle peasants? Theirs is a vacillating attitude. They think that the revolution will not bring them much good. They have rice cooking in their pots and no creditors knocking on their doors at midnight. They, too, judging a thing by whether it ever existed before, knit their brows and think to themselves, "Can the peasant association really last?" "Can the Three People's Principles prevail?" Their conclusion is, "Afraid not!" They imagine it all de-

pends on the will of Heaven and think, "A peasant association? Who
knows if Heaven wills it or not?" In the first period, people from
the association would call on a middle peasant, register in hand, and
say, "Will you please join the peasant association?" The middle peasant would reply, "There's no hurry!" It was not until the second
period, when the peasant associations were already exercising great
power, that the middle peasants came in. They show up better in
the associations than the rich peasants but are not as yet very enthusiastic; they still want to wait and see. It is essential for the peasant
associations to get the middle peasants to join and to do a good deal
more explanatory work among them.

The poor peasants have always been the main force in the bitter
fight in the countryside. They have fought militantly through the two
periods of underground work and of open activity. They are the most
responsive to Communist Party leadership. They are deadly enemies
of the camp of the local tyrants and evil gentry and attack it without
the slightest hesitation. "We joined the peasant association long ago,"
they say to the rich peasants, "why are you still hesitating?" The rich
peasants answer mockingly, "What is there to keep you from joining?
You people have neither a tile over your heads nor a speck of land
under your feet!" It is true the poor peasants are not afraid of losing
anything. Many of them really have "neither a tile over their heads
nor a speck of land under their feet". What, indeed, is there to keep
them from joining the associations? According to the survey of Changsha County, the poor peasants comprise 70 per cent, the middle peasants 20 per cent, and the landlords and the rich peasants 10 per cent
of the population in the rural areas. The 70 per cent, the poor peasants, may be sub-divided into two categories, the utterly destitute
and the less destitute. The utterly destitute,[12] comprising 20 per cent,
are the completely dispossessed, that is, people who have neither land
nor money, are without any means of livelihood, and are forced to
leave home and become mercenaries or hired labourers or wandering
beggars. The less destitute,[13] the other 50 per cent, are the partially
dispossessed, that is, people with just a little land or a little money
who eat up more than they earn and live in toil and distress the year
round, such as the handicraftsmen, the tenant-peasants (not including
the rich tenant-peasants) and the semi-owner-peasants. This great
mass of poor peasants, or altogether 70 per cent of the rural population,
are the backbone of the peasant associations, the vanguard in the
overthrow of the feudal forces and the heroes who have performed

the great revolutionary task which for long years was left undone. Without the poor peasant class (the "riffraff", as the gentry call them), it would have been impossible to bring about the present revolutionary situation in the countryside, or to overthrow the local tyrants and evil gentry and complete the democratic revolution. The poor peasants, being the most revolutionary group, have gained the leadership of the peasant associations. In both the first and second periods almost all the chairmen and committee members in the peasant associations at the lowest level were poor peasants (of the officials in the township associations in Hengshan County the utterly destitute comprise 50 per cent, the less destitute 40 per cent, and poverty-stricken intellectuals 10 per cent). Leadership by the poor peasants is absolutely necessary. Without the poor peasants there would be no revolution. To deny their role is to deny the revolution. To attack them is to attack the revolution. They have never been wrong on the general direction of the revolution. They have discredited the local tyrants and evil gentry. They have beaten down the local tyrants and evil gentry, big and small, and kept them underfoot. Many of their deeds in the period of revolutionary action, which were labelled as "going too far", were in fact the very things the revolution required. Some county governments, county headquarters of the Kuomintang and county peasant associations in Hunan have already made a number of mistakes; some have even sent soldiers to arrest officials of the lower-level associations at the landlords' request. A good many chairmen and committee members of township associations in Hengshan and Hsianghsiang Counties have been thrown in jail. This mistake is very serious and feeds the arrogance of the reactionaries. To judge whether or not it is a mistake, you have only to see how joyful the lawless landlords become and how reactionary sentiments grow, wherever the chairmen or committee members of local peasant associations are arrested. We must combat the counter-revolutionary talk of a "movement of riffraff" and a "movement of lazy peasants" and must be especially careful not to commit the error of helping the local tyrants and evil gentry in their attacks on the poor peasant class. Though a few of the poor peasant leaders undoubtedly did have shortcomings, most of them have changed by now. They themselves are energetically prohibiting gambling and suppressing banditry. Where the peasant association is powerful, gambling has stopped altogether and banditry has vanished. In some places it is literally true that people do not take any articles left by the wayside and that doors are not bolted at night. According to the Hengshan survey, 85 per cent of the poor peasant leaders have made great progress and have proved themselves capable and hard-working. Only 15 per cent retain some bad habits. The most one can call these is "an unhealthy minority", and we must not echo the local tyrants and evil gentry in undiscriminatingly condemning them as "riffraff". This problem of the "unhealthy minority" can be tackled only under the peasant associations' own slogan of "strengthen discipline", by carrying on propaganda among the masses, by educating the "unhealthy minority", and by tightening the associations' discipline; in no circumstances should soldiers be arbitrarily sent to make such arrests as would damage the prestige of the poor peasants and feed the arrogance of the local tyrants and evil gentry. This point requires particular attention.

FOURTEEN GREAT ACHIEVEMENTS

Most critics of the peasant associations allege that they have done a great many bad things. I have already pointed out that the peasants' attack on the local tyrants and evil gentry is entirely revolutionary behaviour and in no way blameworthy. The peasants have done a great many things, and in order to answer people's criticism we must closely examine all their activities, one by one, to see what they have actually done. I have classified and summed up their activities of the last few months; in all, the peasants under the leadership of the peasant associations have the following fourteen great achievements to their credit.

1. ORGANIZING THE PEASANTS INTO PEASANT ASSOCIATIONS

This is the first great achievement of the peasants. In counties like Hsiangtan, Hsianghsiang and Hengshan, nearly all the peasants are organized and there is hardly a remote corner where they are not on the move; these are the best places. In some counties, like Yiyang and Huajung, the bulk of the peasants are organized, with only a small section remaining unorganized; these places are in the second grade. In other counties, like Chengpu and Lingling, while a small section is organized, the bulk of the peasants remain unorganized; these places are in the third grade. Western Hunan, which is under the control of Yuan Tsu-ming,[14] has not yet been reached by the associations' propaganda, and in many of its counties the peasants are completely unorganized; these form a fourth grade. Roughly speaking, the counties in central Hunan, with Changsha as the centre, are the most advanced, those in southern Hunan come second, and western Hunan is only just beginning to organize. According to the figures compiled by the provincial peasant association last November, organizations with a total membership of 1,367,727 have been set up in thirty-seven of the province's seventy-five counties. Of these members about one million were organized during October and November when the power of the associations rose high, while up to September the membership had only been 300,000-400,000. Then came the two months of December and January, and the peasant movement continued its brisk growth. By the end of January the membership must have reached at least two million. As a family generally enters only one name when joining and has an average of five members, the mass following must be about ten million. This astonishing and accelerating rate of expansion explains why the local tyrants, evil gentry and corrupt officials have been isolated, why the public has been amazed at how completely the world has changed since the peasant movement, and why a great revolution has been wrought in the countryside. This is the first great achievement of the peasants under the leadership of their associations.

2. HITTING THE LANDLORDS POLITICALLY

Once the peasants have their organization, the first thing they do is to smash the political prestige and power of the landlord class, and especially of the local tyrants and evil gentry, that is, to pull down landlord authority and build up peasant authority in rural society. This is a most serious and vital struggle. It is the pivotal struggle in the second period, the period of revolutionary action. Without victory in this struggle, no victory is possible in the economic struggle to reduce rent and interest, to secure land and other means of production, and so on. In many places in Hunan like Hsianghsiang, Hengshan and Hsiangtan Counties, this is of course no problem since the authority of the landlords has been overturned and the peasants constitute the sole authority. But in counties like Liling there are still some places (such as Liling's western and southern districts) where the authority of the landlords seems weaker than that of the peasants but, because the political struggle has not been sharp, is in fact surreptitiously competing with it. In such places it is still too early to say that the peasants have gained political victory; they must wage the political struggle more vigorously until the landlords' authority is completely smashed. All in all, the methods used by the peasants to hit the landlords politically are as follows:

Checking the accounts. More often than not the local tyrants and evil gentry have helped themselves to public money passing through their hands, and their books are not in order. Now the peasants are using the checking of accounts as an occasion to bring down a great many of the local tyrants and evil gentry. In many places committees for checking accounts have been established for the express purpose of settling financial scores with them, and the first sign of such a committee makes them shudder. Campaigns of this kind have been carried out in all the counties where the peasant movement is active; they are important not so much for recovering money as for publicizing the crimes of the local tyrants and evil gentry and for knocking them down from their political and social positions.

Imposing fines. The peasants work out fines for such offences as irregularities revealed by the checking of accounts, past outrages against the peasants, current activities which undermine the peasant associations, violations of the ban on gambling and refusal to surrender opium pipes. This local tyrant must pay so much, that member of the evil gentry so much, the sums ranging from tens to thousands of yuan. Naturally, a man who has been fined by the peasants completely loses face.

Levying contributions. The unscrupulous rich landlords are made to contribute for poor relief, for the organization of co-operatives or peasant credit societies, or for other purposes. Though milder than fines, these contributions are also a form of punishment. To avoid trouble, quite a number of landlords make voluntary contributions to the peasant associations.

Minor protests. When someone harms a peasant association by word or deed and the offence is a minor one, the peasants collect in a crowd and swarm into the offender's house to remonstrate with him. He is usually let off after writing a pledge to "cease and desist", in which he explicitly undertakes to stop defaming the peasant association in the future.

Major demonstrations. A big crowd is rallied to demonstrate against a local tyrant or one of the evil gentry who is an enemy of the association. The demonstrators eat at the offender's house, slaughtering his pigs and consuming his grain as a matter of course. Quite a few such cases have occurred. There was a case recently at Machiaho, Hsiangtan County, where a crowd of fifteen thousand peasants went to the houses of six of the evil gentry and demonstrated; the whole affair lasted four days during which more than 130 pigs were killed and eaten. After such demonstrations, the peasants usually impose fines.

"Crowning" the landlords and parading them through the villages. This sort of thing is very common. A tall paper-hat is stuck on the head of one of the local tyrants or evil gentry, bearing the words "Local tyrant so-and-so" or "So-and-so of the evil gentry". He is led by a rope and escorted with big crowds in front and behind. Sometimes brass gongs are beaten and flags waved to attract people's attention. This form of punishment more than any other makes the local tyrants and evil gentry tremble. Anyone who has once been crowned with a tall paper-hat loses face altogether and can never again hold up his head. Hence many of the rich prefer being fined to wearing the tall hat. But wear it they must, if the peasants insist. One ingenious township peasant association arrested an obnoxious member of the gentry and announced that he was to be crowned that very day. The man turned blue with fear. Then the association decided not to crown him that day. They argued that if he were crowned right away, he would become case-hardened and no longer afraid, and that it would be better to let him go home and crown him some other day. Not knowing when he would be crowned, the man was in daily suspense, unable to sit down or sleep at ease.

Locking up the landlords in the county jail. This is a heavier punishment than wearing the tall paper-hat. A local tyrant or one of the evil gentry is arrested and sent to the county jail; he is locked up and the county magistrate has to try him and punish him. Today the people who are locked up are no longer the same. Formerly it was the gentry who sent peasants to be locked up, now it is the other way round.

"Banishment". The peasants have no desire to banish the most notorious criminals among the local tyrants and evil gentry, but would rather arrest or execute them. Afraid of being arrested or executed, they run away. In counties where the peasant movement is well developed, almost all the important local tyrants and evil gentry have fled, and this amounts to banishment. Among them, the top

ones have fled to Shanghai, those of the second rank to Hankow,
those of the third to Changsha, and of the fourth to the county towns.
Of all the fugitive local tyrants and evil gentry, those who have fled
to Shanghai are the safest. Some of those who fled to Hankow, like
the three from Huajung, were eventually captured and brought back.
Those who fled to Changsha are in still greater danger of being
seized at any moment by students in the provincial capital who hail
from their counties; I myself saw two captured in Changsha. Those
who have taken refuge in the county towns are only of the fourth
rank, and the peasantry, having many eyes and ears, can easily track
them down. The financial authorities once explained the difficulties
encountered by the Hunan Provincial Government in raising money
by the fact that the peasants were banishing the well-to-do, which
gives some idea of the extent to which the local tyrants and evil
gentry are not tolerated in their home villages.

Execution. This is confined to the worst local tyrants and evil
gentry and is carried out by the peasants jointly with other sections
of the people. For instance, Yang Chih-tse of Ninghsiang, Chou
Chia-kan of Yuehyang and Fu Tao-nan and Sun Po-chu of Huajung
were shot by the government authorities at the insistence of the
peasants and other sections of the people. In the case of Yen Jung-chiu
of Hsiangtan, the peasants and other sections of the people compelled
the magistrate to agree to hand him over, and the peasants themselves executed him. Liu Chao of Ninghsiang was killed by the
peasants. The execution of Peng Chih-fan of Liling and Chou
Tien-chueh and Tsao Yun of Yiyang is pending, subject to the decision of the "special tribunal for trying local tyrants and evil gentry".
The execution of one such big landlord reverberates through a whole
county and is very effective in eradicating the remaining evils of
feudalism. Every county has these major tyrants, some as many as
several dozen and others at least a few, and the only effective way
of suppressing the reactionaries is to execute at least a few in each
county who are guilty of the most heinous crimes. When the local
tyrants and evil gentry were at the height of their power, they
literally slaughtered peasants without batting an eyelid. Ho Mai-
chuan, for ten years head of the defence corps in the town of Hsin-
kang, Changsha County, was personally responsible for killing almost
a thousand poverty-stricken peasants, which he euphemistically
described as "executing bandits". In my native county of Hsiangtan,
Tang Chun-yen and Lo Shu-lin who headed the defence corps in the

town of Yintien have killed more than fifty people and buried four alive in the fourteen years since 1913. Of the more than fifty they murdered, the first two were perfectly innocent beggars. Tang Chun-yen said, "Let me make a start by killing a couple of beggars!" and so these two lives were snuffed out. Such was the cruelty of the local tyrants and evil gentry in former days, such was the White terror they created in the countryside, and now that the peasants have risen and shot a few and created just a little terror in suppressing the counter-revolutionaries, is there any reason for saying they should not do so?

3. HITTING THE LANDLORDS ECONOMICALLY

Prohibition on sending grain out of the area, forcing up grain prices, and hoarding and cornering. This is one of the great events of recent months in the economic struggle of the Hunan peasants. Since last October the poor peasants have prevented the outflow of the grain of the landlords and rich peasants and have banned the forcing up of grain prices and hoarding and cornering. As a result, the poor peasants have fully achieved their objective; the ban on the outflow of grain is watertight, grain prices have fallen considerably, and hoarding and cornering have disappeared.

Prohibition on increasing rents and deposits;[15] *agitation for reduced rents and deposits.* Last July and August, when the peasant associations were still weak, the landlords, following their long-established practice of maximum exploitation, served notice one after another on their tenants that rents and deposits would be increased. But by October, when the peasant associations had grown considerably in strength and had all come out against the raising of rents and deposits, the landlords dared not breathe another word on the subject. From November onwards, as the peasants have gained ascendancy over the landlords they have taken the further step of agitating for reduced rents and deposits. What a pity, they say, that the peasant associations were not strong enough when rents were being paid last autumn, or we could have reduced them then. The peasants are doing extensive propaganda for rent reduction in the coming autumn, and the landlords are asking how the reductions are to be carried out. As for the reduction of deposits, this is already under way in Hengshan and other counties.

Prohibition on cancelling tenancies. In July and August of last year there were still many instances of landlords cancelling tenancies and re-letting the land. But after October nobody dared cancel a tenancy. Today, the cancelling of tenancies and the re-letting of land are quite out of the question; all that remains as something of a problem is whether a tenancy can be cancelled if the landlord wants to cultivate the land himself. In some places even this is not allowed by the peasants. In others the cancelling of a tenancy may be permitted if the landlord wants to cultivate the land himself, but then the problem of unemployment among the tenant-peasants arises. There is as yet no uniform way of solving this problem.

Reduction of interest. Interest has been generally reduced in Anhua, and there have been reductions in other counties, too. But wherever the peasant associations are powerful, rural money-lending has virtually disappeared, the landlords having completely "stopped lending" for fear that the money will be "communized". What is currently called reduction of interest is confined to old loans. Not only is the interest on such old loans reduced, but the creditor is actually forbidden to press for the repayment of the principal. The poor peasant replies, "Don't blame me. The year is nearly over. I'll pay you back next year."

4. OVERTHROWING THE FEUDAL RULE OF THE LOCAL TYRANTS AND EVIL GENTRY — SMASHING THE *TU* AND *TUAN*[16]

The old organs of political power in the *tu* and *tuan* (*i.e.*, the district and the township), and especially at the *tu* level, just below the county level, used to be almost exclusively in the hands of the local tyrants and evil gentry. The *tu* had jurisdiction over a population of from ten to fifty or sixty thousand people, and had its own armed forces such as the township defence corps, its own fiscal powers such as the power to levy taxes per *mou*[17] of land, and its own judicial powers such as the power to arrest, imprison, try and punish the peasants at will. The evil gentry who ran these organs were virtual monarchs of the countryside. Comparatively speaking, the peasants were not so much concerned with the president of the Republic, the provincial military governor[18] or the county magistrate; their real "bosses" were these rural monarchs. A mere snort from these people, and the peasants knew they had to watch their step. As a consequence of the present revolt in the countryside the authority of the landlord class has generally been struck down, and the organs of rural administration dominated by the local tyrants and evil gentry have naturally collapsed in its wake. The heads of the *tu* and the *tuan* all steer clear of the people, dare not show their faces and push all local matters on to the peasant associations. They put people off with the remark, "It is none of my business!"

Whenever their conversation turns to the heads of the *tu* and the *tuan*, the peasants say angrily, "That bunch! They are finished!"

Yes, the term "finished" truly describes the state of the old organs of rural administration wherever the storm of revolution has raged.

5. OVERTHROWING THE ARMED FORCES OF THE LANDLORDS AND ESTABLISHING THOSE OF THE PEASANTS

The armed forces of the landlord class were smaller in central Hunan than in the western and southern parts of the province. An average of 600 rifles for each county would make a total of 45,000 rifles for all the seventy-five counties; there may, in fact, be more. In the southern and central parts where the peasant movement is well developed, the landlord class cannot hold its own because of the tremendous momentum with which the peasants have risen, and its armed forces have largely capitulated to the peasant associations and taken the side of the peasants; examples of this are to be found in such counties as Ninghsiang, Pingkiang, Liuyang, Changsha, Liling, Hsiangtan, Hsianghsiang, Anhua, Hengshan and Hengyang. In some counties such as Paoching, a small number of the landlords' armed forces are taking a neutral stand, though with a tendency to capitulate. Another small section are opposing the peasant associations, but the peasants are attacking them and may wipe them out before long, as, for example, in such counties as Yichang, Linwu and Chiaho. The armed forces thus taken over from the reactionary landlords are all being reorganized into a "standing household militia"[19] and placed under the new organs of rural self-government, which are organs of the political power of the peasantry. Taking over these old armed forces is one way in which the peasants are building up their own armed forces. A new way is through the setting up of spear corps under the peasant associations. The spears have pointed, double-edged blades mounted on long shafts, and there are now 100,000 of these weapons in the county of Hsianghsiang alone. Other counties like Hsiangtan, Hengshan, Liling and Changsha have 70,000-80,000, or 50,000-60,000, or 30,000-40,000 each. Every county where there is a peasant movement has a rapidly growing spear corps. These peasants thus armed form an "irregular household militia". This multitude equipped with spears, which is larger than the old armed forces mentioned above, is a new-born armed power the mere sight of which makes the local tyrants and evil gentry tremble. The revolutionary authorities in Hunan should see to it that it is built up on a really extensive scale among the more than twenty million peasants in the seventy-five counties of the province, that every peasant, whether young or in his prime, possesses a spear, and that no restrictions are imposed as though a spear were something dreadful. Anyone who is scared at the sight of the spear corps is indeed a weakling! Only the local tyrants and evil gentry are frightened of them, but no revolutionaries should take fright.

6. OVERTHROWING THE POLITICAL POWER OF THE COUNTY MAGISTRATE AND HIS BAILIFFS

That county government cannot be clean until the peasants rise up was proved some time ago in Haifeng, Kwangtung Province. Now we have added proof, particularly in Hunan. In a county where power is in the hands of the local tyrants and evil gentry, the magistrate, whoever he may be, is almost invariably a corrupt official. In a county where the peasants have risen there is clean government, whoever the magistrate. In the counties I visited, the magistrates had to consult the peasant associations on everything in advance. In counties where the peasant power was very strong, the word of the peasant association worked miracles. If it demanded the arrest of a local tyrant in the morning, the magistrate dared not delay till noon; if it demanded arrest by noon, he dared not delay till the afternoon. When the power of the peasants was just beginning to make itself felt in the countryside, the magistrate worked in league with the local tyrants and evil gentry against the peasants. When the peasants' power grew till it matched that of the landlords, the magistrate took the position of trying to accommodate both the landlords and the peasants, accepting some of the peasant association's suggestions while rejecting others. The remark that the word of the peasant association "works miracles" applies only when the power of the landlords has been completely beaten down by that of the peasants. At present the political situation in such counties as Hsianghsiang, Hsiangtan, Liling and Hengshan is as follows:

(1) *All decisions are made by a joint council consisting of the magistrate and the representatives of the revolutionary mass organizations.* The council is convened by the magistrate and meets in his office. In some counties it is called the "joint council of public bodies and the local government", and in others the "council of county affairs". Besides the magistrate himself, the people attending are the representatives of the county peasant association, trade union council, merchant association, women's association, school staff association, student association and Kuomintang headquarters.[20] At such council meetings the magistrate is influenced by the views of the public organizations and invariably does their bidding. The adoption of a democratic committee system of county government should not, therefore, present much of a problem in Hunan. The present county governments are already quite democratic both in form and substance. This situation has been brought about only in the last two or three months, that is, since the peasants have risen all over the countryside and overthrown the power of the local tyrants and evil gentry. It has now come about that the magistrates, seeing their old props collapse and needing other props to retain their posts, have begun to curry favour with the public organizations.

(2) *The judicial assistant has scarcely any cases to handle.* The judicial system in Hunan remains one in which the county magistrate is concurrently in charge of judicial affairs, with an assistant to help him in handling cases. To get rich, the magistrate and his underlings used to rely entirely on collecting taxes and levies, procuring men and provisions for the armed forces, and extorting money in civil and criminal lawsuits by confounding right and wrong, the last being the most regular and reliable source of income. In the last few months, with the downfall of the local tyrants and evil gentry, all the legal pettifoggers have disappeared. What is more, the peasants' problems, big and small, are now all settled in the peasant associations at the various levels. Thus the county judicial assistant simply has nothing to do. The one in Hsianghsiang told me, "When there were no peasant associations, an average of sixty civil or criminal suits were brought to the county government each day; now it receives an average of only four or five a day." So it is that the purses of the magistrates and their underlings perforce remain empty.

(3) *The armed guards, the police and the bailiffs all keep out of the way and dare not go near the villages to practise their extortions.* In the past the villagers were afraid of the townspeople, but now the

townspeople are afraid of the villagers. In particular the vicious curs
kept by the county government — the police, the armed guards and
the bailiffs — are afraid of going to the villages, or if they do so,
they no longer dare to practise their extortions. They tremble at the
sight of the peasants' spears.

7. OVERTHROWING THE CLAN AUTHORITY OF THE ANCESTRAL TEMPLES AND CLAN ELDERS, THE RELIGIOUS AUTHORITY OF TOWN AND VILLAGE GODS, AND THE MASCULINE AUTHORITY OF HUSBANDS

A man in China is usually subjected to the domination of three
systems of authority: (1) the state system (political authority), ranging from the national, provincial and county government down to
that of the township; (2) the clan system (clan authority), ranging
from the central ancestral temple and its branch temples down to
the head of the household; and (3) the supernatural system (religious
authority), ranging from the King of Hell down to the town and
village gods belonging to the nether world, and from the Emperor
of Heaven down to all the various gods and spirits belonging to the
celestial world. As for women, in addition to being dominated by
these three systems of authority, they are also dominated by the men
(the authority of the husband). These four authorities — political,
clan, religious and masculine — are the embodiment of the whole
feudal-patriarchal system and ideology, and are the four thick ropes
binding the Chinese people, particularly the peasants. How the
peasants have overthrown the political authority of the landlords in
the countryside has been described above. The political authority of
the landlords is the backbone of all the other systems of authority.
With that overturned, the clan authority, the religious authority and
the authority of the husband all begin to totter. Where the peasant
association is powerful, the clan elders and administrators of temple
funds no longer dare oppress those lower in the clan hierarchy or
embezzle clan funds. The worst clan elders and administrators, being
local tyrants, have been thrown out. No one any longer dares to
practise the cruel corporal and capital punishments that used to be
inflicted in the ancestral temples, such as flogging, drowning and
burying alive. The old rule barring women and poor people from the
banquets in the ancestral temples has also been broken. The women
of Paikuo in Hengshan County gathered in force and swarmed into

their ancestral temple, firmly planted their backsides in the seats and joined in the eating and drinking, while the venerable clan bigwigs had willy-nilly to let them do as they pleased. At another place, where poor peasants had been excluded from temple banquets, a group of them flocked in and ate and drank their fill, while the local tyrants and evil gentry and other long-gowned gentlemen all took to their heels in fright. Everywhere religious authority totters as the peasant movement develops. In many places the peasant associations have taken over the temples of the gods as their offices. Everywhere they advocate the appropriation of temple property in order to start peasant schools and to defray the expenses of the associations, calling it "public revenue from superstition". In Liling County, prohibiting superstitious practices and smashing idols have become quite the vogue. In its northern districts the peasants have prohibited the incense-burning processions to propitiate the god of pestilence. There were many idols in the Taoist temple at Fupoling in Lukou, but when extra room was needed for the district headquarters of the Kuomintang, they were all piled up in a corner, big and small together, and no peasant raised any objection. Since then, sacrifices to the gods, the performance of religious rites and the offering of sacred lamps have rarely been practised when a death occurs in a family. Because the initiative in this matter was taken by the chairman of the peasant association, Sun Hsiao-shan, he is hated by the local Taoist priests. In the Lungfeng Nunnery in the North Third District, the peasants and primary school teachers chopped up the wooden idols and actually used the wood to cook meat. More than thirty idols in the Tungfu Monastery in the Southern District were burned by the students and peasants together, and only two small images of Lord Pao[21] were snatched up by an old peasant who said, "Don't commit a sin!" In places where the power of the peasants is predominant, only the older peasants and the women still believe in the gods, the younger peasants no longer doing so. Since the latter control the associations, the overthrow of religious authority and the eradication of superstition are going on everywhere. As to the authority of the husband, this has always been weaker among the poor peasants because, out of economic necessity, their womenfolk have to do more manual labour than the women of the richer classes and therefore have more say and greater power of decision in family matters. With the increasing bankruptcy of the rural economy in recent years, the basis for men's domination over women has already been weak-

ened. With the rise of the peasant movement, the women in many
places have now begun to organize rural women's associations; the
opportunity has come for them to lift up their heads, and the authority
of the husband is getting shakier every day. In a word, the whole
feudal-patriarchal system and ideology is tottering with the growth
of the peasants' power. At the present time, however, the peasants
are concentrating on destroying the landlords' political authority.
Wherever it has been wholly destroyed, they are beginning to press
their attack in the three other spheres of the clan, the gods and male
domination. But such attacks have only just begun, and there can be
no thorough overthrow of all three until the peasants have won complete victory in the economic struggle. Therefore, our present task
is to lead the peasants to put their greatest efforts into the political
struggle, so that the landlords' authority is entirely overthrown. The
economic struggle should follow immediately, so that the land problem and the other economic problems of the poor peasants may be
fundamentally solved. As for the clan system, superstition, and inequality between men and women, their abolition will follow as a
natural consequence of victory in the political and economic struggles.
If too much of an effort is made, arbitrarily and prematurely, to
abolish these things, the local tyrants and evil gentry will seize the
pretext to put about such counter-revolutionary propaganda as "the
peasant association has no piety towards ancestors", "the peasant
association is blasphemous and is destroying religion" and "the peasant association stands for the communization of wives", all for the
purpose of undermining the peasant movement. A case in point is
the recent events at Hsianghsiang in Hunan and Yanghsin in Hupeh,
where the landlords exploited the opposition of some peasants to
smashing idols. It is the peasants who made the idols, and when the
time comes they will cast the idols aside with their own hands; there
is no need for anyone else to do it for them prematurely. The Communist Party's propaganda policy in such matters should be, "Draw
the bow without shooting, just indicate the motions."[22] It is for the
peasants themselves to cast aside the idols, pull down the temples
to the martyred virgins and the arches to the chaste and faithful
widows; it is wrong for anybody else to do it for them.

While I was in the countryside, I did some propaganda against
superstition among the peasants. I said:

"If you believe in the Eight Characters,[23] you hope for good luck;
if you believe in geomancy,[24] you hope to benefit from the location

of your ancestral graves. This year within the space of a few months the local tyrants, evil gentry and corrupt officials have all toppled from their pedestals. Is it possible that until a few months ago they all had good luck and enjoyed the benefit of well-sited ancestral graves, while suddenly in the last few months their luck has turned and their ancestral graves have ceased to exert a beneficial influence? The local tyrants and evil gentry jeer at your peasant association and say, 'How odd! Today, the world is a world of committeemen. Look, you can't even go to pass water without bumping into a committee-man!' Quite true, the towns and the villages, the trade unions and the peasant associations, the Kuomintang and the Communist Party, all without exception have their executive committee members — it is indeed a world of committeemen. But is this due to the Eight Characters and the location of the ancestral graves? How strange! The Eight Characters of all the poor wretches in the countryside have suddenly turned auspicious! And their ancestral graves have suddenly started exerting beneficial influences! The gods? Worship them by all means. But if you had only Lord Kuan[25] and the Goddess of Mercy and no peasant association, could you have overthrown the local tyrants and evil gentry? The gods and goddesses are indeed miserable objects. You have worshipped them for centuries, and they have not overthrown a single one of the local tyrants or evil gentry for you! Now you want to have your rent reduced. Let me ask, how will you go about it? Will you believe in the gods or in the peasant association?"

My words made the peasants roar with laughter.

8. SPREADING POLITICAL PROPAGANDA

Even if ten thousand schools of law and political science had been opened, could they have brought as much political education to the people, men and women, young and old, all the way into the remotest corners of the countryside, as the peasant associations have done in so short a time? I don't think they could. "Down with imperialism!" "Down with the warlords!" "Down with the corrupt officials!" "Down with the local tyrants and evil gentry!" — these political slogans have grown wings, they have found their way to the young, the middle-aged and the old, to the women and children in countless villages, they have penetrated into their minds and are on their lips. For instance, watch a group of children at play. If one gets angry with another, if he glares, stamps his foot and shakes his fist, you will then immediately hear from the other the shrill cry of "Down with imperialism!"

In the Hsiangtan area, when the children who pasture the cattle get into a fight, one will act as Tang Sheng-chih, and the other as Yeh Kai-hsin;[26] when one is defeated and runs away, with the other chasing him, it is the pursuer who is Tang Sheng-chih and the pursued Yeh Kai-hsin. As to the song "Down with the Imperialist Powers!" of course almost every child in the towns can sing it, and now many village children can sing it too.

Some of the peasants can also recite Dr. Sun Yat-sen's Testament. They pick out the terms "freedom", "equality", "the Three People's Principles" and "unequal treaties" and apply them, if rather crudely, in their daily life. When somebody who looks like one of the gentry encounters a peasant and stands on his dignity, refusing to make way along a pathway, the peasant will say angrily, "Hey, you local tyrant, don't you know the Three People's Principles?" Formerly when the peasants from the vegetable farms on the outskirts of Changsha entered the city to sell their produce, they used to be pushed around by the police. Now they have found a weapon, which is none other than the Three People's Principles. When a policeman strikes or swears at a peasant selling vegetables, the peasant immediately answers back by invoking the Three People's Principles and that shuts the policeman up. Once in Hsiangtan when a district peasant association and a township peasant association could not see eye to eye, the chairman of the township association declared, "Down with the district peasant association's unequal treaties!"

The spread of political propaganda throughout the rural areas is entirely an achievement of the Communist Party and the peasant associations. Simple slogans, cartoons and speeches have produced such a widespread and speedy effect among the peasants that every one of them seems to have been through a political school. According to the reports of comrades engaged in rural work, political propaganda was very extensive at the time of the three great mass rallies, the anti-British demonstration, the celebration of the October Revolution and the victory celebration for the Northern Expedition. On these occasions, political propaganda was conducted extensively wherever there were peasant associations, arousing the whole countryside with tremendous effect. From now on care should be taken to use every opportunity gradually to enrich the content and clarify the meaning of those simple slogans.

9. PEASANT BANS AND PROHIBITIONS

When the peasant associations, under Communist Party leadership, establish their authority in the countryside, the peasants begin to prohibit or restrict the things they dislike. Gaming, gambling and opium-smoking are the three things that are most strictly forbidden.

Gaming. Where the peasant association is powerful, mahjong, dominoes and card games are completely banned.

The peasant association in the 14th District of Hsianghsiang burned two basketfuls of mahjong sets.

If you go to the countryside, you will find none of these games played; anyone who violates the ban is promptly and strictly punished.

Gambling. Former hardened gamblers are now themselves suppressing gambling; this abuse, too, has been swept away in places where the peasant association is powerful.

Opium-smoking. The prohibition is extremely strict. When the peasant association orders the surrender of opium pipes, no one dares to raise the least objection. In Liling County one of the evil gentry who did not surrender his pipes was arrested and paraded through the villages.

The peasants' campaign to "disarm the opium-smokers" is no less impressive than the disarming of the troops of Wu Pei-fu and Sun Chuan-fang[27] by the Northern Expeditionary Army. Quite a number of venerable fathers of officers in the revolutionary army, old men who were opium-addicts and inseparable from their pipes, have been disarmed by the "emperors" (as the peasants are called derisively by the evil gentry). The "emperors" have banned not only the growing and smoking of opium, but also trafficking in it. A great deal of the opium transported from Kweichow to Kiangsi via the counties of Paoching, Hsianghsiang, Yuhsien and Liling has been intercepted on the way and burned. This has affected government revenues. As a result, out of consideration for the army's need for funds in the Northern Expedition, the provincial peasant association ordered the associations at the lower levels "temporarily to postpone the ban on opium traffic". This, however, has upset and displeased the peasants.

There are many other things besides these three which the peasants have prohibited or restricted, the following being some examples:

The flower drum. Vulgar performances are forbidden in many places.

Sedan-chairs. In many counties, especially Hsianghsiang, there have been cases of smashing sedan-chairs. The peasants, detesting the people who use this conveyance, are always ready to smash the chairs, but the peasant associations forbid them to do so. Association officials tell the peasants, "If you smash the chairs, you only save the rich money and lose the carriers their jobs. Will that not hurt our own people?" Seeing the point, the peasants have worked out a new tactic — considerably to increase the fares charged by the chair-carriers so as to penalize the rich.

Distilling and sugar-making. The use of grain for distilling spirits and making sugar is everywhere prohibited, and the distillers and sugar-refiners are constantly complaining. Distilling is not banned in Futienpu, Hengshan County, but prices are fixed very low, and the wine and spirits dealers, seeing no prospect of profit, have had to stop it.

Pigs. The number of pigs a family can keep is limited, for pigs consume grain.

Chickens and ducks. In Hsianghsiang County the raising of chickens and ducks is prohibited, but the women object. In Hengshan County, each family in Yangtang is allowed to keep only three, and in Futienpu five. In many places the raising of ducks is completely banned, for ducks not only consume grain but also ruin the rice plants and so are worse than chickens.

Feasts. Sumptuous feasts are generally forbidden. In Shaoshan, Hsiangtan County, it has been decided that guests are to be served with only three kinds of animal food, namely, chicken, fish and pork. It is also forbidden to serve bamboo shoots, kelp and lentil noodles. In Hengshan County it has been resolved that eight dishes and no more may be served at a banquet.[28] Only five dishes are allowed in the East Third District in Liling County, and only three meat and three vegetable dishes in the North Second District, while in the West Third District New Year feasts are forbidden entirely. In Hsianghsiang County, there is a ban on all "egg-cake feasts", which are by no means sumptuous. When a family in the Second District of Hsianghsiang gave an "egg-cake feast" at a son's wedding, the peasants, seeing the ban violated, swarmed into the house and broke up the celebration. In the town of Chiamo, Hsianghsiang County, the people have refrained from eating expensive foods and use only fruit when offering ancestral sacrifices.

Oxen. Oxen are a treasured possession of the peasants. "Slaughter an ox in this life and you will be an ox in the next" has become almost a religious tenet; oxen must never be killed. Before the peasants had power, they could only appeal to religious taboo in opposing the slaughter of cattle and had no means of banning it. Since the rise of the peasant associations their jurisdiction has extended even to the cattle, and they have prohibited the slaughter of cattle in the towns. Of the six butcheries in the county town of Hsiangtan, five are now closed and the remaining one slaughters only enfeebled or disabled animals. The slaughter of cattle is totally prohibited throughout the county of Hengshan. A peasant whose ox broke a leg consulted the peasant association before he dared kill it. When the Chamber of Commerce of Chuchow rashly slaughtered a cow, the peasants came into town and demanded an explanation, and the chamber, besides paying a fine, had to let off firecrackers by way of apology.

Tramps and vagabonds. A resolution passed in Liling County prohibited the drumming of New Year greetings or the chanting of praises to the local deities or the singing of lotus rhymes. Various other counties have similar prohibitions, or these practices have disappeared of themselves, as no one observes them any more. The "beggar-bullies" or "vagabonds" who used to be extremely aggressive now have no alternative but to submit to the peasant associations. In Shaoshan, Hsiangtan County, the vagabonds used to make the temple of the Rain God their regular haunt and feared nobody, but since the rise of the associations they have stolen away. The peasant association in Huti Township in the same county caught three such tramps and made them carry clay for the brick kilns. Resolutions have been passed prohibiting the wasteful customs associated with New Year calls and gifts.

Besides these, many other minor prohibitions have been introduced in various places, such as the Liling prohibitions on incense-burning processions to propitiate the god of pestilence, on buying preserves and fruit for ritual presents, burning ritual paper garments during the Festival of Spirits and pasting up good-luck posters at the New Year. At Kushui in Hsianghsiang County, there is a prohibition even on smoking water-pipes. In the Second District, letting off firecrackers and ceremonial guns is forbidden, with a fine of 1.20 yuan for the former and 2.40 yuan for the latter. Religious rites for the dead are prohibited in the 7th and 20th Districts. In the 18th District, it is forbidden to make funeral gifts of money. Things like these, which defy enumeration, may be generally called peasant bans and prohibitions.

They are of great significance in two respects. First, they represent a revolt against bad social customs, such as gaming, gambling and opium-smoking. These customs arose out of the rotten political environment of the landlord class and are swept away once its authority is overthrown. Second, the prohibitions are a form of self-defence against exploitation by city merchants; such are the prohibitions on feasts and on buying preserves and fruit for ritual presents. Manufactured goods are extremely dear and agricultural products are extremely cheap, the peasants are impoverished and ruthlessly exploited by the merchants, and they must therefore encourage frugality to protect themselves. As for the ban on sending grain out of the area, it is imposed to prevent the price from rising because the poor peasants have not enough to feed themselves and have to buy grain on the market. The reason for all this is the peasants' poverty and the contradictions between town and country; it is not a matter of their rejecting manufactured goods or trade between town and country in order to uphold the so-called Doctrine of Oriental Culture.[29] To protect themselves economically, the peasants must organize consumers' co-operatives for the collective buying of goods. It is also necessary for the government to help the peasant associations establish credit (loan) co-operatives. If these things were done, the peasants would naturally find it unnecessary to ban the outflow of grain as a method of keeping down the price, nor would they have to prohibit the inflow of certain manufactured goods in economic self-defence.

10. ELIMINATING BANDITRY

In my opinion, no ruler in any dynasty from Yu, Tang, Wen and Wu down to the Ching emperors and the presidents of the Republic has ever shown as much prowess in eliminating banditry as have the peasant associations today. Wherever the peasant associations are powerful, there is not a trace of banditry. Surprisingly enough, in many places even the pilfering of vegetables has disappeared. In other places there are still some pilferers. But in the counties I visited, even including those that were formerly bandit-ridden, there was no trace of bandits. The reasons are: First, the members of the peasant associations are everywhere spread out over the hills and dales, spear or cudgel in hand, ready to go into action in their hundreds, so that the bandits have nowhere to hide. Second, since the rise of the peasant movement the price of grain has dropped — it was six yuan a picul last spring but only two yuan last winter — and the problem of food has become less serious for the people. Third, members of the secret societies[30] have joined the peasant associations, in which they can openly and legally play the hero and vent their grievances, so that there is no further need for the secret "mountain", "lodge", "shrine" and "river" forms of organization.[31] In killing the pigs and sheep of the local tyrants and evil gentry and imposing heavy levies and fines, they have adequate outlets for their feelings against those who oppressed them. Fourth, the armies are recruiting large numbers of soldiers and many of the "unruly" have joined up. Thus the evil of banditry has ended with the rise of the peasant movement. On this point, even the well-to-do approve of the peasant associations. Their comment is, "The peasant associations? Well, to be fair, there is also something to be said for them."

In prohibiting gaming, gambling and opium-smoking, and in eliminating banditry, the peasant associations have won general approval.

11. ABOLISHING EXORBITANT LEVIES

As the country is not yet unified and the authority of the imperialists and the warlords has not been overthrown, there is as yet no way of removing the heavy burden of government taxes and levies on the peasants or, more explicitly, of removing the burden of expenditure for the revolutionary army. However, the exorbitant levies imposed on the peasants when the local tyrants and evil gentry dominated rural administration, e.g., the surcharge on each *mou* of land, have been abolished or at least reduced with the rise of the peasant movement and the downfall of the local tyrants and evil gentry. This too should be counted among the achievements of the peasant associations.

12. THE MOVEMENT FOR EDUCATION

In China education has always been the exclusive preserve of the landlords, and the peasants have had no access to it. But the landlords' culture is created by the peasants, for its sole source is the peasants' sweat and blood. In China 90 per cent of the people have had no education, and of these the overwhelming majority are peasants. The moment the power of the landlords was overthrown in the rural areas, the peasants' movement for education began. See how the peasants who hitherto detested the schools are today zealously setting up evening classes! They always disliked the "foreign-style school". In my student days, when I went back to the village and saw that the peasants were against the "foreign-style school", I, too, used to identify myself with the general run of "foreign-style students and teachers" and stand up for it, feeling that the peasants were somehow wrong. It was not until 1925, when I lived in the countryside for six months and was already a Communist and had acquired the Marxist viewpoint, that I realized I had been wrong and the peasants right. The texts used in the rural primary schools were entirely about urban things and unsuited to rural needs. Besides, the attitude of the primary school teachers towards the peasants was very bad and, far from being helpful to the peasants, they became objects of dislike. Hence the peasants preferred the old-style schools ("Chinese classes", as they called them) to the modern schools (which they called "foreign classes") and the old-style teachers to the ones in the primary schools. Now the peasants are enthusiastically establishing evening classes, which they call peasant schools. Some have already been opened, others are being organized, and on the average there is one school per township. The peasants are very enthusiastic about these schools, and regard them, and only them, as their own. The funds for the evening schools come from the "public revenue from superstition", from ancestral temple funds, and from other idle public funds or property. The county education boards wanted to use this money to establish primary schools, that is, "foreign-style schools" not suited to the needs of the peasants, while the latter wanted to use it for peasant schools, and the outcome of the dispute was that both got some of the money, though there are places where the peasants got it all. The development of the peasant movement has resulted in a rapid rise in their cultural level. Before long tens of thousands of schools will have sprung up in the villages throughout the province; this is quite different from the empty talk about "universal education", which the intelligentsia and the so-called "educationalists" have been bandying back and forth and which after all this time remains an empty phrase.

13. THE CO-OPERATIVE MOVEMENT

The peasants really need co-operatives, and especially consumers', marketing and credit co-operatives. When they buy goods, the merchants exploit them; when they sell their farm produce, the merchants cheat them; when they borrow money or rice, they are fleeced by the usurers; and they are eager to find a solution to these three problems. During the fighting in the Yangtse valley last winter, when trade routes were cut and the price of salt went up in Hunan, many peasants organized co-operatives to purchase salt. When the landlords deliberately stopped lending, there were many attempts by the peasants to organize credit agencies, because they needed to borrow money. A major problem is the absence of detailed, standard rules of organization. As these spontaneously organized peasant co-operatives often fail to conform to co-operative principles, the comrades working among the peasants are always eagerly enquiring about "rules and regulations". Given proper guidance, the co-operative movement can spread everywhere along with the growth of the peasant associations.

14. BUILDING ROADS AND REPAIRING EMBANKMENTS

This, too, is one of the achievements of the peasant associations. Before there were peasant associations the roads in the countryside were terrible. Roads cannot be repaired without money, and as the wealthy were unwilling to dip into their purses, the roads were left in a bad state. If there was any road work done at all, it was done as an act of charity; a little money was collected from families "wishing to gain merit in the next world", and a few narrow, skimpily paved roads were built. With the rise of the peasant associations orders have been given specifying the required width — three, five, seven or ten feet, according to the requirements of the different routes — and each landlord along a road has been ordered to build a section. Once the order is given, who dares to disobey? In a short time many good roads have appeared. This is no work of charity but the result of compulsion, and a little compulsion of this kind is not at all a bad thing. The same is true of the embankments. The ruthless landlords were always out to take what they could from the tenant-peasants and would never spend even a few coppers on embankment repairs; they would leave the ponds to dry up and the tenant-peasants to starve, caring about nothing but the rent. Now that there are peasant associations, the landlords can be bluntly ordered to repair the embankments. When a landlord refuses, the association will tell him politely, "Very well! If you won't do the repairs, you will contribute grain, a *tou* for each work-day." As this is a bad bargain for the landlord, he hastens to do the repairs. Consequently many defective embankments have been turned into good ones.

All the fourteen deeds enumerated above have been accomplished by the peasants under the leadership of the peasant associations. Would the reader please think it over and say whether any of them is bad in its fundamental spirit and revolutionary significance? Only the local tyrants and evil gentry, I think, will call them bad. Curiously enough, it is reported from Nanchang[32] that Chiang Kai-shek, Chang Ching-chiang[33] and other such gentlemen do not altogether approve of the activities of the Hunan peasants. This opinion is shared by Liu Yueh-chih[34] and other right-wing leaders in Hunan, all of whom say, "They have simply gone Red." But where would the national revolution be without this bit of Red? To talk about "arousing the masses of the people" day in and day out and then to be scared to death when the masses do rise — what difference is there between this and Lord Sheh's love of dragons?[35]

NOTES

[1] Hunan Province was then the centre of the peasant movement in China.

[2] Chao Heng-ti, the ruler of Hunan at the time, was the agent of the Northern warlords. He was overthrown by the Northern Expeditionary Army in 1926.

[3] The Revolution of 1911 overthrew the autocratic regime of the Ching Dynasty. On October 10 of that year, a section of the Ching Dynasty's New Army staged an uprising in Wuchang, Hupeh Province, at the urging of bourgeois and petty-bourgeois revolutionary societies. It was followed by uprisings in other provinces, and very soon the rule of the Ching Dynasty crumbled. On January 1, 1912, the Provisional Government of the Republic of China was set up in Nanking, and Sun Yat-sen was elected Provisional President. The revolution achieved victory through the alliance of the bourgeoisie with the peasants, workers and urban petty bourgeoisie. But state power fell into the hands of the Northern warlord Yuan Shih-kai, and the revolution failed, because the group which led it was conciliationist in nature, failed to give real benefits to the peasants and yielded to imperialist and feudal pressure.

[4] These were the virtues of Confucius, as described by one of his disciples.

[5] The old Chinese phrase, "exceeding the proper limits in righting a wrong", was often quoted for the purpose of restricting people's activities; reforms that remained within the framework of the established order were to be permitted, but activities aiming at the complete destruction of the old order were to be forbidden. Actions within this framework were regarded as "proper", but those that aimed at completely destroying the old order were described as "exceeding the proper limits". It is a convenient doctrine for reformists and opportunists in the revolutionary ranks. Comrade Mao Tse-tung refuted this kind of reformist doctrine.

His remark in the text that "Proper limits have to be exceeded in order to right a wrong, or else the wrong cannot be righted" meant that the mass revolutionary method, and not the revisionist-reformist method, had to be taken to end the old feudal order.

[6] Chiang Kai-shek had not yet been fully exposed as a counter-revolutionary in the winter of 1926 and the spring of 1927 when the Northern Expeditionary Army was marching into the Yangtse valley, and the peasant masses still thought that he was for the revolution. The landlords and rich peasants disliked him and spread the rumour that the Northern Expeditionary Army had suffered defeats and that he had been wounded in the leg. Chiang Kai-shek came to be fully revealed as a counter-revolutionary on April 12, 1927, when he staged his counter-revolutionary coup d'état in Shanghai and elsewhere, massacring the workers, suppressing the peasants and attacking the Communist Party. The landlords and rich peasants then changed their attitude and began to support him.

[7] Kwangtung was the first revolutionary base in the period of the First Revolutionary Civil War (1924-27).

[8] Wu Pei-fu was one of the best-known of the Northern warlords. Together with Tsao Kun, who was notorious for his rigging of the presidential election in 1923 by bribing members of parliament, he belonged to the Chihli (Hopei) clique. He supported Tsao as the leader and the two were generally referred to as "Tsao-Wu". In 1920 after defeating Tuan Chi-jui, warlord of the Anhwei clique, Wu Pei-fu gained control of the Northern warlord government in Peking as an agent of the Anglo-American imperialists; it was he who gave the orders for the massacre, on February 7, 1923, of the workers on strike along the Peking-Hankow Railway. In 1924 he was defeated in the war with Chang Tso-lin (commonly known as the "war between the Chihli and Fengtien cliques"), and he was thereupon ousted from the Peking regime. In 1926 he joined forces with Chang Tso-lin at the instigation of the Japanese and British imperialists, and thus returned to power. When the Northern Expeditionary Army drove northward from Kwangtung in 1926, he was the first foe to be overthrown.

[9] The Three People's Principles were Sun Yat-sen's principles and programme for the bourgeois-democratic revolution in China on the questions of nationalism, democracy and people's livelihood. In 1924, in the Manifesto of the First National Congress of the Kuomintang, Sun Yat-sen restated the Three People's Principles, interpreting nationalism as opposition to imperialism and expressing active support for the movements of the workers and peasants. The old Three People's Principles thus developed into the new, consisting of the Three Great Policies, that is, alliance with Russia, co-operation with the Communist Party, and assistance to the peasants and workers. The new Three People's Principles provided the political basis for co-operation between the Communist Party of China and the Kuomintang during the First Revolutionary Civil War period.

[10] The Chinese term for "long live" is *wansui*, literally "ten thousand years", and was the traditional salute to the emperor; it had become a synonym for "emperor".

[11] Rich peasants should not have been allowed to join the peasant associations, a point which the peasant masses did not yet understand in 1927.

[12] Here the "utterly destitute" means the farm labourers (the rural proletariat) and the rural *lumpen*-proletariat.

[13] The "less destitute" means the rural semi-proletariat.

[14] Yuan Tsu-ming was a warlord of Kweichow Province who controlled the western part of Hunan.

[15] A tenant generally gave his landlord, as a condition of tenancy, a deposit in cash or kind, often amounting to a considerable part of the value of the land. Though this was supposed to be a guarantee for payment of rent, it actually represented a form of extra exploitation.

[16] In Hunan, the *tu* corresponded to the district and the *tuan* to the township. The old administrations of the *tu* and the *tuan* type were instruments of landlord rule.

[17] The tax per *mou* was a surcharge on top of the regular land tax, ruthlessly imposed on the peasants by the landlord regime.

[18] Under the regime of the Northern warlords, the military head of a province was called "military governor". But he was the virtual dictator of the province, with administrative as well as military power gathered in his hands. In league with the imperialists, he maintained a separatist feudal-militarist regime in his locality.

[19] The "standing household militia" was one of the various kinds of armed forces in the countryside. The term "household" is used because some member of almost every household had to join it. After the defeat of the revolution in 1927, the landlords in many places seized control of the militia and turned them into armed counter-revolutionary bands.

[20] At the time, many of the county headquarters of the Kuomintang, under the leadership of the Kuomintang's Central Executive Committee in Wuhan, pursued Dr. Sun Yat-sen's Three Great Policies of alliance with Russia, co-operation with the Communist Party and assistance to the peasants and workers. They constituted the revolutionary alliance of the Communists, the left-wingers of the Kuomintang, and other revolutionaries.

[21] Lord Pao (Pao Cheng) was prefect of Kaifeng, capital of the Northern Sung Dynasty (A.D. 960-1127). He was famous in popular legend as an upright official and a fearless, impartial judge with a knack of passing true verdicts in all the cases he tried.

[22] This reference to archery is taken from *Mencius*. It describes how the expert teacher of archery draws his bow with a histrionic gesture but does not release the arrow. The point is that while Communists should guide the peasants in attaining a full measure of political consciousness, they should leave it to the peasants' own initiative to abolish superstitious and other bad practices, and should not give them orders or do it for them.

[23] The Eight Characters were a method of fortune-telling in China based on the examination of the two cyclic characters each for the year, month, day and hour of a person's birth respectively.

[24] Geomancy refers to the superstition that the location of one's ancestors' graves influences one's fortune. The geomancers claim to be able to tell whether a particular site and its surroundings are auspicious.

[25] Lord Kuan (Kuan Yu, A.D. 160-219), a warrior in the epoch of the Three Kingdoms, was widely worshipped by the Chinese as the God of Loyalty and War.

[26] Tang Sheng-chih was a general who sided with the revolution in the Northern Expedition. Yeh Kai-hsin was a general on the side of the Northern warlords who fought against the revolution.

[27] Sun Chuan-fang was a warlord whose rule extended over the five provinces of Kiangsu, Chekiang, Fukien, Kiangsi and Anhwei. He was responsible for the bloody suppression of the insurrections of the Shanghai workers. His main army

was crushed in the winter of 1926 by the Northern Expeditionary Army in Nanchang and Kiukiang, Kiangsi Province.

[28] In China a dish is served in a bowl or a plate for the whole table, and not individually.

[29] "Oriental Culture" was a reactionary doctrine which rejected modern scientific civilization and favoured the preservation of the backward mode of agricultural production and the feudal culture of the Orient.

[30] For the secret societies, see "Analysis of the Classes in Chinese Society", Note 18, p. 21 of this volume.

[31] "Mountain", "lodge", "shrine" and "river" were names used by primitive secret societies to denote some of their sects.

[32] When Nanchang was captured by the Northern Expeditionary Army in November 1926, Chiang Kai-shek seized the opportunity to establish his general headquarters there. He gathered around himself the right-wing members of the Kuomintang and a number of Northern warlord politicians and, in collusion with the imperialists, hatched his counter-revolutionary plot against Wuhan, the then revolutionary centre. Eventually, on April 12, 1927, he staged his counter-revolutionary coup d'état which was marked by tremendous massacres in Shanghai.

[33] Chang Ching-chiang, a right-wing Kuomintang leader, was a member of Chiang Kai-shek's brain trust.

[34] Liu Yueh-chih was head of the "Left Society", an important anti-Communist group in Hunan.

[35] As told by Liu Hsiang (77-6 B.C.) in his *Hsin Hsu*, Lord Sheh was so fond of dragons that he adorned his whole palace with drawings and carvings of them. But when a real dragon heard of his infatuation and paid him a visit, he was frightened out of his wits. Here Comrade Mao Tse-tung uses this metaphor to show that though Chiang Kai-shek and his like talked about revolution, they were afraid of revolution and against it.

THE SECOND
REVOLUTIONARY CIVIL WAR
PERIOD

WHY IS IT THAT RED POLITICAL POWER CAN EXIST IN CHINA?

October 5, 1928

I. THE INTERNAL POLITICAL SITUATION

The present regime of the new warlords of the Kuomintang remains a regime of the comprador class in the cities and the landlord class in the countryside; it is a regime which has capitulated to imperialism in its foreign relations and which at home has replaced the old warlords with new ones, subjecting the working class and the peasantry to an even more ruthless economic exploitation and political oppression. The bourgeois-democratic revolution which started in Kwangtung Province had gone only halfway when the comprador and landlord classes usurped the leadership and immediately shifted it on to the road of counter-revolution; throughout the country the workers, the peasants, the other sections of the common people, and even the bourgeoisie,[1] have remained under counter-revolutionary rule and obtained not the slightest particle of political or economic emancipation.

Before their capture of Peking and Tientsin, the four cliques of the new Kuomintang warlords, Chiang Kai-shek, the Kwangsi warlords, Feng Yu-hsiang and Yen Hsi-shan,[2] formed a temporary alliance against Chang Tso-lin.[3] As soon as these cities were captured, this alliance broke up, giving way to bitter struggle among the four cliques, and now a war is brewing between the Chiang and the Kwangsi cliques. The contradictions and struggles among the cliques of warlords in China reflect the contradictions and struggles among the imperialist powers. Hence, as long as China is divided among the imperialist powers, the various cliques of warlords cannot under any circumstances

---

This article was part of the resolution, originally entitled "The Political Problems and the Tasks of the Border Area Party Organization", which was drafted by Comrade Mao Tse-tung for the Second Party Congress of the Hunan-Kiangsi Border Area.

come to terms, and whatever compromises they may reach will only be temporary. A temporary compromise today engenders a bigger war tomorrow.

China is in urgent need of a bourgeois-democratic revolution, and this revolution can be completed only under the leadership of the proletariat. Because the proletariat failed to exercise firm leadership in the revolution of 1926-27 which started from Kwangtung and spread towards the Yangtse River, leadership was seized by the comprador and landlord classes and the revolution was replaced by counter-revolution. The bourgeois-democratic revolution thus met with a temporary defeat. This defeat was a heavy blow to the Chinese proletariat and peasantry and also a blow to the Chinese bourgeoisie (but not to the comprador and landlord classes). Yet in the last few months, both in the north and in the south, there has been a growth of organized strikes by the workers in the cities and of insurrections by the peasants in the countryside under the leadership of the Communist Party. Hunger and cold are creating great unrest among the soldiers of the warlord armies. Meanwhile, urged on by the clique headed by Wang Ching-wei and Chen Kung-po, the bourgeoisie is promoting a reform movement of considerable proportions[4] in the coastal areas and along the Yangtse River. This is a new development.

According to the directives of the Communist International and the Central Committee of our Party, the content of China's democratic revolution consists in overthrowing the rule of imperialism and its warlord tools in China so as to complete the national revolution, and in carrying out the agrarian revolution so as to eliminate the feudal exploitation of the peasants by the landlord class. Such a revolutionary movement has been growing day by day since the Tsinan Massacre[5] in May 1928.

II. REASONS FOR THE EMERGENCE AND SURVIVAL OF RED POLITICAL POWER IN CHINA[6]

The long-term survival inside a country of one or more small areas under Red political power completely encircled by a White regime is a phenomenon that has never occurred anywhere else in the world. There are special reasons for this unusual phenomenon. It can exist and develop only under certain conditions.

First, it cannot occur in any imperialist country or in any colony under direct imperialist rule,[7] but can only occur in China which is economically backward, and which is semi-colonial and under indirect imperialist rule. For this unusual phenomenon can occur only in conjunction with another unusual phenomenon, namely, war within the White regime. It is a feature of semi-colonial China that, since the first year of the Republic (1912), the various cliques of old and new warlords have waged incessant wars against one another, supported by imperialism from abroad and by the comprador and landlord classes at home. Such a phenomenon is to be found in none of the imperialist countries nor for that matter in any colony under direct imperialist rule, but only in a country like China which is under indirect imperialist rule. Two things account for its occurrence, namely, a localized agricultural economy (not a unified capitalist economy) and the imperialist policy of marking off spheres of influence in order to divide and exploit. The prolonged splits and wars within the White regime provide a condition for the emergence and persistence of one or more small Red areas under the leadership of the Communist Party amidst the encirclement of the White regime. The independent regime carved out on the borders of Hunan and Kiangsi Provinces is one of many such small areas. In difficult or critical times some comrades often have doubts about the survival of Red political power and become pessimistic. The reason is that they have not found the correct explanation for its emergence and survival. If only we realize that splits and wars will never cease within the White regime in China, we shall have no doubts about the emergence, survival and daily growth of Red political power.

Second, the regions where China's Red political power has first emerged and is able to last for a long time have not been those unaffected by the democratic revolution, such as Szechuan, Kweichow, Yunnan and the northern provinces, but regions such as the provinces of Hunan, Kwangtung, Hupeh and Kiangsi, where the masses of workers, peasants and soldiers rose in great numbers in the course of the bourgeois-democratic revolution of 1926 and 1927. In many parts of these provinces trade unions and peasant associations were formed on a wide scale, and many economic and political struggles were waged by the working class and the peasantry against the landlord class and the bourgeoisie. This is why the people held political power for three days in the city of

Canton and why independent regimes of peasants emerged in Haifeng and Lufeng, in eastern and southern Hunan, in the Hunan-Kiangsi border area and in Huangan, Hupeh Province.[8] As for the present Red Army, it is a split-off from the National Revolutionary Army which underwent democratic political training and came under the influence of the masses of workers and peasants. The elements that make up the Red Army cannot possibly come from armies like those of Yen Hsi-shan and Chang Tso-lin, which have not received any democratic political training or come under the influence of the workers and peasants.

Third, whether it is possible for the people's political power in small areas to last depends on whether the nation-wide revolutionary situation continues to develop. If it does, then the small Red areas will undoubtedly last for a long time, and will, moreover, inevitably become one of the many forces for winning nation-wide political power. If the nation-wide revolutionary situation does not continue to develop but stagnates for a fairly long time, then it will be impossible for the small Red areas to last long. Actually, the revolutionary situation in China is continuing to develop with the continuous splits and wars within the ranks of the comprador and landlord classes and of the international bourgeoisie. Therefore the small Red areas will undoubtedly last for a long time, and will also continue to expand and gradually approach the goal of seizing political power throughout the country.

Fourth, the existence of a regular Red Army of adequate strength is a necessary condition for the existence of Red political power. If we have local Red Guards[9] only but no regular Red Army, then we cannot cope with the regular White forces, but only with the landlords' levies. Therefore, even when the masses of workers and peasants are active, it is definitely impossible to create an independent regime, let alone an independent regime which is durable and grows daily, unless we have regular forces of adequate strength. It follows that the idea of "establishing independent regimes of the workers and the peasants by armed force" is an important one which must be fully grasped by the Communist Party and by the masses of workers and peasants in areas under the independent regime.

Fifth, another important condition in addition to the above is required for the prolonged existence and development of Red political power, namely, that the Communist Party organization should be strong and its policy correct.

III. THE INDEPENDENT REGIME IN THE HUNAN-KIANGSI BORDER AREA AND THE AUGUST DEFEAT

Splits and wars among the warlords weaken the power of the White regime. Thus opportunities are provided for the rise of Red political power in small areas. But fighting among the warlords does not go on every day. Whenever the White regime in one or more provinces enjoys temporary stability, the ruling classes there inevitably combine and do their utmost to destroy Red political power. In areas where all the necessary conditions for its establishment and persistence are not fulfilled, Red political power is in danger of being overthrown by the enemy. This is the reason why many Red regimes emerging at favourable moments before last April in places like Canton, Haifeng and Lufeng, the Hunan-Kiangsi border area, southern Hunan, Liling and Huangan were crushed one after another by the White regime. From April onward the independent regime in the Hunan-Kiangsi border area was confronted with a temporarily stable ruling power in the south, and Hunan and Kiangsi would usually dispatch eight, nine or more regiments — sometimes as many as eighteen — to "suppress" us. Yet with a force of less than four regiments we fought the enemy for four long months, daily enlarging the territory under our independent regime, deepening the agrarian revolution, extending the organizations of the people's political power, and expanding the Red Army and the Red Guards. This was possible because the policies of the Communist Party organizations (local and army) in the Hunan-Kiangsi border area were correct. The policies of the Border Area Special Committee and the Army Committee of the Party were then as follows:

Struggle resolutely against the enemy, set up political power in the middle section of the Lohsiao mountain range,[10] and oppose flightism.

Deepen the agrarian revolution in areas under the independent regime.

Promote the development of the local Party organization with the help of the army Party organization and promote the development of the local armed forces with the help of the regular army.

Concentrate the Red Army units in order to fight the enemy confronting them when the time is opportune, and oppose the division of forces so as to avoid being destroyed one by one.

Adopt the policy of advancing in a series of waves to expand the area under the independent regime, and oppose the policy of expansion by adventurist advance.

Thanks to these proper tactics, to a terrain favourable to our struggle, and to the inadequate co-ordination between the troops invading from Hunan and those invading from Kiangsi, we were able to win a number of victories in the four months from April to July. Although several times stronger than we, the enemy was unable to prevent the constant expansion of our regime, let alone to destroy it, and our regime tended to exert an ever-growing influence on Hunan and Kiangsi. The sole reason for the August defeat was that, failing to realize that the period was one of temporary stability for the ruling classes, some comrades adopted a strategy suited to a period of political splits within the ruling classes and divided our forces for an adventurous advance, thus causing defeat both in the border area and in southern Hunan. Comrade Tu Hsiu-ching, the representative of the Hunan Provincial Committee, failed to grasp the actual situation and disregarded the resolutions of the joint meeting of the Special Committee, the Army Committee and the Yunghsin County Committee of the Party; he just mechanically enforced the order of the Hunan Provincial Committee and echoed the views of the Red Army's 29th Regiment which wanted to evade struggle and return home, and his mistake was exceedingly grave. The situation arising from this defeat was salvaged as a result of the corrective measures taken by the Special Committee and the Army Committee of the Party after September.

IV. THE ROLE OF THE INDEPENDENT REGIME OF THE HUNAN-KIANGSI BORDER AREA IN HUNAN, HUPEH AND KIANGSI

The significance of the armed independent regime of workers and peasants in the Hunan-Kiangsi border area, with Ningkang as its centre, is definitely not confined to the few counties in the border area; this regime will play an immense role in the process of the seizure of political power in Hunan, Hupeh and Kiangsi through the insurrection of the workers and peasants in these three provinces. The following are tasks of great importance for the Party in the border area in connection with the insurrections unfolding in Hunan, Hupeh and Kiangsi: Extend the influence of the agrarian revolution and of the people's political power in the border area to the lower reaches of the rivers in Hunan and Kiangsi and as far as Hupeh; constantly expand the Red Army and enhance its quality through struggle so that it can fulfil its mission in the coming general insurrection of the three provinces; enlarge the local armed forces in the counties, that is, the Red Guards and the workers' and peasants' insurrection detachments, and enhance their quality so that they are able to fight the landlords' levies and small armed units now and safeguard the political power of the border area in the future; gradually reduce the extent to which local work is dependent on the assistance of the Red Army personnel, so that the border area will have its own personnel to take charge of the work and even provide personnel for the Red Army and the expanded territory of the independent regime.

V. ECONOMIC PROBLEMS

The shortage of necessities and cash has become a very big problem for the army and the people inside the White encirclement. Because of the tight enemy blockade, necessities such as salt, cloth and medicines have been very scarce and dear all through the past year in the independent border area, which has upset, sometimes to an acute degree, the lives of the masses of the workers, peasants and petty bourgeoisie,[11] as well as of the soldiers of the Red Army. The Red Army has to fight the enemy and to provision itself at one and the same time. It even lacks funds to pay the daily food allowance of five cents per person, which is provided in addition to grain; the soldiers are undernourished, many are ill, and the wounded in the hospitals are worse off. Such difficulties are of course unavoidable before the nation-wide seizure of political power; yet there is a pressing need to overcome them to some extent, to make life somewhat easier, and especially to secure more adequate supplies for the

Red Army. Unless the Party in the border area can find proper ways to deal with economic problems, the independent regime will have great difficulties during the comparatively long period in which the enemy's rule will remain stable. An adequate solution of these economic problems undoubtedly merits the attention of every Party member.

VI. THE PROBLEM OF MILITARY BASES

The Party in the border area has another task, namely, the consolidation of the military bases at Five Wells[12] and Chiulung. The Five Wells mountain area at the juncture of Yunghsin, Linghsien, Ningkang and Suichuan Counties, and the Chiulung mountain area at the juncture of Yunghsin, Ningkang, Chaling and Lienhua Counties, both of which have topographical advantages, are important military bases not only for the border area at present, but also for insurrections in Hunan, Hupeh and Kiangsi in the future, and this is particularly true of Five Wells, where we have the support of the people as well as a terrain that is especially difficult and strategically important. The way to consolidate these bases is, first, to construct adequate defences, second, to store sufficient grain and, third, to set up comparatively good Red Army hospitals. The Party in the border area must strive to perform these three tasks effectively.

NOTES

[1] By the term "bourgeoisie", Comrade Mao Tse-tung means the national bourgeoisie. For his detailed account of the distinction between this class and the big comprador bourgeoisie, see "On Tactics Against Japanese Imperialism" (December 1935) and "The Chinese Revolution and the Chinese Communist Party" (December 1939).

[2] These four cliques of warlords fought together against Chang Tso-lin and occupied Peking and Tientsin in June 1928.

[3] Chang Tso-lin, who headed the Fengtien clique of warlords, became the most powerful warlord in northern China after defeating Wu Pei-fu in the second Chihli-Fengtien War in 1924. In 1926, with Wu Pei-fu as his ally, he marched on and occupied Peking. In June 1928, while retreating to the Northeast by rail, he was killed *en route* by a bomb planted by the Japanese imperialists whose tool he had been.

[4] This reform movement arose after the Japanese invaders occupied Tsinan on May 3, 1928, and after Chiang Kai-shek openly and brazenly compromised with Japan.

Within the national bourgeoisie which had identified itself with the counter-revolutionary coup d'état of 1927, a section acting in its own interests gradually began to form an opposition to the Chiang Kai-shek regime. The careerist counter-revolutionary group of Wang Ching-wei, Chen Kung-po and others which was active in this movement formed what became known as the "Reorganization Clique" in the Kuomintang.

[5] In 1928 Chiang Kai-shek, backed by British and U.S. imperialism, drove north to attack Chang Tso-lin. The Japanese imperialists then occupied Tsinan, the provincial capital of Shantung, and cut the Tientsin-Pukow railway line to check the northward spread of British and American influence. On May 3 the invading Japanese troops slaughtered large numbers of Chinese in Tsinan. This became known as the Tsinan Massacre.

[6] The organizational form of China's Red political power was similar to that of Soviet political power. A Soviet is a representative council, a political institution created by the Russian working class during the 1905 Revolution. Lenin and Stalin, on the basis of Marxist theory, drew the conclusion that a Soviet republic is the most suitable form of social and political organization for the transition from capitalism to socialism. Under the leadership of the Bolshevik Party of Lenin and Stalin, the Russian October Socialist Revolution in 1917 brought into being for the first time in world history such a socialist Soviet republic, a dictatorship of the proletariat. After the defeat of the 1927 revolution in China, the representative council was adopted as the form of people's political power in various places in the mass revolutionary uprisings led by the Chinese Communist Party and, first and foremost, by Comrade Mao Tse-tung. In its nature political power at that stage of the Chinese revolution was a people's democratic dictatorship of the anti-imperialist, anti-feudal, new-democratic revolution led by the proletariat, which was different from the proletarian dictatorship in the Soviet Union.

[7] During World War II, many colonial countries in the East formerly under the imperialist rule of Britain, the United States, France and the Netherlands were occupied by the Japanese imperialists. Led by their Communist Parties, the masses of workers, peasants and urban petty bourgeoisie and members of the national bourgeoisie in these countries took advantage of the contradictions between the British, U.S., French and Dutch imperialists on the one hand and the Japanese imperialists on the other, organized a broad united front against fascist aggression, built anti-Japanese base areas and waged bitter guerrilla warfare against the Japanese. Thus the political situation existing prior to World War II began to change. When the Japanese imperialists were driven out of these countries at the end of World War II, the imperialists of the United States, Britain, France and the Netherlands attempted to restore their colonial rule, but, having built up armed forces of considerable strength during the anti-Japanese war, these colonial peoples refused to return to the old way of life. Moreover, the imperialist system all over the world was profoundly shaken because the Soviet Union had become strong, because all the imperialist powers, except the United States, had either been overthrown or weakened in the war, and finally because the imperialist front was breached in China by the victorious Chinese revolution. Thus, much as in China, it has become possible for the peoples of all, or at least some, of the colonial countries in the East to maintain big and small revolutionary base areas and revolutionary regimes over a long period of time, and to carry on long-term revolutionary wars in which to surround the cities from the countryside, and then gradually to advance to take the cities and win nation-wide victory. The view held by Comrade Mao Tse-tung in 1928 on the question of establishing independent regimes in colonies under direct imperialist rule has changed as a result of the changes in the situation.

⁸ These were the first counter-attacks which the people under Communist leadership launched in various places against the forces of the counter-revolution after Chiang Kai-shek and Wang Ching-wei successively turned traitor to the revolution in 1927. On December 11, 1927, the workers and revolutionary soldiers of Canton united to stage an uprising, and set up the people's political power. They fought fiercely against the counter-revolutionary forces, which were directly supported by imperialism, but failed because the disparity in strength was too great. Peasants in Haifeng and Lufeng on the eastern coast of Kwangtung Province had started a powerful revolutionary movement during 1923-25 under the leadership of Comrade Peng Pai, a member of the Communist Party, and this movement contributed greatly to the victory of the two eastern campaigns launched from Canton by the National Revolutionary Army against the counter-revolutionary clique headed by Chen Chiung-ming. After Chiang Kai-shek's betrayal of the revolution on April 12, 1927, these peasants staged three uprisings in April, September and October, and established a revolutionary regime which held out until April 1928. In eastern Hunan Province, insurrectionary peasants captured an area embracing Liuyang, Pingkiang, Liling and Chuchow in September 1927. At about the same time, tens of thousands of peasants staged an armed uprising in Hsiaokan, Macheng and Huangan in northeastern Hupeh Province and occupied the county town of Huangan for over thirty days. In southern Hunan, peasants in the counties of Yichang, Chenchow, Leiyang, Yunghsing and Tzehsing rose in arms in January 1928 and set up a revolutionary regime, which lasted for three months.

⁹ The Red Guards were armed units of the masses in the revolutionary base areas, whose members carried on their regular productive work.

¹⁰ The Lohsiao mountain range is a large range running along the borders of Kiangsi and Hunan Provinces. The Chingkang Mountains are in its middle section.

¹¹ By the term "petty bourgeoisie" Comrade Mao Tse-tung means those elements other than the peasants — handicraftsmen, small merchants, professional people of various kinds and petty-bourgeois intellectuals. In China they mostly live in cities, but there are quite a number in the countryside.

¹² Five Wells designates the villages of Big Well, Small Well, Upper Well, Middle Well and Lower Well, in the Chingkang Mountains, which are situated between Yunghsin, Ningkang and Suichuan in western Kiangsi and Linghsien County in eastern Hunan.

THE STRUGGLE IN THE CHINGKANG MOUNTAINS

November 25, 1928

THE INDEPENDENT REGIME
IN THE HUNAN-KIANGSI BORDER AREA
AND THE AUGUST DEFEAT

China is the only country in the world today where one or more small areas under Red political power have emerged in the midst of a White regime which encircles them. We find on analysis that one reason for this phenomenon lies in the incessant splits and wars within China's comprador and landlord classes. So long as these splits and wars continue, it is possible for an armed independent regime of workers and peasants to survive and grow. In addition, its survival and growth require the following conditions: (1) a sound mass base, (2) a sound Party organization, (3) a fairly strong Red Army, (4) terrain favourable to military operations, and (5) economic resources sufficient for sustenance.

An independent regime must vary its strategy against the encircling ruling classes, adopting one strategy when the ruling class regime is temporarily stable and another when it is split up. In a period when the ruling classes are split up, as during the wars between Li Tsung-jen and Tang Sheng-chih in Hunan and Hupeh Provinces[1] and between Chang Fa-kuei and Li Chi-shen in Kwangtung Province,[2] our strategy can be comparatively adventurous and the area carved out by military operations can be comparatively large. However, we must take care to lay a solid foundation in the central districts so that we shall have something secure to rely on when the White terror strikes. In a period when the regime of the ruling classes is

---

This was a report submitted by Comrade Mao Tse-tung to the Central Committee of the Communist Party of China.

73

comparatively stable, as it was in the southern provinces after April this year, our strategy must be one of gradual advance. In such a period, the worst thing in military affairs is to divide our forces for an adventurous advance, and the worst thing in local work (distributing land, establishing political power, expanding the Party and organizing local armed forces) is to scatter our personnel and neglect to lay a solid foundation in the central districts. The defeats which many small Red areas have suffered have been due either to the absence of the requisite objective conditions or to subjective mistakes in tactics. Mistakes in tactics have been made solely because of failure to distinguish clearly between the two kinds of period, that in which the regime of the ruling classes is temporarily stable and that in which it is split up. In a period of temporary stability, some comrades advocated dividing our forces for an adventurous advance and even proposed leaving the defence of extensive areas to the Red Guards alone, as though oblivious of the fact that the enemy could attack not merely with the landlords' levies but even in concentrated operations with regular troops. In local work, they utterly neglected to lay a solid foundation in the central districts and attempted unrestricted expansion regardless of whether it was within our capacity. If anyone advocated a policy of gradual advance in military operations or a policy of concentrating our effort in local work on laying a solid foundation in the central districts so as to secure an invincible position, they dubbed him a "conservative". Their wrong ideas were the root cause of the defeats sustained last August by the Hunan-Kiangsi border area and by the Fourth Red Army in southern Hunan.

Our work in the Hunan-Kiangsi border area began in October last year. At the start, all our Party organizations in the counties were defunct. The local armed forces consisted only of the two units under Yuan Wen-tsai and Wang Tso in the vicinity of the Chingkang Mountains, each unit having sixty rifles in bad repair, while the peasant self-defence corps in the counties of Yunghsin, Lienhua, Chaling and Linghsien had been totally disarmed by the landlord class and the revolutionary ardour of the masses had been stifled. By February this year Ningkang, Yunghsin, Chaling and Suichuan had county Party committees, Linghsien had a special district Party committee, and in Lienhua a Party organization was beginning to function and establish connections with the Wanan County Committee. All the counties except Linghsien had a few local armed units.

In Ningkang, Chaling, Suichuan and Yunghsin, and especially in the two latter counties, there were a good many guerrilla uprisings against the landlords which aroused the masses, and all were fairly successful. In that period the agrarian revolution had not yet been carried very far. The organs of political power were called governments of the workers, peasants and soldiers. Soldiers' committees[3] were set up in the army. When units went on separate missions, action committees were set up to direct them. The leading body of the Party there was the Front Committee (with Mao Tse-tung as secretary), which had been appointed by the Hunan Provincial Committee during the Autumn Harvest Uprising. In early March, upon the request of the Southern Hunan Special Committee, the Front Committee was abolished and reorganized as the Divisional Party Committee (with Ho Ting-ying as secretary), which thus became a body in charge of Party organizations in the army only and without authority over the local Party organizations. Meanwhile, Mao Tse-tung's forces were dispatched to southern Hunan upon the request of the Special Committee there, and consequently the Hunan-Kiangsi border area was occupied by the enemy for more than a month. At the end of March came the defeat in southern Hunan, and in April the forces under Chu Teh and those under Mao Tse-tung, together with the peasant army of southern Hunan, withdrew to Ningkang and began to re-establish the independent regime in the border area.

From April onward the independent regime in the Hunan-Kiangsi border area was confronted with a temporarily stable ruling power in the south, and Hunan and Kiangsi would dispatch at least eight or nine regiments of reactionary forces to "suppress" us and sometimes as many as eighteen. Yet with a force of less than four regiments we fought the enemy for four long months, daily enlarging the territory under our independent regime, deepening the agrarian revolution, extending the people's political power and expanding the Red Army and the Red Guards. This was possible because the policies of the Party organizations (local and army) in the border area were correct. The policies of the Border Area Special Committee (with Mao Tse-tung as secretary) and the Army Committee (with Chen Yi as secretary) of the Party were then as follows:

Struggle resolutely against the enemy, set up political power in the middle section of the Lohsiao mountain range, and oppose flightism.

Deepen the agrarian revolution in areas under the independent regime.

Promote the development of the local Party organization with the help of the army Party organization and promote the development of the local armed forces with the help of the regular army.

Be on the defensive against Hunan with its comparatively strong ruling power, and take the offensive against Kiangsi with its comparatively weak ruling power.

Devote great efforts to the development of Yunghsin, set up an independent regime of the people there and prepare for a prolonged struggle.

Concentrate the Red Army units in order to fight the enemy confronting them when the time is opportune, and oppose the division of forces so as to avoid being destroyed one by one.

Adopt the policy of advancing in a series of waves to expand the area under the independent regime, and oppose the policy of expansion by adventurist advance.

Thanks to these proper tactics, to the terrain of the border area which favoured our struggle, and to the inadequate co-ordination between the troops invading from Hunan and those invading from Kiangsi, we were able to win a number of military victories and expand the people's independent regime in the four months from April to July. Although several times stronger than we, the enemy was unable to prevent the expansion of our regime, let alone to destroy it. Our regime tended to exert an ever-growing influence on Hunan and Kiangsi. The sole reason for the August defeat was that, failing to realize that the period was one of temporary stability for the ruling classes, some comrades adopted a policy suited to a period of splits within the ruling classes and divided our forces for an adventurous advance on southern Hunan, thus causing defeat both in the border area and in southern Hunan. Tu Hsiu-ching, the representative of the Hunan Provincial Committee, and Yang Kai-ming, the secretary of the Border Area Special Committee who had been appointed by the Provincial Committee, failed to grasp the actual situation and, taking advantage of the fact that Mao Tse-tung, Wan Hsi-hsien and other strongly dissenting comrades were far away in Yunghsin, they disregarded the resolutions of the joint meeting of the Army Committee, the Special Committee and the Yunghsin County Committee of the Party, which disapproved of the views of the Hunan Provincial

Committee. They just mechanically enforced the order of the Hunan Provincial Committee to march to southern Hunan and fell in with the desire of the Red Army's 29th Regiment (composed of peasants from Yichang) to evade struggle and return home, thus causing defeat both in the border area and in southern Hunan.

Originally, in mid-July, the Eighth Army from Hunan, under Wu Shang, had invaded Ningkang, penetrated to Yunghsin, sought battle with us in vain (our men tried to attack them from a side road but missed them) and then, being afraid of the masses who supported us, hurriedly retreated to Chaling via Lienhua. In the meantime, the major detachment of the Red Army, which was advancing from Ningkang to attack Linghsien and Chaling, changed its plans on reaching Linghsien and turned towards southern Hunan, while the enemy forces from Kiangsi, consisting of 5 regiments of the Third Army under Wang Chun and Chin Han-ting and 6 regiments of the Sixth Army under Hu Wen-tou, launched a joint assault on Yunghsin. At that point we had only 1 regiment in Yunghsin which, under the cover provided by the broad masses of the people, pinned down these 11 regiments within a radius of thirty *li* of Yunghsin county town for as long as twenty-five days by means of guerrilla attacks from every direction. In the end we lost Yunghsin because of the enemy's fierce assault, and also lost Lienhua and Ningkang shortly afterwards. At that moment internal dissensions suddenly flared up among the Kiangsi enemy forces; the Sixth Army under Hu Wen-tou withdrew in haste and presently engaged Wang Chun's Third Army at Changshu. The other 5 Kiangsi regiments then hastily withdrew to the county town of Yunghsin. Had our major detachment not moved to southern Hunan, it would have been entirely possible to rout this enemy force and extend the area of the independent regime to include Kian, Anfu and Pinghsiang and to link it up with Pingkiang and Liuyang. But as the major detachment was away and the one remaining regiment was much too exhausted, it was decided that some men should remain to defend the Chingkang Mountains in co-operation with the two units under Yuan Wen-tsai and Wang Tso, and that I should take the rest to Kueitung to meet the major detachment and to invite it back. By that time the major detachment was retreating from southern Hunan to Kueitung, and on August 23 we joined forces there.

When the major detachment of the Red Army had arrived in Linghsien in mid-July, the officers and men of the 29th Regiment, who were wavering politically and wanted to return to their homes in southern Hunan, refused to obey orders, while the 28th Regiment was against going to southern Hunan and wanted to go to southern Kiangsi, but in any case did not want to return to Yunghsin. As Tu Hsiu-ching encouraged the 29th Regiment in their mistaken ideas and the Army Committee failed to dissuade them, the major detachment set out from Linghsien for Chenchow on July 17. In an engagement with the enemy forces under Fan Shih-sheng in Chenchow on July 24, it was initially successful but was later defeated and withdrew from the battle. Thereupon, acting on its own, the 29th Regiment hurried homeward to Yichang with the result that one section was annihilated at Lochang by Hu Feng-chang's bandits, another scattered in the Chenchow-Yichang area and has never been heard of since, and no more than a hundred men were mustered again that day. Fortunately, the 28th Regiment, which was the main force, had not suffered great losses and on August 18 it occupied Kueitung. On August 23 the regiment was joined by the troops from the Chingkang Mountains, to which it was decided that the combined forces should return by way of Chungyi and Shangyu. When we reached Chungyi, battalion commander Yuan Chung-chuan defected with an infantry company and an artillery company, and though the two companies were brought back, our regimental commander Wang Erh-cho lost his life in this action. When our men were returning but had not yet reached their destination, enemy units from Hunan and Kiangsi seized the opportunity to attack the Chingkang Mountains on August 30. Using their points of vantage, the defending troops, numbering less than one battalion, fought back, routed the enemy and saved the base.

The causes of our August defeat were as follows: (1) some officers and men, who were wavering and homesick, lost their fighting capacity, while others, who were unwilling to go to southern Hunan, were lacking in enthusiasm; (2) our men were exhausted by long marches in the sweltering summer heat; (3) having ventured several hundred *li* away from Linghsien, our men lost contact with the border area and became isolated; (4) as the masses in southern Hunan had not yet been aroused, the expedition proved to be pure military adventurism; (5) we were uninformed about the enemy situation; and (6) the preparations were inadequate, and officers and men did not understand the purpose of the operation.

THE CURRENT SITUATION IN THE AREA
UNDER THE INDEPENDENT REGIME

Since April this year the Red areas have been gradually extended. After the battle of Lungyuankou (on the borders of Yunghsin and Ningkang) on June 23, in which we defeated the Kiangsi enemy forces for the fourth time, the border area reached the peak of its development, embracing the three counties of Ningkang, Yunghsin and Lienhua, small sections of Kian and Anfu, the northern section of Suichuan, and the southeastern section of Linghsien. In the Red areas the greater part of the land had been distributed and the remainder was being distributed. Organs of political power were set up everywhere in the districts and townships. County governments were set up in Ningkang, Yunghsin, Lienhua and Suichuan, and a border area government was formed. Insurrectionary detachments of workers and peasants were organized in the villages, and Red Guards were formed at the district and county levels. In July the Kiangsi enemy forces launched attacks, and in August the Hunan and Kiangsi enemy forces jointly attacked the Chingkang Mountains. All the county towns and the plains in the border area were occupied by the enemy. The enemy's jackals — the peace preservation corps and the landlords' levies — ran amuck, and White terror raged throughout the towns and countryside. Most of the Party and government organizations collapsed. The rich peasants and the opportunists in the Party went over to the enemy in great numbers. It was not until the battle of the Chingkang Mountains was fought on August 30 that the Hunan enemy forces retreated to Linghsien; but the Kiangsi forces still held all the county towns and most of the villages. However, the enemy has never been able to capture the mountain areas, which include the western and northern districts of Ningkang; the Tienlung, Hsiaohsi-kiang and Wannienshan districts in the northern, western and southern sections of Yunghsin respectively; the Shanghsi district of Lienhua; the Chingkangshan district of Suichuan; and the Tsingshihkang and Tayuan districts of Linghsien. In July and August, in co-ordination with the Red Guards of the various counties, one regiment of the Red Army fought scores of battles, big and small, losing only thirty rifles, before it finally withdrew to the mountains.

As our men were marching back to the Chingkang Mountains via Chungyi and Shangyu, the enemy force from southern Kiangsi, the

Independent 7th Division under Liu Shih-yi, pursued us as far as Suichuan. On September 13 we defeated Liu Shih-yi, captured several hundred rifles and took Suichuan. On September 26 we returned to the Chingkang Mountains. On October 1, at Ningkang, we engaged and defeated one of Hsiung Shih-hui's brigades commanded by Chou Hun-yuan, recovering the entire county of Ningkang. Meanwhile, 126 men of the Hunan enemy forces under Yen Chung-ju, which had been stationed in Kueitung, came over to us and were organized into a special task battalion with Pi Chan-yun as commander. On November 9 we routed one regiment of Chou's brigade at Lungyuankou and the county town of Ningkang. On the next day we advanced and occupied Yunghsin, but withdrew to Ningkang shortly afterwards. At present our area, extending from the southern slopes of the Chingkang Mountains in Suichuan County in the south to the border of Lienhua County in the north, embraces the whole of Ningkang and parts of Suichuan, Linghsien and Yunghsin, forming a narrow unbroken stretch running north to south. The Shanghsi district of Lienhua and the Tienlung and Wannienshan districts of Yunghsin, however, are not firmly linked with this unbroken stretch. The enemy is attempting to destroy our base area by military attacks and economic blockade, and we are now preparing to defeat his attacks.

MILITARY QUESTIONS

Since the struggle in the border area is exclusively military, both the Party and the masses have to be placed on a war footing. How to deal with the enemy, how to fight, has become the central problem in our daily life. An independent regime must be an armed one. Wherever such an area is located, it will be immediately occupied by the enemy if armed forces are lacking or inadequate, or if wrong tactics are used in dealing with the enemy. As the struggle is getting fiercer every day, our problems have become extremely complex and serious.

The Red Army in the border area is drawn from: (1) troops formerly under Yeh Ting and Ho Lung in Chaochow and Swatow;[4] (2) the Guards Regiment of the former National Government at Wuchang;[5] (3) peasants from Pingkiang and Liuyang;[6] (4) peasants from southern Hunan[7] and workers from Shuikoushan;[8] (5) men captured from the forces under Hsu Keh-hsiang, Tang Sheng-chih, Pai Chung-hsi, Chu Pei-teh, Wu Shang and Hsiung Shih-hui; and

(6) peasants from the counties in the border area. However, of the troops formerly commanded by Yeh Ting and Ho Lung, the Guards Regiment and the peasants from Pingkiang and Liuyang, only one-third is left after more than a year's fighting. Casualties have also been heavy among the peasants from southern Hunan. Thus although the first four categories remain the backbone of the Fourth Red Army to this day, they are now far outnumbered by the last two categories. Furthermore, in the latter the peasants are outnumbered by the captured soldiers; without replacement from this source, there would be a serious manpower problem. Even so, the increase in men does not keep pace with the increase in rifles. Rifles are not easily lost, but men are wounded or killed, fall sick or desert and so are lost more easily. The Hunan Provincial Committee has promised to send us workers from Anyuan,[9] and we earnestly hope it will do so.

As to class origin, the Red Army consists partly of workers and peasants and partly of *lumpen*-proletarians. Of course, it is inadvisable to have too many of the latter. But they are able to fight, and as fighting is going on every day with mounting casualties, it is already no easy matter to get replacements even from among them. In these circumstances the only solution is to intensify political training.

The majority of the Red Army soldiers come from the mercenary armies, but their character changes once they are in the Red Army. First of all, the Red Army has abolished the mercenary system, making the men feel they are fighting for themselves and for the people and not for somebody else. So far the Red Army has no system of regular pay, but issues grain, money for cooking oil, salt, firewood and vegetables, and a little pocket money. Land has been allotted to all Red Army officers and men who are natives of the border area, but it is rather difficult to allot land to those from other parts of the country.

After receiving political education, the Red Army soldiers have become class-conscious, learned the essentials of distributing land, setting up political power, arming the workers and peasants, etc., and they know they are fighting for themselves, for the working class and the peasantry. Hence they can endure the hardships of the bitter struggle without complaint. Each company, battalion or regiment has its soldiers' committee which represents the interests of the soldiers and carries on political and mass work.

Experience has proved that the system of Party representatives[10] must not be abolished. The Party representative is particularly important at company level, since Party branches are organized on a company basis. He has to see that the soldiers' committee carries out political training, to guide the work of the mass movements, and to serve concurrently as the secretary of the Party branch. Facts have shown that the better the company Party representative, the sounder the company, and that the company commander can hardly play this important political role. As the casualties among the lower cadres are heavy, captured enemy soldiers often become platoon leaders or company commanders in a very short time; some of those captured in February or March are already battalion commanders. It might seem that since our army is called the Red Army it could do without Party representatives, but this is a gross error. At one time the 28th Regiment in southern Hunan abolished the system, only to restore it later. To rename the Party representatives "directors" would be to confuse them with the directors in the Kuomintang army who are detested by the captured soldiers. A change of name does not affect the nature of the system. Hence we have decided to make no change. Casualties among Party representatives are very heavy, and while we have started classes for training and replenishment, we hope that the Central Committee and the Hunan and Kiangsi Provincial Committees will send us at least thirty comrades who are able to serve as Party representatives.

Ordinarily a soldier needs six months' or a year's training before he can fight, but our soldiers, recruited only yesterday, have to fight today with practically no training. Poor in military technique, they fight on courage alone. As long periods of rest and training are out of the question, the only thing to do is to try and avoid certain engagements if possible and thus gain time for training. We now have a corps of 150 people in training as lower-ranking officers, and we intend to make this course a permanent institution. We hope that the Central Committee and the two Provincial Committees will send us more officers from platoon leader and company commander upwards.

The Hunan Provincial Committee has asked us to attend to the material conditions of the soldiers and make them at least a little better than those of the average worker or peasant. Actually they are worse. In addition to grain, each man receives only five cents a day for cooking oil, salt, firewood and vegetables, and even this is hard to keep up. The monthly cost of these items alone amounts to more than ten thousand silver dollars, which is obtained exclusively through expropriation of the local tyrants.[11] We now have cotton padding for winter clothing for the whole army of five thousand men but are still short of cloth. Cold as the weather is, many of our men are still wearing only two layers of thin clothing. Fortunately we are inured to hardships. What is more, all of us share the same hardships; from the commander of the army to the cook everyone lives on the daily food allowance of five cents, apart from grain. As for pocket money, everybody gets the same amount, whether it is twenty cents, or forty cents.[12] Consequently the soldiers have no complaints against anyone.

After each engagement there are some wounded. Also many officers and men have fallen ill from malnutrition, exposure to cold or other causes. Our hospitals up in the mountains give both Chinese and Western treatment, but are short of doctors and medicines. At present they have over eight hundred patients. The Hunan Provincial Committee promised to obtain drugs for us, but so far we have received none. We still hope the Central Committee and the two Provincial Committees will send us a few doctors with Western training, and some iodine.

Apart from the role played by the Party, the reason why the Red Army has been able to carry on in spite of such poor material conditions and such frequent engagements is its practice of democracy. The officers do not beat the men; officers and men receive equal treatment; soldiers are free to hold meetings and to speak out; trivial formalities have been done away with; and the accounts are open for all to inspect. The soldiers handle the mess arrangements and, out of the daily five cents for cooking oil, salt, firewood and vegetables, they can even save a little for pocket money, amounting to roughly six or seven coppers per person per day, which is called "mess savings". All this gives great satisfaction to the soldiers. The newly captured soldiers in particular feel that our army and the Kuomintang army are worlds apart. They feel spiritually liberated, even though material conditions in the Red Army are not equal to those in the White army. The very soldiers who had no courage in the White army yesterday are very brave in the Red Army today; such is the effect of democracy. The Red Army is like a furnace in which all captured soldiers are transmuted the moment they come over. In China the army needs democracy as much as the people do. Democracy in our army is an important weapon for undermining the feudal mercenary army.[13]

The Party organization now has four levels, the company branch, the battalion committee, the regimental committee and the army committee. In a company there is the branch, with a group in each squad. "The Party branch is organized on a company basis"; this is an important reason why the Red Army has been able to carry on such arduous fighting without falling apart. Two years ago, when we were in the Kuomintang army, our Party had no organizational roots among the soldiers, and even among Yeh Ting's troops[14] there was only one Party branch to each regiment; that is why we could not stand up to any serious test. In the Red Army today the ratio of Party to non-Party people is approximately one to three, or an average of one Party member in every four men. Recently we decided to recruit more Party members among the combat soldiers, so as to attain a fifty-fifty ratio.[15] At present the company branches are short of good Party secretaries, and we ask the Central Committee to send us a number of activists from among those who can no longer function where they are now. Almost all the cadres from southern Hunan are doing Party work in the army. But since some of them were scattered during the retreat in southern Hunan in August, we now have no people to spare.

The local armed forces consist of Red Guards and insurrectionary detachments of workers and peasants. Armed with spears and shotguns, these detachments are organized on a township basis, each township having one detachment whose strength varies with the population. Its job is to suppress counter-revolution, protect the township government and assist the Red Army and Red Guards in battle when the enemy appears. The insurrectionary detachments started in Yunghsin as an underground force, but they have come into the open since we captured the entire county. The organization has now been extended to other counties in the border area and the name remains unchanged. The arms of the Red Guards are mainly five-round rifles but also include some nine-round and single-round rifles. There are 140 rifles in Ningkang, 220 in Yunghsin, 43 in Lienhua, 50 in Chaling, 90 in Linghsien, 130 in Suichuan and 10 in Wanan, making a total of 683. Most of the rifles have been supplied by the Red Army, but a small number were captured from the enemy by the Red Guards themselves. Fighting constantly against the peace preservation corps and levies of the landlords, most of the Red Guards in the counties are steadily increasing their fighting capacity. Before the May 21st Incident,[16] all the counties had peasant self-defence corps. There were 300 rifles in Yuhsien, 300 in Chaling, 60 in Linghsien, 50 in Suichuan, 80 in Yunghsin, 60 in Lienhua, 60 in Ningkang (Yuan Wen-tsai's

men) and 60 in the Chingkang Mountains (Wang Tso's men), totalling
970. After the incident, apart from the rifles in the hands of Yuan's
and Wang's men, which remained intact, only 6 rifles were left in
Suichuan and 1 in Lienhua, all the rest having been seized by the
landlords. The peasant self-defence corps were not able to hold on
to their rifles as a result of the opportunist line. At present the
Red Guards in the counties still have far too few rifles, fewer than
those of the landlords; the Red Army should continue to help them
with arms. The Red Army should do everything, short of reducing
its own fighting capacity, to help arm the people. We have laid it
down that each battalion of the Red Army should consist of four
companies, each with 75 rifles, and, counting the rifles of the special
task company, machine-gun company, trench-mortar company, regimental headquarters and the three battalion headquarters, each
regiment will have 1,075 rifles. Those captured in action should be
used as far as possible for arming the local forces. The commanders
of the Red Guards should be people who have been sent from the
counties to the Red Army training corps and have finished their
training. The Red Army should send fewer and fewer people from
outside areas to command local forces. Chu Pei-teh is arming his peace
preservation corps and levies, while the armed forces of the landlords
in the border counties are of considerable size and fighting capacity.
This makes it all the more urgent to enlarge our local Red forces.

The principle for the Red Army is concentration, and that for the
Red Guards dispersion. At the present time when the reactionary regime
is temporarily stable, the enemy can mass huge forces to attack the
Red Army, and dispersion would not be to the Red Army's advantage.
In our experience, the dispersion of forces has almost always led
to defeat, while the concentration of forces to fight a numerically
inferior, equal or slightly superior enemy force has often led to victory. The Central Committee has instructed us to develop guerrilla
warfare in much too large an area, extending several thousand *li* in
both length and breadth; this is probably due to an overestimation
of our strength. For the Red Guards dispersion is an advantage, and
they are now using this method in their operations in all the counties.

The most effective method in propaganda directed at the enemy
forces is to release captured soldiers and give the wounded medical
treatment. Whenever soldiers, platoon leaders, or company or battalion commanders of the enemy forces are captured, we immediately
conduct propaganda among them; they are divided into those wishing

to stay and those wishing to leave, and the latter are given travelling expenses and set free. This immediately knocks the bottom out of the enemy's slander that "the Communist bandits kill everyone on sight". Writing about this measure, the *Ten-Day Review*, the journal of Yang Chih-sheng's 9th Division, exclaimed: "How vicious!" The Red Army soldiers show great concern for the prisoners and arrange warm farewells for them, and at every "Farewell Party for Our New Brothers" the prisoners respond with speeches of heart-felt gratitude. Medical treatment for the enemy wounded also has a great effect. Clever people on the enemy side like Li Wen-pin have recently imitated us by stopping the killing of prisoners and by giving medical attention to the wounded. Nevertheless, our men rejoin us at the very next engagement, bringing their arms with them, and this has happened twice already. In addition, we do as much written propaganda as possible, for instance, painting slogans. Wherever we go, we cover the walls with them. But we are short of people who can draw and hope the Central Committee and the two Provincial Committees will send us a few.

As for the military bases, the first base, the Chingkang Mountains, is at the juncture of four counties, Ningkang, Linghsien, Suichuan and Yunghsin. The distance between Maoping on the northern slope in Ningkang County and Huangao on the southern slope in Suichuan is 90 *li*. The distance between Nashan on the eastern slope in Yunghsin County and Shuikou on the western slope in Linghsien is 80 *li*. The circumference measures 550 *li*, stretching from Nashan to Lungyuan-kou (both in Yunghsin County), Hsincheng, Maoping, Talung (all in Ningkang County), Shihtu, Shuikou, Hsiatsun (all in Linghsien County), Yingpanhsu, Taichiapu, Tafen, Tuitzechien, Huangao, Wutoukiang and Che-ao (all in Suichuan County) and back to Nashan. In the mountains there are paddy-fields and villages at Big Well, Small Well, Upper Well, Middle Well, Lower Well, Tzeping, Hsiachuang, Hsingchow, Tsaoping, Painihu and Lofu. All these places used to be infested by bandits and deserters but have now been turned into our base area. Its population is under two thousand, and the yield of unhusked rice is less than ten thousand piculs, and so the entire grain for the army has to be supplied from Ningkang, Yung-hsin and Suichuan Counties. All the strategic passes in the mountains are fortified. Our hospitals, bedding and clothing workshops, ordnance department and regimental rear offices are all here. At the present moment grain is being transported to the mountains from Ningkang.

Provided we have adequate supplies, the enemy can never break in. The second base, the Chiulung Mountains, is at the juncture of the four counties of Ningkang, Yunghsin, Lienhua and Chaling. It is less important than the Chingkang Mountains, but serves as the rearmost base for the local armed forces of the four counties, and it too has been fortified. It is essential for an independent Red regime encircled by the White regime to make use of the strategic advantages offered by mountains.

LAND QUESTIONS

The land situation in the border areas. Roughly speaking, more than 60 per cent of the land belonged to the landlords and less than 40 per cent to the peasants. In the Kiangsi sector, landownership was most concentrated in Suichuan County, where about 80 per cent of the land belonged to the landlords. Yunghsin came next with about 70 per cent. In Wanan, Ningkang and Lienhua there were more owner-peasants, but the landlords still owned the bulk of the land, *i.e.*, about 60 per cent of the total, while the peasants owned only 40 per cent. In the Hunan sector, about 70 per cent of the land in both Chaling and Linghsien Counties belonged to the landlords.

The question of the intermediate class. Given this land situation, it is possible to win the support of the majority for the confiscation and redistribution of all the land.[17] The rural population is roughly divided into three classes, the class of big and middle landlords, the intermediate class of small landlords and rich peasants, and the class of middle and poor peasants. The interests of the rich peasants are often interwoven with those of the small landlords. The land of the rich peasants forms only a small percentage of the total, yet if the land of the small landlords is counted in, the amount is considerable. Probably this is more or less the case throughout the country. The land policy which has been adopted in the border areas is complete confiscation and thorough distribution; consequently, in the Red area the big and middle landlord class and the intermediate class are both being attacked. Such is the policy, but in its actual execution we have met with a great deal of obstruction from the intermediate class. In the early days of the revolution the intermediate class ostensibly capitulated to the poor peasant class, but in reality they exploited their traditional social position and clan authority to intimidate the poor peasants for the purpose of delaying the distribution of land.

When no further delay was possible, they concealed their actual holdings, or retained the good land and gave up the poor land. In this period the poor peasants, having long been trampled down and feeling that the victory of the revolution was uncertain, frequently yielded to the intermediate class and dared not take vigorous action. It is taken against the intermediate class in the villages only when the revolution is on the upsurge, for instance, when political power has been seized in one or more counties, the reactionary army has suffered several defeats and the prowess of the Red Army has been repeatedly demonstrated. The most serious instances of delay in land distribution and concealment of landholdings occurred in the southern section of Yunghsin County, where the intermediate class was the largest. The actual land distribution in this area was carried out only after the Red Army won its great victory at Lungyuankou on June 23 and the district government punished several people for delaying distribution. But as the feudal family system prevails in every county, and as all the families in a village or group of villages belong to a single clan, it will be quite a long time before people become conscious of their class and clan sentiment is overcome in the villages.

  The defection of the intermediate class under the White terror. Having been under attack during the revolutionary upsurge, the intermediate class deserted to the enemy as soon as the White terror struck. In Yunghsin and Ningkang it was precisely the small landlords and rich peasants who led the reactionary troops in setting fire to the houses of revolutionary peasants. On the instructions of the reactionaries, they burned down houses and made arrests, and quite brazenly too. When the Red Army returned to the area of Ningkang, Hsincheng, Kucheng and Lungshih, several thousand peasants fled with the reactionaries to Yunghsin, because they were duped by the reactionary propaganda that the Communists would kill them. It was only after we had conducted propaganda to the effect that "peasants who have defected will not be killed" and "peasants who have defected are welcome to come back to reap their crops" that some of them slowly came back.

  When the revolution is at a low ebb in the country as a whole, the most difficult problem in our areas is to keep a firm hold on the intermediate class. The main reason for betrayal by this class is that it has received too heavy a blow from the revolution. But when there is a revolutionary upsurge in the country as a whole, the poor peasant class has something to rely on and becomes bolder, while the intermediate class has something to fear and dare not get out of hand. When the war between Li Tsung-jen and Tang Sheng-chih spread to Hunan, the small landlords in Chaling tried to placate the peasants, and some even sent them pork as a New Year gift (though by then the Red Army had already withdrawn from Chaling to Suichuan). But after the war ended, no one ever heard of such things again. Now that there is a nation-wide tide of counter-revolution, the intermediate class in the White areas, having suffered heavy blows, has attached itself almost wholly to the big landlord class, and the poor peasant class has become isolated. This is indeed a very serious problem.[18]

The pressure of daily life as a cause of the defection of the intermediate class. The Red and the White areas are now facing each other like two countries at war. Owing to the tight enemy blockade and to our mishandling of the petty bourgeoisie, trade between the two areas has almost entirely ceased; necessities such as salt, cloth and medicines are scarce and costly, and agricultural products such as timber, tea and oil cannot be sent out, so that the peasants' cash income is cut off and the people as a whole are affected. Poor peasants are more able to bear such hardships, but the intermediate class will go over to the big landlord class when it can bear them no longer. Unless the splits and wars within the landlord class and among the warlords in China continue, and unless a nation-wide revolutionary situation develops, the small independent Red regimes will come under great economic pressure and it is doubtful whether they will be able to last. For not only is such economic strain intolerable to the intermediate class, but some day it will prove too much even for the workers, poor peasants and Red Army men. In the counties of Yunghsin and Ningkang there was at one time no salt for cooking, and supplies of cloth and medicines, not to mention other things, were entirely cut off. Now salt can be had again but is very expensive. Cloth and medicines are still unobtainable. Timber, tea and oil, which are all produced abundantly in Ningkang, western Yunghsin and northern Suichuan (all within our areas at present), cannot be sent out.[19]

The criterion for land distribution. The township is taken as the unit for land distribution. In hillier regions with less farm land, for instance, in the Hsiaokiang district of Yunghsin, three or four townships were sometimes taken as the unit, but such cases were extremely rare. All the inhabitants, men and women, old and young, received equal shares. A change has now been made in accordance with the Central

Committee's plan whereby labour-power is taken as the criterion, so that a person with labour-power is allotted twice as much land as one without.[20]

The question of concessions to the owner-peasants. This has not yet been discussed in detail. Among the owner-peasants, the rich peasants have requested that productive capacity should be taken as the criterion, that is, that those with more manpower and capital (such as farm implements) should be allotted more land. They feel that neither equal distribution nor distribution according to labour-power is to their advantage. They have indicated that they are willing to put in more effort, which, coupled with the use of their capital, would enable them to raise bigger crops. They will not like it if they are allotted the same amount of land as everybody else and their special efforts and extra capital are ignored (left unused). Land distribution here is still being carried out in the way laid down by the Central Committee. But this question deserves further discussion, and a report will be submitted when conclusions are reached.

The land tax. In Ningkang the tax rate is 20 per cent of the crop, or 5 per cent more than the rate fixed by the Central Committee; it is inadvisable to make any change now as collection is already under way, but the rate will be reduced next year. Then there are the sections of Suichuan, Linghsien and Yunghsin under our regime which are all hilly areas, and where the peasants are so poverty-stricken that any taxation is inadvisable. We have to rely on expropriating the local tyrants in the White areas to cover the expenses of the government and the Red Guards. As for the provisioning of the Red Army, rice is obtained for the time being from the land tax in Ningkang, while cash is obtained solely from expropriation of the local tyrants. During our guerrilla operations in Suichuan in October, we collected more than ten thousand yuan, which will last us some time, and we shall see what can be done when it is spent.

QUESTIONS OF POLITICAL POWER

People's political power has been established everywhere at county, district and township levels, but more in name than in reality. In many places there is no council of workers, peasants and soldiers. The executive committees of the township, district or even county governments were invariably elected at some kind of mass meeting. But mass meetings called on the spur of the moment can neither discuss questions nor help in training the masses politically, and, what is more, they are only too apt to be manipulated by intellectuals or careerists. Some places do have a council, but it is regarded merely as a temporary body for electing the executive committee; once the election is over, authority is monopolized by the committee and the council is never heard of again. Not that there are no councils of workers, peasants and soldiers worthy of the name, but they are very few. The reason is the lack of propaganda and education concerning this new political system. The evil feudal practice of arbitrary dictation is so deeply rooted in the minds of the people and even of the ordinary Party members that it cannot be swept away at once; when anything crops up, they choose the easy way and have no liking for the bothersome democratic system. Democratic centralism can be widely and effectively practised in mass organizations only when its efficacy is demonstrated in revolutionary struggle and the masses understand that it is the best means of mobilizing their forces and is of the utmost help in their struggle. We are drafting a detailed organic law for the councils at all levels (based on the outline drawn up by the Central Committee) in order gradually to correct previous mistakes. In the Red Army, conferences of soldiers' representatives are now being established on a permanent basis and at all levels so as to correct the mistake of having only soldiers' committees and not conferences.

At present, what the masses of the people generally understand by the "government of workers, peasants and soldiers" is the executive committee, because they are still unaware of the powers of the council, and think that the executive committee alone is the real power. An executive committee without a council behind it often acts without regard for the views of the masses, and there are instances everywhere of hesitation and compromise on the confiscation and redistribution of land, of squandering or embezzling funds, and of recoiling before the White forces or fighting only half-heartedly. In addition, the committee seldom meets in full session, all business being decided and handled by its standing committee. In the district and township governments even the standing committee rarely meets, and business is decided and handled separately by the four individuals who work in the office, namely, the chairman, secretary, treasurer and commander of the Red Guards (or insurrectionary detachment). Thus democratic centralism has not become a regular practice even in the work of the government.

In the early days the small landlords and rich peasants scrambled to get on to government committees, especially at the township level. Wearing red ribbons and feigning enthusiasm, they wormed their way into the government committees by trickery and seized control of everything, relegating the poor-peasant members to a minor role. They can be cleared out only when they are unmasked in the course of struggle and the poor peasants assert themselves. Though not widespread, such a state of affairs exists in quite a number of places.

The Party enjoys immense prestige and authority among the masses, the government much less. The reason is that for the sake of convenience the Party handles many things directly and brushes aside the government bodies. There are many such instances. In some places there are no leading Party members' groups in the government organizations, while in others they exist but are not functioning properly. From now on the Party must carry out its task of giving leadership to the government; with the exception of propaganda, the Party's policies and the measures it recommends must be carried out through the government organizations. The Kuomintang's wrong practice of directly imposing orders on the government must be avoided.

QUESTIONS OF PARTY ORGANIZATION

The struggle against opportunism. It may be said that around the time of the May 21st Incident the Party organizations in the border area counties were controlled by opportunists. When the counter-revolution set in, there was very little resolute struggle. In October last year, when the Red Army (the First Regiment of the First Division of the First Army of the Workers' and Peasants' Revolutionary Army) arrived in the border area counties, only a few Party members who had gone into hiding were left and the Party organizations had been entirely destroyed by the enemy. The period from last November to April was one of rebuilding the Party, and the period since May has been one of great expansion. But in the last twelve months manifestations of opportunism continued to be widespread. On the approach of the enemy, some members, lacking the will to fight, hid in remote hills, which they called "lying in ambush". Other members, though very active, resorted to blind insurrection. These were both expressions of petty-bourgeois ideology. After a long period of tempering through struggle and of inner-Party education, such things have become less frequent. In the past year, the same petty-bourgeois ideology also existed in the Red Army. On the approach of the enemy, either reckless battle or precipitate flight would be proposed. Often both ideas emanated from the same individual in the course of the discussions on what military action to take. This opportunist ideology has been gradually corrected through prolonged inner-Party struggle and through lessons learned from actual events, for instance, from the losses incurred in reckless battle and the reverses suffered during precipitate flight.

Localism. The economy in the border area is agricultural, with some places still in the age of the hand-pestle (in the hilly regions the wooden pestle is still in general use for husking rice, while in the plains there are many stone pestles). The unit of social organization everywhere is the clan, consisting of people having the same family name. In the Party organizations in the villages, it often happens that a branch meeting virtually becomes a clan meeting, since branches consist of members bearing the same family name and living close together. In these circumstances it is very hard indeed to build a "militant Bolshevik Party". Such members do not quite understand when they are told that the Communists draw no sharp line of demarcation between one nation and another or between one province and another, or that a sharp line should not be drawn between different counties, districts and townships. Localism exists to a serious extent in the relations between counties and even between districts and townships within the same county. In eliminating localism, reasoning can at best produce only limited results, and it takes White oppression, which is by no means localized, to do much more. For instance, it is only when counter-revolutionary "joint suppression" campaigns by the two provinces make the people share a common lot in struggle that their localism is gradually broken down. Localism is declining as a result of many such lessons.

The question of the native inhabitants and the settlers. There is another peculiar feature in the border counties, namely, the rift between the native inhabitants and the settlers. A very wide rift has long existed between the native inhabitants and the settlers whose forefathers came from the north several hundred years ago; their traditional feuds are deep-seated and they sometimes erupt in violent clashes. The settlers, numbering several millions, live in a zone extending from the Fukien-Kwangtung border all the way along the Hunan-Kiangsi border to southern Hupeh. These settlers, who live in the hilly regions, have been oppressed by the native inhabitants in the plains and have never had any political rights. They welcomed the national revolution of the past two years, thinking that the day had come for them to raise their heads. But unfortunately the revolution failed and they continue to be oppressed by the native inhabitants. Within our own area the problem of the native inhabitants and the settlers exists in Ningkang, Suichuan, Linghsien and Chaling, and is most serious in Ningkang. Under the leadership of the Communist Party, the revolutionaries among the native inhabitants of Ningkang, together with the settlers, overthrew the political power of the native landlords and gained control of the whole county in 1926-27. In June last year the Kiangsi government under Chu Pei-teh turned against the revolution; in September the landlords acted as guides for Chu's troops in the "suppression" campaign against Ningkang and once again stirred up the conflict between the native inhabitants and the settlers. In theory, this rift between the native inhabitants and the settlers ought not to extend into the exploited classes of workers and peasants, much less into the Communist Party. But it does, and it persists by force of long tradition. Here is an example. After the August defeat in the border area, when the native landlords returned to Ningkang, bringing with them the reactionary troops and spreading the rumour that the settlers were going to massacre the native inhabitants, most of the native peasants defected, put on white ribbons and guided the White troops in burning down houses and searching the hills. And when the Red Army routed the White troops in October and November, the native peasants fled with the reactionaries, and their property in turn was seized by the settler-peasants. This situation, reflected in the Party, often leads to senseless conflicts. Our solution is, on the one hand, to announce that "peasants who have defected will not be killed" and "peasants who have defected will also be given land when they return", in order to help them shake off the influence of the landlords and return home without misgivings; on the other hand, it is to get our county governments to order the restoration by settler-peasants of any property they have seized, and to post notices that the native peasants will be protected. Inside the Party, education must be intensified to ensure unity between these two sections of the membership.

The defection of the careerists. During the revolutionary upsurge (in June), many careerists took advantage of the Party's open recruitment of members and sneaked into the Party, with the result that the membership in the border area rapidly rose to more than ten thousand. Since the leaders of the branches and district committees were mostly new members, good inner-Party education was out of the question. As soon as the White terror struck, the careerists defected and acted as guides for the counter-revolutionaries in rounding up our comrades, and the Party organizations in the White areas mostly collapsed. After September the Party carried out a drastic house cleaning and set strict class qualifications for membership. All the Party organizations in Yunghsin and Ningkang Counties were dissolved and a re-registration was undertaken. Though greatly reduced in numbers, the membership has gained in fighting capacity. All Party organizations used to be in the open, but since September underground organizations have been built up to prepare the Party for carrying on its activities when the reactionaries come. At the same time, we have been making every effort to penetrate into the White areas and operate inside the enemy camp. But in the nearby towns the foundations have not yet been laid for Party organization. The reasons are that, first, the enemy is stronger in the towns and, second, our army hurt the interests of the bourgeoisie too much during its occupation of the towns, so that it is difficult for Party members to keep a foothold there. We are now correcting these mistakes and doing our best to build Party organizations in the towns, but so far without much success.

The leading bodies of the Party. The branch executive has been renamed the branch committee. Above the branch there is the district committee, and above that the county committee. Where there are special circumstances, a special district committee is formed between the district and the county levels, as for instance the Peihsiang Special District Committee and the Southeastern Special District Committee in Yunghsin County. In the border area there are altogether five county committees, in Ningkang, Yunghsin, Lienhua, Suichuan and Linghsien. There used to be a county committee in Chaling, but as the work there did not take root, most of the organizations formed last winter and this spring have been crushed by the Whites; consequently, for the last six months we have been able to work only in the hilly regions near Ningkang and Yunghsin, and so the Chaling County Committee has been changed into a special district committee. Comrades were sent to Yuhsien and Anjen Counties, which can be reached only via Chaling, but they have returned without accomplishing anything. The Wanan County Committee was cut off from us by the Whites for more than six months after its joint meeting with us in Suichuan in January, and it was not until September, when the

Red Army reached Wanan in a guerrilla operation, that we resumed
contact. From Wanan eighty revolutionary peasants returned with
our men to the Chingkang Mountains and were organized as the
Wanan Red Guards. There is no Party organization in Anfu. The
County Committee of Kian, which borders on Yunghsin, has got in
touch with us only twice and has given us no help, which is very
strange. In the Shatien area of Kueitung County land distribution
was carried out on two occasions, in March and in August, and Party
organizations have been built up and placed under the Southern Hunan
Special Committee with its centre at Shiherhtung in Lunghsi. Above
the county committees there is the Special Committee of the Hunan-
Kiangsi Border Area. On May 20 the first Party congress of the border
area was held at Maoping in Ningkang County, and it elected twenty-
three people as members of the First Special Committee, with Mao
Tse-tung as secretary. In July the Hunan Provincial Committee sent
over Yang Kai-ming and he became acting secretary. In September
Yang fell ill and Tan Chen-lin took his place. In August, when the
major detachment of the Red Army had gone to southern Hunan
and the White forces were pressing hard on the border area, we
held an emergency meeting at Yunghsin. In October after the Red
Army's return to Ningkang, the second Party congress of the border
area was held at Maoping. In its three-day session beginning on
October 14, it adopted a number of resolutions, including "The
Political Problems and the Tasks of the Border Area Party Organiza-
tion", and elected the following nineteen people as members of the
Second Special Committee, Tan Chen-lin, Chu Teh, Chen Yi, Lung
Chao-ching, Chu Chang-chieh, Liu Tien-chien, Yuan Pan-chu, Tan
Szu-tsung, Tan Ping, Li Chueh-fei, Sung Yi-yueh, Yuan Wen-tsai,
Wang Tso-nung, Chen Cheng-jen, Mao Tse-tung, Wan Hsi-hsien,
Wang Tso, Yang Kai-ming and Ho Ting-ying. A standing committee
of five was formed, with Tan Chen-lin (a worker) as secretary and
Chen Cheng-jen (an intellectual) as deputy secretary. The Sixth Party
Congress of the Red Army was held on November 14 and it elected
an Army Committee of twenty-three members, five of them forming
a standing committee with Chu Teh as secretary. Both the Border
Area Special Committee and the Army Committee are subordinate
to the Front Committee. The Front Committee was reorganized on
November 6, with the following five members designated by the
Central Committee: Mao Tse-tung, Chu Teh, the secretary of the
local Party headquarters (Tan Chen-lin), a worker comrade (Sung

Chiao-sheng) and a peasant comrade (Mao Ko-wen), with Mao Tse-tung as secretary. For the time being, this committee has set up a secretariat, a propaganda section, an organization section, a labour movement commission and a military affairs commission. The Front Committee is in charge of the local Party organizations. It is necessary to retain the Special Committee because sometimes the Front Committee has to move about with the troops. In our opinion the question of proletarian ideological leadership is very important. The Party organizations in the border area counties, which are composed almost exclusively of peasants, will go astray without the ideological leadership of the proletariat. Besides paying close attention to the labour movement in the county towns and other big towns, we should increase the workers' representation in the government bodies. The proportion of workers and poor peasants should also be increased in the leading organs of the Party at all levels.

THE QUESTION OF THE CHARACTER OF THE REVOLUTION

We fully agree with the Communist International's resolution on China. There is no doubt that China is still at the stage of the bourgeois-democratic revolution. The programme for a thorough democratic revolution in China comprises, externally, the overthrow of imperialism so as to achieve complete national liberation, and, internally, the elimination of the power and influence of the comprador class in the cities, the completion of the agrarian revolution in order to abolish feudal relations in the villages, and the overthrow of the government of the warlords. We must go through such a democratic revolution before we can lay a real foundation for the transition to socialism. In the past year we have fought in many places and are keenly aware that the revolutionary tide is on the ebb in the country as a whole. While Red political power has been established in a few small areas, in the country as a whole the people lack the ordinary democratic rights, the workers, the peasants and even the bourgeois democrats do not have freedom of speech or assembly, and the worst crime is to join the Communist Party. Wherever the Red Army goes, the masses are cold and aloof, and only after our propaganda do they slowly move into action. Whatever enemy units we face, there are hardly any cases of mutiny or desertion to our side and we have to fight it out. This holds even for the enemy's Sixth Army which recruited the greatest number of "rebels" after the May 21st Incident. We have an acute sense of our isolation which we keep hoping will end. Only by launching a political and economic struggle for democracy, which will also involve the urban petty bourgeoisie, can we turn the revolution into a seething tide that will surge through the country.

Up to February this year we applied our policy towards the petty bourgeoisie fairly well. In March the representative of the Southern Hunan Special Committee arrived in Ningkang and criticized us for having leaned to the Right, for having done too little burning and killing, and for having failed to carry out the so-called policy of "turning the petty bourgeois into proletarians and then forcing them into the revolution", whereupon the leadership of the Front Committee was reorganized and the policy was changed. In April, after the whole of our army arrived in the border area, there was still not much burning and killing, but the expropriation of the middle merchants in the towns and the collection of compulsory contributions from the small landlords and rich peasants in the countryside were rigorously enforced. The slogan of "All factories to the workers", put forward by the Southern Hunan Special Committee, was also given wide publicity. This ultra-Left policy of attacking the petty bourgeoisie drove most of them to the side of the landlords, with the result that they put on white ribbons and opposed us. With the gradual change of this policy, the situation has been steadily improving. Good results have been achieved in Suichuan in particular, for the merchants in the county town and other market towns no longer fight shy of us, and quite a few speak well of the Red Army. The fair in Tsaolin (held every three days at noon) attracts some twenty thousand people, an attendance which breaks all previous records. This is proof that our policy is now correct. The landlords imposed very heavy taxes and levies on the people; the Pacification Guards[21] of Suichuan levied five toll charges along the seventy-*li* road from Huangao to Tsaolin, no farm produce being exempt. We crushed the Pacification Guards and abolished these tolls, thus winning the support of all the peasants as well as of the small and middle merchants.

The Central Committee wants us to issue a political programme which takes into account the interests of the petty bourgeoisie, and we for our part propose that the Central Committee work out, for general guidance, a programme for the whole democratic revolution which takes into account the workers' interests, the agrarian revolution and national liberation.

A special characteristic of the revolution in China, a country with a predominantly agricultural economy, is the use of military action to develop insurrection. We recommend that the Central Committee should devote great effort to military work.

THE QUESTION OF THE LOCATION OF OUR INDEPENDENT REGIME

The area stretching from northern Kwangtung along the Hunan-Kiangsi border into southern Hupeh lies entirely within the Lohsiao mountain range. We have traversed the whole range, and a comparison of its different sections shows that the middle section, with Ningkang as its centre, is the most suitable for our armed independent regime. The northern section has terrain which is less suitable for our taking either the offensive or the defensive, and it is too close to the enemy's big political centres. Besides, stationing large forces in the area of Liuyang, Liling, Pinghsiang and Tungku would involve a considerable risk, unless we plan a quick seizure of Changsha or Wuhan. The southern section has better terrain than the northern, but our mass base there is not as good as in the middle section, nor can we exert as great a political influence on Hunan and Kiangsi from it as we can from the middle section, from which any move can affect the lower river valleys of the two provinces. The middle section has the following advantages: (1) a mass base, which we have been cultivating for more than a year; (2) a fairly good basis for the Party organizations; (3) local armed forces which have been built up for more than a year and are well experienced in struggle — a rare achievement — and which, coupled with the Fourth Red Army, will prove indestructible in the face of any enemy force; (4) an excellent military base, the Chingkang Mountains, and bases for our local armed forces in all the counties; and (5) the influence it can exert on the two provinces and on the lower valleys of their rivers, an influence endowing it with much more political importance than that possessed by southern Hunan or southern Kiangsi, the influence of either of which can reach out only to its own province, or only to the upper river valley and the hinterland of its own province. The disadvantage of the middle section is that, since it has long been under the independent regime and is confronted by the enemy's large "encirclement and suppression" forces, its economic problems, especially the shortage of cash, are extremely difficult.

As for a plan of action here, the Hunan Provincial Committee advocated three different plans within a few weeks in June and July. First Yuan Teh-sheng came and approved our plan to establish political power in the middle section of the Lohsiao mountain range. Then Tu Hsiu-ching and Yang Kai-ming came and urged that the Red Army should move towards southern Hunan without the least hesitation and leave a force of only two hundred rifles behind to defend the border area together with the Red Guards; this, they said, was the "absolutely correct" policy. The third time, barely ten days later, Yuan Teh-sheng came again with a letter which, besides rebuking us at great length, urged that the Red Army should set out for eastern Hunan; this was again described as the "absolutely correct" policy, to be carried out "without the least hesitation". These rigid directives put us in a real dilemma, because failure to comply would be tantamount to disobedience, while compliance would mean certain defeat. When the second message came, the Army Committee, the Border Area Special Committee and the Yunghsin County Committee of the Party met in a joint session and decided against carrying out the Provincial Committee's instructions, as it was considered dangerous to move towards southern Hunan. But a few days later, Tu Hsiu-ching and Yang Kai-ming, persisting in the Provincial Party Committee's plan and taking advantage of the 29th Regiment's homesickness, dragged the Red Army off to attack the county town of Chenchou, thus bringing defeat both to the border area and to the Red Army. The Red Army lost about half its men, and countless houses were burned down and innumerable people massacred in the border area; county after county fell to the enemy and some of them have not been recovered to this day. As for moving to eastern Hunan, it was certainly inadvisable for the main forces of the Red Army to do so unless there was a split among the ruling landlords of Hunan, Hupeh and Kiangsi Provinces. If we had not advanced on southern Hunan in July, we would not only have averted the August defeat in the border area, but we could also have exploited the fighting between the Kuomintang's Sixth Army and Wang Chun's Kuomintang forces in Changshu, Kiangsi Province, to crush the enemy forces in Yunghsin, overrun Kian and Anfu, and make it possible for our advanced guard to reach Pinghsiang and establish contact with the Fifth Red Army in the northern section of the Lohsiao mountain range. Even if all that had happened, the proper place for our general headquarters should have still been Ningkang, and only guerrilla forces should have been dispatched to eastern Hunan. Since fighting had not broken out among the landlords and since formidable enemy forces were still in Pinghsiang, Chaling and Yuhsien on the Hunan border, we would have been giving the enemy his chance if we had moved our main forces northward. The Central Committee asked us to consider an advance on eastern or on southern Hunan, but either course was very dangerous; although the proposed expedition to eastern Hunan has not been carried out, the expedition to southern Hunan has proved a failure. This painful experience is always worth remembering.

We are not yet in a period when the regime of the landlord class has split up, and the "suppression" forces of the enemy deployed round the border area still number more than ten regiments. But if we can continue to find ways of getting cash (food and clothing no longer being a big problem), then, with the foundation for our work established in the border area, we shall be able to cope with these enemy forces, and even with larger ones. As far as the border area is concerned, it would at once suffer devastation, just as it did in August, if the Red Army moved away. Although not all our Red Guards would be wiped out, the Party and our mass base would receive a crippling blow, and while there are places in the mountains where we might retain a foothold, in the plains we would all have to go underground as in August and September. If the Red Army does not move away, then, building on the foundations we already have, we shall be able gradually to expand to surrounding areas and our prospects will be very bright. If we want to enlarge the Red Army, the only way is to engage the enemy in a prolonged struggle in the vicinity of the Chingkang Mountains where we have a good mass base, namely, in the counties of Ningkang, Yunghsin, Linghsien and Suichuan, utilizing in this struggle the divergence of interests between the enemy forces of Hunan and Kiangsi Provinces, their need to defend themselves on all sides and their consequent inability to concentrate their forces. We can gradually enlarge the Red Army by the use of correct tactics, fighting no battle unless we can win it and capture arms and men. With the preparatory work that had already been done among the masses in the border area between April and July, the Red Army could undoubtedly have been enlarged in August had its major detachment not made its expedition to southern Hunan. Despite that mistake, the Red Army has returned to the border area where the terrain is favourable and the people are friendly, and the prospects are not bad even now. Only through the determination to fight and stamina in fighting in places such as the border area can the Red Army add to its arms and train up good men. The Red Flag has been kept flying in the border area for a whole year. It has incurred the bitter hatred of the landlord class of Hunan, Hupeh and Kiangsi and indeed of that of the whole country, but it is steadily raising the hopes of the workers, peasants and soldiers in the surrounding provinces. Consider the soldiers. Because the warlords are making the "bandit-suppression" campaign against the border area their major task and are issuing such statements as "a year has been spent and a million dollars used up in the effort to suppress the bandits" (Lu Ti-ping), or the Red Army "has 20,000 men with 5,000 rifles" (Wang Chun), the attention of their soldiers and disheartened junior officers is gradually turned towards us, and more and more of them will break away from the enemy to join our ranks, thus providing the Red Army with another source of recruitment. Besides, the fact that the Red Flag has never been lowered in the border area shows at once the strength of the Communist Party and the bankruptcy of the ruling classes, and this is of nation-wide political significance. Therefore, we hold, as we have always held, that it is absolutely necessary and correct to build up and expand Red political power in the middle section of the Lohsiao mountain range.

NOTES

[1] This war took place in October 1927.

[2] This war took place in November and December 1927.

[3] The system of the soldiers' representative conferences and soldiers' committees in the Red Army was later abolished. In 1947, the People's Liberation Army inaugurated a system of armymen's conferences and soldiers' committees, both under the leadership of cadres.

[4] These troops, originally under the command of Comrades Yeh Ting and Ho Lung, staged the Nanchang Uprising of August 1, 1927. They were defeated in their advance on Chaochow and Swatow, Kwangtung Province, and some units, led by Comrades Chu Teh, Lin Piao and Chen Yi, withdrew to southern Hunan via Kiangsi to carry on guerrilla operations. They joined Comrade Mao Tse-tung's forces in the Chingkang Mountains in April 1928.

[5] In the revolutionary days of 1927 most of the cadres in the Guards Regiment of the National Government at Wuchang were members of the Communist Party. At

the end of July 1927, after Wang Ching-wei and his associates had betrayed the revolution, the regiment left Wuchang to join in the uprising at Nanchang. Learning *en route* that the revolutionary forces had already gone south from Nanchang, the regiment made a detour to Hsiushui in western Kiangsi to join the peasant armed forces of Pingkiang and Liuyang.

[6] In the spring of 1927 peasant armed forces of considerable strength were formed in the area of Pingkiang and Liuyang, Hunan Province. On May 21, Hsu Keh-hsiang staged a counter-revolutionary coup in Changsha and massacred the revolutionary masses. The peasant armed forces then marched on Changsha on May 31 to hit back at the counter-revolutionaries, but were stopped by the opportunist Chen Tu-hsiu and turned back. Thereupon a section was reorganized into an independent regiment to engage in guerrilla warfare. After the Nanchang Uprising on August 1, these armed peasants joined forces with the former Guards Regiment of the Wuchang National Government at Hsiushui and Tungku in Kiangsi Province and at Pingkiang and Liuyang in Hunan Province, and staged the Autumn Harvest Uprising in co-ordination with the armed coal miners of Pinghsiang, Kiangsi. In October Comrade Mao Tse-tung led these forces to the Chingkang Mountains.

[7] In early 1928, while Comrade Chu Teh was directing revolutionary guerrilla warfare in southern Hunan, peasant armies were organized in the counties of Yichang, Chenchow, Leiyang, Yunghsing and Tzehsing, where the peasant movement had already taken firm root. Comrade Chu Teh subsequently led them to the Chingkang Mountains to join the forces under Comrade Mao Tse-tung.

[8] Shuikoushan in Changning, Hunan Province, is well known for its lead mines. In 1922 the miners there led by the Communist Party formed a trade union and for years conducted struggles against the counter-revolution. Many of the miners joined the Red Army after the Autumn Harvest Uprising of 1927.

[9] The Anyuan Coal Mines in Pinghsiang County, Kiangsi Province, employing twelve thousand workers, were owned by the Han-Yeh-Ping Iron and Steel Company. From 1921 onwards Party organizations and a miners' union were set up there by the organizers sent by the Hunan Provincial Committee of the Communist Party.

[10] In 1929 the Party representatives in the Red Army were renamed political commissars. In 1931 the company political commissars were renamed political instructors.

[11] Expropriation of the local tyrants was only a temporary measure to defray part of the army's expenses. The expansion of the base areas and the growth of the army made it possible and necessary to defray army expenses through taxation.

[12] This practice of equal cash payment, necessary at the time, remained in force over many years in the Red Army. Later on, however, officers and men received payments which differed slightly according to rank.

[13] Here Comrade Mao Tse-tung lays special stress on the need for a definite measure of democracy in the revolutionary army, since, in the early period of the Red Army, without the stress on democracy it would not have been possible to arouse the revolutionary enthusiasm of the new peasant recruits and the captured White troops who had joined our ranks, nor would it have been possible to eliminate the warlord ways of the reactionary armies which had infected our cadres. Of course, democracy in the army must not transcend the limits of military discipline, which it must serve to strengthen and not weaken. Therefore, while a necessary measure of democracy should be promoted, the demand for ultra-democracy, which amounts to indiscipline, must be combated. Such indiscipline became a matter of serious concern at one point in the early days of the Red Army. For Comrade Mao Tse-tung's

struggle against ultra-democracy in the army, see "On Correcting Mistaken Ideas in the Party", pp. 105-16 of this volume.

[14] Comrade Yeh Ting commanded an independent regiment during the Northern Expedition in 1926. With Communists as its nucleus the regiment became famous as a crack force. It was expanded into the 24th Division after the capture of Wuchang by the revolutionary army and then into the Eleventh Army after the Nanchang Uprising.

[15] Subsequent experience in the Red Army showed that a ratio of one Party member to two non-Party men was adequate. This proportion was generally maintained in the Red Army and later in the People's Liberation Army.

[16] Instigated by Chiang Kai-shek and Wang Ching-wei, the counter-revolutionary Kuomintang army commanders in Hunan, including Hsu Keh-hsiang and Ho Chien, ordered a raid on the provincial headquarters of the trade unions, the peasant associations and other revolutionary organizations in Changsha on May 21, 1927. Communists and revolutionary workers and peasants were arrested and killed en masse. This signalized the open collaboration of the two counter-revolutionary Kuomintang cliques, the Wuhan clique headed by Wang Ching-wei and the Nanking clique headed by Chiang Kai-shek.

[17] Confiscation and redistribution of all the land was a provision in the Land Law promulgated in the Hunan-Kiangsi border area in 1928. Comrade Mao Tse-tung later pointed out that the confiscation of all land, instead of only the land of the landlords, was a mistake stemming from inexperience in agrarian struggles. In the Land Law of Hsingkuo County, Kiangsi, adopted in April 1929, the provision "confiscate all the land" was changed into "confiscate the public land and the land of the landlord class".

[18] In view of the importance of winning over the intermediate class in the countryside, Comrade Mao Tse-tung soon corrected the erroneous policy of dealing too sharply with it. Apart from the present article, Comrade Mao Tse-tung's views on policy towards this class were also set forth in proposals to the Sixth Party Congress of the Red Army (November 1928), including "The Prohibition of Reckless Burning and Killing" and "Protection of the Interests of the Middle and Small Merchants"; in the January 1929 proclamation of the Fourth Red Army, which declared "merchants in the towns who have gradually built up some property are to be left alone so long as they obey the authorities"; in the Land Law of Hsingkuo County adopted in April 1929 (see Note 17), etc.

[19] With the spread of the revolutionary war, the extension of the revolutionary base areas and the adoption of the policy of protecting industry and commerce by the revolutionary government, it became possible to change this situation, and a change did in fact occur later. What was crucial was resolutely to protect the industry and commerce of the national bourgeoisie and oppose ultra-Left policies.

[20] Labour-power is not an appropriate criterion for land distribution. In the Red areas land was in fact redistributed equally on a per capita basis.

[21] The Pacification Guards were a kind of local counter-revolutionary armed force.

ON CORRECTING MISTAKEN IDEAS
IN THE PARTY

December 1929

There are various non-proletarian ideas in the Communist Party organization in the Fourth Red Army which greatly hinder the application of the Party's correct line. Unless these ideas are thoroughly corrected, the Fourth Army cannot possibly shoulder the tasks assigned to it in China's great revolutionary struggle. The source of such incorrect ideas in this Party organization lies, of course, in the fact that its basic units are composed largely of peasants and other elements of petty-bourgeois origin; yet the failure of the Party's leading bodies to wage a concerted and determined struggle against these incorrect ideas and to educate the members in the Party's correct line is also an important cause of their existence and growth. In accordance with the spirit of the September letter of the Central Committee, this congress hereby points out the manifestations of various non-proletarian ideas in the Party organization in the Fourth Army, their sources, and the methods of correcting them, and calls upon all comrades to eliminate them thoroughly.

ON THE PURELY MILITARY VIEWPOINT

The purely military viewpoint is very highly developed among a number of comrades in the Red Army. It manifests itself as follows:

This article was a resolution drawn up by Comrade Mao Tse-tung for the Ninth Party Congress of the Fourth Army of the Red Army. The building of the Chinese people's armed forces was a difficult process. The Chinese Red Army (which became the Eighth Route and New Fourth Armies during the War of Resistance Against Japan and is now the People's Liberation Army) was created on August 1, 1927, during the Nanchang Uprising, and by December 1929 had been in existence

1.   These comrades regard military affairs and politics as opposed
to each other and refuse to recognize that military affairs are only
one means of accomplishing political tasks. Some even say, "If you
are good militarily, naturally you are good politically; if you are not
good militarily, you cannot be any good politically" — this is to go
a step further and give military affairs a leading position over politics.

2.   They think that the task of the Red Army, like that of the
White army, is merely to fight. They do not understand that the
Chinese Red Army is an armed body for carrying out the political
tasks of the revolution. Especially at present, the Red Army should
certainly not confine itself to fighting; besides fighting to destroy the
enemy's military strength, it should shoulder such important tasks as
doing propaganda among the masses, organizing the masses, arming
them, helping them to establish revolutionary political power and
setting up Party organizations. The Red Army fights not merely for
the sake of fighting but in order to conduct propaganda among the
masses, organize them, arm them, and help them to establish revolutionary political power. Without these objectives, fighting loses its
meaning and the Red Army loses the reason for its existence.

3.   Hence, organizationally, these comrades subordinate the departments of the Red Army doing political work to those doing
military work, and put forward the slogan, "Let Army Headquarters
handle outside matters." If allowed to develop, this idea would
involve the danger of estrangement from the masses, control of the
government by the army and departure from proletarian leadership —
it would be to take the path of warlordism like the Kuomintang army.

4.   At the same time, in propaganda work they overlook the
importance of propaganda teams. On the question of mass organization, they neglect the organizing of soldiers' committees in the army
and the organizing of the local workers and peasants. As a result,
both propaganda and organizational work are abandoned.

---

for over two years. During this period the Communist Party organization in the Red
Army learned a great deal and gained quite a rich store of experience in the course
of combating various mistaken ideas. The resolution summed up this experience.
It enabled the Red Army to build itself entirely on a Marxist-Leninist basis and to
eliminate all the influences of armies of the old type. It was carried out not only in
the Fourth Army but also in all other units of the Red Army successively; in this
way the whole Chinese Red Army became a genuine army of the people in every
respect. In the last thirty years or so the Chinese people's armed forces have made
tremendous developments and innovations in their Party activities and political work,
which now present a very different picture, but the basic line remains the same as
that laid down in this resolution.

5. They become conceited when a battle is won and dispirited when a battle is lost.

6. Selfish departmentalism — they think only of the Fourth Army and do not realize that it is an important task of the Red Army to arm the local masses. This is cliquism in a magnified form.

7. Unable to see beyond their limited environment in the Fourth Army, a few comrades believe that no other revolutionary forces exist. Hence their extreme addiction to the idea of conserving strength and avoiding action. This is a remnant of opportunism.

8. Some comrades, disregarding the subjective and objective conditions, suffer from the malady of revolutionary impetuosity; they will not take pains to do minute and detailed work among the masses, but, riddled with illusions, want only to do big things. This is a remnant of putschism.[1]

The sources of the purely military viewpoint are:

1. A low political level. From this flows the failure to recognize the role of political leadership in the army and to recognize that the Red Army and the White army are fundamentally different.

2. The mentality of mercenaries. Many prisoners captured in past battles have joined the Red Army, and such elements bring with them a markedly mercenary outlook, thereby providing a basis in the lower ranks for the purely military viewpoint.

3. From the two preceding causes there arises a third, over-confidence in military strength and absence of confidence in the strength of the masses of the people.

4. The Party's failure actively to attend to and discuss military work is also a reason for the emergence of the purely military viewpoint among a number of comrades.

The methods of correction are as follows:

1. Raise the political level in the Party by means of education, destroy the theoretical roots of the purely military viewpoint, and be clear on the fundamental difference between the Red Army and the White army. At the same time, eliminate the remnants of opportunism and putschism and break down the selfish departmentalism of the Fourth Army.

2. Intensify the political training of officers and men and especially the education of ex-prisoners. At the same time, as far as possible let the local governments select workers and peasants experienced in struggle to join the Red Army, thus organizationally weakening or even eradicating the purely military viewpoint.

3. Arouse the local Party organizations to criticize the Party organizations in the Red Army and the organs of mass political power to criticize the Red Army itself, in order to influence the Party organizations and the officers and men of the Red Army.

4. The Party must actively attend to and discuss military work. All the work must be discussed and decided upon by the Party before being carried out by the rank and file.

5. Draw up Red Army rules and regulations which clearly define its tasks, the relationship between its military and its political apparatus, the relationship between the Red Army and the masses of the people, and the powers and functions of the soldiers' committees and their relationship with the military and political organizations.

ON ULTRA-DEMOCRACY

Since the Fourth Army of the Red Army accepted the directives of the Central Committee, there has been a great decrease in the manifestations of ultra-democracy. For example, Party decisions are now carried out fairly well; and no longer does anyone bring up such erroneous demands as that the Red Army should apply "democratic centralism from the bottom to the top" or should "let the lower levels discuss all problems first, and then let the higher levels decide". Actually, however, this decrease is only temporary and superficial and does not mean that ultra-democratic ideas have already been eliminated. In other words, ultra-democracy is still deep-rooted in the minds of many comrades. Witness the various expressions of reluctance to carry out Party decisions.

The methods of correction are as follows:

1. In the sphere of theory, destroy the roots of ultra-democracy. First, it should be pointed out that the danger of ultra-democracy lies in the fact that it damages or even completely wrecks the Party organization and weakens or even completely undermines the Party's fighting capacity, rendering the Party incapable of fulfilling its fighting tasks and thereby causing the defeat of the revolution. Next, it should be pointed out that the source of ultra-democracy consists in the petty bourgeoisie's individualistic aversion to discipline. When this characteristic is brought into the Party, it develops into ultra-democratic ideas politically and organizationally. These ideas are utterly incompatible with the fighting tasks of the proletariat.

2.   In the sphere of organization, ensure democracy under centralized guidance. It should be done on the following lines:

(1)   The leading bodies of the Party must give a correct line of guidance and find solutions when problems arise, in order to establish themselves as centres of leadership.

(2)   The higher bodies must be familiar with the life of the masses and with the situation in the lower bodies so as to have an objective basis for correct guidance.

(3)   No Party organization at any level should make casual decisions in solving problems. Once a decision is reached, it must be firmly carried out.

(4)   All decisions of any importance made by the Party's higher bodies must be promptly transmitted to the lower bodies and the Party rank and file. The method is to call meetings of activists or general membership meetings of the Party branches or even of the columns[2] (when circumstances permit) and to assign people to make reports at such meetings.

(5)   The lower bodies of the Party and the Party rank and file must discuss the higher bodies' directives in detail in order to understand their meaning thoroughly and decide on the methods of carrying them out.

ON THE DISREGARD OF ORGANIZATIONAL DISCIPLINE

Disregard of organizational discipline in the Party organization in the Fourth Army manifests itself as follows:

A.   Failure of the minority to submit to the majority. For example, when a minority finds its motion voted down, it does not sincerely carry out the Party decisions.

The methods of correction are as follows:

1.   At meetings, all participants should be encouraged to voice their opinions as fully as possible. The rights and wrongs in any controversy should be clarified without compromise or glossing over. In order to reach a clear-cut conclusion, what cannot be settled at one meeting should be discussed at another, provided there is no interference with the work.

2.   One requirement of Party discipline is that the minority should submit to the majority. If the view of the minority has been rejected, it must support the decision passed by the majority. If necessary, it can bring up the matter for reconsideration at the next meeting, but apart from that it must not act against the decision in any way.

B.   Criticism made without regard to organizational discipline:

1.   Inner-Party criticism is a weapon for strengthening the Party organization and increasing its fighting capacity. In the Party organization of the Red Army, however, criticism is not always of this character, and sometimes turns into personal attack. As a result, it damages the Party organization as well as individuals. This is a manifestation of petty-bourgeois individualism. The method of correction is to help Party members understand that the purpose of criticism is to increase the Party's fighting capacity in order to achieve victory in the class struggle and that it should not be used as a means of personal attack.

2.   Many Party members make their criticisms not inside, but outside, the Party. The reason is that the general membership has not yet grasped the importance of the Party organization (its meetings and so forth), and sees no difference between criticism inside and outside the organization. The method of correction is to educate Party members so that they understand the importance of Party organization and make their criticisms of Party committees or comrades at Party meetings.

ON ABSOLUTE EQUALITARIANISM

Absolute equalitarianism became quite serious in the Red Army at one time. Here are some examples. On the matter of allowances to wounded soldiers, there were objections to differentiating between light and serious cases, and the demand was raised for equal allowances for all. When officers rode on horseback, it was regarded not as something necessary for performing their duties but as a sign of inequality. Absolutely equal distribution of supplies was demanded, and there was objection to somewhat larger allotments in special cases. In the hauling of rice, the demand was made that all should carry the same load on their backs, irrespective of age or physical condition. Equality was demanded in the allotment of billets, and the

Headquarters would be abused for occupying larger rooms. Equality was demanded in the assignment of fatigue duties, and there was unwillingness to do a little more than the next man. It even went so far that when there were two wounded men but only one stretcher, neither could be carried away because each refused to yield priority to the other. Absolute equalitarianism, as shown in these examples, is still very serious among officers and soldiers of the Red Army.

Absolute equalitarianism, like ultra-democracy in political matters, is the product of a handicraft and small peasant economy — the only difference being that the one manifests itself in material affairs, while the other manifests itself in political affairs.

The method of correction: We should point out that, before the abolition of capitalism, absolute equalitarianism is a mere illusion of peasants and small proprietors, and that even under socialism there can be no absolute equality, for material things will then be distributed on the principle of "from each according to his ability, to each according to his work" as well as on that of meeting the needs of the work. The distribution of material things in the Red Army must be more or less equal, as in the case of equal pay for officers and men, because this is required by the present circumstances of the struggle. But absolute equalitarianism beyond reason must be opposed because it is not required by the struggle; on the contrary, it hinders the struggle.

ON SUBJECTIVISM

Subjectivism exists to a serious degree among some Party members, causing great harm to the analysis of the political situation and the guidance of the work. The reason is that subjective analysis of a political situation and subjective guidance of work inevitably result either in opportunism or in putschism. As for subjective criticism, loose and groundless talk or suspiciousness, such practices inside the Party often breed unprincipled disputes and undermine the Party organization.

Another point that should be mentioned in connection with inner-Party criticism is that some comrades ignore the major issues and confine their attention to minor points when they make their criticism. They do not understand that the main task of criticism is to point out political and organizational mistakes. As to personal shortcomings, unless they are related to political and organizational mistakes, there is no need to be overcritical and to embarrass the comrades concerned. Moreover, once such criticism develops, there is the great danger that the Party members will concentrate entirely on minor faults, and everyone will become timid and overcautious and forget the Party's political tasks.

The main method of correction is to educate Party members so that a political and scientific spirit pervades their thinking and their Party life. To this end we must: (1) teach Party members to apply the Marxist-Leninist method in analysing a political situation and appraising the class forces, instead of making a subjective analysis and appraisal; (2) direct the attention of Party members to social and economic investigation and study, so as to determine the tactics of struggle and methods of work, and help comrades to understand that without investigation of actual conditions they will fall into the pit of fantasy and putschism; and (3) in inner-Party criticism, guard against subjectivism, arbitrariness and the vulgarization of criticism; statements should be based on facts and criticism should centre on politics.

ON INDIVIDUALISM

The tendency towards individualism in the Red Army Party organization manifests itself as follows:

1.   Retaliation. Some comrades, after being criticized inside the Party by a soldier comrade, look for opportunities to retaliate outside the Party, and one way is to beat or abuse the comrade in question. They also seek to retaliate within the Party. "You have criticized me at this meeting, so I'll find some way to pay you back at the next." Such retaliation arises from purely personal considerations, to the neglect of the interests of the class and of the Party as a whole. Its target is not the enemy class, but individuals in our own ranks. It is a corrosive which weakens the organization and its fighting capacity.

2.   "Small group" mentality. Some comrades consider only the interests of their own small group and ignore the general interest. Although on the surface this does not seem to be the pursuit of personal interests, in reality it exemplifies the narrowest individualism and has a strong corrosive and centrifugal effect. "Small group" mentality used to be rife in the Red Army, and although there has been some

improvement as a result of criticism, there are still survivals and further effort is needed to overcome it.

3. The "employee" mentality. Some comrades do not understand that the Party and the Red Army, of which they are members, are both instruments for carrying out the tasks of the revolution. They do not realize that they themselves are makers of the revolution, but think that their responsibility is merely to their individual superiors and not to the revolution. This passive mentality of an "employee" of the revolution is also a manifestation of individualism. It explains why there are not very many activists who work unconditionally for the revolution. Unless it is eliminated, the number of activists will not grow and the heavy burden of the revolution will remain on the shoulders of a small number of people, much to the detriment of the struggle.

4. Pleasure-seeking. In the Red Army there are also quite a few people whose individualism finds expression in pleasure-seeking. They always hope that their unit will march into big cities. They want to go there not to work but to enjoy themselves. The last thing they want is to work in the Red areas where life is hard.

5. Passivity. Some comrades become passive and stop working whenever anything goes against their wishes. This is mainly due to lack of education, though sometimes it is also due to the leadership's improper conduct of affairs, assignment of work or enforcement of discipline.

6. The desire to leave the army. The number of people who ask for transfers from the Red Army to local work is on the increase. The reason for this does not lie entirely with the individuals but also with: (1) the material hardships of life in the Red Army, (2) exhaustion after long struggle, and (3) the leadership's improper conduct of affairs, assignment of work or enforcement of discipline.

The method of correction is primarily to strengthen education so as to rectify individualism ideologically. Next, it is to conduct affairs, make assignments and enforce discipline in a proper way. In addition, ways must be found to improve the material life of the Red Army, and every available opportunity must be utilized for rest and rehabilitation in order to improve material conditions. In our educational work we must explain that in its social origin individualism is a reflection within the Party of petty-bourgeois and bourgeois ideas.

ON THE IDEOLOGY OF ROVING REBEL BANDS

The political ideology of roving rebel bands has emerged in the Red Army because the proportion of vagabond elements is large and because there are great masses of vagabonds in China, especially in the southern provinces. This ideology manifests itself as follows: (1) Some people want to increase our political influence only by means of roving guerrilla actions, but are unwilling to increase it by undertaking the arduous task of building up base areas and establishing the people's political power. (2) In expanding the Red Army, some people follow the line of "hiring men and buying horses" and "recruiting deserters and accepting mutineers",[3] rather than the line of expanding the local Red Guards and the local troops and thus developing the main forces of the Red Army. (3) Some people lack the patience to carry on arduous struggles together with the masses, and only want to go to the big cities to eat and drink to their hearts' content. All these manifestations of the ideology of roving rebels seriously hamper the Red Army in performing its proper tasks; consequently its eradication is an important objective in the ideological struggle within the Red Army Party organization. It must be understood that the ways of roving rebels of the Huang Chao[4] or Li Chuang[5] type are not permissible under present-day conditions.

The methods of correction are as follows:

1. Intensify education, criticize incorrect ideas, and eradicate the ideology of roving rebel bands.

2. Intensify education among the basic sections of the Red Army and among recently recruited captives to counter the vagabond outlook.

3. Draw active workers and peasants experienced in struggle into the ranks of the Red Army so as to change its composition.

4. Create new units of the Red Army from among the masses of militant workers and peasants.

ON THE REMNANTS OF PUTSCHISM

The Party organization in the Red Army has already waged struggles against putschism, but not yet to a sufficient extent. Therefore, remnants of this ideology still exist in the Red Army. Their manifestations are: (1) blind action regardless of subjective and objective conditions; (2) inadequate and irresolute application of the Party's policies for the cities; (3) slack military discipline, especially in moments of defeat; (4) acts of house-burning by some units; and (5) the practices of shooting deserters and of inflicting corporal punishment, both of which smack of putschism. In its social origins, putschism is a combination of *lumpen*-proletarian and petty-bourgeois ideology.

The methods of correction are as follows:

1. Eradicate putschism ideologically.

2. Correct putschist behaviour through rules, regulations and policies.

NOTES

[1] For a brief period after the defeat of the revolution in 1927, a "Left" putschist tendency arose in the Communist Party. Regarding the Chinese revolution as a "permanent revolution" and the revolutionary situation in China as a "permanent upsurge", the putschist comrades refused to organize an orderly retreat and, adopting the methods of commandism and relying only on a small number of Party members and a small section of the masses, erroneously attempted to stage a series of local uprisings throughout the country, which had no prospect of success. Such putschist activities were widespread at the end of 1927 but gradually subsided in the beginning of 1928, though sentiments in favour of putschism still survived among some comrades.

[2] In the guerrilla system of organization a column corresponded to a division in the regular army, with a complement much more flexible and usually much smaller than that of a regular division.

[3] These two Chinese idioms refer to the methods which some rebels in Chinese history adopted to expand their forces. In the application of these methods, attention was paid to numbers rather than to quality, and people of all sorts were indiscriminately recruited to swell the ranks.

[4] Huang Chao was the leader of the peasant revolts towards the end of the Tang Dynasty. In A.D. 875, starting from his home district Tsaochow (now Hotse County in Shantung), Huang led armed peasants in victorious battles against the imperial forces and styled himself the "Heaven-Storming General". In the course of a decade he swept over most of the provinces in the Yellow, Yangtse, Huai and Pearl river valleys, reaching as far as Kwangsi. He finally broke through the Tungkuan pass, captured the imperial capital of Changan (now Sian in Shensi), and was crowned Emperor of Chi. Internal dissensions and attacks by the non-Han tribal allies of the Tang forces compelled Huang to abandon Changan and retreat to his native district, where he committed suicide. The ten years' war fought by him is one of the most famous peasant wars in Chinese history. Dynastic historians record that "all people suffering from heavy taxes and levies rallied to him". But as he merely carried on roving warfare without ever establishing relatively consolidated base areas, his forces were called "roving rebel bands".

[5] Li Chuang, short for Li Tzu-cheng the King Chuang (the Dare-All King), native of Michih, northern Shensi, was the leader of a peasant revolt which led to the overthrow of the Ming Dynasty. The revolt first started in northern Shensi in 1628. Li joined the forces led by Kao Ying-hsiang and campaigned through Honan and Anhwei and back to Shensi. After Kao's death in 1636, Li succeeded him, becoming King Chuang, and campaigned in and out of the provinces of Shensi, Szechuan, Honan and Hupeh. Finally he captured the imperial capital of Peking in 1644, whereupon the last Ming emperor committed suicide. The chief slogan he spread among the masses was "Support King Chuang, and pay no grain taxes". Another slogan of his to enforce discipline among his men ran: "Any murder means the killing of my father, any rape means the violation of my mother." Thus he won the support of the masses and his movement became the main current of the peasant revolts raging all over the country. As he, too, roamed about without ever establishing relatively consolidated base areas, he was eventually defeated by Wu San-kuei, a Ming general, who colluded with the Ching troops in a joint attack on Li.

A SINGLE SPARK CAN START A PRAIRIE FIRE

January 5, 1930

Some comrades in our Party still do not know how to appraise the current situation correctly and how to settle the attendant question of what action to take. Though they believe that a revolutionary high tide is inevitable, they do not believe it to be imminent. Therefore, they disapprove of the plan to take Kiangsi and only approve of roving guerrilla actions in the three areas on the borders of Fukien, Kwangtung and Kiangsi; at the same time, as they do not have a deep understanding of what it means to establish Red political power in the guerrilla areas, they do not have a deep understanding of the idea of accelerating the nation-wide revolutionary high tide through the consolidation and expansion of Red political power. They seem to think that, since the revolutionary high tide is still remote, it will be labour lost to attempt to establish political power by hard work. Instead, they want to extend our political influence through the easier method of roving guerrilla actions, and, once the masses throughout the country have been won over, or more or less won over, they want to launch a nation-wide armed insurrection which, with the participation of the Red Army, would become a great nation-wide revolution. Their theory that we must first win over the masses on a country-wide scale and in all regions and then establish political power does not accord with the actual state of the Chinese revolution. This theory derives mainly from the failure to understand clearly that China is a semi-colonial country for which many imperialist powers are contending. If one clearly understands this, one will understand first why the unusual phenomenon of prolonged and tangled warfare within the ruling classes is only to be found in China, why this warfare is steadily growing fiercer and spreading, and why

---

This was a letter written by Comrade Mao Tse-tung in criticism of certain pessimistic views then existing in the Party.

there has never been a unified regime. Secondly, one will understand the gravity of the peasant problem and hence why rural uprisings have developed on the present country-wide scale. Thirdly, one will understand the correctness of the slogan of workers' and peasants' democratic political power. Fourthly, one will understand another unusual phenomenon, which is also absent outside China, and which follows from the first (that in China alone there is prolonged and tangled warfare within the ruling classes), namely, the existence and development of the Red Army and the guerrilla forces, and together with them, the existence and development of small Red areas encircled by the White regime. Fifthly, one will understand that in semi-colonial China the establishment and expansion of the Red Army, the guerrilla forces and the Red areas is the highest form of peasant struggle under the leadership of the proletariat, the inevitable outcome of the growth of the semi-colonial peasant struggle, and undoubtedly the most important factor in accelerating the revolutionary high tide throughout the country. And sixthly, one will also understand that the policy which merely calls for roving guerrilla actions cannot accomplish the task of accelerating this nation-wide revolutionary high tide, while the kind of policy adopted by Chu Teh and Mao Tse-tung and also by Fang Chih-min[1] is undoubtedly correct — that is, the policy of establishing base areas; of systematically setting up political power; of deepening the agrarian revolution; of expanding the people's armed forces by a comprehensive process of building up first the township Red Guards, then the district Red Guards, then the county Red Guards, then the local Red Army troops, all the way up to the regular Red Army troops; of spreading political power by advancing in a series of waves, etc., etc. Only thus is it possible to build the confidence of the revolutionary masses throughout the country, as the Soviet Union has built it throughout the world. Only thus is it possible to create tremendous difficulties for the reactionary ruling classes, shake their foundations and hasten their internal disintegration. Only thus is it really possible to create a Red Army which will become the chief weapon for the great revolution of the future. In short, only thus is it possible to hasten the revolutionary high tide.

Comrades who suffer from revolutionary impetuosity overestimate the subjective forces of the revolution[2] and underestimate the forces of the counter-revolution. Such an appraisal stems mainly from subjectivism. In the end, it undoubtedly leads to putschism. On the other hand, underestimating the subjective forces of the revolution and overestimating the forces of the counter-revolution would also constitute an improper appraisal and be certain to produce bad results of another kind. Therefore, in judging the political situation in China it is necessary to understand the following:

1.   Although the subjective forces of the revolution in China are now weak, so also are all organizations (organs of political power, armed forces, political parties, etc.) of the reactionary ruling classes, resting as they do on the backward and fragile social and economic structure of China. This helps to explain why revolution cannot break out at once in the countries of Western Europe where, although the subjective forces of revolution are now perhaps somewhat stronger than in China, the forces of the reactionary ruling classes are many times stronger. In China the revolution will undoubtedly move towards a high tide more rapidly, for although the subjective forces of the revolution at present are weak, the forces of the counter-revolution are relatively weak too.

2.   The subjective forces of the revolution have indeed been greatly weakened since the defeat of the revolution in 1927. The remaining forces are very small and those comrades who judge by appearances alone naturally feel pessimistic. But if we judge by essentials, it is quite another story. Here we can apply the old Chinese saying, "A single spark can start a prairie fire." In other words, our forces, although small at present, will grow very rapidly. In the conditions prevailing in China, their growth is not only possible but indeed inevitable, as the May 30th Movement and the Great Revolution which followed have fully proved. When we look at a thing, we must examine its essence and treat its appearance merely as an usher at the threshold, and once we cross the threshold, we must grasp the essence of the thing; this is the only reliable and scientific method of analysis.

3.   Similarly, in appraising the counter-revolutionary forces, we must never look merely at their appearance, but should examine their essence. In the initial period of our independent regime in the Hunan-Kiangsi border area, some comrades genuinely believed the incorrect appraisal made by the Hunan Provincial Committee and regarded the class enemy as not worth a rap; the two descriptive terms, "terribly shaky" and "extremely panicky", which are standing jokes to this day, were used by the Hunan Provincial Committee at the time (from May to June 1928) in appraising the Hunan ruler

Lu Ti-ping.[3] Such an appraisal necessarily led to putschism in the political sphere. But during the four months from November of that year to February 1929 (before the war between Chiang Kai-shek and the Kwangsi warlords),[4] when the enemy's third "joint suppression expedition"[5] was approaching the Chingkang Mountains, some comrades asked the question, "How long can we keep the Red Flag flying?" As a matter of fact, the struggle in China between Britain, the United States and Japan had by then become quite open, and a state of tangled warfare between Chiang Kai-shek, the Kwangsi clique and Feng Yu-hsiang was taking shape; hence it was actually the time when the counter-revolutionary tide had begun to ebb and the revolutionary tide to rise again. Yet pessimistic ideas were to be found not only in the Red Army and local Party organizations; even the Central Committee was misled by appearances and adopted a pessimistic tone. Its February letter is evidence of the pessimistic analysis made in the Party at that time.

4. The objective situation today is still such that comrades who see only the superficial appearance and not the essence of what is before them are liable to be misled. In particular, when our comrades working in the Red Army are defeated in battle or encircled or pursued by strong enemy forces, they often unwittingly generalize and exaggerate their momentary, specific and limited situation, as though the situation in China and the world as a whole gave no cause for optimism and the prospects of victory for the revolution were remote. The reason they seize on the appearance and brush aside the essence in their observation of things is that they have not made a scientific analysis of the essence of the overall situation. The question whether there will soon be a revolutionary high tide in China can be decided only by making a detailed examination to ascertain whether the contradictions leading to a revolutionary high tide are really developing. Since contradictions are developing in the world between the imperialist countries, between the imperialist countries and their colonies, and between the imperialists and the proletariat in their own countries, there is an intensified need for the imperialists to contend for the domination of China. While the imperialist contention over China becomes more intense, both the contradiction between imperialism and the whole Chinese nation and the contradictions among the imperialists themselves develop simultaneously on Chinese soil, thereby creating the tangled warfare which is expanding and intensifying daily and giving rise to the continuous development of

the contradictions among the different cliques of China's reactionary rulers. In the wake of the contradictions among the reactionary ruling cliques — the tangled warfare among the warlords — comes heavier taxation, which steadily sharpens the contradiction between the broad masses of taxpayers and the reactionary rulers. In the wake of the contradiction between imperialism and China's national industry comes the failure of the Chinese industrialists to obtain concessions from the imperialists, which sharpens the contradiction between the Chinese bourgeoisie and the Chinese working class, with the Chinese capitalists trying to find a way out by frantically exploiting the workers and with the workers resisting. In the wake of imperialist commercial aggression, Chinese merchant-capitalist extortions, heavier government taxation, etc., comes the deepening of the contradiction between the landlord class and the peasantry, that is, exploitation through rent and usury is aggravated and the hatred of the peasants for the landlords grows. Because of the pressure of foreign goods, the exhaustion of the purchasing power of the worker and peasant masses, and the increase in government taxation, more and more dealers in Chinese-made goods and independent producers are being driven into bankruptcy. Because the reactionary government, though short of provisions and funds, endlessly expands its armies and thus constantly extends the warfare, the masses of soldiers are in a constant state of privation. Because of the growth in government taxation, the rise in rent and interest demanded by the landlords and the daily spread of the disasters of war, there are famine and banditry everywhere and the peasant masses and the urban poor can hardly keep alive. Because the schools have no money, many students fear that their education may be interrupted; because production is backward, many graduates have no hope of employment. Once we understand all these contradictions, we shall see in what a desperate situation, in what a chaotic state, China finds herself. We shall also see that the high tide of revolution against the imperialists, the warlords and the landlords is inevitable, and will come very soon. All China is littered with dry faggots which will soon be aflame. The saying, "A single spark can start a prairie fire", is an apt description of how the current situation will develop. We need only look at the strikes by the workers, the uprisings by the peasants, the mutinies of soldiers and the strikes of students which are developing in many places to see that it cannot be long before a "spark" kindles "a prairie fire".

The gist of the above was already contained in the letter from the Front Committee to the Central Committee on April 5, 1929, which reads in part:

The Central Committee's letter [dated February 9, 1929] makes too pessimistic an appraisal of the objective situation and our subjective forces. The Kuomintang's three "suppression" campaigns against the Chingkang Mountains was the high water mark reached by the counter-revolutionary tide. But there it stopped, and since then the counter-revolutionary tide has gradually receded while the revolutionary tide has gradually risen. Although our Party's fighting capacity and organizational strength have been weakened to the extent described by the Central Committee, they will be rapidly restored, and the passivity among comrades in the Party will quickly disappear as the counter-revolutionary tide gradually ebbs. The masses will certainly come over to us. The Kuomintang's policy of massacre only serves to "drive the fish into deep waters",[6] as the saying goes, and reformism no longer has any mass appeal. It is certain that the masses will soon shed their illusions about the Kuomintang. In the emerging situation, no other party will be able to compete with the Communist Party in winning over the masses. The political line and the organizational line laid down by the Party's Sixth National Congress[7] are correct, i.e., the revolution at the present stage is democratic and not socialist, and the present task of the Party [here the words "in the big cities" should have been added][8] is to win over the masses and not to stage immediate insurrections. Nevertheless the revolution will develop swiftly, and we should take a positive attitude in our propaganda and preparations for armed insurrections. In the present chaotic situation we can lead the masses only by positive slogans and a positive attitude. Only by taking such an attitude can the Party recover its fighting capacity. . . . Proletarian leadership is the sole key to victory in the revolution. Building a proletarian foundation for the Party and setting up Party branches in industrial enterprises in key districts are important organizational tasks for the Party at present; but at the same time the major prerequisites for helping the struggle in the cities and hastening the rise of the revolutionary tide are specifically the development of the struggle in the countryside, the establishment of Red political power in small areas, and the creation and expansion of the Red Army. Therefore, it would be wrong to abandon the struggle in the cities, but in our opinion it would also be wrong for any of our Party members to fear the growth of peasant strength lest it should outstrip the workers' strength and harm the revolution. For in the revolution in semi-colonial China, the peasant struggle must always fail if it does not have the leadership of the workers, but the revolution is never harmed if the peasant struggle outstrips the forces of the workers.

The letter also contained the following reply on the question of the Red Army's operational tactics:

> To preserve the Red Army and arouse the masses, the Central Committee asks us to divide our forces into very small units and disperse them over the countryside and to withdraw Chu Teh and Mao Tse-tung from the army, so concealing the major targets. This is an unrealistic view. In the winter of 1927-28, we did plan to disperse our forces over the countryside, with each company or battalion operating on its own and adopting guerrilla tactics in order to arouse the masses while trying not to present a target for the enemy; we have tried this out many times, but have failed every time. The reasons are: (1) most of the soldiers in the main force of the Red Army come from other areas and have a background different from that of the local Red Guards; (2) division into small units results in weak leadership and inability to cope with adverse circumstances, which easily leads to defeat; (3) the units are liable to be crushed by the enemy one by one; (4) the more adverse the circumstances, the greater the need for concentrating our forces and for the leaders to be resolute in struggle, because only thus can we have internal unity against the enemy. Only in favourable circumstances is it advisable to divide our forces for guerrilla operations, and it is only then that the leaders need not stay with the ranks all the time, as they must in adverse circumstances.

The weakness of this passage is that the reasons adduced against the division of forces were of a negative character, which was far from adequate. The positive reason for concentrating our forces is that only concentration will enable us to wipe out comparatively large enemy units and occupy towns. Only after we have wiped out comparatively large enemy units and occupied towns can we arouse the masses on a broad scale and set up political power extending over a number of adjoining counties. Only thus can we make a widespread impact (what we call "extending our political influence"), and contribute effectively to speeding the day of the revolutionary high tide. For instance, both the regime we set up in the Hunan-Kiangsi border area the year before last and the one we set up in western Fukien last year[9] were the product of this policy of concentrating our troops. This is a general principle. But are there not times when our forces should be divided up? Yes, there are. The letter from the Front Committee to the Central Committee says of guerrilla tactics for the Red Army, including the division of forces within a short radius:

> The tactics we have derived from the struggle of the past three years are indeed different from any other tactics, ancient or modern, Chinese or foreign. With our tactics, the masses can be aroused for struggle on an ever-broadening scale, and no enemy, however powerful, can cope with us. Ours are guerrilla tactics. They consist mainly of the following points:
>
> "Divide our forces to arouse the masses, concentrate our forces to deal with the enemy."
>
> "The enemy advances, we retreat; the enemy camps, we harass; the enemy tires, we attack; the enemy retreats, we pursue."
>
> "To extend stable base areas,[10] employ the policy of advancing in waves; when pursued by a powerful enemy, employ the policy of circling around."
>
> "Arouse the largest numbers of the masses in the shortest possible time and by the best possible methods."
>
> These tactics are just like casting a net; at any moment we should be able to cast it or draw it in. We cast it wide to win over the masses and draw it in to deal with the enemy. Such are the tactics we have used for the past three years.

Here, "to cast the net wide" means to divide our forces within a short radius. For example, when we first captured the county town of Yunghsin in the Hunan-Kiangsi border area, we divided the forces of the 29th and 31st Regiments within the boundaries of Yunghsin County. Again, when we captured Yunghsin for the third time, we once more divided our forces by dispatching the 28th Regiment to the border of Anfu County, the 29th to Lienhua, and the 31st to the border of Kian County. And, again, we divided our forces in the counties of southern Kiangsi last April and May, and in the counties of western Fukien last July. As to dividing our forces over a wide radius, it is possible only on the two conditions that circumstances are comparatively favourable and the leading bodies fairly strong. For the purpose of dividing up our forces is to put us in a better position for winning over the masses, for deepening the agrarian revolution and establishing political power, and for expanding the Red Army and the local armed units. It is better not to divide our forces when this purpose cannot be attained or the division of our forces would lead to defeat and to the weakening of the Red Army, as happened in August two years ago when our forces were divided on the Hunan-Kiangsi border for an attack on Chenchou. But there is no doubt that, given the two above-mentioned conditions, we should divide our forces, because division is then more advantageous than concentration.

The Central Committee's February letter was not in the right spirit and had a bad effect on a number of Party comrades in the Fourth Army. At that time the Central Committee also issued a circular stating that war would not necessarily break out between Chiang Kai-shek and the Kwangsi warlords. Since then, however, the appraisals and directives of the Central Committee have in the main been correct. It has already issued another circular correcting the one containing the wrong appraisal. Although it has not made any correction of the letter to the Red Army, its subsequent directives have not been couched in the same pessimistic tone and its views on the Red Army's operations now coincide with ours. Yet the bad effect which this letter had on some comrades persists. Therefore, I feel that it is still necessary to give some explanation.

The plan to take Kiangsi Province within a year was also proposed last April by the Front Committee to the Central Committee, and a decision to that effect was later made at Yutu. The following reasons were given in the letter to the Central Committee:

> The armies of Chiang Kai-shek and the Kwangsi warlords are approaching each other in the vicinity of Kiukiang, and a big battle is imminent. The resumption of mass struggle, coupled with the spread of contradictions among the ruling reactionaries, makes it probable that there will soon be a high tide of revolution. As for how our work should be arranged under these circumstances, we feel that, so far as the southern provinces are concerned, the armed forces of the compradors and landlords in Kwangtung and Hunan Provinces are too strong, and that in Hunan, more-

over, we have lost almost all our mass following, inside as well
as outside the Party, because of the Party's putschist mistakes.
In the three provinces of Fukien, Kiangsi and Chekiang, however,
the situation is different. First, militarily the enemy is weakest
there. In Chekiang, there is only a small provincial force under
Chiang Po-cheng.[11] In Fukien, although there are five groups of
enemy troops totalling fourteen regiments in all, Kuo Feng-
ming's troops have already been smashed; the troops under Chen
Kuo-hui and Lu Hsing-pang[12] are bandits of small fighting capacity; the two brigades of marines stationed along the coast have
never seen action and their fighting capacity is undoubtedly not
high; Chang Chen[13] alone can put up some sort of a fight, but,
according to an analysis made by the Fukien Provincial Committee, even he has only two relatively strong regiments. In
addition, Fukien is now in a state of complete chaos, confusion
and disunity. In Kiangsi, there are sixteen regiments under the
two commands of Chu Pei-teh[14] and Hsiung Shih-hui;[15] they are
stronger than the armed forces of either Fukien or Chekiang,
but far inferior to those of Hunan. Secondly, fewer putschist
mistakes have been made in these three provinces. We are not
clear about the situation in Chekiang, but the Party's organizational and mass base is somewhat better in Kiangsi and Fukien
than in Hunan. Take Kiangsi for example. In northern Kiangsi
we still have some basis in Tehan, Hsiushui and Tungku; in
western Kiangsi the Party and the Red Guards still have some
strength in Ningkang, Yunghsin, Lienhua and Suichuan; in
southern Kiangsi the prospects are still brighter, as the 2nd and
4th Regiments of the Red Army are steadily growing in strength
in the counties of Kian, Yungfeng and Hsingkuo; and what is
more, the Red Army under Fang Chih-min has by no means
been wiped out. All this places us in a position to close in on
Nanchang. We hereby recommend to the Central Committee that
during the period of prolonged warfare among the Kuomintang
warlords, we should contend with Chiang Kai-shek and the
Kwangsi clique for Kiangsi Province and also for western Fukien
and western Chekiang. In these three provinces we should
enlarge the Red Army and create an independent regime of
the masses, with a time limit of one year for accomplishing
this plan.

This proposal to contend for Kiangsi erred only in setting a time limit of one year. It was based not only on conditions within the province itself, but also on the prospect that a nation-wide high tide of revolution would soon arise. For unless we had been convinced that there would soon be a high tide of revolution, we could not possibly have concluded that we could take Kiangsi in a year. The only weakness in the proposal was that it set a time limit of one year, which it should not have done, and so gave a flavour of impetuosity to the word "soon" in the statement, "there will soon be a high tide of revolution". As to the subjective and objective conditions in Kiangsi, they well deserve our attention. Besides the subjective conditions described in the letter to the Central Committee, three objective conditions can now be clearly pointed out. First, the economy of Kiangsi is mainly feudal, the merchant-capitalist class is relatively weak, and the armed forces of the landlords are weaker than in any other southern province. Secondly, Kiangsi has no provincial troops of its own and has always been garrisoned by troops from other provinces. Sent there for the "suppression of Communists" or "suppression of bandits", these troops are unfamiliar with local conditions, their interests are much less directly involved than if they were local troops, and they usually lack enthusiasm. And thirdly, unlike Kwangtung which is close to Hongkong and under British control in almost every respect, Kiangsi is comparatively remote from imperialist influence. Once we have grasped these three points, we can understand why rural uprisings are more widespread and the Red Army and guerrilla units more numerous in Kiangsi than in any other province.

How then should we interpret the word "soon" in the statement, "there will soon be a high tide of revolution"? This is a common question among comrades. Marxists are not fortune-tellers. They should, and indeed can, only indicate the general direction of future developments and changes; they should not and cannot fix the day and the hour in a mechanistic way. But when I say that there will soon be a high tide of revolution in China, I am emphatically not speaking of something which in the words of some people "is possibly coming", something illusory, unattainable and devoid of significance for action. It is like a ship far out at sea whose mast-head can already be seen from the shore; it is like the morning sun in the east whose shimmering rays are visible from a high mountain top; it is like a child about to be born moving restlessly in its mother's womb.

NOTES

[1] Comrade Fang Chih-min, a native of Yiyang, Kiangsi Province, and a member of the Sixth Central Committee of the Communist Party of China, was the founder of the Red area in northeastern Kiangsi and of the Tenth Red Army. In 1934 he led the vanguard detachment of the Red Army in marching north to resist the Japanese invaders. In January 1935 he was captured in battle against the counter-revolutionary Kuomintang troops and in July he died a martyr's death in Nanchang, Kiangsi.

[2] The subjective forces of the revolution mean the organized forces of the revolution.

[3] Lu Ti-ping, a Kuomintang warlord, was the Kuomintang governor of Hunan Province in 1928.

[4] The war of March-April 1929 between Chiang Kai-shek, the Kuomintang warlord in Nanking, and Li Tsung-jen and Pai Chung-hsi, the Kuomintang warlords in Kwangsi Province.

[5] The third invasion of the Red Army's base area on the Chingkang Mountains by the Kuomintang warlords in Hunan and Kiangsi lasting from the end of 1928 to the beginning of 1929.

[6] The quotation is from Mencius, who compared a tyrant who drove his people into seeking a benevolent ruler to the otter which "drives the fish into deep waters".

[7] The Sixth National Congress of the Communist Party of China was held in July 1928. It pointed out that after the defeat in 1927, China's revolution remained bourgeois-democratic in nature, i.e., anti-imperialist and anti-feudal, and that since the inevitable new high tide in the revolution was not yet imminent, the general line for the revolution should be to win over the masses. The Sixth Congress liquidated the 1927 Right capitulationism of Chen Tu-hsiu and also repudiated the "Left" putschism which occurred in the Party at the end of 1927 and the beginning of 1928.

[8] The statement in brackets has been added by the author.

[9] The regime set up in western Fukien came into being in 1929, when the Red Army in the Chingkang Mountains sallied eastward to build a new revolutionary base area and established the people's revolutionary political power in the counties of Lungyen, Yungting and Shanghang in the western part of that province.

[10] Stable base areas were the relatively stable revolutionary base areas established by the Workers' and Peasants' Red Army.

[11] Chiang Po-cheng was then the commander of the Kuomintang peace preservation corps in Chekiang Province.

[12] Chen Kuo-hui and Lu Hsing-pang were two notorious Fukien bandits whose forces had been incorporated into the Kuomintang army.

[13] Chang Chen was a divisional commander of the Kuomintang army.

[14] Chu Pei-teh, a Kuomintang warlord, was then the Kuomintang governor of Kiangsi Province.

[15] Hsiung Shih-hui was then a divisional commander of the Kuomintang army in Kiangsi Province.

PAY ATTENTION TO ECONOMIC WORK

August 20, 1933

The growing intensity of the revolutionary war makes it imperative for us to mobilize the masses in order to launch an immediate campaign on the economic front and undertake all possible and necessary tasks of economic construction. Why? Because all our present efforts should be directed towards gaining victory in the revolutionary war and, first and foremost, towards gaining complete victory in the fight to smash the enemy's fifth "encirclement and suppression" campaign;[1] they should be directed towards securing the material conditions which will guarantee food and other supplies for the Red Army, towards bettering the life of the people and so stimulating their more active participation in the revolutionary war, towards organizing the masses on the economic front and educating them so as to provide fresh mass strength for the war, and towards consolidating the worker-peasant alliance and the democratic dictatorship of workers and peasants and strengthening proletarian leadership by building up the economy. Such economic construction is essential for the attainment of all these objectives. This must be clearly understood by everyone engaged in revolutionary work. Some comrades have thought it impossible to spare time for economic construction because the revolutionary war keeps people busy enough, and they have condemned anyone arguing for it as a "Right deviationist". In their opinion economic construction is impossible in the midst of a revolutionary war and is possible only in the peaceful, tranquil conditions prevailing after final victory. Comrades, such views are wrong. Whoever holds them fails to realize that without building up the economy it is impossible to secure the material prerequisites for the revolutionary war, and the people will become exhausted in the course of a long war. Just consider! The enemy is

---

This speech was delivered at the economic construction conference of seventeen counties in southern Kiangsi in August 1933.

129

enforcing an economic blockade, unscrupulous merchants and reactionaries are disrupting our finance and commerce, and the trade of our Red areas with the outside is seriously hampered. Will not the revolutionary war be seriously affected unless these difficulties are overcome? Salt is very dear, and sometimes even unobtainable. Rice is cheap in the autumn and winter, but it becomes terribly dear in spring and summer. All this directly affects the life of the workers and peasants and prevents any improvement. And does it not affect our basic line — the alliance of workers and peasants? If the workers and peasants become dissatisfied with their living conditions, will it not affect the expansion of our Red Army and the mobilization of the masses for the revolutionary war? Therefore it is utterly wrong to think that no economic construction should be undertaken in the midst of the revolutionary war. Those who think this way often say that everything should be subordinated to the war effort, but they fail to understand that to dispense with economic construction would weaken the war effort rather than subordinate everything to it. Only by extending the work on the economic front and building the economy of the Red areas can we provide an adequate material basis for the revolutionary war, proceed smoothly with our military offensives and strike effective blows at the enemy's "encirclement and suppression" campaigns; only thus can we acquire the resources to enlarge the Red Army and push our front outwards to points thousands of *li* away, so that when the circumstances prove favourable, the Red Army will be able to attack Nanchang and Kiukiang free from all anxiety and, thus relieved of much of the task of provisioning itself, give its undivided attention to fighting; and only thus can we to a certain extent satisfy the material needs of the people so that they will join the Red Army or undertake other revolutionary tasks with even greater enthusiasm. Subordinating everything to the war effort means just this. Among those engaged in revolutionary work in various places, many do not yet understand the importance of economic construction in the revolutionary war, and there are many local governments which give little attention to discussing the problems of economic construction. The economic departments of the local governments are not yet well organized, and some are still without a director; in others some incompetent has been assigned simply to fill the post. The formation of co-operatives is still in the initial stage, and only in a few places has the work of regulating food supplies been started. There has been no propaganda among the people for the work of economic construction (though such propaganda is very important), and mass enthusiasm for it has not been aroused. All this is due to the failure to recognize the importance of economic construction. Through the discussions at this conference and through the reports you will make when you return to your posts, we must create mass enthusiasm for economic construction among all government personnel and among all workers and peasants. The importance of economic construction for the revolutionary war should be made clear to everyone, so that they will do their best to promote the sale of economic construction bonds, develop the co-operative movement, and set up public granaries and storehouses for famine relief everywhere. Each county must establish a sub-department for the regulation of food supplies, with branch offices in important districts and market centres. On the one hand, within our Red areas we should send grain from places with a surplus to those with a deficit, so that it will not pile up in one place and become unobtainable in another and its price will not be too low in one place and too high in another; on the other hand, we should send our grain surplus out of the Red areas in a planned way (*i.e.*, not in unlimited quantities) and bring in necessities from the White areas, thus avoiding exploitation by unscrupulous merchants. We must all do our best to develop agriculture and handicrafts and increase the output of farm implements and lime in order to ensure a bigger crop next year, and we must restore the output of such local products as wolfram, timber, camphor, paper, tobacco, linen, dried mushrooms and peppermint oil to former levels, and market them in the White areas in quantity.

Judged by volume, grain ranks first among the principal outgoing commodities in our trade with the outside areas. About three million piculs of unhusked rice are sent out yearly in exchange for necessary consumer goods, or an average of one picul a head of the three million population; it cannot, surely, be less than this. But who is handling this trade? It is handled entirely by the merchants who exploit us ruthlessly in the process. Last year they bought unhusked rice from the peasants in Wanan and Taiho Counties at fifty cents a picul and sold it in Kanchow for four yuan, making a sevenfold profit. Take another instance. Every year our three million people need about nine million yuan worth of salt and six million yuan worth of cotton cloth. Needless to say, this fifteen million yuan trade in salt and cloth has been entirely in the hands of the merchants; we have done nothing about it. The exploitation by the merchants is really enormous. For instance, they go to Meihsien and buy salt at one yuan for seven catties, and then sell it in our areas at one yuan for twelve ounces. Is this not shocking profiteering? We can no longer ignore such a state of affairs, and from now on we must handle this trade ourselves. Our department of trade with outside areas must make a great effort in this connection.

How shall we use the three million yuan from economic construction bonds? We plan to use it in the following way. One million will be allotted for the Red Army's war expenses, and two million will be loaned as capital to the co-operatives, the Bureau for the Regulation of Food Supplies and the Bureau of External Trade. Of the latter amount, the greater part will be used for expanding our external trade and the rest for expanding production. Our objective is not only to expand production but also to sell our products at fair prices to the White areas and then purchase salt and cloth cheaply for distribution among our people, so as to break the enemy's blockade and check the merchants' exploitation. We must bring about the continued growth of the people's economy, greatly improve the livelihood of the masses and substantially increase our public revenue, thus laying firm material foundations for the revolutionary war and for economic construction.

This is a great task, a great class struggle. But we should ask ourselves, can it be accomplished in the midst of fierce fighting? I think it can. We are not talking about building a railway to Lungyen or, for the time being, even about building a motor road to Kanchow. We are not saying that there should be a complete monopoly of the sale of grain, or that the government should handle all the salt and cloth trade, valued at fifteen million yuan, to the total exclusion of the merchants. This is not the point we are making or what we are trying to do. What we are talking about and trying to do is to develop agriculture and the handicrafts, and send out grain and wolfram in exchange for salt and cloth, starting temporarily with a fund of two million yuan plus the money invested by the people. Is there anything here that we should not undertake, or that we cannot undertake and achieve? We have already started this work and achieved some results. This year's autumn harvest is between 20 and 25 per cent larger than last year's, or more than our original estimate of a 20 per cent increase. In the handicraft industries the production of farm implements and lime is being restored, and we are beginning to restore wolfram production. The output of tobacco, paper and timber is recovering. Much has been accomplished this year in the regulation of food supplies. A start has been made on importing salt. It is on these achievements that we base our firm belief in the possibility of further progress. Is it not clearly wrong to say that economic construction is impossible now and has to wait until the war is over?

It is thus clear that, at the present stage, economic construction must revolve around our central task, the revolutionary war. Today the revolutionary war is our central task, which economic construction should serve, centre on and be subordinated to. It would likewise be wrong to regard economic construction as the centre of all our present work to the neglect of the revolutionary war, or to conduct it apart from the revolutionary war. Not until the civil war is over will it be possible and necessary to regard economic construction as the centre of all our work. In the midst of a civil war, it is sheer delusion to try to carry out such peace-time economic construction as can and should be done in the future but not at present. The tasks for the present are those urgently demanded by the war. Every one of them should serve the war; none is a peace-time undertaking separate from the war. If any comrade entertains the idea of carrying out economic construction apart from the war, he should correct this mistake at once.

It will be impossible to get a rapid campaign going on the economic front without a correct style of leadership and correct methods of work. This, too, presents an important problem which this conference must solve. For the comrades here will have a great deal to do as soon as they return, and will have to give guidance to the many people who will be working with them. In particular, the comrades who are working at the township and city levels and in the co-operatives, the food departments, the trade departments and the purchasing offices, are personally engaged in the practical work of mobilizing the people to organize co-operatives, regulating and transporting food supplies, and managing our trade with the outside areas. If their style of leadership is wrong and if they do not employ correct and efficient methods, the work will be immediately affected, we shall fail to win mass support for the various tasks, and during the coming autumn and winter and next spring and summer we shall be unable to carry out the whole of the Central Government's plan for economic construction. For these reasons I want to direct our comrades' attention to the following.

Firstly, mobilize the masses by various organizational means. In the first place, comrades on the presidiums and in the economic and finance departments of the government bodies at all levels must regularly put on their agenda and discuss, supervise and check up on such items of work as the sale of bonds, the formation of co-operatives, the regulation of food supplies and the promotion of production and trade. Next, the mass organizations, chiefly the trade unions and poor peasant leagues, must be moved into action. The trade unions should mobilize all their members to join these economic struggles. The poor peasant leagues are powerful bases for mobilizing the masses to build up co-operatives and subscribe to bonds, and they should be given vigorous leadership by district and township governments. Furthermore, we must conduct propaganda for economic construction at village or household meetings, explaining clearly how it is related to the revolutionary war and discussing in the most practical terms how to improve the livelihood of the masses and increase our strength for the struggle. We should appeal to the people to subscribe to bonds, develop co-operatives, regulate food supplies, consolidate finances and promote trade; we should call upon them to fight for these slogans and should heighten their enthusiasm. Our objectives cannot be attained unless we use various organizational means to mobilize the masses and conduct propaganda among them in the manner described, that is to say, unless the presidiums and the economic and finance departments of the government bodies at all levels actively attend to discussing and checking up on the work of economic construction, unless they spur the mass organizations into action and hold mass propaganda meetings.

Secondly, we must not be bureaucratic in our methods of mobilizing the masses. Bureaucratic leadership cannot be tolerated in economic construction any more than in any other branch of our revolutionary work. The ugly evil of bureaucracy, which no comrade likes, must be thrown into the cesspit. The methods which all comrades should prefer are those that appeal to the masses, *i.e.*, those which are welcomed by all workers and peasants. One manifestation of bureaucracy is slacking at work due to indifference or perfunctoriness. We must wage a stern struggle against this phenomenon. Commandism is another manifestation. To all appearances, persons given to commandism are not slackers; they give the impression of being hard workers. But in fact co-operatives set up by commandist methods will not succeed, and even if they appear to grow for a time, they cannot be consolidated. In the end the masses will lose faith in them, which will hamper their development. To push the sales of bonds in a commandist way and impose arbitrary quotas, regardless of whether people understand what the bonds are for and of how much they can afford, will ultimately arouse the people's displeasure and make it impossible to achieve good sales. We must reject commandism; what we need is energetic propaganda to convince the masses, and we should develop the co-operatives, promote the sales of bonds and do all the work of economic mobilization in accordance with the actual conditions and the real feelings of the masses.

Thirdly, large numbers of cadres are needed to extend the campaign of economic construction. This is not a matter of scores or hundreds of people, but of thousands and tens of thousands whom we must organize, train and send to the economic construction front. They will be the commanders and the broad masses the soldiers on the economic front. People often sigh over the shortage of cadres. Comrades, is there really a shortage? Innumerable cadres have come to the fore from among the masses who have been steeled in the agrarian struggles, the economic struggles and the revolutionary war. How can we say there is a shortage of cadres? Discard this mistaken view and you will see cadres all around you.

Fourthly, economic construction today is inseparable not only from the general task of the war but from other tasks as well. Only if there is a thorough check-up on land distribution[2] will it be possible to abolish feudal and semi-feudal ownership of land completely, enhance the peasants' enthusiasm for production and swiftly draw the peasant masses into economic construction. Only if the labour laws are resolutely enforced will it be possible to better the life of the workers, bring them speedily into active participation in economic construction and strengthen their leadership of the peasants. Only if there is correct leadership in the elections and in the exposure campaigns[3] which accompany the check-up on land distribution will it be possible to strengthen our government bodies so that they can give more vigorous leadership in the revolutionary war and in all our work, including economic work. The raising of the political and cultural level of the people through cultural and educational work is also a most important task in the development of the economy. That the expansion of the Red Army must not be neglected for a single day goes without saying. Everybody understands that without Red Army victories the economic blockade would be still tighter. On the other hand, economic growth and a better life for the masses will undoubtedly be of great help to the work of expanding the Red Army and inspiring the masses to march eagerly to the front. To sum up, if we achieve all the above tasks, including the very important new one of economic construction, and if we make them all serve the revolutionary war, then victory in the revolutionary war will undoubtedly be ours.

NOTES

[1] Between 1930 and 1934 Chiang Kai-shek launched five large-scale onslaughts against the Red area centred on Juichin, Kiangsi; they were called "encirclement and suppression" campaigns. The fifth of such campaigns began in October 1933, though Chiang Kai-shek had been making active preparations for it since the summer.

[2] A campaign to check up land distribution was carried out in the Red area after the agrarian reform to ascertain whether the land had been properly redistributed.

[3] Exposure campaigns were democratic campaigns in which the people were encouraged to expose misdeeds by the functionaries of the democratic government.

HOW TO DIFFERENTIATE THE CLASSES
IN THE RURAL AREAS

October 1933

I. THE LANDLORD

A landlord is a person who owns land, does not engage in labour himself, or does so only to a very small extent, and lives by exploiting the peasants. The collection of land rent is his main form of exploitation; in addition, he may lend money, hire labour, or engage in industry or commerce. But his exaction of land rent from the peasants is his principal form of exploitation. The administration of communal land and the collection of rent from school land[1] are included in the category of exploitation through land rent.

A bankrupt landlord shall still be classified as a landlord if he does not engage in labour but lives by swindling or robbing others or by receiving assistance from relatives or friends, and is better off than the average middle peasant.

Warlords, officials, local tyrants and evil gentry are political representatives and exceptionally ruthless members of the landlord class. Minor local tyrants and evil gentry are also very often to be found among the rich peasants.

Persons who assist landlords in collecting rent and managing property, who depend on landlord exploitation of the peasants as their main source of income and are better off than the average middle peasant shall be put in the same category as landlords.

Comrade Mao Tse-tung wrote this document in October 1933 to rectify the deviations that had occurred in the work of land reform and to provide a correct solution for the land problem. It was adopted by the Workers' and Peasants' Democratic Central Government of that time as establishing the criteria for determining class status in the rural areas.

Usurers are persons who rely on exploitation by usury as their main source of income, are better off than the average middle peasant, and shall be put in the same category as landlords.

II. THE RICH PEASANT

The rich peasant as a rule owns land. But some rich peasants own only part of their land and rent the remainder. Others have no land of their own at all and rent all their land. The rich peasant generally has rather more and better instruments of production and more liquid capital than the average and engages in labour himself, but always relies on exploitation for part or even the major part of his income. His main form of exploitation is the hiring of labour (long-term labourers). In addition, he may let part of his land and practise exploitation through land rent, or may lend money or engage in industry and commerce. Most rich peasants also engage in the administration of communal land. A person who owns a fair amount of good land, farms some of it himself without hiring labour, but exploits other peasants by means of land rent, loan interest or in other ways, shall also be treated as a rich peasant. Rich peasants regularly practise exploitation and many derive most of their income from this source.

III. THE MIDDLE PEASANT

Many middle peasants own land. Some own only part of their land and rent the rest. Others own no land of their own at all and rent all their land. All of them have a fair number of farm implements. A middle peasant derives his income wholly or mainly from his own labour. As a rule he does not exploit others and in many cases he himself is exploited by others, having to pay a small amount in land rent and in interest on loans. But generally he does not sell his labour power. Some middle peasants (the well-to-do middle peasants) do practise exploitation to a small extent, but this is not their regular or their main source of income.

IV. THE POOR PEASANT

Among the poor peasants some own part of their land and have a few odd farm implements, others own no land at all but only a few odd farm implements. As a rule poor peasants have to rent the land they work on and are subjected to exploitation, having to pay land rent and interest on loans and to hire themselves out to some extent.

In general, a middle peasant does not need to sell his labour power, while the poor peasant has to sell part of his labour power. This is the principal criterion for distinguishing between a middle and a poor peasant.

V. THE WORKER

The worker (including the farm labourer) as a rule owns no land or farm implements, though some do own a very small amount of land and very few farm implements. Workers make their living wholly or mainly by selling their labour power.

NOTES

[1] There were various forms of public land in China's rural areas — land owned by the township or district government, by the ancestral temple of a clan, by a Buddhist or Taoist temple, a Catholic church or a mosque, or land whose income was used for public welfare purposes such as famine relief, or the building and maintenance of bridges and roads, or for educational purposes. In practice, most of such land was controlled by the landlords and rich peasants, and few peasants had any say in its administration.

OUR ECONOMIC POLICY

January 23, 1934

Only the Kuomintang warlords who have brought the areas under their own rule to the brink of bankruptcy have the utter shamelessness to spread the rumour, day in day out, that the Red areas are in a state of total collapse. The imperialists and the Kuomintang are bent on wrecking the Red areas, the work of economic construction now in progress there, and the welfare of the millions of workers and peasants who have achieved liberation. For this purpose, they have pursued a ruthless policy of economic blockade, in addition to organizing forces for military campaigns of "encirclement and suppression". But, leading the broad masses and the Red Army, we have not only smashed one enemy "encirclement and suppression" campaign after another, but have also been doing all the essential work of economic construction within our power in order to defeat this vicious economic blockade. In this respect, too, we have scored one success after another.

The principle governing our economic policy is to proceed with all the essential work of economic construction within our power and concentrate our economic resources on the war effort, and at the same time to improve the life of the people as much as possible, consolidate the worker-peasant alliance in the economic field, ensure proletarian leadership of the peasantry, and strive to secure leadership by the state sector of the economy over the private sector, thus creating the prerequisites for our future advance to socialism.

The focus of our economic construction is to increase agricultural and industrial production, expand our trade with the outside, and develop the co-operatives.

Agriculture in the Red areas is obviously making progress. As compared with 1932, the 1933 agricultural output was 15 per cent higher

---

This report was given by Comrade Mao Tse-tung at the Second National Congress of Workers' and Peasants' Representatives held in Juichin, Kiangsi Province in January 1934.

in southern Kiangsi and western Fukien and 20 per cent higher in the
Fukien-Chekiang-Kiangsi border area. The Szechuan-Shensi border
area has had a good harvest. After a Red area is established, farm
output often declines in the first year or two.[1] But it picks up again as
the peasant masses work with greater enthusiasm after the land is
redistributed and ownership is settled, and after we have given en-
couragement to production. Today in some places farm output has
reached and even exceeded the pre-revolution level. In others, not
only has land that lay waste during the revolutionary uprisings been
reclaimed, but new land has been brought under cultivation. In many
places mutual-aid groups and ploughing teams[2] have been organized
to adjust the use of labour power in the villages, and co-operatives
have been organized to overcome the shortage of draught oxen. Moreover, the women are taking part in production in great numbers. None
of this could have happened in the Kuomintang days. With the land
in the hands of the landlords, the peasants then were neither willing
to improve it nor did they possess the means to do so. Only since we
have distributed the land to the peasants and encouraged and rewarded
production has their labour enthusiasm blossomed forth and great
success in production been achieved. It should be pointed out that in
the present conditions agriculture occupies first place in our economic
construction; it is by agriculture that we solve both the most important
problem of food, and the problem of raw materials such as cotton,
hemp, sugar-cane and bamboo, which are needed for the making of
clothes, sugar, paper and other necessities. The care of forests and
the increase of livestock are also an important part of agriculture.
Within the framework of small-scale peasant economy it is permissible and indeed necessary to draw up suitable plans for the output
of certain important agricultural products and to mobilize the peasants
to strive for their fulfilment. We should pay closer attention and
devote greater efforts to this. We must actively lead the peasants in
solving such difficult and essential problems in production as labour
power, draught oxen, fertilizer, seed and irrigation. In this connection our fundamental task is to adjust the use of labour power in an
organized way and to encourage women to do farm work. The necessary measures to solve the problem of labour power are organizing
mutual-aid groups and ploughing teams and mobilizing and encouraging the whole rural population to help during the busy spring and
summer ploughing seasons. Another big problem is that quite a large
proportion (about 25 per cent) of the peasants are short of draught

oxen. We must attend to organizing draught oxen co-operatives, encouraging the peasants without oxen to buy them for their common use through voluntary subscription to shares. Irrigation, which is the lifeblood of agriculture, also merits close attention. Of course, we cannot as yet bring up the question of state or collective farming, but it is urgently necessary to set up small experimental farms, agricultural research schools and exhibitions of farm produce in various places to stimulate the development of agriculture.

The enemy blockade has made it difficult for us to market goods outside our areas. There has been a decline in production in many handicraft industries in the Red areas, notably tobacco-curing and paper-making. But the difficulties of sending goods out are not entirely insurmountable. We have an extensive market of our own because of the mass demand in our areas. We should systematically restore and develop handicrafts and also certain industries, firstly to supply our own needs and secondly for trade with the outside. In the last two years, and especially since the first half of 1933, many handicrafts and a few industries have begun to look up because of the attention we have begun to devote to them and the gradual development of producers' co-operatives by the people. The most significant fields are tobacco, paper, wolfram, camphor, farm implements and fertilizers (such as lime). Moreover, in our present circumstances we should not neglect the manufacture of our own cotton cloth, medicines and sugar. In the Fukien-Chekiang-Kiangsi border area, some industries have been set up which were previously non-existent, such as paper-making, cloth-making and sugar-refining, and they are doing well. To relieve the shortage of salt, people have begun to extract it from nitre. It requires proper planning to keep industry going. With a scattered handicraft industry, detailed and comprehensive planning is of course impossible. But fairly detailed production plans are absolutely essential for certain important enterprises, and first and foremost for state and co-operative enterprises. Every one of our state and co-operative industrial enterprises must pay attention from the very beginning to making accurate estimates of raw material output and marketing prospects in both the enemy areas and our own.

At the present time, it is particularly necessary for us to organize private external trading according to plan and for the state to handle certain essential commodities directly, for instance, the import of salt and cotton cloth, the export of grain and wolfram, and the adjustment of grain supply within our own areas. Such work was first undertaken in the Fukien-Chekiang-Kiangsi border area and was started in the Central Area in the spring of 1933. With the establishment of the Bureau of External Trade and other agencies, initial successes have been achieved in this connection.

Our economy is made up of three sectors, state enterprise, co-operative enterprise and private enterprise.

At present, state enterprise is limited to what is possible and essential. State-operated industry and commerce have begun to grow and they have boundless prospects.

As regards the private sector of the economy, we shall not hamper it, indeed we shall promote and encourage it, so long as it does not transgress the legal limits set by our government. For the development of private enterprise is essential to the interests of the state and the people at the present stage. Needless to say, private enterprise is now preponderant and will inevitably continue to occupy a dominant position for a considerable time. Today, private undertakings in the Red areas are small in scale.

Co-operative enterprise is growing rapidly. There are altogether 1,423 co-operatives of various kinds, with a total capital of over 300,000 yuan, according to the September 1933 figures for seventeen counties in Kiangsi and Fukien. Consumers' co-operatives and grain co-operatives head the list, with producers' co-operatives coming next. Credit co-operatives have just started functioning. When the co-operative and the state enterprises become co-ordinated and grow over a long period of time, they will become a tremendous force in our economy and will gradually prevail and assume leadership over the private sector. Therefore, the greatest possible development of state enterprise and the extensive development of co-operative enterprise must go hand in hand with encouraging the development of private enterprise.

With the support of the masses, we have issued economic construction bonds to the value of three million yuan in order to develop state enterprise and assist the co-operatives. Such reliance on the strength of the masses is the only possible way to solve the problem of funds for economic construction at this time.

To increase our revenue by developing the economy is a basic principle of our financial policy; it has already brought tangible results in the Fukien-Chekiang-Kiangsi border area and is beginning to do so in the Central Area, too. It is the duty of our financial and economic organizations to apply this principle conscientiously. In this connection, we should make quite sure that the issuing of notes by the state bank is based primarily on the needs of economic development, and only secondarily on purely fiscal needs.

Thrift should be the guiding principle in our government expenditure. It should be made clear to all government workers that corruption and waste are very great crimes. Our campaigns against corruption and waste have already achieved some results, but further efforts are required. Our system of accounting must be guided by the principle of saving every copper for the war effort, for the revolutionary cause and for our economic construction. Our methods of spending state revenue must be strictly different from those of the Kuomintang.

At a time when the country is plunged in economic disaster, when hundreds of millions of people are suffering the terrible hardships of hunger and cold, the people's government in our areas is staunchly pressing ahead with economic construction for the sake of the revolutionary war and in the interests of the nation, regardless of all the difficulties. The situation is perfectly clear — only by defeating imperialism and the Kuomintang and by undertaking planned, organized economic construction can we deliver the people of the whole of China from unprecedented disaster.

NOTES

[1] There was usually a decline in farm output in the first year or two after the establishment of a Red area, chiefly because landownership was not yet settled and the new economic order was not fully established during land redistribution, so that the peasants could not yet set their minds fully on production.

[2] Mutual-aid groups and ploughing teams, based on individual farming, were formed by peasants in the Red areas to facilitate production through a better organization of labour power. On the principle of voluntary participation and mutual benefit, the members did an equal amount of work for each other, or if one could not give another as much help as he received he made up the difference in cash. Apart from helping each other, the teams gave preferential treatment to the families of Red Army soldiers and worked for bereaved old folk without any pay except for meals during the work. As these measures of mutual aid were of great help to production and were carried out on a reasonable basis they won the warm support of the masses.

BE CONCERNED WITH THE WELL-BEING
OF THE MASSES,
PAY ATTENTION TO METHODS OF WORK

January 27, 1934

There are two questions which comrades have failed to stress during the discussion and which, I feel, should be dealt with.

The first concerns the well-being of the masses.

Our central task at present is to mobilize the broad masses to take part in the revolutionary war, overthrow imperialism and the Kuomintang by means of such war, spread the revolution throughout the country, and drive imperialism out of China. Anyone who does not attach enough importance to this central task is not a good revolutionary cadre. If our comrades really comprehend this task and understand that the revolution must at all costs be spread throughout the country, then they should in no way neglect or underestimate the question of the immediate interests, the well-being, of the broad masses. For the revolutionary war is a war of the masses; it can be waged only by mobilizing the masses and relying on them.

If we only mobilize the people to carry on the war and do nothing else, can we succeed in defeating the enemy? Of course not. If we want to win, we must do a great deal more. We must lead the peasants' struggle for land and distribute the land to them, heighten their labour enthusiasm and increase agricultural production, safeguard the interests of the workers, establish co-operatives, develop trade with outside areas, and solve the problems facing the masses — food, shelter and clothing, fuel, rice, cooking oil and salt, sickness and hygiene, and marriage. In short, all the practical problems in the

---

This was part of the concluding speech made by Comrade Mao Tse-tung at the Second National Congress of Workers' and Peasants' Representatives held in Juichin, Kiangsi Province in January 1934.

masses' everyday life should claim our attention. If we attend to these problems, solve them and satisfy the needs of the masses, we shall really become organizers of the well-being of the masses, and they will truly rally round us and give us their warm support. Comrades, will we then be able to arouse them to take part in the revolutionary war? Yes, indeed we will.

Here is the kind of thing we have found among some of our cadres. They talk only about expanding the Red Army, enlarging the transport corps, collecting the land tax and selling bonds; as for other matters, they neither discuss nor attend to them, and even ignore them altogether. For instance, there was a time when the Tingchow Municipal Government concerned itself only with the expansion of the Red Army and with mobilization for the transport corps and paid not the slightest attention to the well-being of the masses. The problems facing the people of Tingchow city were that they had no firewood, no salt was on sale because the capitalists were hoarding it, some people had no houses to live in, and rice was both scarce and dear. These were practical problems for the masses of the people of Tingchow and they eagerly looked to us for help in solving them. But the Tingchow Municipal Government did not discuss any of these matters. That is why when the new workers' and peasants' representative council was elected in the city, a hundred or more representatives were unwilling to attend after the first few council meetings had discussed only the expansion of the Red Army and mobilization for the transport corps, entirely ignoring the well-being of the masses, so that the council was unable to go on meeting. The result was that very little was achieved in regard to the expansion of the Red Army and mobilization for the transport corps. That was one kind of situation.

Comrades! You have probably read the pamphlets given you about two model townships. There the situation is entirely different. What a great number of people have joined the Red Army from Changkang Township in Kiangsi[1] and Tsaihsi Township in Fukien![2] In Changkang 80 per cent of the young men and women have joined the Red Army, and in Tsaihsi the figure is 88 per cent. There has been a big sale of bonds, too, and 4,500 yuan worth have been sold in Changkang which has a population of 1,500. Much has also been done in other fields. What accounts for this? A few examples will make the point clear. In Changkang when fire broke out in a poor peasant's house destroying one and a half rooms, the township government appealed to the masses to contribute money to help him. In another instance, three persons were starving, so the township government and the mutual-aid society immediately gave them rice. During the food shortage last summer, the township government obtained rice from Kunglueh County,[3] more than two hundred *li* away, for the relief of the masses. Excellent work was done along these lines in Tsaihsi as well. Such township governments are really models. They are absolutely different from the Tingchow Municipal Government with its bureaucratic methods of leadership. We should learn from Changkang and Tsaihsi Townships and oppose bureaucratic leaders like those in Tingchow city.

I earnestly suggest to this congress that we pay close attention to the well-being of the masses, from the problems of land and labour to those of fuel, rice, cooking oil and salt. The women want to learn ploughing and harrowing. Whom can we get to teach them? The children want to go to school. Have we set up primary schools? The wooden bridge over there is too narrow and people may fall off. Should we not repair it? Many people suffer from boils and other ailments. What are we going to do about it? All such problems concerning the well-being of the masses should be placed on our agenda. We should discuss them, adopt and carry out decisions and check up on the results. We should convince the masses that we represent their interests, that our lives are intimately bound up with theirs. We should help them to proceed from these things to an understanding of the higher tasks which we have put forward, the tasks of the revolutionary war, so that they will support the revolution and spread it throughout the country, respond to our political appeals and fight to the end for victory in the revolution. The masses in Changkang say, "The Communist Party is really good! It has thought of everything on our behalf." The comrades in Changkang Township are an example to all of us. What admirable people! They have won the genuine affection of the broad masses, who support their call for war mobilization. Do we want to win the support of the masses? Do we want them to devote their strength to the front? If so, we must be with them, arouse their enthusiasm and initiative, be concerned with their well-being, work earnestly and sincerely in their interests and solve all their problems of production and everyday life — the problems of salt, rice, housing, clothing, childbirth, etc. If we do so, the masses will surely support us and regard the revolution as their most glorious banner, as their very life. In the event of a Kuomintang attack on the Red areas they will fight the Kuomintang to the death. There can be no doubt about this, for is it not a plain fact that we have smashed the enemy's first, second, third and fourth "encirclement and suppression" campaigns?

The Kuomintang is now pursuing a policy of blockhouse warfare,[4] feverishly constructing their "tortoise-shells" as though they were iron bastions. Comrades! Are they really iron bastions? Not in the least! Think of the palaces of the feudal emperors over thousands of years, were they not powerful with their walls and moats? Yet they crumbled one after another the moment the masses arose. The tsar of Russia was one of the world's most ferocious rulers, yet when the proletariat and the peasantry rose in revolution, was there anything left of him? No, nothing. His bastions of iron? They all crumbled. Comrades! What is a true bastion of iron? It is the masses, the millions upon millions of people who genuinely and sincerely support the revolution. That is the real iron bastion which no force can smash, no force whatsoever. The counter-revolution cannot smash us; on the contrary, we shall smash it. Rallying millions upon millions of people round the revolutionary government and expanding our revolutionary war, we shall wipe out all counter-revolution and take over the whole of China.

The second question concerns our methods of work.

We are the leaders and organizers of the revolutionary war as well as the leaders and organizers of the life of the masses. To organize the revolutionary war and to improve the life of the masses are our two major tasks. In this respect, we are faced with the serious problem of methods of work. It is not enough to set tasks, we must also solve the problem of the methods for carrying them out. If our task is to cross a river, we cannot cross it without a bridge or a boat. Unless the bridge or boat problem is solved, it is idle to speak of crossing the river. Unless the problem of method is solved, talk about the task is useless. Unless we pay attention to giving leadership to the work of expanding the Red Army and devote particular care to our methods, we will never succeed even though we recite the phrase "Expand the Red Army" a thousand times. Nor can we accomplish our tasks in any other field, for instance, in checking up on land distribution, or in economic construction, or culture and education, or our work in the new areas and the outlying districts, if all we do is to set the tasks without attending to the methods of carrying them out, without combating bureaucratic methods of work and adopting practical and concrete ones, and without discarding commandist methods and adopting the method of patient persuasion.

The comrades in Hsingkuo have done first-rate work and deserve our praise as model workers. Similarly, the comrades in northeastern Kiangsi have done good work and are also model workers. By linking the problem of the well-being of the masses with that of the revolutionary war, the comrades in both these places are simultaneously solving the problems of revolutionary methods of work and of accomplishing their revolutionary tasks. They are working conscientiously, solving problems with minute care and shouldering their revolutionary responsibilities in earnest; they are good organizers and leaders both of revolutionary war and of the well-being of the masses. Elsewhere, too, the comrades have made progress in their work and deserve our praise — as in some parts of the counties of Shanghang, Changting and Yungting in Fukien Province; in Hsikiang and other places in southern Kiangsi Province; in some parts of the counties of Chaling, Yunghsin and Kian in the Hunan-Kiangsi border area; in some parts of Yanghsin County in the Hunan-Hupeh-Kiangsi border area; in districts and townships of many other counties in Kiangsi Province and in the county of Juichin which is directly under our central government.

In all the places under our leadership, there are undoubtedly many active cadres, excellent comrades, who have sprung from the masses. These comrades have a responsibility to help in places where our work is weak and to help comrades who are not yet able to work well. We are in the midst of a great revolutionary war; we must break through the enemy's large-scale "encirclement and suppression" and spread the revolution to all parts of the country. All revolutionary cadres have a tremendous responsibility. After this congress we must adopt effective measures to improve our work, the advanced areas should become even more advanced, and the backward areas should catch up with the advanced. We must create thousands of townships like Changkang and scores of counties like Hsingkuo. They will be our strongholds. From these strongholds we shall go forth to smash the enemy's "encirclement and suppression" campaigns and overthrow the rule of imperialism and the Kuomintang throughout the country.

NOTES

[1] Changkang Township is in Hsingkuo County, Kiangsi Province.

[2] Tsaihsi Township is in Shanghang County, Fukien Province.

[3] Kunglueh County was then in the Red area in Kiangsi, with the town of Tungku lying southeast of Kian County as its centre. It was named after Comrade Huang Kung-lueh, Commander of the Third Army Corps of the Red Army, who laid down his life there in October 1931.

[4] The building of blockhouses round the Red areas was decided upon by Chiang Kai-shek at his military conference held at Lushan, Kiangsi Province in July 1933, as a new military tactic for his fifth "encirclement and suppression" campaign. By the end of January 1934 an estimated total of 2,900 blockhouses had been built in Kiangsi Province. The Japanese aggressors later adopted the same tactic against the Eighth Route and the New Fourth Armies. Experience fully proved that the counter-revolutionary tactic of using blockhouses could be completely foiled and defeated by adhering to Comrade Mao Tse-tung's strategy of people's war.

ON TACTICS AGAINST JAPANESE IMPERIALISM

December 27, 1935

THE CHARACTERISTICS OF THE PRESENT POLITICAL SITUATION

Comrades! A great change has now taken place in the political situation. Our Party has defined its tasks in the light of this changed situation.

What is the present situation?

Its main characteristic is that Japanese imperialism wants to turn China into a colony.

As we all know, for nearly a hundred years China has been a semi-colonial country jointly dominated by several imperialist powers. Owing to the Chinese people's struggle against imperialism and to conflicts among the imperialist powers, China has been able to retain a semi-independent status. For a time World War I gave Japanese imperialism the opportunity of dominating China exclusively. But the treaty surrendering China to Japan, the Twenty-one Demands[1] signed by Yuan Shih-kai,[2] the arch-traitor of that time, was inevitably rendered null and void as a result of the Chinese people's fight against Japanese imperialism and of the intervention by other imperialist powers. In 1922 at the Washington Nine-Power Conference called by the United States, a treaty[3] was signed which once again placed China

---

This report was given by Comrade Mao Tse-tung at the conference of Party activists which was held at Wayaopao, northern Shensi, after the Wayaopao meeting of the Political Bureau of the Central Committee in December 1935. This meeting, one of the most important ever called by the Central Committee of the Communist Party of China, criticized the mistaken view in the Party that the Chinese national bourgeoisie could not be an ally of the workers and peasants in the common fight against Japan, and it decided on the tactics of a national united front. On the basis of the Political Bureau's decisions, Comrade Mao Tse-tung explained in detail the possibility and the importance of re-establishing a united front with the national bourgeoisie on the condition that there must be resistance to Japan. He

under the joint domination of several imperialist powers. But before long the situation changed again. The Incident of September 18, 1931,[4] began the present stage of Japan's colonization of China. As Japanese aggression was temporarily limited to the four northeastern provinces,[5] some people felt that the Japanese imperialists would probably advance no farther. Today things are different. The Japanese imperialists have already shown their intention of penetrating south of the Great Wall and occupying all China. Now they want to convert the whole of China from a semi-colony shared by several imperialist powers into a colony monopolized by Japan. The recent Eastern Hopei Incident[6] and diplomatic talks[7] are clear indications of this trend of events which threatens the survival of the whole Chinese people. This faces all classes and political groups in China with the question of what to do. Resist? Surrender? Or vacillate between the two?

Now let us see how the different classes in China answer this question.

The workers and the peasants are all demanding resistance. The revolution of 1924-27, the agrarian revolution from 1927 to the present day, and the anti-Japanese tide since the Incident of September 18, 1931, have all proved that the working class and peasantry are the most resolute forces in the Chinese revolution.

The petty bourgeoisie is also demanding resistance. Have not the student youth and the urban petty bourgeoisie already started a broad anti-Japanese movement?[8] This section of the Chinese petty bourgeoisie took part in the revolution of 1924-27. Like the peasants, they are small producers in their economic status, and their interests are irreconcilable with those of imperialism. Imperialism and the Chinese counter-revolutionary forces have done them great harm, driving many into unemployment, bankruptcy or semi-bankruptcy. Now, faced with the immediate danger of becoming slaves to a foreign nation, they have no alternative but to resist.

---

stressed the decisive significance of the leading role to be played by the Communist Party and the Red Army in this united front. He pointed out the protracted character of the Chinese revolution, and criticized the narrow-minded closed-doorism and overhastiness with regard to the revolution which had long existed in the Party and which were the basic cause of the serious setbacks of the Party and the Red Army during the Second Revolutionary Civil War. At the same time, he called the Party's attention to the historical lesson of the defeat of the revolution in 1927 which had been caused by Chen Tu-hsiu's Right opportunism, and he showed that Chiang Kai-shek would inevitably try to undermine the forces of the revolution. Thus he enabled the Party to remain clear-headed in the new situation and to save the forces of the revolution from losses, in spite of Chiang Kai-shek's endless

But how do the national bourgeoisie, the comprador and landlord classes, and the Kuomintang face up to this question?

The big local tyrants and evil gentry, the big warlords and the big bureaucrats and compradors have long made up their minds. They maintain, as they have done all along, that revolution of whatever kind is worse than imperialism. They have formed a camp of traitors, for whom the question of whether to become slaves of a foreign nation simply does not exist because they have already lost all sense of nationality and their interests are inseparably linked with imperialism. Their chieftain is Chiang Kai-shek.[9] This camp of traitors are deadly enemies of the Chinese people. Japanese imperialism could not have become so blatant in its aggression were it not for this pack of traitors. They are the running dogs of imperialism.

The national bourgeoisie presents a complicated problem. This class took part in the revolution of 1924-27, but terrified by the flames of revolution, it later deserted to the enemy of the people, the Chiang Kai-shek clique. The question is whether there is any possibility that this class will undergo a change in the present circumstances. We think there is. For the national bourgeoisie is not the same as either the landlord or the comprador class; there is a difference between them. The national bourgeoisie is less feudal than the landlord class and not so comprador as the comprador class. The section having more ties with foreign capital and the Chinese landed interests form the right-wing of the national bourgeoisie; and we shall not, for the moment, consider whether it can change or not. The problem lies with those sections which have few or no such ties. We believe that in the new situation in which China is threatened with being reduced to a colony these sections may change their attitude. The change will be marked by vacillation. On the one hand they dislike imperialism, and on the other they fear thorough revolution, and they vacillate between the two. This explains why they took part in the revolution

intrigues and many armed attacks. In January 1935, at an enlarged meeting of the Political Bureau of the Central Committee which was convened in Tsunyi, Kweichow Province, a new Central Committee leadership headed by Comrade Mao Tse-tung had been established in place of the former "Left" opportunist leadership. However, as that meeting took place during the Red Army's Long March, it had to confine itself to decisions on the most urgent military problems and on the organization of the Secretariat and the Revolutionary Military Commission of the Central Committee. Only when the Red Army had reached northern Shensi after the Long March was it possible for the Central Committee of the Party to deal systematically with the various problems of tactics in the political sphere. A most comprehensive analysis of these problems is given in this report by Comrade Mao Tse-tung.

of 1924-27 and why, in the end, they went over to Chiang Kai-shek's side. In what respect does the present period differ from 1927 when Chiang Kai-shek betrayed the revolution? China was then still a semi-colony, but now she is on the way to becoming a colony. Over the past nine years the national bourgeoisie has deserted its ally, the working class, and made friends with the landlord and comprador classes, but has it gained anything? Nothing, except the bankruptcy or semi-bankruptcy of its industrial and commercial enterprises. Hence we believe that in the present situation the attitude of the national bourgeoisie can change. What will be the extent of the change? The general characteristic of the national bourgeoisie is to vacillate. But at a certain stage of the struggle, one section (the left-wing) may join in, while another section may vacillate towards neutrality.

Whose class interests does the 19th Route Army led by Tsai Ting-kai[10] and others represent? Those of the national bourgeoisie, the upper petty bourgeoisie, and the rich peasants and small landlords in the countryside. Did not Tsai Ting-kai and his associates once fight bitterly against the Red Army? Yes, but they subsequently concluded an anti-Japanese and anti-Chiang alliance with the Red Army. In Kiangsi they had attacked the Red Army, but later in Shanghai they fought the Japanese imperialists; later still, in Fukien they came to terms with the Red Army and turned their guns against Chiang Kai-shek. Whatever course Tsai Ting-kai and his associates may take in the future, and despite their Fukien People's Government's adherence to old practice in failing to arouse the people to struggle, it must be considered beneficial to the revolution that they turned their guns, originally trained on the Red Army, against Japanese imperialism and Chiang Kai-shek. It marked a split within the Kuomintang camp. If the circumstances following the September 18th Incident could cause this group to split away, why cannot the present circumstances give rise to other splits in the Kuomintang? Those Party members who hold that the whole landlord and bourgeois camp is united and permanent and will not change under any circumstances are wrong. They not only fail to appreciate the present grave situation, they have even forgotten history.

Let me speak a little more about the past. In 1926 and 1927, during the time when the revolutionary army advanced on Wuhan, captured it and marched into Honan, Tang Sheng-chih and Feng Yu-hsiang[11] took part in the revolution. In 1933, Feng Yu-hsiang co-operated for a time with the Communist Party in forming the Anti-Japanese Allied Army in Chahar Province.

Take another striking example. Did not the 26th Route Army, which, together with the 19th Route Army, had attacked the Red Army in Kiangsi, stage the Ningtu Uprising[12] in December 1931 and become part of the Red Army? The leaders of the Ningtu Uprising, Chao Po-sheng, Tung Chen-tang and others, have become steadfast comrades in the revolution.

The anti-Japanese operations of Ma Chan-shan[13] in the three northeastern provinces represented another split in the ruling class camp.

All these instances indicate that splits will occur in the enemy camp when all China comes within the range of Japanese bombs, and when the struggle changes its normal pace and suddenly surges forward.

Now, comrades, let us turn to another aspect of the question.

Is it correct to object to our view on the ground that China's national bourgeoisie is politically and economically flabby, and to argue that it cannot possibly change its attitude in spite of the new circumstances? I think not. If weakness is the reason for its inability to change its attitude, why did the national bourgeoisie behave differently in 1924-27 when it did not merely vacillate towards the revolution but actually joined it? Can one say that the weakness of the national bourgeoisie is a new disease, and not one that accompanies it from the very womb? Can one say that the national bourgeoisie is weak today, but was not weak in 1924-27? One of the chief political and economic characteristics of a semi-colonial country is the weakness of its national bourgeoisie. That is exactly why the imperialists dare to bully them, and it follows that one of their characteristics is dislike of imperialism. Of course, so far from denying it, we fully recognize that it is the very weakness of the national bourgeoisie that may make it easy for the imperialists, landlords and compradors to entice them with the bait of some temporary advantage; hence their lack of revolutionary thoroughness. Nevertheless, it cannot be said that in the present circumstances there is no difference between the national bourgeoisie and the landlord and comprador classes.

Therefore, we emphatically assert that when the national crisis reaches a crucial point, splits will occur in the Kuomintang camp. Such splits have revealed themselves in the vacillation of the national bourgeoisie and the emergence of such anti-Japanese figures as Feng

Yu-hsiang, Tsai Ting-kai and Ma Chan-shan, who have become popular
for a time. Basically, these splits are unfavourable to the counter-
revolution and favourable to the revolution. Their possibility is
increased by China's uneven political and economic development, and
the consequent uneven development of the revolution.

Comrades, so much for the positive side of the question. Now let
me take up the negative side, namely, the fact that certain elements
among the national bourgeoisie are often past masters at deceiving
the people. Why? Because apart from the genuine supporters of the
people's revolutionary cause, this class includes many who temporarily
appear as revolutionaries or semi-revolutionaries, and who thus acquire
a deceptive status which makes it difficult for the people to see through
their lack of revolutionary thoroughness and their false trappings.
This increases the responsibility devolving on the Communist Party
to criticize its allies, unmask the fake revolutionaries, and gain the
leadership. To deny the possibility that the national bourgeoisie may
vacillate and join the revolution during great upheavals amounts to
abandoning, or at any rate to minimizing, our Party's task of contending for leadership. For if the national bourgeoisie were exactly
the same as the landlords and compradors and had the same vile and
traitorous visage, there would be little or no problem of contending
with it for leadership.

In making a general analysis of the attitude of the Chinese landlord
class and the bourgeoisie in times of great upheaval, we should also
point to another aspect, namely, that even the landlord and comprador
camp is not completely united. The reason is that China is a semi-
colonial country for which many imperialist powers are contending.
When the struggle is directed against Japanese imperialism, then the
running dogs of the United States or Britain, obeying the varying
tones of their masters' commands, may engage in veiled or even open
strife with the Japanese imperialists and their running dogs. There
have been many instances of such dog-fights and we shall not dwell
on them. We will only mention the fact that Hu Han-min,[14] a Kuomintang politician once detained by Chiang Kai-shek, has recently
added his signature to the Six-Point Programme for Resisting Japan
and Saving the Nation[15] which we have advanced. The warlords
of the Kwangtung and Kwangsi cliques[16] who back Hu Han-min
are also opposing Chiang Kai-shek, under the deceitful slogans of
"Recover our lost territory", and "Resist Japan and at the same time
suppress the bandits"[17] (as against Chiang Kai-shek's slogan of "First

suppress the bandits, then resist Japan"). Is this not rather strange? No, it is not strange at all, but merely a particularly interesting example of a fight between large and small dogs, between well-fed and ill-fed dogs. It is not a big rift, but neither is it small; it is at once an irritating and painful contradiction. But such fights, such rifts, such contradictions are of use to the revolutionary people. We must turn to good account all such fights, rifts and contradictions in the enemy camp and turn them against our present main enemy.

Summing up the question of class relations, we may say that the basic change in the situation, namely, the Japanese invasion of China south of the Great Wall, has changed the relationship among the various classes in China, strengthening the camp of national revolution and weakening that of counter-revolution.

Now let us discuss the situation in the camp of China's national revolution.

First, the Red Army. As you know, comrades, for almost a year and a half the three main contingents of the Chinese Red Army have carried out great shifts of position. The Sixth Army Group led by Jen Pi-shih[18] and other comrades began to shift to Comrade Ho Lung's area[19] in August last year, and in October we ourselves started to shift position.[20] In March this year the Red Army in the Szechuan-Shensi border area[21] began its shift. All three Red Army contingents have abandoned their old positions and moved to new regions. These great shifts have turned the old areas into guerrilla zones. The Red Army has been considerably weakened in the process. From this aspect of the over-all situation, we can see that the enemy has won a temporary and partial victory, while we have suffered a temporary and partial defeat. Is this statement correct? I think it is. For it is a statement of fact. However, some people (Chang Kuo-tao[22] for instance) say that the Central Red Army[23] has failed. Is that correct? No. For it is not a statement of fact. In approaching a problem a Marxist should see the whole as well as the parts. A frog in a well says, "The sky is no bigger than the mouth of the well." That is untrue, for the sky is not just the size of the mouth of the well. If it said, "A part of the sky is the size of the mouth of a well", that would be true, for it tallies with the facts. What we say is that in one respect the Red Army has failed (*i.e.*, failed to maintain its original positions), but in another respect it has won a victory (*i.e.*, in executing the plan of the Long March). In one respect the enemy won a victory (*i.e.*, in occupying our original positions), but in another respect he has failed (*i.e.*, failed to execute his plan of "encirclement and suppression" and of "pursuit and suppression"). That is the only appropriate formulation, for we have completed the Long March.

Speaking of the Long March, one may ask, "What is its significance?" We answer that the Long March is the first of its kind in the annals of history, that it is a manifesto, a propaganda force, a seeding-machine. Since Pan Ku divided the heavens from the earth and the Three Sovereigns and Five Emperors[24] reigned, has history ever witnessed a long march such as ours? For twelve months we were under daily reconnaissance and bombing from the skies by scores of planes, while on land we were encircled and pursued, obstructed and intercepted by a huge force of several hundred thousand men, and we encountered untold difficulties and dangers on the way; yet by using our two legs we swept across a distance of more than twenty thousand *li* through the length and breadth of eleven provinces. Let us ask, has history ever known a long march to equal ours? No, never. The Long March is a manifesto. It has proclaimed to the world that the Red Army is an army of heroes, while the imperialists and their running dogs, Chiang Kai-shek and his like, are impotent. It has proclaimed their utter failure to encircle, pursue, obstruct and intercept us. The Long March is also a propaganda force. It has announced to some 200 million people in eleven provinces that the road of the Red Army is their only road to liberation. Without the Long March, how could the broad masses have learned so quickly about the existence of the great truth which the Red Army embodies? The Long March is also a seeding-machine. In the eleven provinces it has sown many seeds which will sprout, leaf, blossom, and bear fruit, and will yield a harvest in the future. In a word, the Long March has ended with victory for us and defeat for the enemy. Who brought the Long March to victory? The Communist Party. Without the Communist Party, a long march of this kind would have been inconceivable. The Chinese Communist Party, its leadership, its cadres and its members fear no difficulties or hardships. Whoever questions our ability to lead the revolutionary war will fall into the morass of opportunism. A new situation arose as soon as the Long March was over. In the battle of Chihlochen the Central Red Army and the Northwestern Red Army, fighting in fraternal solidarity, shattered the traitor Chiang Kai-shek's campaign of "encirclement and suppression" against the Shensi-Kansu border area[25] and thus laid the cornerstone for the task undertaken by the Central Committee of the Party, the task of setting up the national headquarters of the revolution in northwestern China.

This being the situation with regard to the main body of the Red Army, what about the guerrilla warfare in the southern provinces? Our guerrilla forces there have suffered some setbacks but have not been wiped out. In many places, they are reasserting themselves, growing and expanding.[26]

In the Kuomintang areas, the workers' struggle is now moving beyond the factory walls, and from being an economic struggle is becoming a political struggle. A heroic working-class struggle against the Japanese and the traitors is now in intense ferment and, judging by the situation, it will erupt before long.

The peasants' struggle has never ceased. Harassed by aggression from abroad, by difficulties at home and by natural disasters, the peasants have unleashed widespread struggles in the form of guerrilla warfare, mass uprisings and famine riots. The anti-Japanese guerrilla warfare now going on in the northeastern provinces and eastern Hopei[27] is their reply to the attacks of Japanese imperialism.

The student movement has already grown considerably and will certainly go on doing so. But this movement can sustain itself and break through the martial law imposed by the traitors and the policy of disruption and massacre practised by the police, the secret service agents, the scoundrels in the educational world and the fascists only if it is co-ordinated with the struggles of the workers, peasants and soldiers.

We have already dealt with the vacillation of the national bourgeoisie, the rich peasants and small landlords and the possibility that they may actually participate in the anti-Japanese struggle.

The minority nationalities, and especially the people of Inner Mongolia who are directly menaced by Japanese imperialism, are now rising up in struggle. As time goes on, their struggle will merge with that of the people in northern China and with the operations of the Red Army in the Northwest.

All this indicates that the revolutionary situation is now changing from a localized into a nation-wide one and that it is gradually changing from a state of unevenness to a certain degree of evenness. We are on the eve of a great change. The task of the Party is to form a revolutionary national united front by combining the activities of the Red Army with all the activities of the workers, the peasants, the students, the petty bourgeoisie and the national bourgeoisie throughout the country.

THE NATIONAL UNITED FRONT

Having surveyed the situation with regard to both the counter-revolution and the revolution, we shall find it easy to define the Party's tactical tasks.

What is the basic tactical task of the Party? It is none other than to form a broad revolutionary national united front.

When the revolutionary situation changes, revolutionary tactics and methods of leadership must change accordingly. The task of the Japanese imperialists, the collaborators and the traitors is to turn China into a colony, while our task is to turn China into a free and independent country with full territorial integrity.

To win independence and freedom for China is a great task. It demands that we fight against foreign imperialism and the domestic counter-revolutionary forces. Japanese imperialism is determined to bludgeon its way deep into China. As yet the domestic counter-revolutionary forces of the big landlord and comprador classes are stronger than the people's revolutionary forces. The overthrow of Japanese imperialism and the counter-revolutionary forces in China cannot be accomplished in a day, and we must be prepared to devote a long time to it; it cannot be accomplished by small forces, and we must therefore accumulate great forces. In China, as in the world as a whole, the counter-revolutionary forces are weaker than before and the revolutionary forces stronger. This estimate is correct, representing one aspect of the matter. At the same time, it must be pointed out that the counter-revolutionary forces in China and in the world as a whole are stronger than the revolutionary forces for the time being. This estimate is also correct, representing another aspect of the matter. The uneven political and economic development of China gives rise to the uneven development of her revolution. As a rule, revolution starts, grows and triumphs first in those places in which the counter-revolutionary forces are comparatively weak, while it has yet to start or grows very slowly in those places in which they are strong. Such has long been the situation for the Chinese revolution. It can be predicted that the general revolutionary situation will grow further at certain stages in the future but that the unevenness will remain. The transformation of this unevenness into a general evenness will require a very long time, very great efforts, and the Party's application of a correct line. Seeing that the revolutionary war led by the Communist Party of the Soviet Union[28] took three years to conclude, we must be prepared to devote to the already protracted revolutionary war led by the Chinese Communist Party the longer time necessary to dispose of the domestic and foreign counter-revolutionary forces finally and thoroughly. The kind of impatience that was formerly displayed will never do. Moreover, sound revolutionary tactics must be worked out; we will never achieve great things if we keep on milling around within narrow confines. This does not mean that in China things have to be done slowly; no, they must be done boldly, because the danger of national subjugation does not allow us to slacken for a moment. From now on the revolution will certainly develop much faster than before, for both China and the world are approaching a new period of war and revolution. For all that, China's revolutionary war will remain a protracted one; this follows from the strength of imperialism and the uneven development of the revolution. We say that the present situation is one in which a new high tide in the national revolution is imminent and in which China is on the eve of a great new nation-wide revolution; this is one characteristic of the present revolutionary situation. This is a fact, and it represents one aspect of the matter. But we must also say that imperialism is still a force to be earnestly reckoned with, that the unevenness in the development of the revolutionary forces is a serious weakness, and that to defeat our enemies we must be prepared to fight a protracted war; this is another characteristic of the present revolutionary situation. This, too, is a fact, and represents another aspect of the matter. Both characteristics, both facts, teach and urge us to revise our tactics and change our ways of disposing our forces and carrying on the struggle to suit the situation. The present situation demands that we boldly discard all closed-doorism, form a broad united front and guard against adventurism. We must not plunge into decisive battles until the time is ripe and unless we have the necessary strength.

Here I shall not discuss the relation of adventurism to closed-doorism, or the possible dangers of adventurism as events unfold on a larger scale; that can be left for later. For the moment I shall confine myself to explaining that united front tactics and closed-door tactics are diametrically opposed.

The former requires the recruiting of large forces for the purpose of surrounding and annihilating the enemy.

The latter means fighting single-handed in desperate combat against a formidable enemy.

The advocates of united front tactics say, if we are to make a proper estimate of the possibility of forming a broad revolutionary national united front, a proper estimate must be made of the changes that may occur in the alignment of revolutionary and counter-revolutionary forces in China resulting from the attempt of Japanese imperialism to turn China into a colony. Without a proper estimate of the strong and weak points of the Japanese and Chinese counter-revolutionary forces and of the Chinese revolutionary forces, we shall be unable fully to understand the necessity of organizing a broad revolutionary national united front, or to take firm measures to break down closed-doorism, or to use the united front as a means of organizing and rallying millions of people and all the armies that are potentially friendly to the revolution for the purpose of advancing to strike at our main target, namely, Japanese imperialism and its running dogs, the Chinese traitors, or to use this tactical weapon of ours to strike at the main target before us, but instead we shall aim at a variety of targets so that our bullets will hit not the principal enemy but our lesser enemies or even our allies. This would mean failure to single out the principal enemy and waste of ammunition. It would mean inability to close in and isolate him. It would mean inability to draw to our side all those in the enemy camp and on the enemy front who have joined them under compulsion, and those who were our enemies yesterday but may become our friends today. It would in fact mean helping the enemy, holding back, isolating and constricting the revolution, and bringing it to a low ebb and even to defeat.

The advocates of closed-door tactics say the above arguments are all wrong. The forces of the revolution must be pure, absolutely pure, and the road of the revolution must be straight, absolutely straight. Nothing is correct except what is literally recorded in Holy Writ. The national bourgeoisie is entirely and eternally counter-revolutionary. Not an inch must be conceded to the rich peasants. The yellow trade unions must be fought tooth and nail. If we shake hands with Tsai Ting-kai, we must call him a counter-revolutionary at the same moment. Was there ever a cat that did not love fish or a warlord who was not a counter-revolutionary? Intellectuals are three-day revolutionaries whom it is dangerous to recruit. It follows therefore that closed-doorism is the sole wonder-working magic, while the united front is an opportunist tactic.

Comrades, which is right, the united front or closed-doorism? Which indeed is approved by Marxism-Leninism? I answer without the slightest hesitation — the united front and not closed-doorism. Three-year-olds have many ideas which are right, but they cannot be entrusted with serious national or world affairs because they do not understand them yet. Marxism-Leninism is opposed to the "infantile disorder" found in the revolutionary ranks. This infantile disorder is just what the confirmed exponents of closed-doorism advocate. Like every other activity in the world, revolution always follows a tortuous road and never a straight one. The alignment of forces in the revolutionary and counter-revolutionary camps can change, just as everything else in the world changes. The Party's new tactics of a broad united front start from the two fundamental facts that Japanese imperialism is bent on reducing all China to a colony and that China's revolutionary forces still have serious weaknesses. In order to attack the forces of the counter-revolution, what the revolutionary forces need today is to organize millions upon millions of the masses and move a mighty revolutionary army into action. The plain truth is that only a force of such magnitude can crush the Japanese imperialists and the traitors and collaborators. Therefore, united front tactics are the only Marxist-Leninist tactics. The tactics of closed-doorism are, on the contrary, the tactics of the regal isolationist. Closed-doorism just "drives the fish into deep waters and the sparrows into the thickets", and it will drive the millions upon millions of the masses, this mighty army, over to the enemy's side, which will certainly win his acclaim. In practice, closed-doorism is the faithful servant of the Japanese imperialists and the traitors and collaborators. Its adherents' talk of the "pure" and the "straight" will be condemned by Marxist-Leninists and commended by the Japanese imperialists. We definitely want no closed-doorism; what we want is the revolutionary national united front, which will spell death to the Japanese imperialists and the traitors and collaborators.

THE PEOPLE'S REPUBLIC[29]

If our government has hitherto been based on the alliance of the workers, the peasants and the urban petty bourgeoisie, from now on it must be so transformed as to include also the members of all other classes who are willing to take part in the national revolution.

At the present time, the basic task of such a government should be to oppose the annexation of China by Japanese imperialism. It will have a broader representation so that it may include those who are interested only in the national revolution and not in the agrarian revolution, and even, if they so desire, those who may oppose Japanese imperialism and its running dogs, though they are not opposed to the European and U.S. imperialists because of their close ties with the latter. Therefore, as a matter of principle, the programme of such a government should be in keeping with the basic task of fighting Japanese imperialism and its lackeys, and we should modify our past policies accordingly.

The special feature on the revolutionary side at present is the existence of a well-steeled Communist Party and Red Army. This is of crucial importance. Great difficulties would arise if they did not exist. Why? Because the traitors and collaborators in China are numerous and powerful and are sure to devise every possible means to wreck the united front; they will sow dissension by means of intimidation and bribery and by manoeuvring among various groupings, and will employ their armies to oppress and crush, one by one, all those weaker than themselves who want to part company with them and join us in fighting Japan. All this would hardly be avoidable if the anti-Japanese government and army were to lack this vital factor, i.e., the Communist Party and the Red Army. The revolution failed in 1927 chiefly because, with the opportunist line then prevailing in the Communist Party, no effort was made to expand our own ranks (the workers' and peasants' movement and the armed forces led by the Communist Party), and exclusive reliance was placed on a temporary ally, the Kuomintang. The result was that when imperialism ordered its lackeys, the landlord and comprador classes, to spread their numerous tentacles and draw over first Chiang Kai-shek and then Wang Ching-wei, the revolution suffered defeat. In those days the revolutionary united front had no mainstay, no strong revolutionary armed forces, and so when the defections came thick and fast, the Communist Party was forced to fight single-handed and was powerless to foil the tactics of crushing their opponents one by one which were adopted by the imperialists and the Chinese counter-revolutionaries. True, we had the troops under Ho Lung and Yeh Ting, but they were not yet politically consolidated, and the Party was not very skilled in leading them, so that they were finally defeated. The lesson we paid for with our blood was that the lack of a hard core of revolutionary forces brings the revolution to defeat. Today things are quite different. Now we have a strong Communist Party and a strong Red Army, and we also have the base areas of the Red Army. Not only are the Communist Party and the Red Army serving as the initiator of a national united front against Japan today, but in the future too they will inevitably become the powerful mainstay of China's anti-Japanese government and army, capable of preventing the Japanese imperialists and Chiang Kai-shek from carrying through their policy of disrupting this united front. However, we must be very vigilant because the Japanese imperialists and Chiang Kai-shek will undoubtedly resort to every possible form of intimidation and bribery and of manoeuvring among the various groupings.

Naturally we cannot expect every section of the broad national united front against Japan to be as firm as the Communist Party and the Red Army. In the course of their activities some bad elements may withdraw from the united front under the influence of the enemy. However, we need not fear the loss of such people. While bad elements may drop out under the enemy's influence, good people will come in under ours. The national united front will live and grow as long as the Communist Party and the Red Army live and grow. Such is the leading role of the Communist Party and the Red Army in the national united front. The Communists are no longer political infants and are able to take care of themselves and to handle relations with their allies. If the Japanese imperialists and Chiang Kai-shek can manoeuvre in relation to the revolutionary forces, the Communist Party can do the same in relation to the counter-revolutionary forces. If they can draw bad elements in our ranks over to their side, we can equally well draw their "bad elements" (good ones from our point of view) over to our side. If we can draw a larger number over to our side, this will deplete the enemy's ranks and strengthen ours. In short, two basic forces are now locked in struggle, and in the nature of things all the forces in between will have to line up on one side or the other. The Japanese imperialists' policy of subjugating China and Chiang Kai-shek's policy of betraying China will inevitably drive many people over to our side — either directly into joining the ranks of the Communist Party and the Red Army or into forming a united front with us. This will come about unless we pursue closed-door tactics.

Why change the "workers' and peasants' republic" into a "people's republic"?

Our government represents not only the workers and peasants but the whole nation. This has been implicit in our slogan of a workers' and peasants' democratic republic, because the workers and peasants constitute 80 to 90 per cent of the population. The Ten-Point Programme[30] adopted by the Sixth National Congress of our Party embodies the interests of the whole nation and not of the workers and peasants alone. But the present situation requires us to change our slogan, to change it into one of a people's republic. The reason is that Japanese invasion has altered class relations in China, and it is now possible not only for the petty bourgeoisie but even for the national bourgeoisie to join the anti-Japanese struggle.

The people's republic will definitely not represent the interests of the enemy classes. On the contrary, it will stand in direct opposition to the landlord and comprador classes, the lackeys of imperialism, and will not count them among the people. In the same way, Chiang Kai-shek's "National Government of the Republic of China" represents only the wealthiest, but not the common people whom it does not count as part of the nation. As 80 to 90 per cent of China's population is made up of workers and peasants, the people's republic ought to represent their interests first and foremost. However, by throwing off imperialist oppression to make China free and independent and by throwing off landlord oppression to free China from semi-feudalism, the people's republic will benefit not only the workers and peasants but other sections of the people too. The sum total of the interests of the workers, peasants and the rest of the people constitutes the interests of the whole Chinese nation. The comprador and the landlord classes also live on Chinese soil, but as they have no regard for the national interests, their interests clash with those of the majority. This small minority are the only ones that we break with and are clashing with, and we therefore have the right to call ourselves the representatives of the whole nation.

There is, of course, a clash of interests between the working class and the national bourgeoisie. We shall not be able to extend the national revolution successfully unless the working class, the vanguard of the national revolution, is accorded political and economic rights and is enabled to direct its strength against imperialism and its running dogs, the traitors. However if the national bourgeoisie joins the anti-imperialist united front, the working class and the national bourgeoisie will have interests in common. In the period of the bourgeois-democratic revolution, the people's republic will not expropriate private property other than imperialist and feudal private property, and so far from confiscating the national bourgeoisie's industrial and commercial enterprises, it will encourage their development. We shall protect every national capitalist who does not support the imperialists or the Chinese traitors. In the stage of democratic revolution there are limits to the struggle between labour and capital. The labour laws of the people's republic will protect the interests of the workers, but will not prevent the national bourgeoisie from making profits or developing their industrial and commercial enterprises, because such development is bad for imperialism and good for the Chinese people. Thus it is clear that the people's republic will represent the interests of all strata opposed to imperialism and the feudal forces. The government of the people's republic will be based primarily on the workers and peasants, but will also include representatives of the other classes which are opposed to imperialism and the feudal forces.

But is it not dangerous to let the representatives of such classes join the government of the people's republic? No. The workers and peasants are the basic masses of the republic. In giving the urban petty bourgeoisie, the intellectuals and other sections of the population who support the anti-imperialist and anti-feudal programme the right to have a voice in the government of the people's republic and to work in it, the right to vote and stand for election, we must not allow the interests of the workers and peasants, the basic masses, to be violated. The essential part of our programme must be the protection of their interests. With their representatives comprising the majority in this government and with the Communist Party exercising leadership and working within it, there is a guarantee that the participation of other classes will present no danger. It is perfectly obvious that the Chinese revolution at the present stage is still a bourgeois-democratic and not a proletarian socialist revolution in nature. Only the counter-revolutionary Trotskyites[31] talk such nonsense as that China has already completed her bourgeois-democratic revolution and that any further revolution can only be socialist. The revolution of 1924-27 was a bourgeois-democratic revolution, which was not carried to completion but failed. The agrarian revolution which we have led since 1927 is also a bourgeois-democratic revolution, because it is directed not against capitalism, but against imperialism and feudalism. This will remain true of our revolution for quite a long time to come.

Basically, the workers, the peasants and the urban petty bourgeoisie are still the motive forces of the revolution, but now there may be the national bourgeoisie as well.

The change in the revolution will come later. In the future the democratic revolution will inevitably be transformed into a socialist revolution. As to when the transition will take place, that will depend on the presence of the necessary conditions, and it may take quite a long time. We should not hold forth about transition until all the necessary political and economic conditions are present and until it is advantageous and not detrimental to the overwhelming majority of the people throughout China. It is wrong to have any doubts on this matter and expect the transition to take place soon, as some of our comrades did when they maintained that the transition in the revolution would begin the moment the democratic revolution began to triumph in key provinces. They did so because they failed to understand what kind of country China is politically and economically and to realize that, compared with Russia, China will find it more difficult, and require much more time and effort, to complete her democratic revolution politically and economically.

INTERNATIONAL SUPPORT

Finally, a word is necessary about the relation between the Chinese and the world revolution.

Ever since the monster of imperialism came into being, the affairs of the world have become so closely interwoven that it is impossible to separate them. We Chinese have the spirit to fight the enemy to the last drop of our blood, the determination to recover our lost territory by our own efforts, and the ability to stand on our own feet in the family of nations. But this does not mean that we can dispense with international support; no, today international support is necessary for the revolutionary struggle of any nation or country. There is the old adage, "In the Spring and Autumn Era there were no righteous wars."[32] This is even truer of imperialism today, for it is only the oppressed nations and the oppressed classes that can wage just wars. All wars anywhere in the world in which the people rise up to fight their oppressors are just struggles. The February and October Revolutions in Russia were just wars. The revolutions of the people in various European countries after World War I were just struggles. In China, the Anti-Opium War,[33] the War of the Taiping Heavenly Kingdom,[34] the Yi Ho Tuan War,[35] the Revolutionary War of 1911,[36] the Northern Expedition of 1926-27, the Agrarian Revolutionary War from 1927 to the present, and the present resistance to Japan and punitive actions against traitors — these are all just wars. Now, in the mounting tide of nation-wide struggle against Japan and of world-wide struggle against fascism, just wars will spread all over China and the globe. All just wars support each other, while all unjust wars should be turned into just wars — this is the Leninist line.[37] Our war against Japan needs the support of the people of the whole world and, above all, the support of the people of the Soviet Union, which they will certainly give us because they and we are bound together in a common cause. In the past, the Chinese revolutionary forces were temporarily cut off from the world revolutionary forces by Chiang Kai-shek, and in this sense we were isolated. Now the situation has changed, and changed to our advantage. Henceforth it will continue to change to our advantage. We can no longer be isolated. This provides a necessary condition for China's victory in the war against Japan and for victory in the Chinese revolution.

NOTES

[1] The Twenty-one Demands on the Yuan Shih-kai government were presented by the Japanese imperialists on January 18, 1915. On May 7, they sent an ultimatum demanding a reply within forty-eight hours. The demands were divided into five parts. The first four contained the following: to transfer to Japan the rights Germany had seized in Shantung and to grant Japan additional rights in the province; to grant rights to the Japanese to lease or own land in southern Manchuria and eastern Mongolia and to establish residence, engage in industry and commerce, and have exclusive railway building and mining rights there; to reorganize the Han-Yeh-Ping Iron and Steel Company as a joint Sino-Japanese enterprise; and to undertake not to lease or cede any harbours or islands along China's coastline to any third power. The fifth part contained demands that Japan should control China's political, financial, military and police affairs and should build vital railway lines connecting the provinces of Hupeh, Kiangsi and Kwangtung. Yuan Shih-kai accepted all the demands except those in the fifth part, about which he pleaded for "further negotiations". Thanks to the unanimous opposition of the Chinese people, Japan failed to get her demands implemented.

[2] Yuan Shih-kai was the head of the Northern warlords in the last years of the Ching Dynasty. After the Ching Dynasty was overthrown by the Revolution of

1911, he usurped the presidency of the Republic and organized the first government of the Northern warlords, which represented the big landlord and big comprador classes. He did this by relying on counter-revolutionary armed force and on the support of the imperialists and by taking advantage of the conciliationist nature of the bourgeoisie then leading the revolution. In 1915 he wanted to make himself emperor and, to gain the support of the Japanese imperialists, accepted the Twenty-one Demands with which Japan aimed at obtaining exclusive control of all China. In December of the same year an uprising against his assumption of the throne took place in Yunnan Province and promptly won country-wide response and support. Yuan Shih-kai died in Peking in June 1916.

[3] The Nine-Power Conference in Washington was called by the U.S. government in November 1921; China, Britain, France, Italy, Belgium, the Netherlands, Portugal and Japan were invited. It was a struggle between the United States and Japan for hegemony in the Far East. On February 6, 1922, a nine-power treaty was concluded on the basis of the principle, advanced by the United States, of the "open door" or "equal opportunities for all nations in China". The aim of this treaty was to create a situation in which the imperialist powers had joint control of China, and it actually cleared the way for exclusive domination by the U.S. imperialists, the purpose being to frustrate Japan's plans for exclusive domination.

[4] On September 18, 1931, the Japanese "Kwantung Army" in northeastern China seized Shenyang. Under Chiang Kai-shek's order of "absolute non-resistance", the Chinese troops at Shenyang and elsewhere in the Northeast (the Northeastern Army) withdrew to the south of Shanhaikuan, and consequently the Japanese forces rapidly occupied the provinces of Liaoning, Kirin and Heilungkiang. This act of Japanese aggression has become known as the "September 18th Incident".

[5] The "four northeastern provinces" were then Liaoning, Kirin, Heilungkiang and Jehol, which correspond to the present Liaoning, Kirin and Heilungkiang Provinces, the northeastern part of Hopei Province north of the Great Wall and the eastern part of the Inner Mongolian Autonomous Region. After the September 18th Incident, the Japanese invaders occupied Liaoning, Kirin and Heilungkiang and later, in 1933, seized Jehol.

[6] At the instigation of the Japanese, a puppet regime called the "Eastern Hopei Anti-Communist Autonomous Administration" was established in twenty-two counties in eastern Hopei by the Kuomintang traitor Yin Ju-keng on November 25, 1935. This became known as the Eastern Hopei Incident.

[7] The diplomatic talks between the Chiang Kai-shek government and the Japanese government discussed the so-called "Three Principles of Hirota", *i.e.*, the "Three Principles for Dealing with China" put forward by Japanese Foreign Minister Hirota, namely, (1) suppression by China of all anti-Japanese movements; (2) establishment of economic co-operation between China, Japan and "Manchukuo"; and (3) joint defence by China and Japan against communism. On January 21, 1936, Hirota told the Diet that the Chinese government "has accepted the three principles proposed by the Empire".

[8] The year 1935 witnessed a new upsurge in the popular patriotic movement throughout the country. Students in Peking, under the leadership of the Communist Party of China, held a patriotic demonstration on December 9, putting forward such slogans as "Stop the civil war and unite to resist foreign aggression" and "Down with Japanese imperialism". This movement broke through the long reign of terror imposed by the Kuomintang government in league with the Japanese invaders and very quickly won the people's support throughout the country. It is

known as the "December 9th Movement". The outcome was that new changes manifested themselves in the relations among the various classes in the country, and the Anti-Japanese National United Front proposed by the Communist Party of China became the openly advocated policy of all patriotic people. The Chiang Kai-shek government with its traitorous policy became very isolated.

[9] At the time of this report Chiang Kai-shek, after selling out the Northeast to Japan, was selling out northern China while actively keeping up his fighting against the Red Army. Therefore the Chinese Communist Party had to do its best to expose him as a traitor, and naturally he was not included in the Anti-Japanese National United Front proposed by the Party. But already in this report Comrade Mao Tse-tung mentioned the possible disintegration of the camp of the Chinese landlord and comprador classes as a result of the contradictions among the imperialist powers. And Japan's attack on northern China did subsequently lead to serious clashes of interest between Japanese and Anglo-American imperialism. The Chinese Communist Party maintained that the Chiang Kai-shek clique, with its close ties with Anglo-American imperialist interests, might change its attitude to Japan at its masters' bidding, and therefore it adopted the policy of compelling Chiang Kai-shek to resist Japan. On its return to northern Shensi from Shansi, in May 1936 the Red Army appealed directly to the Nanking Kuomintang government for an end to the civil war and for united resistance to Japan. In August of the same year, the Central Committee of the Chinese Communist Party addressed a letter to the Kuomintang's Central Executive Committee, calling for the formation of a bi-partisan united front against Japan and negotiations between the representatives of both parties. But Chiang Kai-shek rejected these proposals. It was not until December 1936 when Chiang Kai-shek was detained in Sian by Kuomintang army officers who favoured alliance with the Communists against Japan that he was compelled to accept the Communist Party's demand for ending the civil war and resisting Japan.

[10] Tsai Ting-kai was deputy commander of the Kuomintang's 19th Route Army and commander of one of its corps, the two other leaders being Chen Ming-shu and Chiang Kuang-nai. This army, which had fought the Red Army in Kiangsi, was transferred to Shanghai after the September 18th Incident. The mounting anti-Japanese tide of the people in Shanghai and the whole country had a great impact on the 19th Route Army. When the Japanese marines attacked in Shanghai during the night of January 28, 1932, the Army and the people of Shanghai put up a joint resistance. However, the battle was lost through the treachery of Chiang Kai-shek and Wang Ching-wei. Later, on Chiang's orders, the 19th Route Army was transferred to Fukien to fight the Red Army again. But the leaders of the Army gradually came to realize the futility of such fighting. In November 1933, allying themselves with Kuomintang forces under Li Chi-shen and others, they publicly renounced Chiang Kai-shek, established the "People's Revolutionary Government of the Republic of China" in Fukien, and concluded an agreement with the Red Army to resist Japan and oppose Chiang Kai-shek. The 19th Route Army and Fukien People's Government collapsed under the attacks of Chiang's troops. From then on, Tsai Ting-kai and others gradually moved towards a position of co-operation with the Communist Party.

[11] Feng Yu-hsiang, together with the forces under his command in Suiyuan Province, announced his break with the Northern warlord clique and joined the revolution when the revolutionary Northern Expeditionary Army reached Wuhan in September 1926. Early in 1927, his troops moved in from Shensi to attack Honan Province in co-ordination with the Northern Expeditionary Army. Although Feng

participated in anti-Communist activities following the betrayal of the revolution by Chiang Kai-shek and Wang Ching-wei in 1927, there was always a clash of interests between him and the Chiang Kai-shek clique. After Japan invaded China on September 18, 1931 he favoured resistance and in May 1933 co-operated with the Communist Party in forming the people's Anti-Japanese Allied Army in Chang-chiakou. His efforts came to naught in August under the pressure of both Chiang Kai-shek's forces and the Japanese invaders. In his later years Feng continued to co-operate with the Communist Party.

[12] An uprising took place at Ningtu, Kiangsi in December 1931 within the Kuomintang's 26th Route Army, which was sent by Chiang Kai-shek to attack the Red Army in Kiangsi Province. Led by Comrades Chao Po-sheng and Tung Chen-tang, more than ten thousand officers and men rose up and joined the Red Army in response to the Communist call for resistance to Japan.

[13] Ma Chan-shan was an officer of the Kuomintang's Northeastern Army whose troops were stationed in Heilungkiang. He and his men fought the Japanese invaders who drove towards Heilungkiang via Liaoning after the September 18th Incident.

[14] Hu Han-min, a well-known Kuomintang politician, was an opponent of Dr. Sun Yat-sen's policy of co-operation with the Chinese Communist Party and was Chiang Kai-shek's accomplice in the counter-revolutionary coup d'état of April 12, 1927. Later he fell out with Chiang in a struggle for power and was held in detention by the latter. Set free after the September 18th Incident, he left Nanking for Canton where he instigated the warlords of Kwangtung and Kwangsi to oppose Chiang Kai-shek's Nanking government for a considerable period of time.

[15] The Six-Point Programme for Resisting Japan and Saving the Nation was the "Chinese People's Basic Programme for Fighting Japan" put forward by the Chinese Communist Party in 1934 and published over the signatures of Soong Ching Ling (Mme. Sun Yat-sen) and others. The programme consisted of the following points: (1) mobilize all sea, land and air forces to fight Japan; (2) mobilize the people throughout the country; (3) arm all the people; (4) confiscate the property of the Japanese imperialists in China and of the traitors to defray war expenditure; (5) establish an all-China committee for national armed defence, to be elected by the representatives of workers, peasants, soldiers, students and businessmen; and (6) form an alliance with all the forces opposed to the Japanese imperialists, and establish friendly relations with all countries observing benevolent neutrality.

[16] These warlords were Chen Chi-tang of Kwangtung and Li Tsung-jen and Pai Chung-hsi of Kwangsi.

[17] The Chiang Kai-shek gang of bandits described the revolutionary people as "bandits" and their armed attacks upon and massacre of the revolutionary people as "bandit suppression".

[18] Comrade Jen Pi-shih was a veteran member of the Chinese Communist Party and one of its first organizers. He was a member of the Party's Central Committee from its Fifth National Congress in 1927 onwards. He was elected to the Political Bureau at the Fourth Plenary Session of the Sixth Central Committee in 1931. In 1933 he served as secretary of the Provincial Party Committee of the Hunan-Kiangsi Border Area and concurrently as political commissar of the Sixth Army Group of the Red Army. When the Sixth and Second Army Groups joined forces and formed the Second Front Army, he was appointed its political commissar. He was Director of the General Political Department of the Eighth Route Army in the first years of the War of Resistance. In 1940 he began to serve in the Secretariat of the Party's

Central Committee. At the First Plenary Session of the Seventh Central Committee in 1945 he was again elected a member of the Political Bureau and of the Secretariat. Comrade Jen Pi-shih died in Peking on October 27, 1950.

[19] The Sixth Army Group of the Chinese Workers' and Peasants' Red Army, originally stationed in the Hunan-Kiangsi border area, broke through the enemy's siege and shifted its position in August 1934 on the orders of the Party's Central Committee. In October it joined forces with the Second Army Group led by Comrade Ho Lung in eastern Kweichow, and together they formed the Second Front Army of the Red Army and created the Hunan-Hupeh-Szechuan-Kweichow revolutionary base area.

[20] In October 1934 the First, Third and Fifth Army Groups of the Chinese Workers' and Peasants' Red Army (that is, the First Front Army of the Red Army, also known as the Central Red Army) set out from Changting and Ninghua in western Fukien and from Juichin, Yutu and other places in southern Kiangsi and started a major strategic movement. In traversing the eleven provinces of Fukien, Kiangsi, Kwangtung, Hunan, Kwangsi, Kweichow, Szechuan, Yunnan, Sikang, Kansu and Shensi, crossing perpetually snow-capped mountains and trackless grasslands, sustaining untold hardships and frustrating the enemy's repeated encirclements, pursuits, obstructions and interceptions, the Red Army covered 25,000 *li* (12,500 kilometres) on this march and finally arrived triumphantly at the revolutionary base area in northern Shensi in October 1935.

[21] The Red Army in the Szechuan-Shensi border area was the Fourth Front Army of the Chinese Workers' and Peasants' Red Army. In March 1935, it shifted from its base in the Szechuan-Shensi border area to the borders of Szechuan and Sikang Provinces. In June, it joined forces with the First Front Army in Maokung in western Szechuan and advanced northward by two routes, a right route and a left route. But on arriving in the Maoerhkai area near Sungpan in September, Chang Kuo-tao of the Fourth Front Army led the troops on the left route in a southward direction, in defiance of the Central Committee's orders, thus causing a disruption in the Red Army. The Second Front Army, which had broken through the enemy's siege and left the Hunan-Hupeh-Szechuan-Kweichow border area, arrived at Kantze, Sikang Province, in June 1936 via Hunan, Kweichow and Yunnan, and there it joined forces with the Fourth Front Army. Acting against Chang Kuo-tao's wishes, the comrades in the Fourth Front Army resumed the shift northward together with the Second Front Army. In October, the entire Second Front Army and a part of the Fourth Front Army arrived in northern Shensi and succeeded in joining forces with the First Front Army.

[22] Chang Kuo-tao was a renegade from the Chinese revolution. Speculating on the revolution, he joined the Chinese Communist Party in his youth. In the Party he made many mistakes and ended by committing grave crimes. Most notoriously, in 1935 he opposed the Red Army's northward march, advocating a defeatist and liquidationist withdrawal by the Red Army to the minority-nationality areas on the Szechuan-Sikang border, and he engaged in openly traitorous activities against the Party and the Central Committee, established his own bogus central committee, disrupted the unity of the Party and the Red Army, and caused heavy losses to its Fourth Front Army. Thanks to patient education by Comrade Mao Tse-tung and the Central Committee, the Fourth Front Army and its numerous cadres soon came back under the correct leadership of the Central Committee and played an honourable part in subsequent struggles. Chang Kuo-tao, however, proved incorrigible, escaped

by himself from the Shensi-Kansu-Ningsia Border Region in the spring of 1938 and joined the Kuomintang secret police.

[23] The Central Red Army, or the First Front Army, refers to the Red Army that was built up in the Kiangsi-Fukien area directly under the leadership of the Central Committee of the Chinese Communist Party.

[24] Pan Ku, according to Chinese mythology, was the creator of the world and the first ruler of mankind. The Three Sovereigns and Five Emperors were legendary rulers in ancient China.

[25] In July 1935, the Kuomintang troops started their third "encirclement and suppression" campaign against the Shensi-Kansu revolutionary base area. The 26th Army Corps of the Northern Shensi Red Army routed two enemy brigades in the eastern sector and drove the enemy to the east of the Yellow River. In September, the 25th Army Corps of the Red Army, which had been operating in the Hupeh-Honan-Anhwei base area, joined forces with the Northern Shensi Red Army after arriving in northern Shensi via southern Shensi and eastern Kansu, and together they formed the 15th Army Group of the Red Army. In the Kanchuan-Laoshan campaign, this army group wiped out most of the enemy 110th Division, killed its divisional commander and in a subsequent action destroyed four battalions of the enemy's 107th Division at Yulinchiao, Kanchuan County. The enemy organized new attacks and put Tung Ying-pin (an army corps commander of the Northeastern Army) in command of five divisions, which mounted an attack along two routes; the division on the east route drove northward by way of Lochuan and Fuhsien and the other four divisions on the west route drove along the Hulu River towards Fuhsien, northern Shensi, via Chingyang and Hoshui in Kansu. By October, the Central Red Army reached northern Shensi. In the following month the Central Red Army and the 15th Army Group jointly wiped out the enemy's 109th Division in Chihlochen, southwest of Fuhsien, and eliminated one regiment of the enemy's 106th Division at Heishuisze in the course of pursuit. Thus the enemy's third "encirclement and suppression" campaign against the Shensi-Kansu border area was completely smashed.

[26] When the main forces of the Red Army in southern China shifted position during 1934-35, they left behind some units to operate as guerrillas. These guerrilla units held out in the following fourteen base areas in eight provinces: southern Chekiang, northern Fukien, eastern Fukien, southern Fukien, western Fukien, northeastern Kiangsi, the Fukien-Kiangsi border, the Kwangtung-Kiangsi border, southern Hunan, the Hunan-Kiangsi border, the Hunan-Hupeh-Kiangsi border, the Hupeh-Honan-Anhwei border, the Tungpai Mountains in southern Honan and Hainan Island off the coast of Kwangtung.

[27] After the Japanese imperialists occupied the Northeast in 1931, the Chinese Communist Party called upon the people to put up armed resistance. It organized anti-Japanese guerrilla units, formed the Northeastern People's Revolutionary Army and rendered assistance to various volunteer forces fighting the enemy. In 1934, under the leadership of the Party, all these forces were reorganized into the single Northeast Anti-Japanese United Army, with the outstanding Communist Yang Ching-yu as Commander-in-Chief. This army kept up anti-Japanese guerrilla war in the Northeast for a long time. The anti-Japanese guerrilla war in eastern Hopei refers to the peasant uprising against Japan there in May 1935.

[28] The revolutionary war led by the Communist Party of the Soviet Union refers to the fighting from 1918 to 1920 in which the Soviet people beat off armed interven-

tion by Britain, the United States, France, Japan, Poland, etc., and suppressed the White Guard rebellion.

[29] The political power and the policies of a people's republic, as here enunciated by Comrade Mao Tse-tung, were made a reality in the people's Liberated Areas under the leadership of the Communist Party during the War of Resistance. That was why the Party was able to lead the people behind the enemy lines in waging a victorious war against the Japanese invaders. After Japan's surrender, the Third Revolutionary Civil War broke out. As the war went on, the area liberated by the people gradually extended to the whole of China, and in this way the unified People's Republic of China was born. Thus Comrade Mao Tse-tung's ideal of a people's republic was eventually realized throughout the country.

[30] The Sixth National Congress of the Communist Party of China held in July 1928 adopted the following Ten-Point Programme: (1) overthrow imperialist rule; (2) confiscate foreign capitalist enterprises and banks; (3) unify China and recognize the right of the nationalities to self-determination; (4) overthrow the Kuomintang warlord government; (5) establish a government of councils of workers, peasants and soldiers; (6) institute the eight-hour day, increase wages, and establish unemployment relief and social insurance; (7) confiscate the land of all landlords and distribute the land among the peasants; (8) improve the living conditions of the soldiers, give land and jobs to ex-soldiers; (9) abolish all exorbitant taxes and miscellaneous levies and adopt a consolidated progressive tax; and (10) unite with the world proletariat, unite with the Soviet Union.

[31] Originally an anti-Leninist faction in the Russian working-class movement, the Trotskyite group later degenerated into a downright counter-revolutionary gang. In his report to the plenary session of the Central Committee of the C.P.S.U. (B.) in 1937, Comrade Stalin explained the course this group of renegades had run as follows:

> In the past, seven or eight years ago, Trotskyism was one of such political trends in the working class, an anti-Leninist trend, it is true, and therefore profoundly mistaken, but nevertheless a political trend. . . . Present-day Trotskyism is not a political trend in the working class, but a gang without principle and without ideas, of wreckers and diversionists, intelligence service agents, spies, murderers, a gang of sworn enemies of the working class, working in the pay of the intelligence services of foreign states.

After the failure of the Chinese revolution in 1927, a small number of Trotskyites appeared in China, too. Ganging up with Chen Tu-hsiu and other renegades, they formed a small counter-revolutionary clique in 1929 and spread such counter-revolutionary propaganda as that the Kuomintang had already completed the bourgeois-democratic revolution, and they became a dirty imperialist and Kuomintang instrument against the people. The Chinese Trotskyites shamelessly joined the Kuomintang secret service. After the September 18th Incident, to fulfil the order given by the criminal renegade Trotsky "not to impede the occupation of China by imperial Japan", they began collaborating with Japanese secret agents, received subsidies from them and engaged in all kinds of activities facilitating Japanese aggression.

[32] This quotation is from *Mencius*. Mencius made this remark because in the period known as the Spring and Autumn Era (722-481 B.C.) the feudal princes of China incessantly fought one another for power.

[33] Faced with the opposition of the Chinese people to her traffic in opium, Britain sent forces in 1840-42 to invade Kwangtung and other coastal regions of China, under the pretext of protecting trade. Led by Lin Tse-hsu, the troops in

Kwangtung fought a war of resistance. A "Quell-the-British Corps" which was spontaneously organized by the people of Canton also dealt the British aggressors severe blows.

[34] The War of the Taiping Heavenly Kingdom was a peasant revolutionary war in the middle of the 19th century against the feudal rule and national oppression of the Ching Dynasty. In January 1851 Hung Hsiu-chuan, Yang Hsiu-ching and other leaders of this revolution staged an uprising in Chintien Village of Kueiping County in Kwangsi and proclaimed the founding of the Taiping Heavenly Kingdom. In 1852 the peasant army, proceeding northward from Kwangsi, marched through Hunan, Hupeh, Kiangsi and Anhwei and in 1853 captured Nanking, the main city on the lower Yangtse. A part of the forces then continued the drive north and pushed to the vicinity of Tientsin. However, the Taiping army failed to build stable base areas in the places it occupied, and also, after establishing its capital in Nanking, the leading group in the army committed many political and military errors; therefore it could not withstand the combined onslaught of the counter-revolutionary forces of the Ching government and of the British, U.S. and French aggressors, and it was finally defeated in 1864.

[35] The Yi Ho Tuan War was the vast spontaneous movement of the peasants and handicraftsmen in northern China in 1900. Forming themselves into mystical secret societies, these peasants and handicraftsmen carried on armed struggle against the imperialists. But the movement was put down with indescribable savagery, and Peking and Tientsin were occupied by the joint forces of eight imperialist powers.

[36] For the Revolution of 1911, see "Report on an Investigation of the Peasant Movement in Hunan", Note 3, p. 56 of this volume.

[37] See V. I. Lenin, "The War Programme of the Proletarian Revolution", *Collected Works*, Russ. ed., Moscow, 1950, Vol. XXIII. See also *History of the Communist Party of the Soviet Union (Bolsheviks), Short Course*, Chapter 6, Section 3.

PROBLEMS OF STRATEGY
IN CHINA'S REVOLUTIONARY WAR

December 1936

CHAPTER I

HOW TO STUDY WAR

1. THE LAWS OF WAR ARE DEVELOPMENTAL

The laws of war are a problem which anyone directing a war must study and solve.

The laws of revolutionary war are a problem which anyone directing a revolutionary war must study and solve.

The laws of China's revolutionary war are a problem which anyone directing China's revolutionary war must study and solve.

We are now engaged in a war; our war is a revolutionary war; and our revolutionary war is being waged in this semi-colonial and semi-feudal country of China. Therefore, we must study not only the laws of war in general, but the specific laws of revolutionary war, and the even more specific laws of revolutionary war in China.

It is well known that when you do anything, unless you understand its actual circumstances, its nature and its relations to other things, you will not know the laws governing it, or know how to do it, or be able to do it well.

Comrade Mao Tse-tung wrote this work to sum up the experience of the Second Revolutionary Civil War and used it for his lectures at the Red Army College in northern Shensi. Only five chapters were completed. The chapters on the strategic offensive, political work and other problems were left undone because he was too busy in consequence of the Sian Incident. This work, a result of a major inner-Party controversy on military questions during the Second Revolutionary Civil War, gives expression to one line in military affairs as against another. The enlarged meeting of the Political Bureau of the Central Committee held at Tsunyi in January 1935 settled

War is the highest form of struggle for resolving contradictions, when they have developed to a certain stage, between classes, nations, states, or political groups, and it has existed ever since the emergence of private property and of classes. Unless you understand the actual circumstances of war, its nature and its relations to other things, you will not know the laws of war, or know how to direct war, or be able to win victory.

Revolutionary war, whether a revolutionary class war or a revolutionary national war, has its own specific circumstances and nature, in addition to the circumstances and nature of war in general. Therefore, besides the general laws of war, it has specific laws of its own. Unless you understand its specific circumstances and nature, unless you understand its specific laws, you will not be able to direct a revolutionary war and wage it successfully.

China's revolutionary war, whether civil war or national war, is waged in the specific environment of China and so has its own specific circumstances and nature distinguishing it both from war in general and from revolutionary war in general. Therefore, besides the laws of war in general and of revolutionary war in general, it has specific laws of its own. Unless you understand them, you will not be able to win in China's revolutionary war.

Therefore, we must study the laws of war in general, we must also study the laws of revolutionary war, and, finally, we must study the laws of China's revolutionary war.

Some people hold a wrong view, which we refuted long ago. They say that it is enough merely to study the laws of war in general, or, to put it more concretely, that it is enough merely to follow the military manuals published by the reactionary Chinese government or the reactionary military academies in China. They do not see that these manuals give merely the laws of war in general and moreover are wholly copied from abroad, and that if we copy and apply them exactly without the slightest change in form or content, we shall be "cutting the feet to fit the shoes" and be defeated. Their argument is: why should knowledge which has been acquired at the cost of

the controversy about the military line, reaffirmed Comrade Mao Tse-tung's views and repudiated the erroneous line. In October 1935 the Central Committee moved to northern Shensi, and in December Comrade Mao Tse-tung made a report "On Tactics Against Japanese Imperialism" in which problems concerning the political line of the Party in the Second Revolutionary Civil War were systematically solved. He wrote this work a year later, in 1936, to explain the problems of strategy in China's revolutionary war in a systematic way.

blood be of no use? They fail to see that although we must cherish the earlier experience thus acquired, we must also cherish experience acquired at the cost of our own blood.

Others hold a second wrong view, which we also refuted long ago. They say that it is enough merely to study the experience of revolutionary war in Russia, or, to put it more concretely, that it is enough merely to follow the laws by which the civil war in the Soviet Union was directed and the military manuals published by Soviet military organizations. They do not see that these laws and manuals embody the specific characteristics of the civil war and the Red Army in the Soviet Union, and that if we copy and apply them without allowing any change, we shall also be "cutting the feet to fit the shoes" and be defeated. Their argument is: since our war, like the war in the Soviet Union, is a revolutionary war, and since the Soviet Union won victory, how then can there be any alternative but to follow the Soviet example? They fail to see that while we should set special store by the war experience of the Soviet Union, because it is the most recent experience of revolutionary war and was acquired under the guidance of Lenin and Stalin, we should likewise cherish the experience of China's revolutionary war, because there are many factors that are specific to the Chinese revolution and the Chinese Red Army.

Still others hold a third wrong view, which we likewise refuted long ago. They say that the most valuable experience is that of the Northern Expedition of 1926-27 and that we must learn from it, or, to put it more concretely, that we must imitate the Northern Expedition in driving straight ahead to seize the big cities. They fail to see that while the experience of the Northern Expedition should be studied, it should not be copied and applied mechanically, because the circumstances of our present war are different. We should take from the Northern Expedition only what still applies today, and work out something of our own in the light of present conditions.

Thus the different laws for directing different wars are determined by the different circumstances of those wars — differences in their time, place and nature. As regards the time factor, both war and its laws develop; each historical stage has its special characteristics, and hence the laws of war in each historical stage have their special characteristics and cannot be mechanically applied in another stage. As for the nature of war, since revolutionary war and counter-revolutionary war both have their special characteristics, the laws governing them also have their own characteristics, and those applying to one cannot be mechanically transferred to the other. As for the factor of place, since each country or nation, especially a large country or nation, has its own characteristics, the laws of war for each country or nation also have their own characteristics, and here, too, those applying to one cannot be mechanically transferred to the other. In studying the laws for directing wars that occur at different historical stages, that differ in nature and that are waged in different places and by different nations, we must fix our attention on the characteristics and development of each, and must oppose a mechanical approach to the problem of war.

Nor is this all. It signifies progress and development in a commander who is initially capable of commanding only a small formation, if he becomes capable of commanding a big one. There is also a difference between operating in one locality and in many. It likewise signifies progress and development in a commander who is initially capable of operating only in a locality he knows well, if he becomes capable of operating in many other localities. Owing to technical, tactical and strategic developments on the enemy side and on our own, the circumstances also differ from stage to stage within a given war. It signifies still more progress and development in a commander who is capable of exercising command in a war at its lower stages, if he becomes capable of exercising command in its higher stages. A commander who remains capable of commanding only a formation of a certain size, only in a certain locality and at a certain stage in the development of a war shows that he has made no progress and has not developed. There are some people who, contented with a single skill or a peep-hole view, never make any progress; they may play some role in the revolution at a given place and time, but not a significant one. We need directors of war who can play a significant role. All the laws for directing war develop as history develops and as war develops; nothing is changeless.

2. THE AIM OF WAR IS TO ELIMINATE WAR

War, this monster of mutual slaughter among men, will be finally eliminated by the progress of human society, and in the not too distant future too. But there is only one way to eliminate it and that is to oppose war with war, to oppose counter-revolutionary war with revolutionary war, to oppose national counter-revolutionary war with national revolutionary war, and to oppose counter-revolutionary class war with revolutionary class war. History knows only two kinds of war, just and unjust. We support just wars and oppose unjust wars. All counter-revolutionary wars are unjust, all revolutionary wars are just. Mankind's era of wars will be brought to an end by our own efforts, and beyond doubt the war we wage is part of the final battle. But also beyond doubt the war we face will be part of the biggest and most ruthless of all wars. The biggest and most ruthless of unjust counter-revolutionary wars is hanging over us, and the vast majority of mankind will be ravaged unless we raise the banner of a just war. The banner of mankind's just war is the banner of mankind's salvation. The banner of China's just war is the banner of China's salvation. A war waged by the great majority of mankind and of the Chinese people is beyond doubt a just war, a most lofty and glorious undertaking for the salvation of mankind and China, and a bridge to a new era in world history. When human society advances to the point where classes and states are eliminated, there will be no more wars, counter-revolutionary or revolutionary, unjust or just; that will be the era of perpetual peace for mankind. Our study of the laws of revolutionary war springs from the desire to eliminate all wars; herein lies the distinction between us Communists and all the exploiting classes.

3. STRATEGY IS THE STUDY OF THE LAWS OF A WAR SITUATION AS A WHOLE

Wherever there is war, there is a war situation as a whole. The war situation as a whole may cover the entire world, may cover an entire country, or may cover an independent guerrilla zone or an independent major operational front. Any war situation which acquires a comprehensive consideration of its various aspects and stages forms a war situation as a whole.

The task of the science of strategy is to study those laws for directing a war that govern a war situation as a whole. The task of the science of campaigns and the science of tactics[1] is to study those laws for directing a war that govern a partial situation.

Why is it necessary for the commander of a campaign or a tactical operation to understand the laws of strategy to some degree? Because an understanding of the whole facilitates the handling of the part, and because the part is subordinate to the whole. The view that strategic victory is determined by tactical successes alone is wrong because it overlooks the fact that victory or defeat in a war is first and foremost a question of whether the situation as a whole and its various stages are properly taken into account. If there are serious defects or mistakes in taking the situation as a whole and its various stages into account, the war is sure to be lost. "One careless move loses the whole game" refers to a move affecting the situation as a whole, a move decisive for the whole situation, and not to a move of a partial nature, a move which is not decisive for the whole situation. As in chess, so in war.

But the situation as a whole cannot be detached from its parts and become independent of them, for it is made up of all its parts. Sometimes certain parts may suffer destruction or defeat without seriously affecting the situation as a whole, because they are not decisive for it. Some defeats or failures in tactical operations or campaigns do not lead to deterioration in the war situation as a whole, because they are not of decisive significance. But the loss of most of the campaigns making up the war situation as a whole, or of one or two decisive campaigns, immediately changes the whole situation. Here, "most of the campaigns" or "one or two campaigns" are decisive. In the history of war, there are instances where defeat in a single battle nullified all the advantages of a series of victories, and there are also instances where victory in a single battle after many defeats opened up a new situation. In those instances the "series of victories" and the "many defeats" were partial in nature and not decisive for the situation as a whole, while "defeat in a single battle" or "victory in a single battle" played the decisive role. All this explains the importance of taking into account the situation as a whole. What is most important for the person in over-all command is to concentrate on attending to the war situation as a whole. The main point is that, according to the circumstances, he should concern himself with the problems of the grouping of his military units and formations, the relations between campaigns, the relations between various operational stages, and the relations between our activities as a whole and the enemy's activities as a whole — all these problems demand his greatest care and effort, and if he ignores them and immerses himself in secondary problems, he can hardly avoid setbacks.

The relationship between the whole and the part holds not only for the relationship between strategy and campaign but also for that between campaign and tactics. Examples are to be found in the relation between the operations of a division and those of its regiments and battalions, and in the relation between the operations of a company and those of its platoons and squads. The commanding officer at any level should centre his attention on the most important and decisive problem or action in the whole situation he is handling, and not on other problems or actions.

What is important or decisive should be determined not by general or abstract considerations, but according to the concrete circumstances. In a military operation the direction and point of assault should be selected according to the actual situation of the enemy, the terrain, and the strength of our own forces at the moment. One must see to it that the soldiers do not overeat when supplies are abundant, and take care that they do not go hungry when supplies are short. In the White areas the mere leakage of a piece of information may cause defeat in a subsequent engagement, but in the Red areas such leakage is often not a very serious matter. It is necessary for the high commanders to participate personally in certain battles but not in others. For a military school, the most important question is the selection of a director and instructors and the adoption of a training programme. For a mass meeting, the main thing is mobilizing the masses to attend and putting forward suitable slogans. And so on and so forth. In a word, the principle is to centre our attention on the important links that have a bearing on the situation as a whole.

The only way to study the laws governing a war situation as a whole is to do some hard thinking. For what pertains to the situation as a whole is not visible to the eye, and we can understand it only by hard thinking; there is no other way. But because the situation as a whole is made up of parts, people with experience of the parts, experience of campaigns and tactics, can understand matters of a higher order provided they are willing to think hard. The problems of strategy include the following:

Giving proper consideration to the relation between the enemy and ourselves.

Giving proper consideration to the relation between various campaigns or between various operational stages.

Giving proper consideration to those parts which have a bearing on (are decisive for) the situation as a whole.

Giving proper consideration to the special features contained in the general situation.

Giving proper consideration to the relation between the front and the rear.

Giving proper consideration to the distinction as well as the connection between losses and replacements, between fighting and resting, between concentration and dispersion, between attack and defence, between advance and retreat, between concealment and exposure, between the main attack and supplementary attacks, between assault and containing action, between centralized command and decentralized command, between protracted war and war of quick decision, between positional war and mobile war, between our own forces and friendly forces, between one military arm and another, between higher and lower levels, between cadres and the rank and file, between old and new soldiers, between senior and junior cadres, between old and new cadres, between Red areas and White areas, between old Red areas and new ones, between the central district and the borders of a given base area, between the warm season and the cold season, between victory and defeat, between large and small troop formations, between the regular army and the guerrilla forces, between destroying the enemy and winning over the masses, between expanding the Red Army and consolidating it, between military work and political work, between past and present tasks, between present and future tasks, between tasks arising from one set of circumstances and tasks arising from another, between fixed fronts and fluid fronts, between civil war and national war, between one historical stage and another, etc., etc.

None of these problems of strategy is visible to the eye, and yet, if we think hard, we can comprehend, grasp and master them all, that is, we can raise the important problems concerning a war or concerning military operations to the higher plane of principle and solve them. Our task in studying the problems of strategy is to attain this goal.

4. THE IMPORTANT THING IS TO BE GOOD AT LEARNING

Why have we organized the Red Army? For the purpose of defeating the enemy. Why do we study the laws of war? For the purpose of applying them in war.

To learn is no easy matter and to apply what one has learned is even harder. Many people appear impressive when discoursing on military science in classrooms or in books, but when it comes to actual fighting, some win battles and others lose them. Both the history of war and our own experience in war have proved this point.

Where then does the crux lie?

In real life, we cannot ask for "ever-victorious generals", who are few and far between in history. What we can ask for is generals who are brave and sagacious and who normally win their battles in the course of a war, generals who combine wisdom with courage. To become both wise and courageous one must acquire a method, a method to be employed in learning as well as in applying what has been learned.

What method? The method is to familiarize ourselves with all aspects of the enemy situation and our own, to discover the laws governing the actions of both sides and to make use of these laws in our own operations.

The military manuals issued in many countries point both to the necessity of a "flexible application of principles according to circumstances" and to the measures to be taken in case of defeat. They point to the former in order to warn a commander against subjectively committing mistakes through too rigid an application of principles, and to the latter in order to enable him to cope with the situation after he has committed subjective mistakes or after unexpected and irresistible changes have occurred in the objective circumstances.

Why are subjective mistakes made? Because the way the forces in a war or a battle are disposed or directed does not fit the conditions of the given time and place, because subjective direction does not correspond to, or is at variance with, the objective conditions, in other words, because the contradiction between the subjective and the objective has not been resolved. People can hardly avoid such situations whatever they are doing, but some people prove themselves more competent than others. As in any job we demand a comparatively high degree of competence, so in war we demand more victories or, conversely, fewer defeats. Here the crux is to bring the subjective and the objective into proper correspondence with each other.

Take an example in tactics. If the point chosen for attack is on one of the enemy's flanks and it is located precisely where his weak spot happens to be, and in consequence the assault succeeds, then the subjective corresponds with the objective, that is, the commander's reconnaissance, judgement and decision have corresponded with the enemy's actual situation and dispositions. If the point chosen for attack is on another flank or in the centre and the attack hits a snag and makes no headway, then such correspondence is lacking. If the attack is properly timed, if the reserves are used neither too late nor too early, and if all the other dispositions and operations in the battle are such as to favour us and not the enemy, then the subjective direction throughout the battle completely corresponds with the objective situation. Such complete correspondence is extremely rare in a war or a battle, in which the belligerents are groups of live human beings bearing arms and keeping their secrets from each other; this is quite unlike handling inanimate objects or routine matters. But if the direction given by the commander corresponds in the main with the actual situation, that is, if the decisive elements in the direction correspond with the actual situation, then there is a basis for victory.

A commander's correct dispositions stem from his correct decisions, his correct decisions stem from his correct judgements, and his correct judgements stem from a thorough and necessary reconnaissance and from pondering on and piecing together the data of various kinds gathered through reconnaissance. He applies all possible and necessary methods of reconnaissance, and ponders on the information gathered about the enemy's situation, discarding the dross and selecting the essential, eliminating the false and retaining the true, proceeding from the one to the other and from the outside to the inside; then, he takes the conditions on his own side into account, and makes a study of both sides and their interrelations, thereby forming his judgements, making up his mind and working out his plans. Such is the complete process of knowing a situation which a military man goes through before he formulates a strategic plan, a campaign plan or a battle plan. But instead of doing this, a careless military man bases his military plans on his own wishful thinking, and hence his plans are fanciful and do not correspond with reality. A rash military man relying solely upon enthusiasm is bound to be tricked by the enemy, or lured on by some superficial or partial aspect of the enemy's situation, or swayed by irresponsible suggestions from subordinates that are not based on real knowledge or deep insight, and so he runs his head against a brick wall, because he does not know or does not want to know that every military plan must be based on the necessary reconnaissance and on careful consideration of the enemy's situation, his own situation, and their interrelations.

The process of knowing a situation goes on not only before the formulation of a military plan but also after. In carrying out the plan from the moment it is put into effect to the end of the operation, there is another process of knowing the situation, namely, the process of practice. In the course of this process, it is necessary to examine anew whether the plan worked out in the preceding process corresponds with reality. If it does not correspond with reality, or if it does not fully do so, then in the light of our new knowledge, it becomes necessary to form new judgements, make new decisions and change the original plan so as to meet the new situation. The plan is partially changed in almost every operation, and sometimes it is even changed completely. A rash man who does not understand the need for such alterations or is unwilling to make them, but who acts blindly, will inevitably run his head against a brick wall.

The above applies to a strategic action, a campaign or a battle. Provided he is modest and willing to learn, an experienced military man will be able to familiarize himself with the character of his own forces (commanders, men, arms, supplies, etc., and their sum total), with the character of the enemy forces (likewise, commanders, men, arms, supplies, etc., and their sum total) and with all other conditions related to the war, such as politics, economics, geography and weather; such a military man will have a better grasp in directing a war or an operation and will be more likely to win victories. He will achieve this because, over a long period of time, he has come to know the situation on the enemy side and his own, discovered the laws of action, and resolved the contradictions between the subjective and the objective. This process of knowing is extremely important; without such a long period of experience, it would be difficult to understand and grasp the laws of an entire war. Neither a beginner nor a person who fights only on paper can become a really able high-ranking commander; only one who has learned through actual fighting in war can do so.

All military laws and military theories which are in the nature of principles are the experience of past wars summed up by people in former days or in our own times. We should seriously study these lessons, paid for in blood, which are a heritage of past wars. That is one point. But there is another. We should put these conclusions to the test of our own experience, assimilating what is useful, rejecting what is useless, and adding what is specifically our own. The latter is very important, for otherwise we cannot direct a war.

Reading is learning, but applying is also learning and the more important kind of learning at that. Our chief method is to learn warfare through warfare. A person who has had no opportunity to go to school can also learn warfare — he can learn through fighting in war. A revolutionary war is a mass undertaking; it is often not a matter of first learning and then doing, but of doing and then learning, for doing is itself learning. There is a gap between the ordinary civilian and the soldier, but it is no Great Wall, and it can be quickly closed, and the way to close it is to take part in revolution, in war. By saying that it is not easy to learn and to apply, we mean that it is hard to learn thoroughly and to apply skilfully. By saying that civilians can very quickly become soldiers, we mean that it is not difficult to cross the threshold. To put the two statements together, we may cite the Chinese adage, "Nothing in the world is difficult for one who sets his mind to it." To cross the threshold is not difficult, and mastery, too, is possible provided one sets one's mind to the task and is good at learning.

The laws of war, like the laws governing all other things, are reflections in our minds of objective realities; everything outside of the mind is objective reality. Consequently what has to be learned and known includes the state of affairs on the enemy side and that on our side, both of which should be regarded as the object of study, while the mind (the capacity to think) alone is the subject performing the study. Some people are good at knowing themselves and poor at knowing their enemy, and some are the other way round; neither can solve the problem of learning and applying the laws of war. There is a saying in the book of Sun Wu Tzu, the great military scientist of ancient China, "Know the enemy and know yourself, and you can fight a hundred battles with no danger of defeat",[2] which refers both to the stage of learning and to the stage of application, both to knowing the laws of the development of objective reality and to deciding on our own action in accordance with these laws in order to overcome the enemy facing us. We should not take this saying lightly.

War is the highest form of struggle between nations, states, classes, or political groups, and all the laws of war are applied by warring nations, states, classes, or political groups for the purpose of achieving victory for themselves. Unquestionably, victory or defeat in war is determined mainly by the military, political, economic and natural conditions on both sides. But not by these alone. It is also determined by each side's subjective ability in directing the war. In his endeavour to win a war, a military man cannot overstep the limitations imposed by the material conditions; within these limitations, however, he can and must strive for victory. The stage of action for a military man is built upon objective material conditions, but on that stage he can direct the performance of many a drama, full of sound and colour, power and grandeur. Therefore, given the objective material foundations, *i.e.*, the military, political, economic and natural conditions, our Red Army commanders must display their prowess and marshal all their forces to crush the national and class enemies and to transform this evil world. Here is where our subjective ability in directing war can and must be exercised. We do not permit any of our Red Army commanders to become a blundering hothead; we decidedly want every Red Army commander to become a hero who is both brave and sagacious, who possesses both all-conquering courage and the ability to remain master of the situation throughout the changes and vicissitudes of the entire war. Swimming in the ocean of war, he not only must not flounder but must make sure of reaching the opposite shore with measured strokes. The laws for directing war constitute the art of swimming in the ocean of war.

So much for our methods.

CHAPTER II

THE CHINESE COMMUNIST PARTY AND
CHINA'S REVOLUTIONARY WAR

China's revolutionary war, which began in 1924, has passed through two stages, the first from 1924 to 1927, and the second from 1927 to 1936; the stage of national revolutionary war against Japan will now commence. In all three of its stages this revolutionary war has been, is and will be fought under the leadership of the Chinese proletariat and its party, the Chinese Communist Party. The chief enemies in China's revolutionary war are imperialism and the feudal forces. Although the Chinese bourgeoisie may take part in the revolutionary war at certain historical junctures, yet its selfishness and lack of political and economic independence render it both unwilling and unable to lead China's revolutionary war on to the road of complete victory. The masses of China's peasantry and urban petty bourgeoisie wish to take an active part in the revolutionary war and to carry it to complete victory. They are the main forces in the revolutionary war, but, being small-scale producers, they are limited in their political outlook (and some of the unemployed masses have anarchist views), so that they are unable to give correct leadership in the war. Therefore, in an era when the proletariat has already appeared on the political stage, the responsibility for leading China's revolutionary war inevitably falls on the shoulders of the Chinese Communist Party. In this era, any revolutionary war will definitely end in defeat if it lacks, or runs counter to, the leadership of the proletariat and the Communist Party. Of all the social strata and political groupings in semi-colonial China, the proletariat and the Communist Party are the ones most free from narrow-mindedness and selfishness, are politically the most far-sighted, the best organized and the readiest to learn with an open mind from the experience of the vanguard class, the proletariat, and its political party throughout the world and to make use of this experience in their own cause. Hence only the proletariat and the Communist Party can lead the peasantry, the urban petty bourgeoisie and bourgeoisie, can overcome the narrow-mindedness of the peasantry and the petty bourgeoisie, the destructiveness of the unemployed masses, and also (provided the Communist Party does not err in its policy) the vacillation and lack of thoroughness of the bourgeoisie — and can lead the revolution and the war on to the road of victory.

The revolutionary war of 1924-27 was waged, basically speaking, in conditions in which the international proletariat and the Chinese proletariat and its party exerted political influence on the Chinese national bourgeoisie and its parties and entered into political co-operation with them. However, this revolutionary war failed at the critical juncture, first of all because the big bourgeoisie turned traitor, and at the same time because the opportunists within the revolutionary ranks voluntarily surrendered the leadership of the revolution.

The Agrarian Revolutionary War, lasting from 1927 to the present, has been waged under new conditions. The enemy in this war is not imperialism alone but also the alliance of the big bourgeoisie and the big landlords. And the national bourgeoisie has become a tail to the big bourgeoisie. This revolutionary war is led by the Communist Party alone, which has established absolute leadership over it. This absolute leadership is the most important condition enabling the revolutionary war to be carried through firmly to the end. Without it, it is inconceivable that the revolutionary war could have been carried on with such perseverance.

The Chinese Communist Party has led China's revolutionary war courageously and resolutely, and for fifteen long years[3] has demonstrated to the whole nation that it is the people's friend, fighting at all times in the forefront of the revolutionary war in defence of the people's interests and for their freedom and liberation.

By its arduous struggles and by the martyrdom of hundreds of thousands of its heroic members and tens of thousands of its heroic cadres, the Communist Party of China has played a great educative role among hundreds of millions of people throughout the country. The Party's great historic achievements in its revolutionary struggles have provided the prerequisite for the survival and salvation of China at this critical juncture when she is being invaded by a national enemy; and this prerequisite is the existence of a political leadership enjoying the confidence of the vast majority of the people and chosen by them after long years of testing. Today, the people accept what the Communist Party says more readily than what any other political party says. Were it not for the arduous struggles of the Chinese Communist Party in the last fifteen years, it would be impossible to save China in the face of the new menace of subjugation.

Besides the errors of the Right opportunism of Chen Tu-hsiu[4] and the "Left" opportunism of Li Li-san,[5] the Chinese Communist Party has committed two other errors in the course of the revolutionary war. The first error was the "Left" opportunism of 1931-34,[6] which resulted in serious losses in the Agrarian Revolutionary War so that, instead of our defeating the enemy's fifth campaign of "encirclement and suppression", we lost our base areas and the Red Army was weakened. This error was corrected at the enlarged meeting of the Political Bureau of the Central Committee at Tsunyi in January 1935. The second was the Right opportunism of Chang Kuo-tao in 1935-36[7] which grew to such an extent that it undermined the discipline of the Party and of the Red Army and caused serious losses to part of the Red Army's main forces. But this error was also finally rectified, thanks to the correct leadership of the Central Committee and the political consciousness of Party members, commanders and fighters in the Red Army. Of course all these errors were harmful to our Party, to our revolution and the war, but in the end we overcame them, and in doing so our Party and our Red Army have steeled themselves and become still stronger.

The Chinese Communist Party has led and continues to lead the stirring, magnificent and victorious revolutionary war. This war is not only the banner of China's liberation, but has international revolutionary significance as well. The eyes of the revolutionary people the world over are upon us. In the new stage, the stage of the anti-Japanese national revolutionary war, we shall lead the Chinese revolution to its completion and exert a profound influence on the revolution in the East and in the whole world. Our revolutionary war has proved that we need a correct Marxist military line as well as a correct Marxist political line. Fifteen years of revolution and war have hammered out such political and military lines. We believe that from now on, in the new stage of the war, these lines will be further developed, filled out and enriched in new circumstances, so that we can attain our aim of defeating the national enemy. History tells us that correct political and military lines do not emerge and develop spontaneously and tranquilly, but only in the course of struggle. These lines must combat "Left" opportunism on the one hand and Right opportunism on the other. Without combating and thoroughly overcoming these harmful tendencies which damage the revolution and the revolutionary war, it would be impossible to establish a correct line and win victory in this war. It is for this reason that I often refer to erroneous views in this pamphlet.

CHAPTER III

CHARACTERISTICS OF
CHINA'S REVOLUTIONARY WAR

1. THE IMPORTANCE OF THE SUBJECT

People who do not admit, do not know, or do not want to know that China's revolutionary war has its own characteristics have equated the war waged by the Red Army against the Kuomintang forces with war in general or with the civil war in the Soviet Union. The experience of the civil war in the Soviet Union directed by Lenin and Stalin has a world-wide significance. All Communist Parties, including the Chinese Communist Party, regard this experience and its theoretical summing-up by Lenin and Stalin as their guide. But this does not mean that we should apply it mechanically to our own conditions. In many of its aspects China's revolutionary war has characteristics distinguishing it from the civil war in the Soviet Union. Of course it is wrong to take no account of these characteristics or deny their existence. This point has been fully borne out in our ten years of war.

Our enemy has made similar mistakes. He did not recognize that fighting against the Red Army required a different strategy and different tactics from those used in fighting other forces. Relying on his superiority in various respects, he took us lightly and stuck to his old methods of warfare. This was the case both before and during his fourth "encirclement and suppression" campaign in 1933, with the result that he suffered a series of defeats. In the Kuomintang army a new approach to the problem was suggested first by the reactionary Kuomintang general Liu Wei-yuan and then by Tai Yueh. Their idea was eventually accepted by Chiang Kai-shek. That was how Chiang Kai-shek's Officers' Training Corps at Lushan[8] came into being and how the new reactionary military principles[9] applied in the fifth campaign of "encirclement and suppression" were evolved.

But when the enemy changed his military principles to suit operations against the Red Army, there appeared in our ranks a group of people who reverted to the "old ways". They urged a return to ways suited to the general run of things, refused to go into the specific circumstances of each case, rejected the experience gained in the Red Army's history of sanguinary battles, belittled the strength of imperialism and the Kuomintang as well as that of the Kuomintang army, and turned a blind eye to the new reactionary principles adopted by the enemy. As a result, all the revolutionary bases except the Shensi-Kansu border area were lost, the Red Army was reduced from 300,000 to a few tens of thousands, the membership of the Chinese Communist Party fell from 300,000 to a few tens of thousands, and the Party organizations in the Kuomintang areas were almost all destroyed. In short, we paid a severe penalty, which was historic in its significance. This group of people called themselves Marxist-Leninists, but actually they had not learned an iota of Marxism-Leninism. Lenin said that the most essential thing in Marxism, the living soul of Marxism, is the concrete analysis of concrete conditions.[10] That was precisely the point these comrades of ours forgot.

Hence one can see that, without an understanding of the characteristics of China's revolutionary war, it is impossible to direct it and lead it to victory.

2. WHAT ARE THE CHARACTERISTICS OF CHINA'S REVOLUTIONARY WAR?

What then are the characteristics of China's revolutionary war? I think there are four principal ones.

The first is that China is a vast, semi-colonial country which is unevenly developed politically and economically and which has gone through the revolution of 1924-27.

This characteristic indicates that it is possible for China's revolutionary war to develop and attain victory. We already pointed this out (at the First Party Congress of the Hunan-Kiangsi Border Area)[11] when in late 1927 and early 1928, soon after guerrilla warfare was started in China, some comrades in the Chingkang Mountains in the Hunan-Kiangsi border area raised the question, "How long can we keep the Red Flag flying?" For this was a most fundamental question. Without answering this question of whether China's revolutionary base areas and the Chinese Red Army could survive and develop, we could not have advanced a single step. The Sixth National Congress of the Chinese Communist Party in 1928 again gave the answer to the question. Since then the Chinese revolutionary movement has had a correct theoretical basis.

Let us now analyse this characteristic.

China's political and economic development is uneven — a weak capitalist economy coexists with a preponderant semi-feudal economy; a few modern industrial and commercial cities coexist with a vast stagnant countryside; several million industrial workers coexist with several hundred millions of peasants and handicraftsmen labouring under the old system; big warlords controlling the central government coexist with small warlords controlling the provinces; two kinds of reactionary armies, the so-called Central Army under Chiang Kai-shek and "miscellaneous troops" under the warlords in the provinces, exist side by side; a few railways, steamship lines and motor roads exist side by side with a vast number of wheelbarrow paths and foot-paths many of which are difficult to negotiate even on foot.

China is a semi-colonial country — disunity among the imperialist powers makes for disunity among the ruling groups in China. There is a difference between a semi-colonial country controlled by several countries and a colony controlled by a single country.

China is a vast country — "When it is dark in the east, it is light in the west; when things are dark in the south, there is still light in the north." Hence one need not worry about lack of room for manoeuvre.

China has gone through a great revolution — this has provided the seeds from which the Red Army has grown, provided the leader of the Red Army, namely, the Chinese Communist Party, and provided the masses with experience of participation in a revolution.

We say, therefore, that the first characteristic of China's revolutionary war is that it is waged in a vast semi-colonial country which is unevenly developed politically and economically and which has gone through a revolution. This characteristic basically determines our military strategy and tactics as well as our political strategy and tactics.

The second characteristic is that our enemy is big and powerful.

How do matters stand with the Kuomintang, the enemy of the Red Army? It is a party that has seized political power and has more or less stabilized its power. It has gained the support of the world's principal counter-revolutionary states. It has remodelled its army which has thus become different from any other army in Chinese history and on the whole similar to the armies of modern states; this army is much better supplied with weapons and *matériel* than the Red Army, and is larger than any army in Chinese history, or for that matter than the standing army of any other country. There is a world of difference between the Kuomintang army and the Red Army. The Kuomintang controls the key positions or lifelines in the politics, economy, communications and culture of China; its political power is nation-wide.

The Chinese Red Army is thus confronted with a big and powerful enemy. This is the second characteristic of China's revolutionary war. It necessarily makes the military operations of the Red Army different in many ways from those of wars in general and from those of the civil war in the Soviet Union or of the Northern Expedition.

The third characteristic is that the Red Army is small and weak.

The Chinese Red Army, starting as guerrilla units, came into being after the defeat of the first great revolution. This occurred in a period of relative political and economic stability in the reactionary capitalist countries of the world as well as in a period of reaction in China.

Our political power exists in scattered and isolated mountainous or remote regions and receives no outside help whatsoever. Economic and cultural conditions in the revolutionary base areas are backward compared with those in the Kuomintang areas. The revolutionary base areas embrace only rural districts and small towns. These areas were extremely small in the beginning and have not grown much larger since. Moreover, they are fluid and not stationary, and the Red Army has no really consolidated bases.

The Red Army is numerically small, its arms are poor, and it has great difficulty in obtaining supplies such as food, bedding and clothing.

This characteristic presents a sharp contrast to the preceding one. From this sharp contrast have arisen the strategy and tactics of the Red Army.

The fourth characteristic is Communist Party leadership and the agrarian revolution.

This characteristic is the inevitable consequence of the first one. It has given rise to two features. On the one hand, despite the fact that China's revolutionary war is taking place in a period of reaction in China and throughout the capitalist world, victory is possible because it is under the leadership of the Communist Party and has the support of the peasantry. Thanks to this support, our base areas, small as they are, are politically very powerful and stand firmly opposed to the enormous Kuomintang regime, while militarily they place great difficulties in the way of the Kuomintang attacks. Small as it is, the Red Army has great fighting capacity, because its members, led by the Communist Party, are born of the agrarian revolution and are fighting for their own interests, and because its commanders and fighters are politically united.

The Kuomintang, on the other hand, presents a sharp contrast. It opposes the agrarian revolution and therefore has no support from the peasantry. Though it has a large army, the Kuomintang cannot make its soldiers and the many lower-ranking officers, who were originally small producers, risk their lives willingly for it. Its officers and men are politically divided, which reduces its fighting capacity.

3. OUR STRATEGY AND TACTICS ENSUING
FROM THESE CHARACTERISTICS

Thus the four principal characteristics of China's revolutionary war are: a vast semi-colonial country which is unevenly developed politically and economically and which has gone through a great revolution; a big and powerful enemy; a small and weak Red Army; and the agrarian revolution. These characteristics determine the line for guiding China's revolutionary war as well as many of its strategic and tactical principles. It follows from the first and fourth characteristics that it is possible for the Chinese Red Army to grow and defeat its enemy. It follows from the second and third characteristics that it is impossible for the Chinese Red Army to grow very rapidly or defeat its enemy quickly; in other words, the war will be protracted and may even be lost if it is mishandled.

These are the two aspects of China's revolutionary war. They exist simultaneously, that is, there are favourable factors and there are difficulties. This is the fundamental law of China's revolutionary war, from which many other laws ensue. The history of our ten years of war has proved the validity of this law. He who has eyes but fails to see this fundamental law cannot direct China's revolutionary war, cannot lead the Red Army to victories.

It is clear that we must correctly settle all the following matters of principle:

Determine our strategic orientation correctly, oppose adventurism when on the offensive, oppose conservatism when on the defensive, and oppose flightism when shifting from one place to another.

Oppose guerrilla-ism in the Red Army, while recognizing the guerrilla character of its operations.

Oppose protracted campaigns and a strategy of quick decision, and uphold the strategy of protracted war and campaigns of quick decision.

Oppose fixed battle lines and positional warfare, and favour fluid battle lines and mobile warfare.

Oppose fighting merely to rout the enemy, and uphold fighting to annihilate the enemy.

Oppose the strategy of striking with two "fists" in two directions at the same time, and uphold the strategy of striking with one "fist" in one direction at one time.[12]

Oppose the principle of maintaining one large rear area, and uphold the principle of small rear areas.

Oppose an absolutely centralized command, and favour a relatively centralized command.

Oppose the purely military viewpoint and the ways of roving rebels,[13] and recognize that the Red Army is a propagandist and organizer of the Chinese revolution.

Oppose bandit ways,[14] and uphold strict political discipline.

Oppose warlord ways, and favour both democracy within proper limits and an authoritative discipline in the army.

Oppose an incorrect, sectarian policy on cadres, and uphold the correct policy on cadres.

Oppose the policy of isolation, and affirm the policy of winning over all possible allies.

Oppose keeping the Red Army at its old stage, and strive to develop it to a new stage.

Our present discussion of the problems of strategy is intended to elucidate these matters carefully in the light of the historical experience gained in China's ten years of bloody revolutionary war.

CHAPTER IV

"ENCIRCLEMENT AND SUPPRESSION" AND COUNTER-CAMPAIGNS AGAINST IT — THE MAIN PATTERN OF CHINA'S CIVIL WAR

In the ten years since our guerrilla war began, every independent Red guerrilla unit, every Red Army unit or every revolutionary base area has been regularly subjected by the enemy to "encirclement and suppression". The enemy looks upon the Red Army as a monster and seeks to capture it the moment it shows itself. He is for ever pursuing the Red Army and for ever trying to encircle it. For ten years this pattern of warfare has not changed, and unless the civil war gives place to a national war, the pattern will remain the same till the day the enemy becomes the weaker contestant and the Red Army the stronger.

The Red Army's operations take the form of counter-campaigns against "encirclement and suppression". For us victory means chiefly victory in combating "encirclement and suppression", that is, strategic

victory and victories in campaigns. The fight against each "encirclement and suppression" campaign constitutes a counter-campaign, which
usually comprises several or even scores of battles, big and small.
Until an "encirclement and suppression" campaign has been basically
smashed, one cannot speak of strategic victory or of victory in the
counter-campaign as a whole, even though many battles may have
been won. The history of the Red Army's decade of war is a history
of counter-campaigns against "encirclement and suppression".

In the enemy's "encirclement and suppression" campaigns and the
Red Army's counter-campaigns against them, the two forms of fighting,
offensive and defensive, are both employed, and here there is no difference from any other war, ancient or modern, in China or elsewhere.
The special characteristic of China's civil war, however, is the repeated
alternation of the two forms over a long period of time. In each
"encirclement and suppression" campaign, the enemy employs the
offensive against the Red Army's defensive, and the Red Army
employs the defensive against his offensive; this is the first stage of a
counter-campaign against "encirclement and suppression". Then the
enemy employs the defensive against the Red Army's offensive, and
the Red Army employs the offensive against his defensive; this is
the second stage of the counter-campaign. Every "encirclement and
suppression" campaign has these two stages, and they alternate over
a long period.

By repeated alternation over a long period we mean the repetition
of this pattern of warfare and these forms of fighting. This is a fact
obvious to everybody. An "encirclement and suppression" campaign
and a counter-campaign against it — such is the repeated pattern of the
war. In each campaign the alternation in the forms of fighting consists
of the first stage in which the enemy employs the offensive against our
defensive and we meet his offensive with our defensive, and of the
second stage in which the enemy employs the defensive against our
offensive and we meet his defensive with our offensive.

As for the content of a campaign or of a battle, it does not consist
of mere repetition but is different each time. This, too, is a fact and
obvious to everybody. In this connection it has become a rule that with
each campaign and each counter-campaign, the scale becomes larger,
the situation more complicated and the fighting more intense.

But this does not mean that there are no ups and downs. After the
enemy's fifth "encirclement and suppression" campaign, the Red Army
was greatly weakened, and all the base areas in the south were lost.

Having shifted to the northwest, the Red Army now no longer holds
a vital position threatening the internal enemy as it did in the south,
and as a result the scale of the "encirclement and suppression"
campaigns has become smaller, the situation simpler and the fighting
less intense.

What constitutes a defeat for the Red Army? Strategically
speaking, there is a defeat only when a counter-campaign against
"encirclement and suppression" fails completely, but even then the
defeat is only partial and temporary. For only the total destruction of
the Red Army would constitute complete defeat in the civil war; but
this has never happened. The loss of extensive base areas and the
shift of the Red Army constituted a temporary and partial defeat, not
a final and complete one, even though this partial defeat entailed
losing 90 per cent of the Party membership, of the armed forces and
of the base areas. We call this shift the continuation of our defensive
and the enemy's pursuit the continuation of his offensive. That is to
say, in the course of the struggle between the enemy's "encirclement
and suppression" and our counter-campaign we allowed our defensive
to be broken by the enemy's offensive instead of turning from the
defensive to the offensive; and so our defensive turned into a retreat
and the enemy's offensive into a pursuit. But when the Red Army
reached a new area, as for example when we shifted from Kiangsi
Province and various other regions to Shensi Province, the repetition
of "encirclement and suppression" campaigns began afresh. That is
why we say that the Red Army's strategic retreat (the Long March)
was a continuation of its strategic defensive and the enemy's strategic
pursuit was a continuation of his strategic offensive.

In the Chinese civil war, as in all other wars, ancient or modern,
in China or abroad, there are only two basic forms of fighting, attack
and defence. The special characteristic of China's civil war consists in
the long-term repetition of "encirclement and suppression" campaigns
and of our counter-campaigns together with the long-term alternation
in the two forms of fighting, attack and defence, with the inclusion
of the phenomenon of the great strategic shift of more than ten thousand
kilometres (the Long March).[15]

A defeat for the enemy is much the same. It is a strategic defeat
for the enemy when his "encirclement and suppression" campaign is
broken and our defensive becomes an offensive, when the enemy turns
to the defensive and has to reorganize before launching another
"encirclement and suppression" campaign. The enemy has not had

to make a strategic shift of more than ten thousand kilometres such as we have, because he rules the whole country and is much stronger than we are. But there have been partial shifts of his forces. Sometimes, enemy forces in White strongholds encircled by the Red Army in some base areas have broken through our encirclement and withdrawn to the White areas to organize new offensives. If the civil war is prolonged and the Red Army's victories become more extensive, there will be more of this sort of thing. But the enemy cannot achieve the same results as the Red Army, because he does not have the help of the people and because his officers and men are not united. If he were to imitate the Red Army's long-distance shift, he would certainly be wiped out.

In the period of the Li Li-san line in 1930, Comrade Li Li-san failed to understand the protracted nature of China's civil war and for that reason did not perceive the law that in the course of this war there is repetition over a long period of "encirclement and suppression" campaigns and of their defeat (by that time there had already been three in the Hunan-Kiangsi border area and two in Fukien). Hence, in an attempt to achieve rapid victory for the revolution, he ordered the Red Army, which was then still in its infancy, to attack Wuhan, and also ordered a nation-wide armed uprising. Thus he committed the error of "Left" opportunism.

Likewise the "Left" opportunists of 1931-34 did not believe in the law of the repetition of "encirclement and suppression" campaigns. Some responsible comrades in our base area along the Hupeh-Honan-Anhwei border held an "auxiliary force" theory, maintaining that the Kuomintang army had become merely an auxiliary force after the defeat of its third "encirclement and suppression" campaign and that the imperialists themselves would have to take the field as the main force in further attacks on the Red Army. The strategy based on this estimate was that the Red Army should attack Wuhan. In principle, this fitted in with the views of those comrades in Kiangsi who called for a Red Army attack on Nanchang, were against the work of linking up the base areas and the tactics of luring the enemy in deep, regarded the seizure of the capital and other key cities of a province as the starting point for victory in that province, and held that "the fight against the fifth 'encirclement and suppression' campaign represents the decisive battle between the road of revolution and the road of colonialism". This "Left" opportunism was the source of the wrong line adopted in the struggles against the fourth "encirclement and suppression" campaign in the Hupeh-Honan-Anhwei border area and in those against the fifth in the Central Area in Kiangsi; and it rendered the Red Army helpless before these fierce enemy campaigns and brought enormous losses to the Chinese revolution.

The view that the Red Army should under no circumstances adopt defensive methods was directly related to this "Left" opportunism, which denied the repetition of "encirclement and suppression" campaigns, and it, too, was entirely erroneous.

The proposition that a revolution or a revolutionary war is an offensive is of course correct. A revolution or a revolutionary war in its emergence and growth from a small force to a big force, from the absence of political power to the seizure of political power, from the absence of a Red Army to the creation of a Red Army, and from the absence of revolutionary base areas to their establishment, must be on the offensive and cannot be conservative; and tendencies towards conservatism must be opposed.

The only entirely correct proposition is that a revolution or a revolutionary war is an offensive but also involves defence and retreat. To defend in order to attack, to retreat in order to advance, to move against the flanks in order to move against the front, and to take a roundabout route in order to get on to the direct route — this is inevitable in the process of development of many phenomena, especially military movements.

Of the two propositions stated above, the first may be correct in the political sphere, but it is incorrect when transposed to the military sphere. Moreover, it is correct politically only in one situation (when the revolution is advancing), but incorrect when transposed to another situation (when the revolution is in retreat, in general retreat as in Russia in 1906[16] and in China in 1927, or in partial retreat as in Russia at the time of the Treaty of Brest-Litovsk in 1918).[17] Only the second proposition is entirely correct and true. The "Left" opportunism of 1931-34, which mechanically opposed the employment of defensive military measures, was nothing but infantile thinking.

When will the pattern of repeated "encirclement and suppression" campaigns come to an end? In my opinion, if the civil war is prolonged, this repetition will cease when a fundamental change takes place in the balance of forces. It will cease when the Red Army has become stronger than the enemy. Then we shall be encircling and suppressing the enemy and he will be resorting to counter-campaigns, but political and military conditions will not allow him to attain the same position as that of the Red Army in its counter-campaigns. It can be definitely asserted that by then the pattern of repeated "encirclement and suppression" campaigns will have largely, if not completely, come to an end.

CHAPTER V

THE STRATEGIC DEFENSIVE

Under this heading I would like to discuss the following problems: (1) active and passive defence; (2) preparations for combating "encirclement and suppression" campaigns; (3) strategic retreat; (4) strategic counter-offensive; (5) starting the counter-offensive; (6) concentration of troops; (7) mobile warfare; (8) war of quick decision; and (9) war of annihilation.

1. ACTIVE AND PASSIVE DEFENCE

Why do we begin by discussing defence? After the failure of China's first national united front of 1924-27, the revolution became a most intense and ruthless class war. While the enemy ruled the whole country, we had only small armed forces; consequently, from the very beginning we have had to wage a bitter struggle against his "encirclement and suppression" campaigns. Our offensives have been closely linked with our efforts to break them, and our fate depends entirely on whether or not we are able to do so. The process of breaking an "encirclement and suppression" campaign is usually circuitous and not as direct as one would wish. The primary problem, and a serious one too, is how to conserve our strength and await an opportunity to defeat the enemy. Therefore, the strategic defensive is the most complicated and most important problem facing the Red Army in its operations.

In our ten years of war two deviations often arose with regard to the strategic defensive; one was to belittle the enemy, the other was to be terrified of him.

As a result of belittling the enemy, many guerrilla units suffered defeat, and on several occasions the Red Army was unable to break the enemy's "encirclement and suppression".

When the revolutionary guerrilla units first came into existence, their leaders often failed to assess the enemy's situation and our own correctly. Because they had been successful in organizing sudden armed uprisings in certain places or mutinies among the White troops, they saw only the momentarily favourable circumstances, or failed to see the grave situation actually confronting them, and so usually underestimated the enemy. Moreover, they had no understanding of their own weaknesses (*i.e.*, lack of experience and smallness of forces). It was an objective fact that the enemy was strong and we were weak, and yet some people refused to give it thought, talked only of attack but never of defence or retreat, thus mentally disarming themselves in the matter of defence, and hence misdirected their actions. Many guerrilla units were defeated on this account.

Examples in which the Red Army, for this reason, failed to break the enemy's "encirclement and suppression" campaigns were its defeat in 1928 in the Haifeng-Lufeng area of Kwangtung Province,[18] and its loss of freedom of action in 1932 in the fourth counter-campaign against the enemy's "encirclement and suppression" in the Hupeh-Honan-Anhwei border area, where the Red Army acted on the theory that the Kuomintang army was merely an auxiliary force.

There are many instances of setbacks which were due to being terrified of the enemy.

As against those who underestimated him, some people greatly overestimated him and also greatly underestimated our own strength, as a result of which they adopted an unwarranted policy of retreat and likewise disarmed themselves mentally in the matter of defence. This resulted in the defeat of some guerrilla units, or the failure of certain Red Army campaigns, or the loss of base areas.

The most striking example of the loss of a base area was that of the Central Base Area in Kiangsi during the fifth counter-campaign against "encirclement and suppression". The mistake here arose from a Rightist viewpoint. The leaders feared the enemy as if he were a tiger, set up defences everywhere, fought defensive actions at every step and did not dare to advance to the enemy's rear and attack him there, which would have been to our advantage, or boldly to lure the enemy troops in deep so as to herd them together and annihilate them. As a result, the whole base area was lost and the Red Army had to undertake the Long March of over 12,000 kilometres. However, this kind of mistake was usually preceded by a "Left" error of underestimating the enemy. The military adventurism of attacking the key cities in 1932 was the root cause of the line of passive defence subsequently adopted in coping with the enemy's fifth "encirclement and suppression" campaign.

The most extreme example of being terrified of the enemy was the retreatism of the "Chang Kuo-tao line". The defeat of the Western Column of the Fourth Front Red Army west of the Yellow River[19] marked the final bankruptcy of this line.

Active defence is also known as offensive defence, or defence through decisive engagements. Passive defence is also known as purely defensive defence or pure defence. Passive defence is actually a spurious kind of defence, and the only real defence is active defence, defence for the purpose of counter-attacking and taking the offensive. As far as I know, there is no military manual of value nor any sensible military expert, ancient or modern, Chinese or foreign, that does not oppose passive defence, whether in strategy or tactics. Only a complete fool or a madman would cherish passive defence as a talisman. However, there are people in this world who do such things. That is an error in war, a manifestation of conservatism in military matters, which we must resolutely oppose.

The military experts of the newer and rapidly developing imperialist countries, namely, Germany and Japan, trumpet the advantages of the strategic offensive and come out against the strategic defensive. This kind of military thinking is absolutely unsuited to China's revolutionary war. These military experts assert that a serious weakness of the defensive is that it shakes popular morale, instead of inspiring it. This applies to countries where class contradictions are acute and the war benefits only the reactionary ruling strata or the reactionary political groups in power. But our situation is different. With the slogan of defending the revolutionary base areas and defending China, we can rally the overwhelming majority of the people to fight with one heart and one mind, because we are the oppressed and the victims of aggression. It was also by using the form of the defensive that the Red Army of the Soviet Union defeated its enemies during the civil war. When the imperialist countries organized the Whites for attack, the war was waged under the slogan of defending the Soviets; even when the October Uprising was being prepared, the military mobilization was carried out under the slogan of defending the capital. In every just war the defensive not only has a lulling effect on politically alien elements, it also makes possible the rallying of the backward sections of the masses to join in the war.

When Marx said that once an armed uprising is started there must not be a moment's pause in the attack,[20] he meant that the masses, having taken the enemy unawares in an insurrection, must give the reactionary rulers no chance to retain or recover their political power, must seize this moment to beat the nation's reactionary ruling forces when they are unprepared, and must not rest content with the victories already won, underestimate the enemy, slacken their attacks or hesitate to press forward, and so let slip the opportunity of destroying the enemy, bringing failure to the revolution. This is correct. It does not mean, however, that when we are already locked in battle with an enemy who enjoys superiority, we revolutionaries should not adopt defensive measures even when we are hard pressed. Only a prize idiot would think in this way.

Taken as a whole, our war has been an offensive against the Kuomintang, but militarily it has assumed the form of breaking the enemy's "encirclement and suppression".

Militarily speaking, our warfare consists of the alternate use of the defensive and the offensive. In our case it makes no difference whether the offensive is said to follow or to precede the defensive, because the crux of the matter is to break the "encirclement and suppression". The defensive continues until an "encirclement and suppression" campaign is broken, whereupon the offensive begins, these being but two stages of the same thing; and one such enemy campaign is closely followed by another. Of the two stages, the defensive is the more complicated and the more important. It involves numerous problems of how to break the "encirclement and suppression". The basic principle here is to stand for active defence and oppose passive defence.

In our civil war, when the strength of the Red Army surpasses that of the enemy, we shall, in general, no longer need the strategic defensive. Our policy then will be the strategic offensive alone. This change will depend on an over-all change in the balance of forces. By that time the only remaining defensive measures will be of a partial character.

2. PREPARATIONS FOR COMBATING "ENCIRCLEMENT AND SUPPRESSION" CAMPAIGNS

Unless we have made necessary and sufficient preparations against a planned enemy "encirclement and suppression" campaign, we shall certainly be forced into a passive position. To accept battle in haste is to fight without being sure of victory. Therefore, when the enemy is preparing an "encirclement and suppression" campaign, it is absolutely necessary for us to prepare our counter-campaign. To be opposed to such preparations, as some people in our ranks were at one time, is childish and ridiculous.

There is a difficult problem here on which controversy may easily arise. When should we conclude our offensive and switch to the phase of preparing our counter-campaign against "encirclement and suppression"? When we are victoriously on the offensive and the enemy is on the defensive, his preparations for the next "encirclement and suppression" campaign are conducted in secret, and therefore it is difficult for us to know when his offensive will begin. If our work of preparing the counter-campaign begins too early, it is bound to reduce the gains from our offensive and will sometimes even have certain harmful effects on the Red Army and the people. For the chief measures in the preparatory phase are the military preparations for withdrawal and the political mobilization for them. Sometimes, if we start preparing too early, this will turn into waiting for the enemy; after waiting a long time without the enemy's appearing, we will have to renew our offensive. And sometimes, the enemy will start his offensive just as our new offensive is beginning, thus putting us in a difficult position. Hence the choice of the right moment to begin our preparations is an important problem. The right moment should be determined with due regard both to the enemy's situation and our own and to the relation between the two. In order to know the enemy's situation, we should collect information on his political, military and financial position and the state of public opinion in his territory. In analysing such information we must take the total strength of the enemy into full account and must not exaggerate the extent of his past defeats, but on the other hand we must not fail to take into account his internal contradictions, his financial difficulties, the effect of his past defeats, etc. As for our side, we must not exaggerate the extent of our past victories, but neither should we fail to take full account of their effect.

Generally speaking, however, on the question of timing the preparations, it is preferable to start them too early rather than too late. For the former involves smaller losses and has the advantage that preparedness averts peril and puts us in a fundamentally invincible position.

The essential problems during the preparatory phase are the preparations for the withdrawal of the Red Army, political mobilization, recruitment, arrangements for finance and provisions, and the handling of politically alien elements.

By preparations for the Red Army's withdrawal we mean taking care that it does not move in a direction jeopardizing the withdrawal or advance too far in its attacks or become too fatigued. These are the things the main forces of the Red Army must attend to on the eve of a large-scale enemy offensive. At such a time, the Red Army must devote its attention mainly to planning the selection and preparation of the battle areas, the acquisition of supplies, and the enlargement and training of its own forces.

Political mobilization is a problem of prime importance in the struggle against "encirclement and suppression". That is to say, we should tell the Red Army and the people in the base area clearly, resolutely and fully that the enemy's offensive is inevitable and imminent and will do serious harm to the people, but at the same time, we should tell them about his weaknesses, the factors favourable to the Red Army, our indomitable will to victory and our general plan of work. We should call upon the Red Army and the entire population to fight against the enemy's "encirclement and suppression" campaign and defend the base area. Except where military secrets are concerned, political mobilization must be carried out openly, and, what is more, every effort should be made to extend it to all who might possibly support the revolutionary cause. The key link here is to convince the cadres.

Recruitment of new soldiers should be based on two considerations, first, on the level of political consciousness of the people and the size of the population and, second, on the current state of the Red Army and the possible extent of its losses in the whole course of the counter-campaign.

Needless to say, the problems of finance and food are of great importance to the counter-campaign. We must take the possibility of a prolonged enemy campaign into account. It is necessary to make an estimate of the minimum material requirements — chiefly of the Red Army but also of the people in the revolutionary base area — for the entire struggle against the enemy's "encirclement and suppression" campaign.

With regard to politically alien elements we should not be off our guard, but neither should we be unduly apprehensive of treachery on their part and adopt excessive precautionary measures. Distinction should be made between the landlords, the merchants and the rich peasants, and the main point is to explain things to them politically and win their neutrality, while at the same time organizing the masses of the people to keep an eye on them. Only against the very few elements who are most dangerous should stern measures like arrest be taken.

The extent of success in a struggle against "encirclement and suppression" is closely related to the degree to which the tasks of the preparatory phase have been fulfilled. Relaxation of preparatory work which is due to underestimation of the enemy and panic which is due to being terrified of the enemy's attacks are harmful tendencies, and both should be resolutely opposed. What we need is an enthusiastic but calm state of mind and intense but orderly work.

3. STRATEGIC RETREAT

A strategic retreat is a planned strategic step taken by an inferior force for the purpose of conserving its strength and biding its time to defeat the enemy, when it finds itself confronted with a superior force whose offensive it is unable to smash quickly. But military adventurists stubbornly oppose such a step and advocate "engaging the enemy outside the gates".

We all know that when two boxers fight, the clever boxer usually gives a little ground at first, while the foolish one rushes in furiously and uses up all his resources at the very start, and in the end he is often beaten by the man who has given ground.

In the novel *Shui Hu Chuan*,[21] the drill master Hung, challenging Lin Chung to a fight on Chai Chin's estate, shouts, "Come on! Come on! Come on!" In the end it is the retreating Lin Chung who spots Hung's weak point and floors him with one blow.

During the Spring and Autumn Era, when the states of Lu and Chi[22] were at war, Duke Chuang of Lu wanted to attack before the Chi troops had tired themselves out, but Tsao Kuei prevented him. When instead he adopted the tactic of "the enemy tires, we attack", he defeated the Chi army. This is a classic example from China's military history of a weak force defeating a strong force. Here is the account given by the historian Tsochiu Ming:[23]

> In the spring the Chi troops invaded us. The Duke was about to fight. Tsao Kuei requested an audience. His neighbours said,

"This is the business of meat-eating officials, why meddle with it?"
Tsao replied, "Meat-eaters are fools, they cannot plan ahead."
So he saw the Duke. And he asked, "What will you rely on when
you fight?" The Duke answered, "I never dare to keep all my
food and clothing for my own enjoyment, but always share them
with others." Tsao said, "Such paltry charity cannot reach all.
The people will not follow you." The Duke said, "I never offer
to the gods less sacrificial beasts, jade or silk than are due to them.
I keep good faith." Tsao said, "Such paltry faith wins no trust.
The gods will not bless you." The Duke said, "Though unable
personally to attend to the details of all trials, big and small, I
always demand the facts." Tsao said, "That shows your devotion
to your people. You can give battle. When you do so, I beg to
follow you." The Duke and he rode in the same chariot. The battle
was joined at Changshao. When the Duke was about to sound
the drum for the attack, Tsao said, "Not yet." When the men
of Chi had drummed thrice, Tsao said, "Now we can drum." The
army of Chi was routed. The Duke wanted to pursue. Again Tsao
said, "Not yet." He got down from the chariot to examine the
enemy's wheel-tracks, then mounted the arm-rest of the chariot
to look afar. He said, "Now we can pursue!" So began the pursuit
of the Chi troops. After the victory the Duke asked Tsao why he
had given such advice. Tsao replied, "A battle depends upon
courage. At the first drum courage is aroused, at the second it
flags, and with the third it runs out. When the enemy's courage
ran out, ours was still high and so we won. It is difficult to fathom
the moves of a great state, and I feared an ambush. But when I
examined the enemy's wheel-tracks and found them criss-crossing
and looked afar and saw his banners drooping, I advised pursuit."

That was a case of a weak state resisting a strong state. The story
speaks of the political preparations before a battle — winning the
confidence of the people; it speaks of a battlefield favourable for
switching over to the counter-offensive — Changshao; it indicates the
favourable time for starting the counter-offensive — when the enemy's
courage is running out and one's own is high; and it points to the
moment for starting the pursuit — when the enemy's tracks are criss-
crossed and his banners are drooping. Though the battle was not a
big one, it illustrates the principles of the strategic defensive. China's
military history contains numerous instances of victories won on these

principles. In such famous battles as the Battle of Chengkao between the states of Chu and Han,[24] the Battle of Kunyang between the states of Hsin and Han,[25] the Battle of Kuantu between Yuan Shao and Tsao Tsao,[26] the Battle of Chihpi between the states of Wu and Wei,[27] the Battle of Yiling between the states of Wu and Shu,[28] and the Battle of Feishui between the states of Chin and Tsin,[29] in each case the contending sides were unequal, and the weaker side, yielding some ground at first, gained mastery by striking only after the enemy had struck and so defeated the stronger side.

Our war began in the autumn of 1927, and we then had no experience at all. The Nanchang Uprising[30] and the Canton Uprising[31] failed, and in the Autumn Harvest Uprising[32] the Red Army in the Hunan-Hupeh-Kiangsi border area also suffered several defeats and shifted to the Chingkang Mountains on the Hunan-Kiangsi border. In the following April the units which had survived the defeat of the Nanchang Uprising also moved to the Chingkang Mountains by way of southern Hunan. By May 1928, however, basic principles of guerrilla warfare, simple in nature and suited to the conditions of the time, had already been evolved, that is, the sixteen-character formula: "The enemy advances, we retreat; the enemy camps, we harass; the enemy tires, we attack; the enemy retreats, we pursue." This sixteen-character formulation of military principles was accepted by the Central Committee before the Li Li-san line. Later our operational principles were developed a step further. At the time of our first counter-campaign against "encirclement and suppression" in the Kiangsi base area, the principle of "luring the enemy in deep" was put forward and, moreover, successfully applied. By the time the enemy's third "encirclement and suppression" campaign was defeated, a complete set of operational principles for the Red Army had taken shape. This marked a new stage in the development of our military principles, which were greatly enriched in content and underwent many changes in form, mainly in the sense that although they basically remained the same as in the sixteen-character formula, they transcended their originally simple nature. The sixteen-character formula covered the basic principles for combating "encirclement and suppression"; it covered the two stages of the strategic defensive and the strategic offensive, and within the defensive, it covered the two stages of the strategic retreat and the strategic counter-offensive. What came later was only a development of this formula.

But beginning from January 1932, after the publication of the Party's resolution entitled "Struggle for Victory First in One or More Provinces After Smashing the Third 'Encirclement and Suppression' Campaign", which contained serious errors of principle, the "Left" opportunists attacked these correct principles, finally abrogated the whole set and instituted a complete set of contrary "new principles" or "regular principles". From then on, the old principles were no longer to be considered as regular but were to be rejected as "guerrilla-ism". The opposition to "guerrilla-ism" reigned for three whole years. Its first stage was military adventurism, in the second it turned into military conservatism and, finally, in the third stage it became flightism. It was not until the Central Committee held the enlarged meeting of the Political Bureau at Tsunyi, Kweichow Province, in January 1935 that this wrong line was declared bankrupt and the correctness of the old line reaffirmed. But at what a cost!

Those comrades who vigorously opposed "guerrilla-ism" argued along the following lines. It was wrong to lure the enemy in deep because we had to abandon so much territory. Although battles had been won in this way, was not the situation different now? Moreover, was it not better to defeat the enemy without abandoning territory? And was it not better still to defeat the enemy in his own areas, or on the borders between his areas and ours? The old practices had had nothing "regular" about them and were methods used only by guerrillas. Now our own state had been established and our Red Army had become a regular army. Our fight against Chiang Kai-shek had become a war between two states, between two great armies. History should not repeat itself, and everything pertaining to "guerrilla-ism" should be totally discarded. The new principles were "completely Marxist", while the old had been created by guerrilla units in the mountains, and there was no Marxism in the mountains. The new principles were the antithesis of the old. They were: "Pit one against ten, pit ten against a hundred, fight bravely and determinedly, and exploit victories by hot pursuit"; "Attack on all fronts"; "Seize key cities"; and "Strike with two 'fists' in two directions at the same time". When the enemy attacked, the methods of dealing with him were: "Engage the enemy outside the gates", "Gain mastery by striking first", "Don't let our pots and pans be smashed", "Don't give up an inch of territory" and "Divide the forces into six routes". The war was "the decisive battle between the road of revolution and the road of colonialism", a war of short swift thrusts, blockhouse warfare, war of attrition, "protracted war". There were, further, the policy of maintaining a great rear area and an absolutely centralized command. Finally there was a large-scale "house-moving". And anyone who did not accept these things was to be punished, labelled an opportunist, and so on and so forth.

Without a doubt these theories and practices were all wrong. They were nothing but subjectivism. Under favourable circumstances this subjectivism manifested itself in petty-bourgeois revolutionary fanaticism and impetuosity, but in times of adversity, as the situation worsened, it changed successively into desperate recklessness, conservatism and flightism. They were the theories and practices of hotheads and ignoramuses; they did not have the slightest flavour of Marxism about them; indeed they were anti-Marxist.

Here we shall discuss only strategic retreat, which in Kiangsi was called "luring the enemy in deep" and in Szechuan "contracting the front". No previous theorist or practitioner of war has ever denied that this is the policy a weak army fighting a strong army must adopt in the initial stage of a war. It has been said by a foreign military expert that in strategically defensive operations, decisive battles are usually avoided in the beginning, and are sought only when conditions have become favourable. That is entirely correct and we have nothing to add to it.

The object of strategic retreat is to conserve military strength and prepare for the counter-offensive. Retreat is necessary because not to retreat a step before the onset of a strong enemy inevitably means to jeopardize the preservation of one's own forces. In the past, however, many people were stubbornly opposed to retreat, considering it to be an "opportunist line of pure defence". Our history has proved that their opposition was entirely wrong.

To prepare for a counter-offensive, we must select or create conditions favourable to ourselves but unfavourable to the enemy, so as to bring about a change in the balance of forces, before we go on to the stage of the counter-offensive.

In the light of our past experience, during the stage of retreat we should in general secure at least two of the following conditions before we can consider the situation as being favourable to us and unfavourable to the enemy and before we can go over to the counter-offensive. These conditions are:

(1) The population actively supports the Red Army.
(2) The terrain is favourable for operations.
(3) All the main forces of the Red Army are concentrated.

(4)   The enemy's weak spots have been discovered.
(5)   The enemy has been reduced to a tired and demoralized state.
(6)   The enemy has been induced to make mistakes.

The first condition, active support of the population, is the most important one for the Red Army. It means having a base area. Moreover, given this condition, it is easy to achieve conditions 4, 5 and 6. Therefore, when the enemy launches a full-scale offensive, the Red Army generally withdraws from the White area into the base area, because that is where the population is most active in supporting the Red Army against the White army. Also, there is a difference between the borders and the central district of a base area; in the latter the people are better at blocking the passage of information to the enemy, better at reconnaissance, transportation, joining in the fighting, and so on. Thus when we were combating the first, second and third "encirclement and suppression" campaigns in Kiangsi, all the places selected as "terminal points for the retreat" were situated where the first condition, popular support, was excellent or quite good. This characteristic of our base areas made the Red Army's operations very different from ordinary operations and was the main reason why the enemy subsequently had to resort to the policy of blockhouse warfare.

One advantage of operating on interior lines is that it makes it possible for the retreating army to choose terrain favourable to itself and force the attacking army to fight on its terms. In order to defeat a strong army, a weak army must carefully choose favourable terrain as a battleground. But this condition alone is not enough and must be accompanied by others. The first of these is popular support. The next is a vulnerable enemy, for instance, an enemy who is tired or has made mistakes, or an advancing enemy column that is comparatively poor in fighting capacity. In the absence of these conditions, even if we have found excellent terrain, we have to disregard it and continue to retreat in order to secure them. In the White areas there is no lack of good terrain, but we do not have the favourable condition of active popular support. If other conditions are not yet fulfilled, the Red Army has no alternative but to retreat towards its base area. Distinctions such as those between the White areas and the Red areas also usually exist between the borders and the central district of a base area.

Except for local units and containing forces, all our assault troops should, on principle, be concentrated. When attacking an enemy who is on the defensive strategically, the Red Army usually disperses its own forces. Once the enemy launches a full-scale offensive, the Red Army effects a "retreat towards the centre". The terminal point chosen for the retreat is usually in the central section of the base area, but sometimes it is in the frontal or rear sections, as circumstances require. By such a retreat towards the centre all the main forces of the Red Army can be concentrated.

Another essential condition for a weak army fighting a strong one is to pick out the enemy's weaker units for attack. But at the beginning of the enemy's offensive we usually do not know which of his advancing columns is the strongest and which the second strongest, which is the weakest and which the second weakest, and so a process of reconnaissance is required. This often takes a considerable time. That is another reason why strategic retreat is necessary.

If the attacking enemy is far more numerous and much stronger than we are, we can accomplish a change in the balance of forces only when the enemy has penetrated deeply into our base area and tasted all the bitterness it holds for him. As the chief of staff of one of Chiang Kai-shek's brigades remarked during the third "encirclement and suppression" campaign, "Our stout men have worn themselves thin and our thin men have worn themselves to death." Or, in the words of Chen Ming-shu, Commander-in-Chief of the Western Route of the Kuomintang's "Encirclement and Suppression" Army, "Everywhere the National Army gropes in the dark, while the Red Army walks in broad daylight." By then the enemy army, although still strong, is much weakened, its soldiers are tired, its morale is sagging and many of its weak spots are revealed. But the Red Army, though weak, has conserved its strength and stored up its energy, and is waiting at its ease for the fatigued enemy. At such a time it is generally possible to attain a certain parity between the two sides, or to change the enemy's absolute superiority to relative superiority and our absolute inferiority to relative inferiority, and occasionally even to become superior to the enemy. When fighting against the third "encirclement and suppression" campaign in Kiangsi, the Red Army executed a retreat to the extreme limit (to concentrate in the rear section of the base area); if it had not done so, it could not have defeated the enemy because the enemy's "encirclement and suppression" forces were then over ten times the size of the Red Army. When Sun Wu Tzu said, "Avoid the enemy when he is full of vigour, strike when he is fatigued and withdraws", he was referring to tiring and demoralizing the enemy so as to reduce his superiority.

Finally, the object of retreat is to induce the enemy to make mistakes or to detect his mistakes. One must realize that an enemy commander, however wise, cannot avoid making some mistakes over a relatively long period of time, and hence it is always possible for us to exploit the openings he leaves us. The enemy is liable to make mistakes, just as we ourselves sometimes miscalculate and give him openings to exploit. In addition, we can induce the enemy to make mistakes by our own actions, for instance, by "counterfeiting an appearance", as Sun Wu Tzu called it, that is, by making a feint to the east but attacking in the west. If we are to do this, the terminal point for the retreat cannot be rigidly limited to a definite area. Sometimes when we have retreated to the predetermined area and not yet found openings to exploit, we have to retreat farther and wait for the enemy to give us an opening.

The favourable conditions which we seek by retreating are in general those stated above. But this does not mean that a counter-offensive cannot be launched until all these conditions are present. The presence of all of them at the same time is neither possible nor necessary. But a weak force operating on interior lines against a strong enemy should strive to secure such conditions as are necessary in the light of the enemy's actual situation. All views to the contrary are incorrect.

The decision on the terminal point for retreat should depend on the situation as a whole. It is wrong to decide on a place which, considered in relation to only part of the situation, appears to be favourable for our passing to the counter-offensive, if it is not also advantageous from the point of view of the situation as a whole. For at the start of our counter-offensive we must take subsequent developments into consideration, and our counter-offensives always begin on a partial scale. Sometimes the terminal point for retreat should be fixed in the frontal section of the base area, as it was during our second and fourth counter-campaigns against "encirclement and suppression" in Kiangsi and our third counter-campaign in the Shensi-Kansu area. At times it should be in the middle section of the base area, as in our first counter-campaign in Kiangsi. At other times, it should be fixed in the rear section of the base area, as in our third counter-campaign in Kiangsi. In all these cases the decision was taken by correlating the partial situation with the situation as a whole. But during the fifth counter-campaign in Kiangsi, our army gave no consideration whatsoever to retreat, because it did not take account of either the partial or the total situation, and this was really rash and foolhardy conduct. A situation is made up of a number of factors; in considering the relation between a part of the situation and the whole, we should base our judgements on whether the factors on the enemy's side and on ours, as manifested in both the partial and the whole situation, are to a certain extent favourable for our starting a counter-offensive.

The terminal points for retreat in a base area can be generally divided into three types, those in the frontal, those in the middle, and those in the rear section of the base area. Does this, however, mean refusing to fight in the White areas altogether? No. It is only when we have to deal with a large-scale campaign of enemy "encirclement and suppression" that we refuse to fight in the White areas. It is only when there is a wide disparity between the enemy's strength and ours that, acting on the principle of conserving our strength and biding our time to defeat the enemy, we advocate retreating to the base area and luring him in deep, for only by so doing can we create or find conditions favourable for our counter-offensive. If the situation is not so serious, or if it is so serious that the Red Army cannot begin its counter-offensive even in the base area, or if the counter-offensive is not going well and a further retreat is necessary to bring about a change in the situation, then we should recognize, theoretically at least, that the terminal point for the retreat may be fixed in a White area, though we have had very little experience of this kind.

In general, the terminal points for retreat in a White area can also be divided into three types: (1) those in front of our base area, (2) those on its flanks, and (3) those behind it. Here is an example of the first type.

> During our first counter-campaign against "encirclement and suppression" in Kiangsi, had it not been for the disunity inside the Red Army and the split in the local Party organization (the two difficult problems created by the Li Li-san line and the A-B Group),[33] it is conceivable that we might have concentrated our forces within the triangle formed by Kian, Nanfeng and Changshu and launched a counter-offensive. For the enemy force advancing from the area between the Kan and Fu Rivers was not very greatly superior to the Red Army in strength (100,000 against 40,000). Though the popular support there was not as active as in the base area, the terrain was favourable; moreover, it would have

been possible to smash, one by one, the enemy forces advancing along separate routes.

Now for an example of the second type.

During our third counter-campaign in Kiangsi, if the enemy's offensive had not been on so large a scale, if one of the enemy's columns had advanced from Chienning, Lichuan and Taining on the Fukien-Kiangsi border, and if that column had not been too strong for us to attack, it is likewise conceivable that the Red Army might have massed its forces in the White area in western Fukien and crushed that column first, without having to make a thousand-*li* detour through Juichin to Hsingkuo.

Finally, an example of the third type.

During that same third counter-campaign in Kiangsi, if the enemy's main force had headed south instead of west, we might have been compelled to withdraw to the Huichang-Hsunwu-Anyuan area (a White area), in order to induce the enemy to move further south; the Red Army could have then driven northward into the interior of the base area, by which time the enemy force in the north of the base area would not have been very large.

The above, however, are all hypothetical examples not based on actual experience; they should be regarded as exceptional and not treated as general principles. When the enemy launches a large-scale "encirclement and suppression" campaign, our general principle is to lure him in deep, withdraw into the base area and fight him there, because this is our surest method of smashing his offensive.

Those who advocate "engaging the enemy outside the gates" oppose strategic retreat, arguing that to retreat means to lose territory, to bring harm on the people ("to let our pots and pans be smashed", as they call it), and to give rise to unfavourable repercussions outside. During our fifth counter-campaign, they argued that every time we retreated a step the enemy would push his blockhouses forward a step, so that our base areas would continuously shrink and we would have no way of recovering lost ground. Even though luring the enemy deep into our territory might have been useful in the past, it would be useless against the enemy's fifth "encirclement and suppression" campaign in which he adopted the policy of blockhouse warfare. The only way to deal with this campaign, they said, was to divide up our forces for resistance and make short swift thrusts at the enemy.

It is easy to give an answer to such views, and our history has already done so. As for loss of territory, it often happens that only by loss can loss be avoided; this is the principle of "Give in order to take". If what we lose is territory and what we gain is victory over the enemy, plus recovery and also expansion of our territory, then it is a paying proposition. In a business transaction, if a buyer does not "lose" some money, he cannot obtain goods; if a seller does not "lose" some goods, he cannot obtain money. The losses incurred in a revolutionary movement involve destruction, and what is gained is construction of a progressive character. Sleep and rest involve loss of time, but energy is gained for tomorrow's work. If any fool does not understand this and refuses to sleep, he will have no energy the next day, and that is a losing proposition. We lost out in the fifth counter-campaign for precisely such reasons. Reluctance to give up part of our territory resulted in the loss of it all. Abyssinia, too, lost all her territory when she fought the enemy head-on, though that was not the sole cause of her defeat.

The same holds true on the question of bringing damage on the people. If you refuse to let the pots and pans of some households be smashed over a short period of time, you will cause the smashing of the pots and pans of all the people to go on over a long period of time. If you are afraid of unfavourable short-term political repercussions, you will have to pay the price in unfavourable long-term political repercussions. After the October Revolution, if the Russian Bolsheviks had acted on the opinions of the "Left Communists" and refused to sign the peace treaty with Germany, the new-born Soviets would have been in danger of early death.[34]

Such seemingly revolutionary "Left" opinions originate from the revolutionary impetuosity of the petty-bourgeois intellectuals as well as from the narrow conservatism of the peasant small producers. People holding such opinions look at problems only one-sidedly and are unable to take a comprehensive view of the situation as a whole; they are unwilling to link the interests of today with those of tomorrow or the interests of the part with those of the whole, but cling like grim death to the partial and the temporary. Certainly, we should cling tenaciously to the partial and the temporary when, in the concrete circumstances of the time, they are favourable — and especially when they are decisive — for the whole current situation and the whole period, or otherwise we shall become advocates of letting things slide and doing nothing about them. That is why a retreat must have a terminal point. We must not go by the short-sightedness of the small producer. We should learn the wisdom of the Bolsheviks. The naked eye is not enough, we must have the aid of the telescope and the microscope. The Marxist method is our telescope and microscope in political and military matters.

Of course, strategic retreat has its difficulties. To pick the time for beginning the retreat, to select the terminal point, to convince the cadres and the people politically — these are difficult problems demanding solution.

The problem of timing the beginning of the retreat is very important. If in the course of our first counter-campaign against "encirclement and suppression" in Kiangsi Province our retreat had not been carried out just when it was, that is, if it had been delayed, then at the very least the extent of our victory would have been affected. Both a premature and a belated retreat, of course, bring losses. But generally speaking, a belated retreat brings more losses than a premature one. A well-timed retreat, which enables us to keep all the initiative, is of great assistance to us in switching to the counter-offensive when, having reached the terminal point for our retreat, we have regrouped our forces and are waiting at our ease for the fatigued enemy. When smashing the enemy's first, second and fourth campaigns of "encirclement and suppression" in Kiangsi, we were able to handle him confidently and without haste. It was only during the third campaign that the Red Army was very fatigued by the detour it had hastily had to make in order to reassemble, because we had not expected the enemy to launch a new offensive so quickly after suffering such a crushing defeat in the second campaign (we ended our second counter-campaign on May 29, 1931, and Chiang Kai-shek began his third "encirclement and suppression" campaign on July 1). The timing of the retreat is decided in the same way as the timing of the preparatory phase of a counter-campaign which we discussed earlier, that is, entirely on the basis of the requisite information we have collected and of the appraisal of the general situation on the enemy side and on our own.

It is extremely difficult to convince the cadres and the people of the necessity of strategic retreat when they have had no experience of it, and when the prestige of the army leadership is not yet such that it can concentrate the authority for deciding on strategic retreat in the hands of a few persons or of a single person and at the same time enjoy the confidence of the cadres. Because the cadres lacked experience and had no faith in strategic retreat, great difficulties were encountered at the beginning of our first and fourth counter-campaigns and during the whole of the fifth. During the first counter-campaign the cadres, under the influence of the Li Li-san line, were in favour not of retreat but of attack until they were convinced otherwise. In the fourth counter-campaign the cadres, under the influence of military adventurism, objected to making preparations for retreat. In the fifth, they at first persisted in the military adventurist view, which opposed luring the enemy in deep, but later turned to military conservatism. Another case is that of the adherents of the Chang Kuo-tao line, who did not admit the impossibility of establishing our bases in the regions of the Tibetan and the Hui peoples[35] until they ran up against a brick wall. Experience is essential for the cadres, and failure is indeed the mother of success. But it is also necessary to learn with an open mind from other people's experience, and it is sheer "narrow empiricism" to insist on one's own personal experience in all matters and, in its absence, to adhere stubbornly to one's own opinions and reject other people's experience. Our war has suffered in no small measure on this account.

The people's lack of faith in the need for a strategic retreat, which was due to their inexperience, was never greater than in our first counter-campaign in Kiangsi. At that time the local Party organizations and the masses of the people in the counties of Kian, Hsingkuo and Yungfeng were all opposed to the Red Army's withdrawal. But after the experience of the first counter-campaign, no such problem occurred in the subsequent ones. Everyone was convinced that the loss of territory in the base area and the sufferings of the people were temporary and was confident that the Red Army could smash the enemy's "encirclement and suppression". However, whether or not the people have faith is closely tied up with whether or not the cadres have faith, and hence the first and foremost task is to convince the cadres.

Strategic retreat is aimed solely at switching over to the counter-offensive and is merely the first stage of the strategic defensive. The decisive link in the entire strategy is whether victory can be won in the stage of the counter-offensive which follows.

4. STRATEGIC COUNTER-OFFENSIVE

To defeat the offensive of an enemy who enjoys absolute superiority we rely on the situation created during the stage of our strategic retreat, a situation which is favourable to ourselves, unfavourable to the enemy and different from that at the beginning of his offensive. It takes many elements to make up such a situation. All this has been dealt with above.

However, the presence of these conditions and of a situation favourable to ourselves and unfavourable to the enemy does not mean that we have already defeated him. Such conditions and such a situation provide the possibility for our victory and his defeat, but do not constitute the reality of victory or defeat; they have not yet brought actual victory or defeat to either army. To bring about victory or defeat a decisive battle between the two armies is necessary. Only a decisive battle can settle the question as to which army is the victor and which the vanquished. This is the sole task in the stage of strategic counter-offensive. The counter-offensive is a long process, the most fascinating, the most dynamic, and also the final stage of a defensive campaign. What is called active defence refers chiefly to this strategic counter-offensive, which is in the nature of a decisive engagement.

Conditions and situation are created not only in the stage of the strategic retreat, but continue to be created in that of the counter-offensive. Whether in form or in nature, they are not exactly the same in the latter stage as in the former.

What might remain the same in form and in nature, for example, is the fact that the enemy troops will be even more fatigued and depleted, which is simply a continuation of their fatigue and depletion in the previous stage.

But wholly new conditions and a wholly new situation are bound to emerge. Thus, when the enemy has suffered one or more defeats, the conditions advantageous to us and disadvantageous to him will not be confined to his fatigue, etc., but a new factor will have been added, namely, that he has suffered defeats. New changes will take place in the situation, too. When the enemy begins to manoeuvre his troops in a disorderly way and to make false moves, the relative strengths of the two opposing armies will naturally no longer be the same as before.

But if it is not the enemy's forces but ours that have suffered one or more defeats, then both the conditions and the situation will change in the opposite direction. That is to say, the enemy's disadvantages will be reduced, while on our side disadvantages will emerge and even grow. That again will be something entirely new and different.

A defeat for either side will lead directly and speedily to a new effort by the defeated side to avert disaster, to extricate itself from the new conditions and the new situation unfavourable to it and favourable to the enemy and to re-create such conditions and such a situation as are favourable to it and unfavourable to its opponent, in order to bring pressure to bear on the latter.

The effort of the winning side will be exactly the opposite. It will strive to exploit its victory and inflict still greater damage on the enemy, add to the conditions that are in its favour and further improve its situation, and prevent the enemy from succeeding in extricating himself from his unfavourable conditions and unfavourable situation and averting disaster.

Thus, for either side, the struggle at the stage of the decisive battle is the most intense, the most complicated and the most changeful as well as the most difficult and trying in the whole war or the whole campaign; it is the most exacting time of all from the point of view of command.

In the stage of counter-offensive, there are many problems, the chief of which are the starting of the counter-offensive, the concentration of troops, mobile warfare, war of quick decision and war of annihilation.

Whether in a counter-offensive or in an offensive, the principles with regard to these problems do not differ in their basic character. In this sense we may say that a counter-offensive is an offensive.

Still, it is not exactly an offensive. The principles of the counter-offensive are applied when the enemy is on the offensive. The principles of the offensive are applied when the enemy is on the defensive. In this sense, there are certain differences between a counter-offensive and an offensive.

For this reason, although the various operational problems are all included in the discussion of the counter-offensive in the present chapter on the strategic defensive, and although the chapter on the strategic offensive will deal only with other problems in order to avoid repetition, we should not overlook either the similarities or the differences between the counter-offensive and the offensive when it comes to actual application.

5. STARTING THE COUNTER-OFFENSIVE

The problem of starting a counter-offensive is the problem of the "initial battle" or "prelude".

Many bourgeois military experts advise caution in the initial battle, whether one is on the strategic defensive or on the strategic offensive, but more especially when on the defensive. In the past we, too, have stressed this as a serious point. Our operations against the five enemy campaigns of "encirclement and suppression" in Kiangsi Province have given us rich experience, a study of which will not be without benefit.

In his first campaign, the enemy employed about 100,000 men, divided into eight columns, to advance southward from the Kian-Chienning line against the Red Army's base area. The Red Army had about 40,000 men and was concentrated in the area of Huangpi and Hsiaopu in Ningtu County, Kiangsi Province.

The situation was as follows:

(1) The "suppression" forces did not exceed 100,000 men, none of whom were Chiang Kai-shek's own troops, and the general situation was not very grave.

(2) The enemy division under Lo Lin, defending Kian, was located across the Kan River to the west.

(3) The three enemy divisions under Kung Ping-fan, Chang Hui-tsan and Tan Tao-yuan had advanced and occupied the Futien-Tungku-Lungkang-Yuantou sector southeast of Kian and northwest of Ningtu. The main body of Chang Hui-tsan's division was at Lungkang and that of Tan Tao-yuan's division at Yuantou. It was not advisable to select Futien and Tungku as the battleground, as the inhabitants, misled by the A-B Group, were for a time mistrustful of and opposed to the Red Army.

(4) The enemy division under Liu Ho-ting was far away in Chienning in the White area of Fukien, and was unlikely to cross into Kiangsi.

(5) The two enemy divisions under Mao Ping-wen and Hsu Keh-hsiang had entered the Toupi-Lokou-Tungshao sector lying between Kuangchang and Ningtu. Toupi was a White area, Lokou a guerrilla zone, and Tungshao, where there were A-B Group elements, was a place from which information was liable to leak out. Furthermore, if we were to attack Mao Ping-wen and Hsu Keh-hsiang and then drive westward, the three enemy divisions in the west under Chang Hui-tsan, Tan Tao-yuan and Kung Ping-fan might join forces, thus making it difficult for us to win victory and impossible to bring the issue to a final solution.

(6) The two divisions under Chang Hui-tsan and Tan Tao-yuan, which made up the enemy's main force, were troops belonging to Lu Ti-ping, who was commander-in-chief of this "encirclement and suppression" campaign and governor of Kiangsi Province, and Chang Hui-tsan was the field commander. To wipe out these two divisions would be practically to smash the campaign. Each division had about fourteen thousand men and Chang's was divided between two places, so that if we attacked one division at a time we would enjoy absolute superiority.

(7) The Lungkang-Yuantou sector, where the main forces of the Chang and Tan divisions were located, was close to our concentrations, and there was good popular support to cover our approach.

(8) The terrain in Lungkang was good. Yuantou was not easy to attack. But were the enemy to advance to Hsiaopu to attack us, we would have good terrain there too.

(9) We could mass the largest number of troops in the Lungkang sector. In Hsingkuo, less than a hundred *li* to the southwest of Lungkang, we had an independent division of over one thousand men, which could manoeuvre in the enemy's rear.

(10) If our troops made a breakthrough at the centre and breached the enemy's front, his columns to the east and west would be cut into two widely separated groups.

For the above reasons, we decided that our first battle should be against Chang Hui-tsan's main force, and we successfully hit two of his brigades and his divisional headquarters, capturing the entire force of nine thousand men and the divisional commander himself, without letting a single man or horse escape. This one victory scared Tan's division into fleeing towards Tungshao and Hsu's division into fleeing towards Toupi. Our troops then pursued Tan's division and wiped out half of it. We fought two battles in five days (December 27, 1930 to January 1, 1931), and, fearing defeat, the enemy forces in Futien, Tungku and Toupi retreated in disorder. So ended the first campaign of "encirclement and suppression".

The situation in the second campaign was as follows:

(1) The "suppression" forces numbering 200,000 were under the command of Ho Ying-chin with headquarters at Nanchang.

(2) As in the first enemy campaign, none of the forces were Chiang Kai-shek's own troops. Among them the 19th Route Army

under Tsai Ting-kai, the 26th under Sun Lien-chung and the 8th under Chu Shao-liang were strong, or fairly strong, while all the rest were rather weak.

(3) The A-B Group had been cleaned up, and the entire population of the base area supported the Red Army.

(4) The 5th Route Army under Wang Chin-yu, newly arrived from the north, was afraid of us, and, generally speaking, so were the two divisions on its left flank under Kuo Hua-tsung and Hao Meng-ling.

(5) If our troops attacked Futien first and then swept across to the east, we could expand the base area to the Chienning-Lichuan-Taining sector on the Fukien-Kiangsi border and acquire supplies to help smash the next "encirclement and suppression" campaign. But if we were to thrust westward, we would come up against the Kan River and have no room for expansion after the battle. To turn east again after the battle would tire our troops and waste time.

(6) Though our army (numbering over 30,000 men) was somewhat smaller than in the first campaign, it had had four months in which to recuperate and build up energy.

For these reasons, we decided, for our first battle, to engage the forces of Wang Chin-yu and of Kung Ping-fan (totalling 11 regiments) in the Futien sector. After winning this battle we attacked Kuo Hua-tsung, Sun Lien-chung, Chu Shao-liang and Liu Ho-ting in succession. In fifteen days (from May 16 to May 30, 1931) we marched seven hundred *li*, fought five battles, captured more than twenty thousand rifles and roundly smashed the enemy's "encirclement and suppression" campaign. When fighting Wang Chin-yu, we were between the two enemy forces under Tsai Ting-kai and Kuo Hua-tsung, some ten *li* from the latter and forty *li* from the former, and some people said we were "getting into a blind alley", but we got through all the same. This was mainly due to the popular support we enjoyed in the base area and to the lack of co-ordination among the enemy units. After Kuo Hua-tsung's division was defeated, Hao Meng-ling's division fled by night back to Yungfeng, and so avoided disaster.

The situation in the third "encirclement and suppression" campaign was as follows:

(1) Chiang Kai-shek personally took the field as commander-in-chief. Under him there were three subordinate commanders,

each in charge of a column — the left, the right and the centre. The central column was commanded by Ho Ying-chin, who, like Chiang Kai-shek, had his headquarters in Nanchang, the right was commanded by Chen Ming-shu with headquarters at Kian, and the left by Chu Shao-liang with headquarters at Nanfeng.

(2) The "suppression" forces numbered 300,000. The main forces, totalling about 100,000 men, were Chiang Kai-shek's own troops and consisted of 5 divisions (of 9 regiments each), commanded by Chen Cheng, Lo Cho-ying, Chao Kuan-tao, Wei Li-huang and Chiang Ting-wen respectively. Besides these, there were 3 divisions (totalling 40,000 men) under Chiang Kuang-nai, Tsai Ting-kai and Han Teh-chin. Then there was Sun Lien-chung's army of 20,000. In addition, there were other, weaker forces that were likewise not Chiang's own troops.

(3) The enemy's strategy in this "suppression" campaign was to "drive straight in", which was vastly different from the strategy of "consolidating at every step" he used in the second campaign. The aim was to press the Red Army back against the Kan River and annihilate it there.

(4) There was an interval of only one month between the end of the second enemy campaign and the beginning of the third. The Red Army (then about 30,000 strong) had had neither rest nor replenishments after much hard fighting and had just made a detour of a thousand *li* to concentrate at Hsingkuo in the western part of the southern Kiangsi base area, when the enemy pressed it hard from several directions.

In this situation the plan we first decided on was to move from Hsingkuo by way of Wanan, make a breakthrough at Futien, and then sweep from west to east across the enemy's rear communication lines, thus letting the enemy's main forces make a deep but useless penetration into our base area in southern Kiangsi; this was to be the first phase of our operation. Then when the enemy turned back northward, inevitably very fatigued, we were to seize the opportunity to strike at his vulnerable units; that was to be the second phase of our operation. The heart of this plan was to avoid the enemy's main forces and strike at his weak spots. But when our forces were advancing on Futien, we were detected by the enemy, who rushed the two divisions under Chen Cheng and Lo Cho-ying to the scene. We had to change our plan and fall back to Kaohsinghsu in the

western part of Hsingkuo County, which, together with its environs
of less than a hundred square *li*, was then the only place for our troops
to concentrate in. The day after our concentration we decided to
make a thrust eastward towards Lientang in eastern Hsingkuo County,
Liangtsun in southern Yungfeng County and Huangpi in northern
Ningtu County. That same night, under cover of darkness, we passed
through the forty-*li* gap between Chiang Ting-wen's division and the
forces of Chiang Kuang-nai, Tsai Ting-kai and Han Teh-chin, and
swung to Lientang. On the second day we skirmished with the forward
units under Shangkuan Yun-hsiang (who was in command of Hao
Meng-ling's division as well as his own). The first battle was fought
on the third day with Shangkuan Yun-hsiang's division and the second
battle on the fourth day with Hao Meng-ling's division; after a three-
day march we reached Huangpi and fought our third battle against
Mao Ping-wen's division. We won all three battles and captured over
ten thousand rifles. At this point all the main enemy forces, which
had been advancing westward and southward, turned eastward.
Focusing on Huangpi, they converged at furious speed to seek battle
and closed in on us in a major compact encirclement. We slipped
through in the high mountains that lay in the twenty-*li* gap between
the forces of Chiang Kuang-nai, Tsai Ting-kai and Han Teh-chin on
the one side and Chen Cheng and Lo Cho-ying on the other, and
thus, returning from the east to the west, reassembled within the
borders of Hsingkuo County. By the time the enemy discovered this
fact and began advancing west again, our forces had already had a
fortnight's rest, whereas the enemy forces, hungry, exhausted and
demoralized, were no good for fighting and so decided to retreat.
Taking advantage of their retreat, we attacked the forces of Chiang
Kuang-nai, Tsai Ting-kai, Chiang Ting-wen and Han Teh-chin, wiping
out one of Chiang Ting-wen's brigades and Han Teh-chin's entire
division. As for the divisions under Chiang Kuang-nai and Tsai
Ting-kai, the fight resulted in a stalemate and they got away.

The situation in the fourth "encirclement and suppression" campaign was as follows. The enemy was advancing on Kuangchang in
three columns; the eastern one was his main force, while the two
divisions forming his western column were exposed to us and were
also very close to the area where our forces were concentrated. Thus
we had the opportunity to attack his western column in southern
Yihuang County first, and at one stroke we annihilated the two
divisions under Li Ming and Chen Shih-chi. As the enemy then sent

two divisions from the eastern column to give support to his central column and advanced further, we were again able to wipe out a division in southern Yihuang County. In these two battles we captured more than ten thousand rifles and, in the main, smashed this campaign of "encirclement and suppression".

In his fifth campaign the enemy advanced by means of his new strategy of building blockhouses and first occupied Lichuan. But, in attempting to recover Lichuan and engage the enemy outside the base area, we made an attack north of Lichuan at Hsiaoshih, which was an enemy strongpoint and was situated, moreover, in the White area. Failing to win the battle, we shifted our attack to Tzehsichiao, which was also an enemy strongpoint situated in the White area southeast of Hsiaoshih, and again we failed. Then in seeking battle we milled around between the enemy's main forces and his block-houses and were reduced to complete passivity. All through our fifth counter-campaign against "encirclement and suppression", which lasted a whole year, we showed not the slightest initiative or drive. In the end we had to withdraw from our Kiangsi base area.

Our army's experience in these five counter-campaigns against "encirclement and suppression" proves that the first battle in the counter-offensive is of the greatest importance for the Red Army, which is on the defensive, if it is to smash a large and powerful enemy "suppression" force. Victory or defeat in the first battle has a tremendous effect upon the entire situation, all the way to the final engagement. Hence we arrive at the following conclusions.

First, the first battle must be won. We should strike only when positively certain that the enemy's situation, the terrain and popular support are all in our favour and not in his. Otherwise we should rather fall back and carefully bide our time. There will always be opportunities; we should not rashly accept battle. In our first counter-campaign we originally planned to strike at Tan Tao-yuan's troops; we advanced twice but each time had to restrain ourselves and pull back, because they would not budge from their commanding position on the Yuantou heights. A few days later we sought out Chang Hui-tsan's troops, which were more vulnerable to our attack. In our second counter-campaign our army advanced to Tungku where, for the sole purpose of waiting for Wang Chin-yu's men to leave their strongpoint at Futien, we encamped close to the enemy for twenty-five days even at the risk of leakage of information; we rejected all impatient suggestions for a quick attack and finally attained our aim. In our third counter-campaign, although the storm was breaking all around us and we had made a detour of a thousand *li*, and although the enemy had discovered our plan to outflank him, we nevertheless exercised patience, turned back, changed our tactics to a breakthrough in the centre, and finally fought the first battle successfully at Lientang. In our fourth counter-campaign, after our attack on Nanfeng had failed, we unhesitatingly withdrew, wheeled round to the enemy's right flank, and reassembled our forces in the area of Tungshao, where-upon we launched our great and victorious battle in southern Yihuang County. It was only in the fifth counter-campaign that the importance of the first battle was not recognized at all. Taking alarm at the loss of the single county town of Lichuan, our forces marched north to meet the enemy in an attempt to recover it. Then, the unexpected encounter at Hsunkou, which had resulted in a victory (with the annihilation of an enemy division), was not treated as the first battle, nor were the changes that were bound to ensue foreseen, but instead Hsiaoshih was rashly attacked with no assurance of success. Thus the initiative was lost at the very first move, and that is really the worst and most stupid way to fight.

Second, the plan for the first battle must be the prelude to, and an organic part of, the plan for the whole campaign. Without a good plan for the whole campaign it is absolutely impossible to fight a really good first battle. That is to say, even though victory is won in the first battle, if the battle harms rather than helps the campaign as a whole, such a victory can only be reckoned a defeat (as in the case of the battle of Hsunkou in the fifth campaign). Hence, before fighting the first battle one must have a general idea of how the second, third, fourth, and even the final battle will be fought, and consider what changes will ensue in the enemy's situation as a whole if we win, or lose, each of the succeeding battles. Although the result may not — and, in fact, definitely will not — turn out exactly as we expect, we must think everything out carefully and realistically in the light of the general situation on both sides. Without a grasp of the situation as a whole, it is impossible to make any really good move on the chessboard.

Third, one must also consider what will happen in the next strategic stage of the war. Whoever directs strategy will not be doing his duty if he occupies himself only with the counter-offensive and neglects the measures to be taken after it succeeds, or in case it fails. In a particular strategic stage, he should take into consideration the succeeding stages, or, at the very least, the following one. Even though future changes are difficult to foresee and the farther ahead one looks the more blurred things seem, a general calculation is possible and an appraisal of distant prospects is necessary. In war as well as in politics, planning only one step at a time as one goes along is a harmful way of directing matters. After each step, it is necessary to examine the ensuing concrete changes and to modify or develop one's strategic and operational plans accordingly, or otherwise one is liable to make the mistake of rushing straight ahead regardless of danger. However, it is absolutely essential to have a long-term plan which has been thought out in its general outline and which covers an entire strategic stage or even several strategic stages. Failure to make such a plan will lead to the mistake of hesitating and allowing oneself to be tied down, which in fact serves the enemy's strategic objects and reduces one to a passive position. It must be borne in mind that the enemy's supreme command is not lacking in strategic insight. Only when we have trained ourselves to be a head taller than the enemy will strategic victories be possible. During the enemy's fifth "encirclement and suppression" campaign, failure to do so was the main reason for the errors in strategic direction under the "Left" opportunist and the Chang Kuo-tao lines. In short, in the stage of retreat we must see ahead to the stage of the counter-offensive, in the stage of the counter-offensive we must see ahead to that of the offensive, and in the stage of the offensive we must again see ahead to a stage of retreat. Not to do so but to confine ourselves to considerations of the moment is to court defeat.

The first battle must be won. The plan for the whole campaign must be taken into account. And the strategic stage that comes next must be taken into account. These are the three principles we must never forget when we begin a counter-offensive, that is, when we fight the first battle.

6. CONCENTRATION OF TROOPS

The concentration of troops seems easy but is quite hard in practice. Everybody knows that the best way is to use a large force to defeat a small one, and yet many people fail to do so and on the contrary often divide their forces up. The reason is that such military leaders have no head for strategy and are confused by complicated circumstances; hence, they are at the mercy of these circumstances, lose their initiative and have recourse to passive response.

No matter how complicated, grave and harsh the circumstances, what a military leader needs most of all is the ability to function independently in organizing and employing the forces under his command. He may often be forced into a passive position by the enemy, but the important thing is to regain the initiative quickly. Failure to do so spells defeat.

The initiative is not something imaginary but is concrete and material. Here the most important thing is to conserve and mass an armed force that is as large as possible and full of fighting spirit.

It is easy to fall into a passive position in defensive warfare, which gives far less scope for the full exercise of initiative than does offensive warfare. However, defensive warfare, which is passive in form, can be active in content, and can be switched from the stage in which it is passive in form to the stage in which it is active both in form and in content. In appearance a fully planned strategic retreat is made under compulsion, but in reality it is effected in order to conserve our strength and bide our time to defeat the enemy, to lure him in deep and prepare for our counter-offensive. On the other hand, refusal to retreat and hasty acceptance of battle (as in the battle of Hsiaoshih) may appear a serious effort to gain the initiative, while in reality it is passive. Not only is a strategic counter-offensive active in content, but in form, too, it discards the passive posture of the period of retreat. In relation to the enemy, our counter-offensive represents our effort to make him relinquish the initiative and put him in a passive position.

Concentration of troops, mobile warfare, war of quick decision and war of annihilation are all necessary conditions for the full achievement of this aim. And of these, concentration of troops is the first and most essential.

This concentration is necessary for the purpose of reversing the situation as between the enemy and ourselves. First, its purpose is to reverse the situation as regards advance and retreat. Previously it was the enemy who was advancing and we who were retreating; now we seek a situation in which we advance and he retreats. When we concentrate our troops and win a battle, then in that battle we gain the above purpose, and this influences the whole campaign.

Second, its purpose is to reverse the situation with regard to attack and defence. In defensive warfare the retreat to the prescribed terminal point belongs basically to the passive, or "defence", stage. The counter-offensive belongs to the active, or "attack", stage. Although the strategic defensive retains its defensive character throughout its duration, still as compared with the retreat the counter-offensive already represents a change not only in form but in content. The counter-offensive is transitional between the strategic defensive and the strategic offensive, and in the nature of a prelude to the strategic offensive; it is precisely for the purpose of the counter-offensive that troops are concentrated.

Third, its purpose is to reverse the situation with regard to interior and exterior lines. An army operating on strategically interior lines suffers from many disadvantages, and this is especially so in the case of the Red Army, confronted as it is with "encirclement and suppression". But in campaigns and battles we can and absolutely must change this situation. We can turn a big "encirclement and suppression" campaign waged by the enemy against us into a number of small, separate campaigns of encirclement and suppression waged by us against the enemy. We can change the converging attack directed by the enemy against us on the plane of strategy into converging attacks directed by us against the enemy on the plane of campaigns and battles. We can change the enemy's strategic superiority over us into our superiority over him in campaigns and battles. We can put the enemy who is in a strong position strategically into a weak position in campaigns and battles. At the same time we can change our own strategically weak position into a strong position in campaigns and battles. This is what we call exterior-line operations within interior-line operations, encirclement and suppression within "encirclement and suppression", blockade within blockade, the offensive within the defensive, superiority within inferiority, strength within weakness, advantage within disadvantage, and initiative within passivity. The winning of victory in the strategic defensive depends basically on this measure — concentration of troops.

In the war annals of the Chinese Red Army, this has often been an important controversial issue. In the battle of Kian on October 4, 1930, our advance and attack were begun before our forces were fully concentrated, but fortunately the enemy force (Teng Ying's division) fled of its own accord; by itself our attack was ineffective.

Beginning from 1932, there was the slogan "Attack on all fronts", which called for attacks from the base area in all directions — north, south, east and west. This is wrong not only for the strategic defensive but even for the strategic offensive. As long as there is no fundamental change in the over-all balance of forces, both strategy and tactics involve the defensive and the offensive, containing actions and assaults, and "attacks on all fronts" are in fact extremely rare. This slogan expresses the military equalitarianism which accompanies military adventurism.

In 1933 the exponents of military equalitarianism put forward the theory of "striking with two 'fists'" and splitting the main force of the Red Army in two, to seek victories simultaneously in two strategic directions. As a result, one fist remained idle while the other was tired out with fighting, and we failed to win the greatest victory possible at the time. In my opinion, when we face a powerful enemy, we should employ our army, whatever its size, in only one main direction at a time, not two. I am not objecting to operations in two or more directions, but at any given time there ought to be only one main direction. The Chinese Red Army, which entered the arena of the civil war as a small and weak force, has since repeatedly defeated its powerful antagonist and won victories that have astonished the world, and it has done so by relying largely on the employment of concentrated strength. Any one of its great victories can prove this point. When we say, "Pit one against ten, pit ten against a hundred", we are speaking of strategy, of the whole war and the over-all balance of forces, and in the strategic sense that is just what we have been doing. However, we are not speaking of campaigns and tactics, in which we must never do so. Whether in counter-offensives or offensives, we should always concentrate a big force to strike at one part of the enemy forces. We suffered every time we did not concentrate our troops, as in the battles against Tan Tao-yuan in the Tungshao area of Ningtu County in Kiangsi Province in January 1931, against the 19th Route Army in the Kaohsinghsu area of Hsingkuo County in Kiangsi in August 1931, against Chen Chi-tang in the Shuikouhsu area of Nanhsiung County in Kwangtung Province in July 1932, and against Chen Cheng in the Tuantsun area of Lichuan County in Kiangsi in March 1934. In the past, battles such as those of Shuikouhsu and Tuantsun were generally deemed victories or even big victories (in the former we routed twenty regiments under Chen Chi-tang, in the latter twelve regiments under Chen Cheng), but we never welcomed such victories and in a certain sense even regarded them as defeats. For, in our opinion, a battle has little significance when there are no prisoners or war booty, or when they do not outweigh the losses.

Our strategy is "pit one against ten" and our tactics are "pit ten against one" — this is one of our fundamental principles for gaining mastery over the enemy.

Military equalitarianism reached its extreme point in our fifth counter-campaign against "encirclement and suppression" in 1934. It was thought that we could beat the enemy by "dividing the forces into six routes" and "resisting on all fronts", but instead we were beaten by the enemy, and the reason was fear of losing territory. Naturally one can scarcely avoid loss of territory when concentrating the main forces in one direction while leaving only containing forces in others. But this loss is temporary and partial and is compensated for by victory in the place where the assault is made. After such a victory is won, territory lost in the area of the containing forces can be recovered. The enemy's first, second, third and fourth campaigns of "encirclement and suppression" all entailed the loss of territory — particularly the third campaign, in which the Kiangsi base area of the Red Army was almost completely lost — but in the end we not only recovered but extended our territory.

Failure to appreciate the strength of the people in the base area has often given rise to unwarranted fear of moving the Red Army too far away from the base area. This happened when the Red Army in Kiangsi made a long drive to attack Changchow in Fukien Province in 1932, and also when it wheeled around to attack Fukien after the victory in our fourth counter-campaign in 1933. There was fear in the first case that the enemy would seize the entire base area, and in the second that he would seize part of it; consequently there was opposition to concentrating our forces and advocacy of dividing them up for defence, but in the end all this proved to be wrong. As far as the enemy is concerned, he is afraid to advance into our base area, but the main danger in his eyes is a Red Army that has driven into the White area. His attention is always fixed on the whereabouts of the main force of the Red Army, and he rarely takes his eyes off it to concentrate on the base area. Even when the Red Army is on the defensive, it is still the centre of the enemy's attention. Part of his over-all plan is to reduce the size of our base area, but if the Red Army concentrates its main force to annihilate one of his columns, the enemy's supreme command will be compelled to focus greater attention on the Red Army and concentrate larger forces against it. Hence it is possible to wreck an enemy plan for reducing the size of a base area.

Also, it was wrong to say, "In the fifth 'encirclement and suppression' campaign which is being carried on by means of blockhouse warfare, it is impossible for us to operate with concentrated forces, and all we can do is to divide them up for defence and for short swift thrusts." The enemy's tactics of pushing forward 3, 5, 8, or 10 *li* at a time and building blockhouses at each halt were entirely the result of the Red Army's practice of fighting defensive actions at every successive point. The situation would certainly have been different if our army had abandoned the tactics of point-by-point defence on interior lines and, when possible and necessary, had turned and driven into the enemy's interior lines. The principle of concentration of forces is precisely the means for defeating the enemy's blockhouse warfare.

The kind of concentration of forces we advocate does not mean the abandonment of people's guerrilla warfare. To abandon small-scale guerrilla warfare and "concentrate every single rifle in the Red Army", as advocated by the Li Li-san line, has long since been proved wrong. Considering the revolutionary war as a whole, the operations of the people's guerrillas and those of the main forces of the Red Army complement each other like a man's right arm and left arm, and if we had only the main forces of the Red Army without the people's guerrillas, we would be like a warrior with only one arm. In concrete terms, and especially with regard to military operations, when we talk of the people in the base area as a factor, we mean that we have an armed people. That is the main reason why the enemy is afraid to approach our base area.

It is also necessary to employ Red Army detachments for operations in secondary directions; not all the forces of the Red Army should be concentrated. The kind of concentration we advocate is based on the principle of guaranteeing absolute or relative superiority on the battlefield. To cope with a strong enemy or to fight on a battlefield of vital importance, we must have an absolutely superior force; for instance, a force of 40,000 was concentrated to fight the 9,000 men under Chang Hui-tsan on December 30, 1930, in the first battle of our first counter-campaign. To cope with a weaker enemy or to fight on a battlefield of no great importance, a relatively superior force is sufficient; for instance, only some 10,000 Red Army men were employed to fight Liu Ho-ting's division of 7,000 men in Chienning on May 29, 1931, in the last battle of our second counter-campaign.

That is not to say we must have numerical superiority on every occasion. In certain circumstances, we may go into battle with a relatively or absolutely inferior force. Take the case of going into battle with a relatively inferior force when we have only a rather small Red Army force in a certain area (it is not that we have more troops and have not concentrated them). Then, in order to smash the attack of the stronger enemy in conditions where popular support, terrain and weather are greatly in our favour, it is of course necessary to concentrate the main part of our Red Army force for a surprise attack on a segment of one flank of the enemy while containing his centre and his other flank with guerrillas or small detachments, and in this way victory can be won. In our surprise attack on this segment of the enemy flank, the principle of using a superior force against an inferior force, of using the many to defeat the few, still applies. The same principle also applies when we go into battle with an absolutely inferior force, for example, when a guerrilla force makes a surprise attack on a large White army force, but is attacking only a small part of it.

As for the argument that the concentration of a large force for action in a single battle area is subject to the limitations of terrain, roads, supplies and billeting facilities, it should be evaluated according to the circumstances. There is a difference in the degree to which these limitations affect the Red Army and the White army, as the Red Army can stand greater hardships than the White army.

We use the few to defeat the many — this we say to the rulers of China as a whole. We use the many to defeat the few — this we say to each separate enemy force on the battlefield. That is no longer a secret, and in general the enemy is by now well acquainted with our way. However, he can neither prevent our victories nor avoid his own losses, because he does not know when and where we shall act. This we keep secret. The Red Army generally operates by surprise attacks.

7. MOBILE WARFARE

Mobile warfare or positional warfare? Our answer is mobile warfare. So long as we lack a large army or reserves of ammunition, and so long as there is only a single Red Army force to do the fighting in each base area, positional warfare is generally useless to us. For us, positional warfare is generally inapplicable in attack as well as in defence.

One of the outstanding characteristics of the Red Army's operations, which follows from the fact that the enemy is powerful while the Red Army is deficient in technical equipment, is the absence of fixed battle lines.

The Red Army's battle lines are determined by the direction in which it is operating. As its operational direction often shifts, its battle lines are fluid. Though the main direction does not change in a given period of time, within its ambit the secondary directions may shift at any moment; when we find ourselves checked in one direction, we must turn to another. If, after a time, we also find ourselves checked in the main direction, then we must change it too.

In a revolutionary civil war, there cannot be fixed battle lines, which was also the case in the Soviet Union. The difference between the Soviet Army and ours is that its battle lines were not so fluid as ours. There cannot be absolutely fixed battle lines in any war, because the vicissitudes of victory and defeat, advance and retreat, preclude it. But relatively fixed battle lines are often to be found in the general run of wars. Exceptions occur only where an army faces a much stronger enemy, as is the case with the Chinese Red Army in its present stage.

Fluidity of battle lines leads to fluidity in the size of our base areas. Our base areas are constantly expanding and contracting, and often as one base area falls another rises. This fluidity of territory is entirely a result of the fluidity of the war.

Fluidity in the war and in our territory produces fluidity in all fields of construction in our base areas. Construction plans covering several years are out of the question. Frequent changes of plan are all in the day's work.

It is to our advantage to recognize this characteristic. We must base our planning on it and must not have illusions about a war of advance without any retreats, take alarm at any temporary fluidity of our territory or of the rear areas of our army, or endeavour to draw up detailed long-term plans. We must adapt our thinking and our work to the circumstances, be ready to sit down as well as to march on, and always have our marching rations handy. It is only by exerting ourselves in today's fluid way of life that tomorrow we can secure relative stability, and eventually full stability.

The exponents of the strategy of "regular warfare" which dominated our fifth counter-campaign denied this fluidity and opposed what they called "guerrilla-ism". Those comrades who opposed fluidity managed affairs as though they were the rulers of a big state, and the result was an extraordinary and immense fluidity — the 25,000-*li* Long March.

Our workers' and peasants' democratic republic is a state, but today it is not yet a full-fledged one. Today we are still in the period of strategic defensive in the civil war, the form of our political power is still far from that of a full-fledged state, our army is still much inferior to the enemy both in numbers and technical equipment, our territory is still very small, and our enemy is constantly out to destroy us and will never rest content till he has done so. In defining our policy on the basis of these facts, we should not repudiate guerrilla-ism in general terms but should honestly admit the guerrilla character of the Red Army. It is no use being ashamed of this. On the contrary, this guerrilla character is precisely our distinguishing feature, our strong point, and our means of defeating the enemy. We should be prepared to discard it, but we cannot do so today. In the future this guerrilla character will definitely become something to be ashamed of and to be discarded, but today it is invaluable and we must stick to it.

"Fight when you can win, move away when you can't win" — this is the popular way of describing our mobile warfare today. There is no military expert anywhere in the world who approves only of fighting and never of moving, though few people do as much moving as we do. We generally spend more time in moving than in fighting and would be doing well if we fought an average of one sizable battle a month. All our "moving" is for the purpose of "fighting", and all our strategy and tactics are built on "fighting". Nevertheless, there are times when it is inadvisable for us to fight. In the first place, it is inadvisable to fight when the force confronting us is too large; second, it is sometimes inadvisable to fight when the force confronting us, though not so large, is very close to other enemy forces; third, it is generally inadvisable to fight an enemy force that is not isolated and is strongly entrenched; fourth, it is inadvisable to continue an engagement in which there is no prospect of victory. In any one of these situations we are prepared to move away. Such moving away is both permissible and necessary. For our recognition of the necessity of moving away is based on our recognition of the necessity of fighting. Herein lies the fundamental characteristic of the Red Army's mobile warfare.

Mobile warfare is primary, but we do not reject positional warfare where it is possible and necessary. It should be admitted that positional warfare should be employed for the tenacious defence of particular key points in a containing action during the strategic defensive, and when, during the strategic offensive, we encounter an enemy force that is isolated and cut off from help. We have had considerable experience in defeating the enemy by such positional warfare; we have cracked open many enemy cities, blockhouses and forts and broken through fairly well-fortified enemy field positions. In future we shall increase our efforts and remedy our inadequacies in this respect. We should by all means advocate positional attack or defence when circumstances require and permit it. At the present time, what we are opposed to is the general use of positional warfare or putting it on an equal footing with mobile warfare; that is impermissible.

During the ten years' civil war, have there been no changes whatsoever in the guerrilla character of the Red Army, its lack of fixed battle lines, the fluidity of its base areas, or the fluidity of construction work in its base areas? Yes, there have been changes. The period from the days in the Chingkang Mountains to our first counter-campaign against "encirclement and suppression" in Kiangsi was the first stage, the stage in which the guerrilla character and fluidity were very pronounced, the Red Army being in its infancy and the base areas still being guerrilla zones. In the second stage, comprising the period from the first to the third counter-campaign, both the guerrilla character and the fluidity were considerably reduced, front armies having been formed and base areas with a population of several millions established. In the third stage, which comprised the period from the end of the third to the fifth counter-campaign, the guerrilla character and the fluidity were further reduced, and a central government and a revolutionary military commission had already been set up. The fourth stage was the Long March. The mistaken rejection of guerrilla warfare and fluidity on a small scale had led to guerrilla warfare and fluidity on a great scale. Now we are in the fifth stage. Because of our failure to smash the fifth "encirclement and suppression" campaign and because of this great fluidity, the Red Army and the base areas have been greatly reduced, but we have planted our feet in the Northwest and consolidated and developed the Shensi-Kansu-Ningsia Border Region, our base area here. The three front armies which form the main forces of the Red Army have been brought under a unified command, which is unprecedented.

Going by the nature of our strategy, we may also say the period from the days in the Chingkang Mountains to our fourth counter-campaign was one stage, the period of the fifth counter-campaign was another, and the period from the Long March to the present is the third. During the fifth counter-campaign the correct policy of the past was wrongly discarded; today we have correctly discarded the wrong policy adopted during the fifth counter-campaign and revived the earlier and correct policy. However, we have not thrown out everything in the fifth counter-campaign, nor revived everything that preceded it. We have revived only what was good in the past, and discarded only the mistakes of the period of the fifth counter-campaign.

Guerrilla-ism has two aspects. One is irregularity, that is, decentralization, lack of uniformity, absence of strict discipline, and simple methods of work. These features stemmed from the Red Army's infancy, and some of them were just what was needed at the time. As the Red Army reaches a higher stage, we must gradually and consciously eliminate them so as to make the Red Army more centralized, more unified, more disciplined and more thorough in its work — in short, more regular in character. In the directing of operations we should also gradually and consciously reduce such guerrilla characteristics as are no longer required at a higher stage. Refusal to make progress in this respect and obstinate adherence to the old stage are impermissible and harmful, and are detrimental to large-scale operations.

The other aspect of guerrilla-ism consists of the principle of mobile warfare, the guerrilla character of both strategic and tactical operations which is still necessary at present, the inevitable fluidity of our base areas, flexibility in planning the development of the base areas, and the rejection of premature regularization in building the Red Army. In this connection, it is equally impermissible, disadvantageous and harmful to our present operations to deny the facts of history, oppose the retention of what is useful, and rashly leave the present stage in order to rush blindly towards a "new stage", which as yet is beyond reach and has no real significance.

We are now on the eve of a new stage with respect to the Red
Army's technical equipment and organization. We must be prepared
to go over to this new stage. Not to prepare ourselves would be
wrong and harmful to our future warfare. In the future, when the
technical and organizational conditions in the Red Army have
changed and the building of the Red Army has entered a new stage,
its operational directions and battle lines will become more stable;
there will be more positional warfare; the fluidity of the war, of
our territory and of our construction work will be greatly reduced
and finally disappear; and we will no longer be handicapped by
present limitations, such as the enemy's superiority and his strongly
entrenched positions.

At present we oppose both the wrong measures of the period of
the domination of "Left" opportunism and the revival of many of the
irregular features which the Red Army had in its infancy but which
are now unnecessary. But we should be resolute in restoring the many
valuable principles of army building and of strategy and tactics by
which the Red Army has consistently won its victories. We must sum
up all that is good from the past in a systematic, more highly developed
and richer military line, in order to win victories over the enemy today
and prepare to go over to the new stage in the future.

The waging of mobile warfare involves many problems, such as
reconnaissance, judgement, decision, combat disposition, command,
concealment, concentration, advance, deployment, attack, pursuit,
surprise attack, positional attack, positional defence, encounter action,
retreat, night fighting, special operations, evading the strong and
attacking the weak, besieging the enemy in order to strike at his
reinforcements, feint attack, defence against aircraft, operating
amongst several enemy forces, by-passing operations, consecutive
operations, operating without a rear, the need for rest and building
up energy. These problems exhibited many specific features in the
history of the Red Army, features which should be methodically dealt
with and summed up in the science of campaigns, and I shall not go
into them here.

8. WAR OF QUICK DECISION

A strategically protracted war and campaigns or battles of quick
decision are two aspects of the same thing, two principles which should

receive equal and simultaneous emphasis in civil wars and which are also applicable in anti-imperialist wars.

Because the reactionary forces are very strong, revolutionary forces grow only gradually, and this fact determines the protracted nature of our war. Here impatience is harmful and advocacy of "quick decision" incorrect. To wage a revolutionary war for ten years, as we have done, might be surprising in other countries, but for us it is like the opening sections in an "eight-legged essay" — the "presentation, amplification and preliminary exposition of the theme"[36] — and many exciting parts are yet to follow. No doubt developments in the future will be greatly accelerated under the influence of domestic and international conditions. As changes have already taken place in the international and domestic situation and greater changes are coming, it can be said that we have outgrown the past state of slow development and fighting in isolation. But we should not expect successes overnight. The aspiration to "wipe out the enemy before breakfast" is admirable, but it is bad to make concrete plans to do so. As China's reactionary forces are backed by many imperialist powers, our revolutionary war will continue to be a protracted one until China's revolutionary forces have built up enough strength to breach the main positions of our internal and external enemies, and until the international revolutionary forces have crushed or contained most of the international reactionary forces. To proceed from this point in formulating our strategy of long-term warfare is one of the important principles guiding our strategy.

The reverse is true of campaigns and battles — here the principle is not protractedness but quick decision. Quick decision is sought in campaigns and battles, and this is true at all times and in all countries. In a war as a whole, too, quick decision is sought at all times and in all countries, and a long drawn-out war is considered harmful. China's war, however, must be handled with the greatest patience and treated as a protracted war. During the period of the Li Li-san line, some people ridiculed our way of doing things as "shadow-boxing tactics" (meaning our tactics of fighting many battles back and forth before going on to seize the big cities), and said that we would not see the victory of the revolution until our hair turned white. Such impatience was proved wrong long ago. But if their criticism had been applied not to strategy but to campaigns and battles, they would have been perfectly right, and for the following reasons. First, the Red Army has no sources from which to replenish its arms and especially its ammunition; second, the White forces consist of many armies while there is only one Red Army, which must be prepared to fight one operation after another in quick succession in order to smash each campaign of "encirclement and suppression"; and third, though the White armies advance separately, most of them keep fairly close to one another, and if we fail to gain a quick decision in attacking one of them, all the others will converge upon us. For these reasons we have to fight battles of quick decision. It is usual for us to conclude a battle in a few hours, or in a day or two. It is only when our plan is to "besiege the enemy in order to strike at his reinforcements" and our purpose is to strike not at the besieged enemy but at his reinforcements that we are prepared for a certain degree of protractedness in our besieging operations; but even then we seek a quick decision against the reinforcements. A plan of protracted operations is often applied in campaigns or battles when we are strategically on the defensive and are tenaciously defending positions on a holding front, or when, in a strategic offensive, we are attacking isolated enemy forces cut off from help, or are eliminating White strongholds within our base areas. But protracted operations of this kind help rather than hinder the main Red Army force in its battles of quick decision.

A quick decision cannot be achieved simply by wanting it, but requires many specific conditions. The main requirements are: adequate preparations, seizing the opportune moment, concentration of superior forces, encircling and outflanking tactics, favourable terrain, and striking at the enemy when he is on the move, or when he is stationary but has not yet consolidated his positions. Unless these requirements are satisfied, it is impossible to achieve quick decision in a campaign or battle.

The smashing of an enemy "encirclement and suppression" is a major campaign, but the principle of quick decision and not that of protractedness still applies. For the manpower, financial resources and military strength of a base area do not allow protractedness.

While quick decision is the general principle, we must oppose undue impatience. It is altogether necessary that the highest military and political leading body of a revolutionary base area, having taken into account the circumstances in its base area and the situation of the enemy, should not be overawed by his truculence, dispirited by hardships that can be endured, or dejected by setbacks, but should have the requisite patience and stamina. The smashing of the first enemy "encirclement and suppression" campaign in Kiangsi Province took only one week from the first battle to the last; the second was smashed in barely a fortnight; the third dragged on for three months before it was smashed; the fourth took three weeks; and the fifth taxed our endurance for a whole year. When we were compelled to break through the enemy's encirclement after the failure to smash his fifth campaign, we showed an unjustifiable haste. In the circumstances then obtaining, we could well have held out for another two or three months, giving the troops some time for rest and reorganization. If that had been done, and if the leadership had been a little wiser after our breakthrough, the outcome would have been very different.

For all that, the principle of shortening the duration of a campaign by every possible means remains valid. Campaign and battle plans should call for our maximum effort in concentration of troops, mobile warfare, and so on, so as to ensure the destruction of the enemy's effective strength on the interior lines (that is, in the base area) and the quick defeat of his "encirclement and suppression" campaign, but where it is evident that the campaign cannot be terminated on our interior lines, we should employ the main Red Army force to break through the enemy's encirclement and switch to our exterior lines (that is, the enemy's interior lines) in order to defeat him there. Now that the enemy has developed his blockhouse warfare to a high degree, this will become our usual method of operation. At the time of the Fukien Incident,[37] two months after the commencement of our fifth counter-campaign, the main forces of the Red Army should undoubtedly have thrust into the Kiangsu-Chekiang-Anhwei-Kiangsi region, with Chekiang as the centre, and swept over the length and breadth of the area between Hangchow, Soochow, Nanking, Wuhu, Nanchang and Foochow, turning our strategic defensive into a strategic offensive, menacing the enemy's vital centres and seeking battles in the vast areas where there were no blockhouses. By such means we could have compelled the enemy, who was attacking southern Kiangsi and western Fukien, to turn back to defend his vital centres, broken his attack on the base area in Kiangsi and rendered aid to Fukien People's Government — we certainly could have aided it by this means. As this plan was rejected, the enemy's fifth "encirclement and suppression" campaign could not be broken, and the People's Government in Fukien inevitably collapsed. Even after a year's fighting, though it had become inopportune for us to advance on Chekiang, we could still have turned to the strategic offensive in another direction by moving our main forces towards Hunan, that is, by driving into central Hunan instead of going through Hunan to Kweichow, and in this way we could have manoeuvred the enemy from Kiangsi into Hunan and destroyed him there. As this plan, too, was rejected, all hope of breaking the enemy's fifth campaign was finally dashed, and we had no alternative but to set out on the Long March.

9. WAR OF ANNIHILATION

It is inappropriate to advocate a "contest of attrition" for the Chinese Red Army today. A "contest of treasures" not between Dragon Kings but between a Dragon King and a beggar would be rather ludicrous. For the Red Army which gets almost all its supplies from the enemy, war of annihilation is the basic policy. Only by annihilating the enemy's effective strength can we smash his "encirclement and suppression" campaigns and expand our revolutionary base areas. Inflicting casualties is a means of annihilating the enemy, or otherwise there would be no sense to it. We incur losses ourselves in inflicting casualties on the enemy, but we replenish ourselves by annihilating his units, thereby not only making good our losses but adding to the strength of our army. A battle in which the enemy is routed is not basically decisive in a contest with a foe of great strength. A battle of annihilation, on the other hand, produces a great and immediate impact on any enemy. Injuring all of a man's ten fingers is not as effective as chopping off one, and routing ten enemy divisions is not as effective as annihilating one of them.

Our policy for dealing with the enemy's first, second, third and fourth "encirclement and suppression" campaigns was war of annihilation. The forces annihilated in each campaign constituted only part of his total strength, and yet all these "encirclement and suppression" campaigns were smashed. In our fifth counter-campaign, however, the opposite policy was pursued, which in fact helped the enemy to attain his aims.

War of annihilation entails the concentration of superior forces and the adoption of encircling or outflanking tactics. We cannot have the former without the latter. Conditions such as popular support, favourable terrain, a vulnerable enemy force and the advantage of surprise are all indispensable for the purpose of annihilation.

Merely routing one enemy force or permitting it to escape has meaning only if, in the battle or campaign as a whole, our main force is concentrating its operations of annihilation against another enemy force, or otherwise it is meaningless. Here the losses are justified by the gains.

In establishing our own war industry we must not allow ourselves to become dependent on it. Our basic policy is to rely on the war industries of the imperialist countries and of our domestic enemy. We have a claim on the output of the arsenals of London as well as of Hanyang, and, what is more, it is delivered to us by the enemy's transport corps. This is the sober truth, it is not a jest.

NOTES

[1] The science of strategy, the science of campaigns and the science of tactics are all components of Chinese military science. The science of strategy deals with the laws that govern the war situation as a whole. The science of campaigns deals with the laws that govern campaigns and is applied in directing campaigns. The science of tactics deals with the laws that govern battles and is applied in directing battles.

[2] Sun Wu Tzu, or Sun Wu, was a famous Chinese military scientist in the 5th century B.C., who wrote *Sun Tzu*, a treatise on war containing thirteen chapters. This quotation is from Chapter 3, "The Strategy of Attack".

[3] When Comrade Mao Tse-tung wrote this article in 1936, it was exactly fifteen years since the founding of the Chinese Communist Party in July 1921.

[4] Chen Tu-hsiu was originally a professor at Peking University and became famous as an editor of *New Youth*. He was one of the founders of the Communist Party of China. Owing to his reputation at the time of the May 4th Movement and owing to the Party's immaturity in its initial period, he became General Secretary of the Party. In the last period of the revolution of 1924-27, the Rightist thinking in the Party represented by Chen Tu-hsiu developed into a line of capitulationism. Comrade Mao Tse-tung has observed that the capitulationists at that time "voluntarily gave up the Party's leadership of the peasant masses, urban petty bourgeoisie and middle bourgeoisie, and in particular gave up the Party's leadership of the armed forces, thus causing the defeat of the revolution" ("The Present Situation and Our Tasks", *Selected Works of Mao Tse-tung*, Eng. ed., FLP, Peking, 1961, Vol. IV, p. 171). After the defeat of 1927 Chen Tu-hsiu and a handful of other capitulationists lost faith in the future of the revolution and became liquidationists. They took the reactionary Trotskyist stand and together with the Trotskyites formed a small anti-Party group. Consequently Chen Tu-hsiu was expelled from the Party in November 1929. He died in 1942.

[5] The "Left" opportunism of Li Li-san, generally known as the "Li Li-san line", refers to the "Left" opportunist line which existed in the Party for about four months beginning from June 1930 and which was represented by Comrade Li Li-san, then the

most influential leader of the Central Committee of the Communist Party of China. The Li Li-san line had the following characteristics: It violated the policy of the Party's Sixth National Congress; it denied that mass strength had to be built up for the revolution and denied that the development of the revolution was uneven; it regarded as "extremely erroneous . . . localism and conservatism characteristic of peasant mentality" the ideas of Comrade Mao Tse-tung that for a long time we should devote our attention mainly to creating rural base areas, use the rural areas to encircle the cities and use these bases to advance a high tide of country-wide revolution; and it held that preparations should be made for immediate insurrections in all parts of the country. On the basis of this erroneous line, Comrade Li Li-san drew up an adventurist plan for organizing immediate armed insurrections in the key cities throughout the country. At the same time, he refused to recognize the uneven development of the world revolution, holding that the general outbreak of the Chinese revolution would inevitably lead to a general outbreak of world revolution, without which the Chinese revolution could not be successful; he also refused to recognize the protracted nature of China's bourgeois-democratic revolution, holding that the beginnings of victory in one or more provinces would mark the beginning of the transition to socialist revolution, and thus formulated a number of inappropriate "Left" adventurist policies. Comrade Mao Tse-tung opposed this erroneous line, and the broad masses of cadres and members in the Party also demanded its rectification. At the Third Plenary Session of the Party's Sixth Central Committee in September 1930 Comrade Li Li-san admitted the mistakes that had been pointed out and then relinquished his leading position in the Central Committee. Over a long period of time Comrade Li Li-san corrected his wrong views, and so he was re-elected to the Central Committee at the Seventh National Congress of the Party.

[6] The Third Plenary Session of the Sixth Central Committee of the Party held in September 1930, and the subsequent central leading body adopted many positive measures to put an end to the Li Li-san line. But later a number of Party comrades who were inexperienced in practical revolutionary struggle, with Chen Shao-yu (Wang Ming) and Chin Pang-hsien (Po Ku) in the lead, came out against the Central Committee's measures. In the pamphlet, *The Two Lines* or *The Struggle for the Further Bolshevization of the Communist Party of China*, they most emphatically declared that the main danger then existing in the Party was not "Left" opportunism but "Right opportunism" and, to justify their own activities, they "criticized" the Li Li-san line as "Rightist". They put forward a new political programme which continued, revived or developed the Li Li-san line and other "Left" ideas and policies in a new guise, and set themselves against the correct line of Comrade Mao Tse-tung. It was mainly to criticize the military mistakes of this new "Left" opportunist line that Comrade Mao Tse-tung wrote the present article, "Problems of Strategy in China's Revolutionary War". This line was dominant in the Party from the Fourth Plenary Session of the Sixth Central Committee in January 1931 to the meeting of the Political Bureau convened by the Central Committee at Tsunyi, Kweichow Province, in January 1935, which ended the dominance of this erroneous line and established the new central leadership headed by Comrade Mao Tse-tung. The erroneous "Left" line dominated the Party for a particularly long time (four years) and brought extremely heavy losses, with disastrous consequences, to the Party and the revolution. A loss of 90 per cent was inflicted on the Chinese Communist Party, the Chinese Red Army and its base areas, tens of millions of people in the revolutionary base areas were made to suffer the

cruel oppression of the Kuomintang, and the progress of the Chinese revolution was retarded. The overwhelming majority of the errant comrades have realized and corrected their mistakes through a long process of learning from experience and have done much good work for the Party and the people. Under Comrade Mao Tse-tung's leadership they are now united with the masses of other comrades in the Party on the basis of a common political understanding.

[7] For the Right opportunism of Chang Kuo-tao, see "On Tactics Against Japanese Imperialism", Notes 21 and 22, pp. 175-76 of this volume.

[8] The Officers' Training Corps at Lushan was an organization set up by Chiang Kai-shek in July 1933 on Lushan Mountain in Kiukiang, Kiangsi Province, for training anti-Communist military cadres. Officers of Chiang Kai-shek's armed forces were sent there in rotation to receive fascist military and political training from German, Italian and American instructors.

[9] These new military principles largely constituted the Chiang Kai-shek gang's policy of "blockhouse warfare" in accordance with which it advanced gradually and entrenched itself at every step.

[10] See V. I. Lenin, " 'Communism' ", in which Lenin, criticizing the Hungarian Communist Bela Kun, said that he "gives up the most essential thing in Marxism, the living soul of Marxism, the concrete analysis of concrete conditions" (*Collected Works*, Russ. ed., Moscow, 1950, Vol. XXXI, p. 143).

[11] The First Party Congress of the Hunan-Kiangsi Border Area was held on May 20, 1928 at Maoping, Ningkang County.

[12] For an explanation, see pp. 236-37 of this volume.

[13] For roving rebels, see "On Correcting Mistaken Ideas in the Party", Notes 4 and 5, pp. 115-16 of this volume.

[14] "Bandit ways" refers to plundering and looting resulting from lack of discipline, organization and clear political direction.

[15] The Long March of 25,000 *li* (12,500 kilometres) was made by the Red Army from Kiangsi Province to northern Shensi Province. For further reference, see "On Tactics Against Japanese Imperialism", Note 20, p. 175 of this volume.

[16] The period after the December uprising of 1905 was defeated, in which the revolutionary tide in Russia gradually receded. See *History of the Communist Party of the Soviet Union (Bolsheviks), Short Course*, Chapter 3, Sections 5 and 6.

[17] The peace treaty of Brest-Litovsk was concluded between Soviet Russia and Germany in March 1918. Confronted with obviously superior enemy forces, the revolutionary forces had to make a temporary retreat in order to prevent the German imperialists from launching an attack on the new-born Soviet Republic, which as yet had no army of its own. The conclusion of this treaty gained time for the Soviet Republic to consolidate the political power of the proletariat, reorganize its economy and build up the Red Army. It enabled the proletariat to maintain its leadership over the peasantry and build up sufficient strength to defeat the White Guards and the armed intervention of Britain, the United States, France, Japan, Poland and other countries in 1918-20.

[18] On October 30, 1927 the peasants of the Haifeng-Lufeng area of Kwangtung Province launched their third insurrection under the leadership of the Communist Party of China. They occupied Haifeng and Lufeng and the surrounding area, organized a Red Army and established the democratic political power of the workers and

peasants. They were later defeated because they made the mistake of underestimating the enemy.

[19] The Fourth Front Army and the Second Front Army of the Red Army joined forces in the autumn of 1936 and shifted northward from the northeastern part of Sikang. Chang Kuo-tao was then still persisting in his anti-Party stand and in his policy of retreat and liquidation. In October of the same year, when the Second and Fourth Front Armies arrived in Kansu, he ordered the advance units of the Fourth Front Army, numbering more than 20,000, to organize the Western Column for crossing the Yellow River and advancing westward to Chinghai. This Column was practically defeated after suffering blows in battles in December 1936 and was completely defeated in March 1937.

[20] See letter from Karl Marx to L. Kugelmann on the Paris Commune.

[21] *Shui Hu Chuan (Heroes of the Marshes)* is a celebrated Chinese novel describing a peasant war. The novel is attributed to Shih Nai-an who lived around the end of the Yuan Dynasty and the beginning of the Ming Dynasty (14th century). Lin Chung and Chai Chin are both heroes in this novel. Hung is the drill master on Chai Chin's estate.

[22] Lu and Chi were two feudal states in the Spring and Autumn Era (722-481 B.C.). Chi was a big state in the central part of the present Shantung Province, and Lu was a smaller one in the southern part. Duke Chuang reigned over Lu from 693 to 662 B.C.

[23] Tsochiu Ming was the author of *Tso Chuan*, a classical chronicle of the Chou Dynasty. For the passage quoted, see the section in *Tso Chuan* entitled "The 10th Year of Duke Chuang" (684 B.C.).

[24] The ancient town of Chengkao, in the northwest of the present Chengkao County, Honan Province, was of great military importance. It was the scene of battles fought in 203 B.C. between Liu Pang, King of Han, and Hsiang Yu, King of Chu. At first Hsiang Yu captured Hsingyang and Chengkao and Liu Pang's troops were almost routed. Liu Pang waited until the opportune moment when Hsiang Yu's troops were in midstream crossing the Szeshui River, and then crushed them and recaptured Chengkao.

[25] The ancient town of Kunyang, in the north of the present Yehhsien County, Honan Province, was the place where Liu Hsiu, founder of the Eastern Han Dynasty, defeated the troops of Wang Mang, Emperor of the Hsin Dynasty, in A.D. 23. There was a huge numerical disparity between the two sides, Liu Hsiu's forces totalling 8,000 to 9,000 men as against Wang Mang's 400,000. But taking advantage of the negligence of Wang Mang's generals, Wang Hsun and Wang Yi, who underestimated the enemy, Liu Hsiu with only 3,000 picked troops put Wang Mang's main forces to rout. He followed up this victory by crushing the rest of the enemy troops.

[26] Kuantu was in the northeast of the present Chungmou County, Honan Province, and the scene of the battle between the armies of Tsao Tsao and Yuan Shao in A.D. 200. Yuan Shao had an army of 100,000, while Tsao Tsao had only a meagre force and was short of supplies. Taking advantage of lack of vigilance on the part of Yuan Shao's troops, who belittled the enemy, Tsao Tsao dispatched his light-footed soldiers to spring a surprise attack on them and set their supplies on fire. Yuan Shao's army was thrown into confusion and its main force wiped out.

[27] The state of Wu was ruled by Sun Chuan, and the state of Wei by Tsao Tsao. Chihpi is situated on the south bank of the Yangtse River, to the northeast of Chiayu, Hupeh Province. In A.D. 208 Tsao Tsao led an army of over 500,000 men, which he

proclaimed to be 800,000 strong, to launch an attack on Sun Chuan. The latter, in alliance with Tsao Tsao's antagonist Liu Pei, mustered a force of 30,000. Knowing that Tsao Tsao's army was plagued by epidemics and was unaccustomed to action afloat, the allied forces of Sun Chuan and Liu Pei set fire to Tsao Tsao's fleet and crushed his army.

[28] Yiling, to the east of the present Ichang, Hupeh Province, was the place where Lu Hsun, a general of the state of Wu, defeated the army of Liu Pei, ruler of Shu, in A.D. 222. Liu Pei's troops scored successive victories at the beginning of the war and penetrated five or six hundred *li* into the territory of Wu as far as Yiling. Lu Hsun, who was defending Yiling, avoided battle for over seven months until Liu Pei "was at his wits' end and his troops were exhausted and demoralized". Then he crushed Liu Pei's troops by taking advantage of a favourable wind to set fire to their tents.

[29] Hsieh Hsuan, a general of Eastern Tsin Dynasty, defeated Fu Chien, ruler of the state of Chin, in A.D. 383 at the Feishui River in Anhwei Province. Fu Chien had an infantry force of more than 600,000, a cavalry force of 270,000 and a guards corps of more than 30,000, while the land and river forces of Eastern Tsin numbered only 80,000. When the armies lined up on opposite banks of the Feishui River, Hsieh Hsuan, taking advantage of the overconfidence and conceit of the enemy troops, requested Fu Chien to move his troops back so as to leave room for the Eastern Tsin troops to cross the river and fight it out. Fu Chien complied, but when he ordered withdrawal, his troops got into a panic and could not be stopped. Seizing the opportunity, the Eastern Tsin troops crossed the river, launched an offensive and crushed the enemy.

[30] Nanchang, capital of Kiangsi Province, was the scene of the famous uprising on August 1, 1927 led by the Communist Party of China in order to combat the counter-revolution of Chiang Kai-shek and Wang Ching-wei and to continue the revolution of 1924-27. More than thirty thousand troops took part in the uprising which was led by Comrades Chou En-lai, Chu Teh, Ho Lung and Yeh Ting. The insurrectionary army withdrew from Nanchang on August 5 as planned, but suffered a defeat when approaching Chaochow and Swatow in Kwangtung Province. Led by Comrades Chu Teh, Chen Yi and Lin Piao, part of the troops later fought their way to the Chingkang Mountains and joined forces with the 1st Division of the First Workers' and Peasants' Revolutionary Army under Comrade Mao Tse-tung.

[31] See "Why Is It That Red Political Power Can Exist in China?", Note 8, p. 72 of this volume.

[32] The famous Autumn Harvest Uprising under the leadership of Comrade Mao Tse-tung was launched in September 1927 by the people's armed forces of Hsiushui, Pinghsiang, Pingkiang and Liuyang Counties on the Hunan-Kiangsi border, who formed the 1st Division of the First Workers' and Peasants' Revolutionary Army. Comrade Mao Tse-tung led this force to the Chingkang Mountains where a revolutionary base was established.

[33] The A-B (initials for "Anti-Bolshevik") Group was a counter-revolutionary organization of undercover Kuomintang agents in the Red areas.

[34] See V. I. Lenin, "Theses on the Question of the Immediate Conclusion of a Separate and Annexationist Peace", "Strange and Monstrous", "A Serious Lesson and a Serious Responsibility", "Report on War and Peace", *Selected Works*, in two volumes, Eng. ed., FLPH, Moscow, 1952, Vol. II, Part 1, and also *History of the Communist Party of the Soviet Union (Bolsheviks), Short Course*, Chapter 7, Section 7.

³⁵ The regions referred to here are those inhabited by the Tibetans in Sikang and the Hui people in Kansu, Chinghai and Sinkiang Provinces.

³⁶ The "eight-legged essay" was the prescribed form in the imperial competitive examinations in feudal China from the 15th to the 19th century. The main body of the essay was made up of the inceptive paragraph, the middle paragraph, the rear paragraph and the concluding paragraph, with each paragraph comprising two parts. Here Comrade Mao Tse-tung is using the development of the theme in this kind of essay as a metaphor to illustrate the development of the revolution through its various stages. However, Comrade Mao Tse-tung generally uses the term "eight-legged essay" to ridicule dogmatism.

³⁷ In November 1933, under the influence of the people's anti-Japanese upsurge throughout China, the leaders of the Kuomintang's 19th Route Army, in alliance with the Kuomintang forces under Li Chi-shen, publicly renounced Chiang Kai-shek and established the "People's Revolutionary Government of the Republic of China" in Fukien, concluding an agreement with the Red Army to attack Chiang Kai-shek and resist Japan. This episode was referred to as the Fukien Incident. The 19th Route Army and Fukien People's Government, however, collapsed under the attacks of Chiang Kai-shek's troops.

A STATEMENT ON CHIANG KAI-SHEK'S STATEMENT

December 28, 1936

In Sian Chiang Kai-shek accepted the demand for resistance to Japan put forward by Generals Chang Hsueh-liang and Yang Hu-cheng and the people of the Northwest and, as an initial step, he has ordered his civil war troops to withdraw from the provinces of Shensi and Kansu. This marks the beginning of Chiang's reversal of his wrong policy in the past decade.[1] It is a blow to the intrigues conducted by the Japanese imperialists and the Chinese "punitive" group[2] to stage-manage a civil war, foment splits and get Chiang killed in the Sian Incident. Their disappointment is already apparent. The indication that Chiang Kai-shek is beginning to wake up may be considered a sign of the Kuomintang's willingness to end the wrong policy it has pursued for ten years.

On December 26 Chiang Kai-shek issued a statement in Loyang, the so-called "Admonition to Chang Hsueh-liang and Yang Hu-cheng", which is so ambiguous and evasive as to be an interesting specimen among China's political documents. If Chiang really wants to draw a serious lesson from the incident and try to revitalize the Kuomintang, and if he wants to end his consistently wrong policy of compromise in foreign affairs and of civil war and oppression at home, so that the Kuomintang will no longer stand opposed to the wishes of the people, then as a token of good faith he should have produced a better piece of writing, repenting his political past and setting a new course for the future. The statement of December 26 cannot meet the demands of the Chinese masses.

However, it does contain one praiseworthy passage, in which Chiang asserts that "promises must be kept and action must be resolute". This means that, although he did not sign the terms set forth

by Chang and Yang in Sian, he is willing to accept such demands as
are beneficial to the state and the nation and will not break his word
on the grounds that he did not sign. We shall see whether, after he
has withdrawn his troops, Chiang will act in good faith and carry
out the terms he has accepted. The terms are:

(1) to reorganize the Kuomintang and the National Government, expel the pro-Japanese group and admit anti-Japanese
elements;

(2) to release the patriotic leaders in Shanghai[3] and all other
political prisoners, and guarantee the freedoms and rights of the
people;

(3) to end the policy of "suppressing the Communists" and
enter into an alliance with the Red Army to resist Japan;

(4) to convene a national salvation conference, representing
all parties, groups, sections of the population and armies, to decide
on the policy of resisting Japan and saving the nation;

(5) to enter into co-operation with countries sympathetic to
China's resistance to Japan; and

(6) to adopt other specific ways and means to save the nation.

The fulfilment of these terms requires above all good faith, and also
some courage. We shall judge Chiang by his future actions.

But his statement contains the remark that the Sian Incident was
brought about under the pressure of "reactionaries". It is a pity that
he did not explain what kind of people he meant by "reactionaries",
nor is it clear how the word "reactionary" is defined in Chiang's
dictionary. However, what is certain is that the Sian Incident took
place under the influence of the following forces:

(1) the mounting indignation against Japan among the troops
of Generals Chang and Yang and among the revolutionary people
of the Northwest;

(2) the mounting indignation against Japan among the people
of the whole country;

(3) the growth of the Left forces in the Kuomintang;

(4) the demand by the groups in power in various provinces
for resistance to Japan and for the salvation of the nation;

(5) the stand taken by the Communist Party for a national
united front against Japan; and

(6) the development of the world peace front.

All these are indisputable facts. It is just these forces that Chiang calls "reactionary"; while other people call them revolutionary, Chiang calls them "reactionary" — that is all. Since he declared in Sian that he would fight Japan in earnest, presumably he will not resume violent attacks on the revolutionary forces immediately after leaving Sian; not only does his own political life and that of his group hang upon his good faith, but they now have confronting them and obstructing their political path a force which has expanded to their detriment — the "punitive" group which tried to get him killed in the Sian Incident. We therefore advise Chiang Kai-shek to revise his political dictionary, changing the word "reactionary" to "revolutionary", for it is better to use terms corresponding to the facts.

Chiang should remember that he owes his safe departure from Sian to the mediation of the Communist Party, as well as to the efforts of Generals Chang and Yang, the leaders in the Sian Incident. Throughout the incident, the Communist Party stood for a peaceful settlement and made every effort to that end, acting solely in the interests of national survival. Had the civil war spread and had Chang and Yang kept Chiang Kai-shek in custody for long, the incident could only have developed in favour of the Japanese imperialists and the Chinese "punitive" group. It was in these circumstances that the Communist Party firmly exposed the intrigues of the Japanese imperialists and of Wang Ching-wei,[4] Ho Ying-chin[5] and other members of the Chinese "punitive" group, and firmly advocated a peaceful settlement, which happened to coincide with the views of Generals Chang Hsueh-liang and Yang Hu-cheng and such members of the Kuomintang as T. V. Soong.[6] This is exactly what the people throughout the country call for, because they bitterly detest the present civil war.

Chiang was set free upon his acceptance of the Sian terms. From now on the question is whether he will carry out to the letter his pledge that "promises must be kept and action must be resolute", and strictly fulfil all the terms for saving the nation. The nation will not permit any further hesitation on his part or allow him any discount in fulfilling the terms. If he wavers on the issue of resisting Japan or delays in fulfilling his pledge, then the nation-wide revolutionary tide will sweep him away. Chiang and his group should bear in mind the old saying: "If a man does not keep his word, what is he good for?"

If Chiang can clean up the dirt created by the Kuomintang's reactionary policy over the past ten years, thoroughly correct his fundamental errors of compromise in foreign affairs and of civil war and oppression at home, immediately join the anti-Japanese front uniting all parties and groups and really take the military and political measures that can save the nation, then of course the Communist Party will support him. As early as August 25, the Communist Party promised such support to Chiang and the Kuomintang in its letter to the Kuomintang.[7] The people throughout the country have known for fifteen years that the Communist Party observes the maxim, "Promises must be kept and action must be resolute." They undoubtedly have more confidence in the words and deeds of the Communist Party than in those of any other party or group in China.

NOTES

[1] Under the influence of the Chinese Red Army and the people's anti-Japanese movement, the Kuomintang's Northeastern Army headed by Chang Hsueh-liang and the Kuomintang's 17th Route Army headed by Yang Hu-cheng agreed to the anti-Japanese national united front proposed by the Communist Party of China and demanded that Chiang Kai-shek should unite with the Communist Party to resist Japan. He refused, became still more active in his military preparations for the "suppression of the Communists" and massacred young people in Sian who were anti-Japanese. Chang Hsueh-liang and Yang Hu-cheng took joint action and arrested Chiang Kai-shek. This was the famous Sian Incident of December 12, 1936. He was forced to accept the terms of unity with the Communist Party and resistance to Japan, and was then set free to return to Nanking.

[2] The Chinese "punitive" group consisted of the pro-Japanese elements in the Kuomintang government in Nanking who tried to wrest power from Chiang Kai-shek during the Sian Incident. With Wang Ching-wei and Ho Ying-chin as their leaders, they advocated a "punitive expedition" against Chang Hsueh-liang and Yang Hu-cheng. Availing themselves of the incident, they prepared to start large-scale civil war in order to clear the way for the Japanese invaders and wrest political power from Chiang Kai-shek.

[3] Seven leaders of the patriotic anti-Japanese movement in Shanghai had been arrested by Chiang Kai-shek's government in November 1936. They were Shen Chun-ju, Chang Nai-chi, Tsou Tao-fen, Li Kung-pu, Sha Chien-li, Shih Liang and Wang Tsao-shih. They were kept in prison till July 1937.

[4] Wang Ching-wei was the head of the pro-Japanese group in the Kuomintang. He had stood for compromise with the Japanese imperialists ever since their invasion of the Northeast in 1931. In December 1938 he left Chungking, openly capitulated to the Japanese invaders, and set up a puppet government in Nanking.

[5] Ho Ying-chin, a Kuomintang warlord, was another leader of the pro-Japanese group. During the Sian Incident he actively plotted civil war by deploying Kuomintang

troops for an attack on Shensi along the Lunghai Railway. He planned to kill Chiang Kai-shek by bombing Sian, in order to take over Chiang's position.

⁶ T. V. Soong was a pro-American member of the Kuomintang. Championing U.S. interests he, too, favoured a peaceful settlement of the Sian Incident, because U.S. imperialism was at loggerheads with Japanese imperialism with which it was then contending for supremacy in the Far East.

⁷ This letter sternly criticized the Kuomintang's reactionary rule and the decisions of the Second Plenary Session of its Central Executive Committee. It also set out the Communist Party's policy of forming an anti-Japanese national united front and renewing its co-operation with the Kuomintang. The main part of the letter reads:

In talking about "centralization and unification", the Second Plenary Session of the Central Executive Committee of your party is really confusing cause and effect. It must be emphasized that the civil war and disunity of the last ten years have been entirely caused by the disastrous policy of dependence on imperialism pursued by your party and your party's government, and especially the policy of non-resistance to Japan persisted in ever since the Incident of September 18, 1931. Under the slogan of "Internal pacification before resistance to foreign invasion", your party and your party's government have been carrying on incessant civil war and launching numerous encirclement campaigns against the Red Army, and have spared no effort in suppressing the patriotic and democratic movements of the people throughout the country. Being blind to the fact that Japanese imperialism is China's deadliest enemy, you have had no qualms even in recent months about abandoning northeastern and northern China, you have used all your strength to fight the Red Army and wage factional struggles within your own party, you have blocked the Red Army on its way to fight the Japanese and harassed its rear, you have ignored the nation-wide demand for resistance to Japan and have deprived the people of their freedoms and rights. Patriotism is penalized and innocent people are in jail everywhere; treason is rewarded and traitors are jubilant over their new appointments and honours. To seek centralization and unification by means of this wrong policy is like "climbing a tree to seek fish" and will produce exactly the opposite results. We wish to warn you gentlemen that if you do not make a fundamental change in your erroneous policy, and if you do not direct your hatred against the Japanese imperialists but continue to direct it against your own countrymen, you will find it impossible even to maintain the *status quo*, and any talk about centralization, unification and a so-called "modern state" will remain idle chatter. What the whole nation demands is centralization and unification for fighting Japan and saving the nation, not for fawning on the foreigners and persecuting our own people. The people are now eagerly demanding a government that can really save their country and themselves, a really democratic republic. They demand a democratic republican government which will serve their interests. The programme of such a government must principally provide for: first, resistance to foreign aggression; second, democratic rights for the people; and third, development of the national economy and elimination, or at least alleviation, of the people's sufferings. If there is any sense in your talk about a "modern state", this is the only programme genuinely meeting the needs of colonial and semi-colonial China in the present era. With eager hopes and firm determination the people are struggling for the realization of these objectives. But your party and your party's government are pursuing a policy that runs counter to their hopes, and you will never win their confidence. The Chinese Communist Party and the Chinese Red Army hereby solemnly declare: we stand for the setting up of a unified democratic republic for the whole country and the convening of a parliament elected by universal suffrage, and we support an anti-Japanese national salvation congress representative of all the people and all the anti-Japanese armed forces in the country, and a unified national defence government for the whole country. We hereby declare: as soon as a unified democratic republic is set up for the whole of China, the Red areas will become one of its component parts, the representatives of the people of the Red areas will attend the all-China parliament, and the same democratic system will be set up in the Red areas as in other parts of China. We hold that the national defence council, which the Second Plenary Session of the Central Executive Committee of your party has decided to organize, and the national assembly, which your party and your party's government are in process of convening, cannot achieve centralization and unification for resisting Japan and saving the nation. According to the regulations of the national defence council passed by the Second Plenary Session of the Central Executive Committee of your party, this council will be confined to a few officials who hold power in your party and your party's government, and its task is merely to serve as an advisory body to that government. It is only too clear that such a council cannot achieve anything or win any confidence among the people. The same applies to the national assembly which you gentlemen propose to convene; according to the "Draft Constitution of the Republic of China" and the "Organic Law and Election Law of the National Assembly" passed by your party's government, this assembly will be merely an organ manipulated by a few officials of your party and your party's government, it will be nothing but an appendage for them, or a piece of ornamentation. A national defence council and a national assembly of this kind have nothing at all in common with the all-China congress for resistance to Japan and for national salvation — the national defence council — and the Chinese democratic republic and its parliament which our Party has proposed. We hold that a national defence council for resistance to Japan and national salvation must include representatives of all the political parties and groups, all walks of life and all the armed forces, and must constitute a real organ of authority to decide the major policies for resisting Japan and saving the nation, and that a unified national defence government must be formed from this council. The national assembly must be a parliament elected by universal suffrage and the supreme organ of authority of the democratic republic of China. Only such a national defence council and such an all-China parliament will win the approval, support and participation of the people of the whole country and place the great cause of saving the nation and the people on a firm, unshakable foundation. Mere fine words are useless and will not win the people's approval. The failure of the various conferences held by your party and your party's government is the best proof of this. The declaration of the Second Plenary Session of the Central Executive Committee of your party stated, "Dangers and obstacles are only to be expected; but we will never, because of the difficulties and troubles that beset the nation, relax in the fulfilment of our duty." And again, "As to the survival of the nation, naturally our party will work for it persistently, body and soul." True enough, being the ruling party in the largest part of China, your party must bear the political responsibility for all past deeds. In view of the fact that the Kuomintang government is a one-party dictatorship, your party can never escape this responsibility. In particular, you can never shift onto others your responsibility for the loss of almost half of China, resulting from the absolutely wrong policy which your party has pursued since the September 18th Incident against the wishes of all the people and the interests of the whole nation. As we and all the people see it, since half of China has been abandoned by your party, it certainly cannot evade its duty of recovering the territory and restoring China's sovereignty. At the same time, even within your party many men of conscience are now clearly awake to the horrors of national subjugation and the inviolability of the people's will; they are beginning to turn in a new direction and feel indignant and dissatisfied with those in their midst who have brought disaster both to their party and to the nation. The Chinese Communist Party has full sympathy with this new turn and warmly applauds the noble spirit and awakening of these patriotic and conscientious members of the Kuomintang, their readiness to make sacrifices in the struggle, and their courage to introduce reforms when the nation is on the brink of ruin. We know that the number of awakened and patriotic people is increasing daily in your party's central and provincial headquarters, in its central and provincial governments, in educational, scientific, artistic, journalistic and industrial circles, among the women and in religious and medical circles, within the police service, among all kinds of popular organizations, and in particular among the broad ranks of the army and among both old and new Kuomintang members as well as Kuomintang leaders at various levels; this is very heartening. The Chinese Communist Party is always ready to join hands with these members of the Kuomintang and form a solid national united front with them to fight the nation's deadliest enemy, Japanese imperialism. We hope that they will speedily grow into a dominant force in the Kuomintang and prevail over those wicked and shameless members who have ignored the interests of the nation and virtually become Japanese agents and collaborators — members who are a disgrace to Dr. Sun Yat-sen's memory — and we hope that they will thus be able to revive the spirit of Dr. Sun's revolutionary Three People's Principles, reaffirm his Three Great Policies of alliance with Russia, co-operation with the Communist Party and assistance to the peasants and workers, and "work persistently, body and soul" for the realization of the revolutionary Three People's Principles, of the Three Great Policies and of Dr. Sun's revolutionary Testament. We hope that, together with the patriotic leaders of all political parties and groups and of all walks of life and together with all patriotic people, they will resolutely shoulder the responsibility of continuing Dr. Sun's revolutionary cause and will throw themselves into the struggle to drive out the Japanese imperialists and save the Chinese nation from subjugation, to win democratic rights for the people, to develop China's national economy and free the vast majority of its people from their sufferings, and to bring into being the democratic republic of China with a democratic parliament and democratic government. The Chinese Communist Party hereby declares to all members of the Kuomintang: if you really do this, we shall resolutely support you and are ready to form with you a solid revolutionary united front like that of the great revolutionary period of 1924-27 against imperialist and feudal oppression, for this is the only correct way today to save the nation from subjugation and ensure its survival.

THE TASKS OF
THE CHINESE COMMUNIST PARTY IN THE
PERIOD OF RESISTANCE TO JAPAN

May 3, 1937

THE PRESENT STAGE OF DEVELOPMENT OF CHINA'S EXTERNAL AND INTERNAL CONTRADICTIONS

1. As the contradiction between China and Japan has become the principal one and China's internal contradictions have dropped into a secondary and subordinate place, changes have occurred in China's international relations and internal class relations, giving rise to a new stage of development in the current situation.

2. China has long been in the grip of two acute and basic contradictions, the contradiction between China and imperialism and the contradiction between feudalism and the masses of the people. In 1927 the bourgeoisie, represented by the Kuomintang, betrayed the revolution and sold China's national interests to imperialism, thus creating a situation in which the state power of the workers and peasants stood in sharp antagonism to that of the Kuomintang, and, of necessity, the task of the national and democratic revolution devolved upon the Chinese Communist Party alone.

3. Since the Incident of September 18, 1931 and especially since the Northern China Incident of 1935,[1] the following changes have taken place in these contradictions:

(1) The contradiction between China and imperialism in general has given way to the particularly salient and sharp contradiction between China and Japanese imperialism. Japanese imperialism is carrying out a policy of total conquest of China. Consequently, the contradictions between China and certain other imperialist powers

Comrade Mao Tse-tung delivered this report at the National Conference of the Communist Party of China, held in Yenan in May 1937.

263

have been relegated to a secondary position, while the rift between these powers and Japan has been widened. Consequently also, the Chinese Communist Party and the Chinese people are faced with the task of linking China's anti-Japanese national united front with the world peace front. This means that China should not only unite with the Soviet Union, which has been the consistently good friend of the Chinese people, but as far as possible should work for joint opposition to Japanese imperialism with those imperialist countries which, at the present time, are willing to maintain peace and are against new wars of aggression. The aim of our united front must be resistance to Japan, and not simultaneous opposition to all the imperialist powers.

(2) The contradiction between China and Japan has changed internal class relations within China and has confronted the bourgeoisie and even the warlords with the question of survival, so that they and their political parties have been undergoing a gradual change in their political attitude. This has placed the task of establishing an anti-Japanese national united front before the Chinese Communist Party and the Chinese people. Our united front should include the bourgeoisie and all who agree to the defence of the motherland; it should represent national solidarity against the foreign foe. This task not only must, but can, be fulfilled.

(3) The contradiction between China and Japan has changed matters for the masses throughout the country (the proletariat, the peasantry and the urban petty bourgeoisie) and for the Communist Party, and it has changed the Party's policy. More and more people have risen to fight for national salvation. The policy proclaimed by the Communist Party after the September 18th Incident was to conclude agreements with those sections of the Kuomintang which were willing to co-operate with us for resistance, subject to three conditions (stop attacking the revolutionary base areas, guarantee the freedoms and rights of the people, arm the people), and it has developed into a policy of establishing an anti-Japanese united front of the whole nation. This is the reason for the following steps taken by our Party: in 1935, the August declaration[2] and the December resolution;[3] in 1936, the abandonment of the "anti-Chiang Kai-shek" slogan in May,[4] the letter to the Kuomintang in August,[5] the resolution on the democratic republic in September,[6] and the insistence on a peaceful settlement of the Sian Incident in December; and in 1937, the February telegram to the Third Plenary Session of the Central Executive Committee of the Kuomintang.[7]

(4)   Because of the contradiction between China and Japan, a change has also occurred in the Chinese warlord regimes and the civil wars among them, which are the product of the imperialist policy of spheres of influence and of China's semi-colonial economic conditions. Japanese imperialism fosters such separate regimes and civil wars for the purpose of facilitating exclusive Japanese domination of China. Certain other imperialist powers are temporarily in favour of unity and peace in China in their own interests. The Chinese Communist Party and the Chinese people on their part are exerting their utmost efforts against civil wars and splits and for peace and unity.

(5)   In terms of relative political importance the development of the national contradiction between China and Japan has demoted the domestic contradictions between classes and between political groupings to a secondary and subordinate place. But they still exist and have by no means diminished or disappeared. The same is true of the contradictions between China and the imperialist powers other than Japan. Therefore, the Chinese Communist Party and the Chinese people are faced with the following task — to make the appropriate adjustments with regard to those internal and external contradictions which can and must be adjusted at present so as to fit in with the general task of unity against Japan. This is the reason for the Chinese Communist Party's policies of peace and unity, democracy, bettering the life of the people and negotiations with foreign countries that are opposed to Japan.

4.   The first stage of the new period in the Chinese revolution began on December 9, 1935 and ended when the Kuomintang's Central Executive Committee held its Third Plenary Session in February 1937. The major events in this stage were the movements for national salvation among the students and cultural and press circles; the Red Army's entry into the Northwest; the Communist Party's work of propaganda and organization for its anti-Japanese national united front policy; the anti-Japanese strikes in Shanghai and Tsingtao;[8] the relative stiffening of British policy towards Japan;[9] the Kwangtung-Kwangsi Incident;[10] the resistance in Suiyuan and the movement in its support;[11] Nanking's somewhat firmer attitude in the Sino-Japanese negotiations;[12] the Sian Incident; and finally, the Third Plenary Session of the Central Executive Committee of the Kuomintang in Nanking.[13] These events all centred on the basic contradiction, which is the antagonism between China and Japan; they all centred directly on the historical need for an anti-Japanese national united front.

The basic task of the revolution at this stage was to struggle for internal peace and stop the internal armed conflicts, so that there could be unity against Japan. During this stage the Communist Party issued its call, "Stop the civil war and unite against Japan", a call which in the main has been put into effect, and thereby created the primary prerequisite for the actual establishment of an anti-Japanese national united front.

5. Owing to the presence of the pro-Japanese group inside the Kuomintang, it made no definite or thoroughgoing change in its policy at the Third Plenary Session of its Central Executive Committee and did not concretely solve any problem. However, owing to the pressure of the people and to developments in its own ranks, the Kuomintang had to begin to change its wrong policy of the previous ten years, that is, it had to turn away from the policy of civil war, dictatorship and non-resistance to Japan and to move in the direction of peace, democracy and resistance to Japan, and it had to begin accepting the policy of an anti-Japanese national united front; this initial change revealed itself at the Third Plenary Session of its Central Executive Committee. From now on the demand must be for a thorough change in Kuomintang policy. In order to attain this goal our Party and the people throughout the country must develop the movement for resistance to Japan and for democracy still more extensively, must go a step further in criticizing the Kuomintang, pushing it into action and keeping up the pressure, must unite with all those within the Kuomintang who stand for peace, democracy and resistance to Japan, and must help the hesitant waverers forward and throw out the pro-Japanese elements.

6. The present stage is the second one in the new period. Both the previous and present stages are stages of transition towards nationwide armed resistance to Japan. If in the previous stage the principal task was the fight for peace, then in the present stage the principal task is the fight for democracy. It must be understood that just as a genuine and solid anti-Japanese national united front cannot be established without internal peace, so it cannot be established without internal democracy. Hence at the present stage of development the fight for democracy is the central link in the revolutionary task. If we fail to see the importance of democracy clearly and slacken our fight for it, we shall be unable to establish a genuine and solid anti-Japanese national united front.

THE STRUGGLE FOR DEMOCRACY AND FREEDOM

7.   Japanese imperialism is now intensifying its preparations for the invasion of China south of the Great Wall. In concert with the intensified preparations of Hitler and Mussolini for predatory war in the West, Japan is exerting every ounce of energy in the East in order to prepare the ground, according to a definite plan, for the subjugation of China at a single stroke — she is creating the military, political, economic and ideological conditions at home and the diplomatic conditions internationally, and fostering the pro-Japanese forces in China. Japan's propaganda about "Sino-Japanese collaboration" and a certain relaxation in her diplomatic measures stem precisely from the tactical needs of her policy of aggression on the eve of war. China is now approaching the critical moment of decision between survival and extinction and must rush preparations for resisting Japan and saving the nation. We are certainly not against preparation; what we are against is the doctrine of protracted preparation and the frivolous, dissipated and gluttonous life of civil and military officialdom which imperils the nation; such things actually help the enemy and must be quickly swept away.

8.   Political, military, economic and educational preparations for national defence are all necessary for armed resistance to save the nation, and none of them should be delayed for a moment. But the key that will ensure victory for our armed resistance is the winning of political democracy and freedom. Armed resistance requires domestic peace and unity, but the peace already won cannot be consolidated and internal unity cannot be strengthened without democracy and freedom. Armed resistance requires the mobilization of the people, but there is no way of mobilizing them without democracy and freedom. Unless peace and unity are consolidated, unless the people are mobilized, our armed resistance will meet the same fate as Abyssinia's. Abyssinia was defeated mainly because her feudal regime could not achieve solid internal unity and rouse the initiative of her people. Without democracy, a genuine and solid national united front against Japan cannot be established in China and its goals cannot be attained.

9.   China must at once start democratic changes in the two following respects. First, in the matter of the political system, the reactionary Kuomintang dictatorship of one party and one class must be changed

into a democratic government based on the co-operation of all parties and all classes. In this respect, a start should be made by changing the undemocratic procedures for electing and convening the national assembly, and by holding democratic elections to the assembly and ensuring freedom in the conduct of its meetings, after which it will be necessary to go on to framing and adopting a truly democratic constitution, convening a truly democratic parliament, and electing a genuinely democratic government that will carry out genuinely democratic policies. Only thus can internal peace be truly consolidated, internal armed hostilities ended and internal unity strengthened, enabling the whole nation to unite and resist the foreign foe. It is possible that Japanese imperialism will attack us before the changes are completed. Therefore, in order to be able to resist and thoroughly crush the Japanese attack when it comes, we must quickly go ahead with the reforms and be prepared to accomplish them fully in the course of our armed resistance. The people of the whole country and the patriots of all parties should throw off their former indifference towards the question of a national assembly and a constitution, and should concentrate on the movement for a national assembly and a constitution, a movement that is important for national defence; they should subject the Kuomintang, the party in power, to severe criticism, and press and impel it to give up its one-party, one-class dictatorship and act according to the opinions of the people. In the next few months of this year, a broad democratic movement must be set going throughout the country, with the immediate objective of completely democratizing the national assembly and the constitution. The second matter concerns freedom of speech, assembly and association for the people. Without such freedom, it will be impossible to carry out the democratic reconstruction of the political system, mobilize the people for the war of resistance and victoriously defend the motherland and recover the lost territories. In the next few months the nation-wide democratic movement should strive for at least a minimal achievement of such freedoms, which must include the release of political prisoners, the removal of the ban on political parties, etc. Democratic reconstruction of the political system and freedom and rights for the people constitute an important part of the programme of the anti-Japanese national united front; at the same time they are prerequisites for the establishment of a genuine and solid anti-Japanese national united front.

10. Our enemies — the Japanese imperialists, the Chinese traitors, the pro-Japanese elements and the Trotskyites — have been doing their utmost to wreck every move for peace and unity, democracy and freedom in China and for armed resistance to Japan. In the past, while we were fighting strenuously for peace and unity, they were doing all they could to foment civil war and splits. At present and in the near future, while we fight strenuously for democracy and freedom, they will no doubt resort to their wrecking again. Their general objective is to thwart us in our task of armed resistance in defence of the motherland and to accomplish their aggressive plan for subjugating China. From now on, in the struggle for democracy and freedom, we must not only exert ourselves in propaganda, agitation and criticism directed towards the Kuomintang die-hards and the backward sections of the people, but must also fully expose and firmly combat the intrigues of the Japanese imperialists and of the pro-Japanese elements and Trotskyites who serve as their running dogs in the invasion of China.

11. For the sake of internal peace, democracy and armed resistance and for the sake of establishing the anti-Japanese national united front, the Chinese Communist Party has made the following four pledges in its telegram to the Third Plenary Session of the Central Executive Committee of the Kuomintang:

(1) the Communist-led government in the Shensi-Kansu-Ningsia revolutionary base area will be renamed the Government of the Special Region of the Republic of China and the Red Army will be redesignated as part of the National Revolutionary Army, and they will come under the direction of the Central Government in Nanking and its Military Council respectively;

(2) a thoroughly democratic system will be applied in the areas under the Government of the Special Region;

(3) the policy of overthrowing the Kuomintang by armed force will be discontinued; and

(4) the confiscation of the land of the landlords will be discontinued.

These pledges are necessary as well as permissible. For only thus can we transform the state of antagonism between the two different regimes within the country and achieve unity for common action against the enemy, in line with the changes in the relative political importance of China's external and internal contradictions. These are principled and conditional concessions, made with the aim of obtaining in return what the whole nation needs — peace, democracy and armed resistance. Moreover, the concessions have limits. The preservation of the Communist Party's leadership over the Special Region and in the Red Army, and the preservation of the Communist Party's independence and freedom of criticism in its relations with the Kuomintang — these are the limits beyond which it is impermissible to go. Concessions mean concessions by both parties: the Kuomintang abandons the policy of civil war, dictatorship and non-resistance to the foreign foe, and the Communist Party abandons the policy of maintaining antagonism between the two regimes. We exchange the latter for the former and resume our co-operation with the Kuomintang to fight for national salvation. To describe this as capitulation by the Communist Party is nothing but Ah Q-ism[14] or malicious slander.

12. Does the Communist Party agree with the Three People's Principles? Our answer is, Yes, we do.[15] The Three People's Principles have undergone changes in the course of their history. The revolutionary Three People's Principles of Dr. Sun Yat-sen won the people's confidence and became the banner of the victorious revolution of 1924-27 because they were resolutely applied as a result of his co-operation with the Communist Party. In 1927, however, the Kuomintang turned on the Communist Party (the party purge[16] and the anti-Communist war) and pursued an opposite policy, bringing the revolution down in defeat and endangering the nation; consequently the people lost confidence in the Three People's Principles. Now that there is an extremely grave national crisis and the Kuomintang cannot continue to rule in the same old way, the people of the whole country and the patriots within the Kuomintang are urgently demanding co-operation between the two parties. Consequently, it is completely in keeping with the historical requirements of the Chinese revolution that the essence of the Three People's Principles should be revived and restored, and that the two parties should resume their co-operation, in accordance with the Principle of Nationalism, or the struggle for national independence and liberation, the Principle of Democracy, or the attainment of internal democracy and freedom, and the Principle of People's Livelihood, or the promotion of the people's welfare, and they should lead the people to put these principles resolutely into practice. This ought to be clearly grasped by every member of the Communist Party. Communists will never abandon their ideal of socialism and communism, which they will

attain by going through the stage of the bourgeois-democratic revolution. The Chinese Communist Party has its own political and economic programme. Its maximum programme is socialism and communism, which is different from the Three People's Principles. Even its programme for the period of the democratic revolution is more thoroughgoing than that of any other party in China. But the Communist Party's programme for the democratic revolution and the programme of the Three People's Principles as proclaimed by the Kuomintang's First National Congress are basically not in conflict. Therefore, far from rejecting the Three People's Principles, we are ready staunchly to put them into practice; moreover, we ask the Kuomintang to implement them together with us, and we call upon the whole nation to put them into effect. We hold that the Communist Party, the Kuomintang and the people of the whole country should unite and fight for these three great objectives of national independence, democracy and freedom, and the people's livelihood.

13. Was our past slogan of a workers' and peasants' democratic republic wrong? No, it was not. Since the bourgeoisie, and particularly the big bourgeoisie, withdrew from the revolution, became retainers of imperialism and the feudal forces and turned into enemies of the people, the only remaining motive forces of the revolution were the proletariat, the peasantry and the urban petty bourgeoisie, and the only remaining revolutionary party was the Communist Party, which, as such, inevitably had to shoulder the responsibility for organizing the revolution. The Communist Party alone continued to hold aloft the banner of revolution, preserved the revolutionary tradition, put forward the slogan of a workers' and peasants' democratic republic and fought hard for it for many years. This slogan was not in conflict with the task of bourgeois-democratic revolution but signified that we were resolutely carrying out this task. Not a single item of policy adopted in our actual struggle was out of keeping with this task. Our policy, including the confiscation of the land of the landlords and the enforcement of the eight-hour working day, never went beyond the bounds of capitalist private ownership; our policy was not to put socialism in practice then. What will be the composition of the new democratic republic? It will consist of the proletariat, the peasantry, the urban petty bourgeoisie, the bourgeoisie, and all those in the country who agree with the national and democratic revolution; it will be the alliance of these classes in the national and democratic revolution. The salient feature here is the inclusion

of the bourgeoisie; the reason is that in the present circumstances there is a possibility that the bourgeoisie will once again co-operate with us and join in the resistance to Japan, and the party of the proletariat should therefore not repel but welcome them and revive its alliance with them for the common struggle, so as to help the Chinese revolution forward. In order to end the internal armed conflict, the Communist Party is willing to discontinue the policy of forcible confiscation of the land of the landlords and is prepared to solve the land problem by legislative and other appropriate means in the course of building the new democratic republic. The first question to be settled is whether China's land will be owned by the Japanese or by the Chinese. Since the solution of the land problem of the peasants is predicated on the defence of China, it is absolutely necessary for us to turn from the method of forcible confiscation to appropriate new methods.

It was correct to put forward the slogan of a workers' and peasants' democratic republic in the past, and it is correct to drop it today.

14. To establish the national united front for joint resistance to the enemy, it is necessary properly to resolve certain internal contradictions, the principle here being that the solution should help strengthen and extend the anti-Japanese national united front and not weaken or narrow it. During the stage of the democratic revolution, it is impossible to avoid contradictions and struggles between classes, parties and political groupings, but it is both possible and essential to put an end to such struggles as are detrimental to unity and to resisting Japan (the civil war, the antagonistic conflict between the political parties, provincial separatism, feudal political and economic oppression on the one hand, and the policy of insurrection and excessive economic demands harmful to the resistance on the other, etc.), and to continue such struggles as benefit unity and resistance to Japan (for freedom of criticism, for the independence of the political parties, for the improvement of the political and economic life of the people, etc.).

15. Within the over-all task of fighting for an anti-Japanese national united front and a unified democratic republic, the tasks of the Red Army and the anti-Japanese base area are:

(1) To suit the circumstances of war against Japan, the Red Army should immediately be reorganized into the National Rev-

olutionary Army and become a model army in that war by raising the level of its military, political and cultural education.

(2)   Our base area should become a component part of the state, apply its democratic system under the new conditions, reorganize its peace preservation corps, clear out traitors and saboteurs, and become a region that is a model of resistance and democracy.

(3)   Essential economic construction should be conducted in this area and the livelihood of the people should be improved.

(4)   Essential cultural work should be carried out.

OUR RESPONSIBILITY TO LEAD

16.   It is a law confirmed by Chinese history that the Chinese bourgeoisie, which may participate in fighting imperialism and feudalism in certain historical circumstances, vacillates and turns traitor in others, because of its economic and political flabbiness. Thus it is history's verdict that China's bourgeois-democratic revolution against imperialism and feudalism is a task that can be completed, not under the leadership of the bourgeoisie, but only under that of the proletariat. What is more, it is possible to overcome the bourgeoisie's inherent vacillation and lack of thoroughness and to prevent the miscarriage of the revolution only by bringing the perseverance and thoroughness of the proletariat in the democratic revolution into full play. Is the proletariat to follow the bourgeoisie, or is the bourgeoisie to follow the proletariat? This question of responsibility for leadership in the Chinese revolution is the linchpin upon which the success or failure of the revolution depends. The experience of 1924-27 shows how the revolution forged ahead when the bourgeoisie followed the political leadership of the proletariat and met defeat when the proletariat became the political tail of the bourgeoisie through the fault of the Communist Party.[17] This piece of history should not be allowed to repeat itself. In the present circumstances, without the political leadership of the proletariat and its party it is impossible to establish an anti-Japanese national united front, to attain the objectives of peace, democracy and armed resistance and to defend the motherland, and impossible to set up a unified democratic republic. Today the bourgeoisie, represented by the Kuomintang, is still very passive

and conservative, and the proof of this is its long hesitation about accepting the anti-Japanese national united front initiated by the Communist Party. This situation increases the responsibility of the proletariat and its party for giving political leadership. To function as the general staff in resisting Japan and saving the nation is a responsibility the Communist Party cannot relinquish, an obligation it cannot decline.

17. How does the proletariat give political leadership through its party to all the revolutionary classes in the country? First, by putting forward basic political slogans that accord with the course of historical development and by putting forward slogans of action for each stage of development and each major turn of events in order to translate these political slogans into reality. For instance, we have put forward the basic slogans for "an anti-Japanese national united front" and for "a unified democratic republic", but we have also put forward the slogans, "end the civil war", "fight for democracy" and "carry out armed resistance", as specific objectives for concerted action by the entire nation; without such specific objectives political leadership is out of the question. Second, the proletariat, and especially its vanguard the Communist Party, should set an example through its boundless enthusiasm and loyalty in achieving the specific objectives when the whole country goes into action for them. In the fight to fulfil all the tasks of the anti-Japanese national united front and the democratic republic, Communists should be the most far-sighted, the most self-sacrificing, the most resolute, and the least prejudiced in sizing up situations, and should rely on the majority of the masses and win their support. Third, the Communist Party should establish proper relations with its allies and develop and consolidate its alliance with them, while adhering to the principle of never relinquishing its defined political objectives. Fourth, it should expand the ranks of the Communist Party and maintain its ideological unity and strict discipline. It is by doing all these things that the Communist Party gives effect to its political leadership of the people throughout China. They constitute the foundation for guaranteeing our political leadership and for ensuring that the revolution will win complete victory and not be disrupted by the vacillations of our allies.

18. When internal peace is achieved and co-operation is established between the two parties, changes will have to be made in the forms of struggle, organization and work which we adopted when the line was one of maintaining a regime antagonistic to that of the Kuo-

mintang. They will mainly be changes from military to peaceful forms and from illegal to legal forms. It will not be easy to make these changes and we shall have to learn afresh. The retraining of our cadres thus becomes a key link.

19. Many comrades have been asking questions about the nature of the democratic republic and its future. Our answer is: as to its class nature, the republic will be an alliance of all revolutionary classes, and as to its future, it may move towards socialism. Our democratic republic is to be established in the course of national armed resistance under the leadership of the proletariat and in the new international environment (with socialism victorious in the Soviet Union and the approach of a new period of world revolution). Therefore, though it will still be a bourgeois-democratic state socially and economically, yet it will be different from the general run of bourgeois republics because, in concrete political terms, it will have to be a state based on the alliance of the working class, the peasantry, the petty bourgeoisie and the bourgeoisie. Thus, as to the future of the democratic republic, though it may move in a capitalist direction, the possibility also exists that it will turn towards socialism, and the party of the Chinese proletariat should struggle hard for the latter prospect.

20. The fight against closed-doorism and adventurism and also against tailism is essential to the accomplishment of the Party's tasks. In the mass movements our Party has a traditional tendency towards rank closed-doorism, haughty sectarianism, and adventurism; this ugly tendency hinders the Party in establishing an anti-Japanese national united front and winning over the majority of the masses. It is absolutely necessary to wipe out this tendency in each and every field of work. What we ask is: rely on the majority and take the whole situation into account. There must be no revival of the Chen Tu-hsiu type of tailism, which is a reflection of bourgeois reformism in the ranks of the proletariat. To debase the class stand of the Party, to obscure its distinctive features, to sacrifice the interests of the workers and peasants to suit the needs of bourgeois reformism, is sure to lead the revolution to defeat. What we ask is: carry out firm revolutionary policies and strive for complete victory in the bourgeois-democratic revolution. To overcome the undesirable tendencies we have described, it is absolutely necessary to raise the Marxist-Leninist theoretical level of the whole Party, for Marxism-Leninism alone is the compass which can guide the Chinese revolution to victory.

NOTES

[1] The Northern China Incident took place in 1935 when the Japanese carried on aggression against northern China and the Kuomintang government headed by Chiang Kai-shek betrayed our sovereignty and humiliated our nation. In May of that year, the Japanese demanded that the Kuomintang government grant them administrative authority over northern China, and in June Ho Ying-chin, the Kuomintang government's representative there, submitted and signed an agreement with Yoshijiro Umezu, commander of the invading forces in northern China, which became known as the "Ho-Umezu Agreement". By its terms China forfeited much of her sovereignty in the provinces of Hopei and Chahar. In October, at the instigation of the Japanese invaders, some Chinese traitors staged a revolt in Hsiangho, Hopei Province, and seized the county town. In November, a number of Chinese traitors were put up by the Japanese invaders to start a self-styled movement of autonomy in the five provinces of northern China, and a puppet "Anti-Communist Autonomous Administration" was established in eastern Hopei. To meet the Japanese demand for "special administration for northern China", the Kuomintang government appointed Sung Cheh-yuan and others to form a "Political Council for Hopei and Chahar".

[2] This declaration was issued by the Chinese Communist Party on August 1, 1935. Its main points are contained in the following extracts:

"At this moment when our country and our people are threatened with imminent destruction, the Communist Party once again appeals to all fellow-countrymen: whatever the past or present differences of political opinion and of interests among the political parties, whatever the differences of view and of interests among our countrymen in their various walks of life, whatever the past or present hostilities between the various armies, we should all truly awaken to the realization that 'brothers quarrelling at home, join forces against attacks from without' and, first and foremost, we should stop the civil war so as to concentrate the nation's resources (manpower, material and financial resources, and the armed forces) on the fight for the sacred cause of resisting Japan and saving the nation. Once again the Communist Party solemnly declares: if the Kuomintang troops cease their attacks on the Red Army and if any units carry out resistance to Japan, then the Red Army, regardless of any old feuds or present conflicts or differences on domestic issues, will not only immediately cease its hostile actions against these units, but willingly work closely with them to save the nation."

"The Communist Party is willing to initiate a national defence government of this kind; for the joint formation of such a national defence government it is ready to hold immediate talks with all those willing to join the cause of resisting Japan and saving the nation — all political parties, all organizations (trade unions, peasant associations, student unions, chambers of commerce, educational associations, journalists' societies, associations of teachers and other staff of schools, fellow-townsmen's associations, the Chih Kung Tang, the Association for National Armed Self-Defence, the Anti-Japanese Association, the Association for National Salvation, etc.), all prominent public figures, scholars and statesmen and all local military and administrative bodies. The national defence government emerging out of these negotiations should be a provisional organ of leadership for saving the nation from subjugation and ensuring its survival. It should endeavour to convene a delegate body truly representative of all our countrymen (with delegates democratically elected by all the various circles of workers, peasants, soldiers, government personnel, businessmen and students, by all parties and all organizations willing to resist Japan and save the nation, and by all overseas Chinese and all the nationalities within China's boundaries) to discuss all problems relating to armed resistance and national salvation in more specific terms. The Communist Party will do its very best to help convene such an assembly of representatives of the people and to carry out all its decisions."

"An anti-Japanese united army should be formed of all troops willing to fight Japan. A single general headquarters of this army should be set up under the leadership of the national defence government. The question of whether this headquarters should be composed of representatives elected by the officers and men of the various anti-Japanese army units or be formed in some other way should be decided by the representatives of all circles and by the will of the people. The Red Army will unreservedly be the first to join this united army and fulfil its duty in resisting Japan and saving the nation. To enable the national defence government and the anti-Japanese united army effectively to discharge their immense responsibilities for national defence and for resisting Japan, the Communist Party hereby appeals to the whole nation: those who have money give money, those who have guns give guns, those who have grain give grain, those who have labour power give labour power, and those who have special skill contribute special skill, so that all our fellow-countrymen will be mobilized and all weapons, old or modern, will be used to arm the people in millions upon millions."

[3] The December resolution was the "Resolution on the Present Political Situation and the Tasks of the Party", adopted at the meeting of the Political Bureau of the Central Committee of the Chinese Communist Party at Wayaopao, northern Shensi, on December 25, 1935. It made a comprehensive analysis of the current internal and international situation and the changes in class relations in China, and formulated the Party's policy. The resolution runs in part as follows:

The present situation shows that the attempts of Japanese imperialism to annex China have shocked the whole country and the whole world. Changes have taken place or are taking place in the relations between all classes, strata, political parties and armed forces in China's political life. There is a realignment of forces in both the national revolutionary front and the national counter-revolutionary front. Therefore, the Party's tactical line is to arouse, unite and organize the revolutionary forces throughout the country and among all the nationalities to oppose the chief enemy confronting them, namely, Japanese imperialism and the arch-traitor Chiang Kai-shek. All people, all parties, all armed forces and all classes, in so far as they are opposed to Japanese imperialism and the traitor Chiang Kai-shek, should unite and wage the sacred national revolutionary war, drive the Japanese imperialists out of China, overthrow the rule of their running dogs in China, achieve the complete liberation of the Chinese nation and safeguard China's independence and territorial integrity. Only by establishing the broadest anti-Japanese national united front (embracing the lower and upper strata) can we defeat Japanese imperialism and its running dog, Chiang Kai-shek. Of course, different individuals, different organizations, different social classes and strata and the various armed forces join the anti-Japanese national revolution from different motives and with different class standpoints. Some do so in order to hold on to their positions, some to gain leadership in the movement so that it will not go beyond the limits they allow, and some genuinely to work for the complete liberation of the Chinese nation. Precisely because their motives and their standpoints differ, some will vacillate or turn traitor at the very start of the struggle, some will become indifferent or withdraw from the fight midway, and some will determinedly fight to the end. Nevertheless, our task is to unite not only all possible basic forces but also all potential allies likely to resist Japan, and enable the people throughout the country who have labour power to give labour power, those who have money to give money, those who have guns to give guns, and those who have knowledge to contribute knowledge, leaving no patriotic Chinese outside the anti-Japanese front. Such is the general line of the Party's tactics for the broadest possible national united front. Only by pursuing this line can we mobilize the forces of the whole people to deal with the common enemy, Japanese imperialism and the traitor Chiang Kai-shek. The Chinese working class and peasantry remain the basic motive forces of the Chinese revolution. The broad masses of the petty bourgeoisie and the revolutionary intellectuals are their most reliable allies in the national revolution. A solid alliance of the workers, the peasants and the petty bourgeoisie is the basic force for defeating Japanese imperialism and the traitors and collaborators. When a section of the national bourgeoisie and the warlords gives moral support, maintains benevolent neutrality or directly participates in the struggle against Japan and the traitors and collaborators, this will serve to expand the anti-Japanese front, however much it may disapprove of the agrarian revolution and Red political power. For the total strength of the counter-revolution will thus be reduced and the total strength of the revolution increased. To this end, the Party should adopt appropriate ways and means to win these forces over to the anti-Japanese front. Moreover, unity is by no means prevalent even in the camp of the landlord and comprador classes. Since the contention for China among many imperialist powers has generated contending groups of traitors in their service with contradictions and conflicts among them, the Party should employ a variety of methods to ensure that for the time being some of these counter-revolutionary forces do not actively oppose the anti-Japanese front. The same tactics should be applied in dealing with the imperialist powers other than Japan. In arousing, uniting and organizing the forces of the people throughout the country to fight the common enemy, the Party should resolutely and unswervingly combat all tendencies towards vacillation, compromise, capitulation and betrayal within the anti-Japanese united front. Those who disrupt the Chinese people's anti-Japanese movement are traitors or collaborators whom we should all join in hitting hard. The Communist Party should win the leadership of the anti-Japanese front by being resolute and right in its words and deeds against the Japanese imperialists and the traitors and collaborators. Only under the Communist Party's leadership can the anti-Japanese movement be completely victorious. With regard to the masses in the anti-Japanese war, it is necessary to satisfy their demands in matters affecting their basic interests (the demand of the peasants for land and the demand of the workers, the soldiers, the urban poor and the intellectuals for better living). Only by satisfying their demands will we be able to mobilize still broader sections of the masses to join the anti-Japanese ranks, keep up the anti-Japanese movement, and lead the movement to complete victory. And only thus can the Party win leadership in the anti-Japanese war.

See "On Tactics Against Japanese Imperialism", pp. 153-78 of this volume.

⁴ The Red Army sent an open telegram on May 5, 1936 demanding that the
Nanking government end the civil war, conduct peace negotiations with the Communists for unity against Japan. The text reads as follows:

To the Military Council of the Nanking National Government; to all land,
sea and air forces; to all parties, all political groups; all public bodies, all
newspapers; and to all fellow-countrymen refusing to be slaves to a foreign
nation:

After crossing the Yellow River on its eastward expedition, the Anti-
Japanese Vanguard of the Chinese People's Red Army, organized by the
Revolutionary Military Commission of the Chinese Red Army, was everywhere
victorious and won support from all over the country. But when it occupied
the Tatung-Puchow Railway and was energetically preparing to drive eastward
into Hopei to engage the Japanese imperialists directly, Chiang Kai-shek sent
more than ten divisions into Shansi and co-operated with Yen Hsi-shan in
barring its advance against the Japanese. He also ordered the troops under
Chang Hsueh-liang and Yang Hu-cheng, as well as the troops in northern
Shensi, to march on the Shensi-Kansu Red area to harass our anti-Japanese
rear. In order to be able to reach and fight the Japanese, the people's Anti-
Japanese Vanguard should have concentrated its entire strength and wiped out
Chiang's troops blocking the way. But after much deliberation, the Revolutionary
Military Commission of the Red Army decided that a battle to the finish between
the two sides in the present national crisis would only damage China's strength
for national defence and delight the Japanese imperialists, whichever side
emerged victorious. Furthermore, there are quite a number of patriotic officers
and men in Chiang Kai-shek's and Yen Hsi-shan's armies who are willing to
end the civil war and unite to resist Japan, and it is really against their con-
sciences to obey Chiang's and Yen's orders and block the Red Army on its way
to fight the Japanese. Therefore, in spite of its numerous victories in Shansi,
the Revolutionary Military Commission of the Red Army has withdrawn the
people's Anti-Japanese Vanguard to the west of the Yellow River in order to
preserve China's strength for national defence and thereby help to bring nearer
the war of resistance against Japan, resolutely carry out our repeated declara-
tions to the nation on ending the civil war and uniting to resist Japan, and
hasten the final awakening of Chiang Kai-shek and the patriotic officers and
men in his army. With this demonstration of our good faith to the Nanking
government, to all the country's land, sea and air forces and to the whole
nation, we are ready to arrange a cease-fire with all the armed units attacking the
anti-Japanese Red Army within one month and to enter into peace negotiations
with them in order to end the civil war and resist Japan. The Revolutionary
Military Commission of the Red Army hereby solemnly advises the gentlemen
of the Nanking government at this critical juncture, when our country and people
are threatened with imminent destruction, to make a determined effort to atone
for past misdeeds and end the civil war in the whole country, to join forces
against attacks from without in the spirit of brothers quarrelling at home, and
first of all end the civil war in Shensi, Kansu and Shansi, whereupon both sides
should appoint delegates to discuss specific measures for resisting Japan and
saving the nation. This will be a blessing to the nation and the country as well
as for your own good. However, if you obstinately refuse to listen to reason
and prefer to be traitors and collaborators, your rule will surely collapse in the
end and you will be spurned and overthrown by the whole nation. The old
saying runs, "A thousand pointing fingers accuse, and a man dies even without

a sickness." Or as another saying goes, "The butcher who lays down his knife at once becomes a Buddha." These are words for you gentlemen to digest and ponder. And the Revolutionary Military Commission of the Red Army calls upon all organizations, all parties and all people in the country, who refuse to be slaves to a foreign nation, to support our proposal for a cease-fire and peace negotiations, and for unity against Japan, to organize committees for hastening the cessation of the civil war and to send representatives to the front to stop the firing on both sides and to supervise the full implementation of this proposal.

[5] See "A Statement on Chiang Kai-shek's Statement", Note 7, pp. 259-61 of this volume.

[6] The slogan of "A people's republic" was first put forward in the "Resolution on the Present Political Situation and the Tasks of the Party", adopted at the meeting of the Political Bureau of the Central Committee of the Chinese Communist Party held in December 1935, and in the report by Comrade Mao Tse-tung "On Tactics Against Japanese Imperialism". Later circumstances made it necessary for the Party to adopt the policy of forcing Chiang Kai-shek to resist Japan, and, as the slogan would have been unacceptable to the Chiang Kai-shek clique, it was changed into "A democratic republic" in the Party's letter of August 1936 to the Kuomintang. The slogan of a democratic republic was subsequently explained in more concrete terms in the "Resolution on the New Situation in the Movement to Resist Japan and Save the Nation, and on the Democratic Republic", which the Central Committee of the Party adopted in September of the same year. Though different in form, the two slogans are in essence the same. The following two extracts concerning the democratic republic are from the September 1936 resolution of the Party's Central Committee:

"The Central Committee holds that in the present situation it is necessary to put forward the slogan of 'establish a democratic republic', because this is the best way to unite all the anti-Japanese forces to safeguard China's territorial integrity and avert the calamity of the destruction of China and of the subjugation of her people, and also because this is the most fitting slogan for the formation of a united front based on the democratic demands of the broad masses of the people. By 'a democratic republic' we mean a democracy which is geographically more extensive than that of the workers' and peasants' democratic dictatorship in one part of China and a political system which is far more progressive than the one-party dictatorship of the Kuomintang in the main parts of China; it will therefore offer a better guarantee of the wide development of armed resistance to Japan and the achievement of complete victory. Moreover, the democratic republic will not only enable the broadest sections of the Chinese people to take part in the country's political life and enhance their political consciousness and organized strength, but also give the Chinese proletariat and its leader, the Communist Party, scope for activity in the struggle for the future victory of socialism. Therefore, the Chinese Communist Party proclaims its active support of the movement for a democratic republic. It also declares that when the democratic republic is established through the length and breadth of China and a parliament elected by universal suffrage is convened, the Red areas will at once become an organic part of the republic, the people of the Red areas will elect their representatives to the parliament, and the same democratic system will be put into practice in the Red areas."

"The Central Committee stresses that we shall impel the Kuomintang government in Nanking to resist Japan and we shall create the prerequisites for the democratic republic only by extending the Chinese people's movement of armed resistance and national salvation, by broadening the anti-Japanese national united front of all political parties, people of all walks of life and all armies, by strengthening the Chinese Communist Party's role of political leadership in the national united front, by greatly consolidating the Red political power and the Red Army, and by waging a determined struggle against all words and deeds which betray our sovereignty and humiliate our nation or weaken the forces of the national united front. It is impossible for the democratic republic to become a reality without bitter and sustained struggles, without the mobilization of the entire Chinese nation, and without a high tide of revolution. In the course of the struggle for the democratic republic, the Chinese Communist Party should insist that the democratic republic should begin by carrying out the Ten-Point Programme for Resisting Japan and Saving the Nation proposed by our Party and go on until it finally fulfils the basic tasks of the Chinese bourgeois-democratic revolution."

[7] This telegram was dispatched on February 10, 1937. The full text reads as follows:

To the Third Plenary Session of the Central Executive Committee of the Kuomintang

Gentlemen:

It is a matter of national rejoicing that the Sian Incident has been settled peacefully. From now on it will be possible for the policy of internal peace and for unity and solidarity against foreign aggression to be carried out; this is a blessing to the nation and the country. At this moment when the Japanese invaders are running amuck and the survival of the Chinese nation hangs by a thread, our Party eagerly hopes that, in accordance with this policy, the Third Plenary Session of the Central Executive Committee of your party will decide on the following as the national policy:

(1) end all civil wars and concentrate the country's strength in a united effort to meet the foreign aggression;

(2) guarantee freedom of speech, assembly and association, and release all political prisoners;

(3) call a conference of representatives of all political parties, people of all walks of life and all armies, and concentrate the nation's talents in a common endeavour to save the country;

(4) speedily complete all preparations for resisting Japan; and

(5) improve the livelihood of the people.

If the Third Plenary Session of your Central Executive Committee can succeed in resolutely and firmly deciding on this as the national policy, our Party will pledge the following as an expression of our good faith in solidarity against foreign aggression:

(1) the policy of armed insurrection to overthrow the National Government will be discontinued throughout the country;

(2) the Workers' and Peasants' Democratic Government will be renamed the Government of the Special Region of the Republic of China and the Red Army will be redesignated as part of the National Revolutionary Army, and they will come under the direction of the Central Government in Nanking and its Military Council respectively;

(3) a thoroughly democratic system based on universal suffrage will be put into effect in the areas under the Government of the Special Region; and

(4) the policy of confiscating the land of the landlords will be discontinued and the common programme of the anti-Japanese national united front resolutely carried out.

[8] In November and December 1936, big strikes broke out among 45,000 workers in twenty-six Japanese and Chinese-owned textile mills in Shanghai. In December all the workers of the Japanese-owned textile mills in Tsingtao struck in sympathy. The Shanghai workers won their strike, their wages were increased five per cent retrospectively from November, and the employers undertook not to sack workers arbitrarily or assault or abuse them. But the strike in Tsingtao was suppressed by Japanese marines.

[9] Britain and the United States began to change their attitude towards Japan and exerted some influence on the Chiang Kai-shek government in its policy towards Japan after Japanese imperialism occupied Shanhaikuan and penetrated into northern China in 1933, and especially after the conclusion of the "Ho-Umezu Agreement" (see Note 1, p. 276) in 1935, which directly jeopardized their imperialist interests in northern and central China. During the Sian Incident of 1936, Britain suggested rejection of Japanese demands prejudicial to British interests in China and even intimated that, provided the Chiang Kai-shek government maintained its rule over the Chinese people, it would not be a bad thing for it to "form some sort of alliance with the Communist Party" so as to deal a blow to the Japanese policy of aggression.

[10] In June 1936, Li Tsung-jen and Pai Chung-hsi, warlords of Kwangsi, and Chen Chi-tang, warlord of Kwangtung, jointly declared their opposition to Chiang Kai-shek under the pretext of "resisting Japan and saving the nation". In August their opposition melted away before Chiang Kai-shek's tactics of bribery and divide and rule.

[11] The Japanese forces and puppet troops began to invade Suiyuan in August 1936. In November, the Chinese troops there fought back and the people throughout the country started a movement in support of their fight.

[12] After the "Ho-Umezu Agreement" of 1935, the Nanking Kuomintang government took a firmer attitude towards Japan under the pressure of the people's rising anti-Japanese sentiment and under the impact of the stiffer policy the British and U.S. imperialists were adopting towards Japan. The Kuomintang government used stalling tactics in the negotiations with Japan from September to December 1936, which ended without result.

[13] This was the meeting of the Central Executive Committee of the Kuomintang on February 15, 1937 after the peaceful settlement of the Sian Incident.

[14] Ah Q is the leading character in The True Story of Ah Q, the famous novel by the great Chinese writer Lu Hsun. Ah Q typifies all those who compensate themselves for their failures and setbacks in real life by regarding them as moral or spiritual victories.

[15] In the stage of China's bourgeois-democratic revolution, the Communists agreed with the basic points of Sun Yat-sen's programme and co-operated with him, which did not mean that they agreed with the bourgeois and petty-bourgeois world outlook or ideological system of which he was the exponent. As the vanguard of the Chinese proletariat, the Chinese Communists had an entirely different world outlook or ideological system and theoretical approach to the national and other problems, from those of Sun Yat-sen.

[16] Reorganized by Sun Yat-sen in 1924, the Kuomintang became a revolutionary alliance of several classes, which members of the Communist Party joined

in their individual capacity. After its betrayal of the revolution in 1927, the Kuomintang carried out what it called a "party purge" throughout the country, butchering the Communists and many of its own left-wingers who genuinely supported Dr. Sun Yat-sen's Three Great Policies. From then on the Kuomintang became the counter-revolutionary political party of the big landlords and big bourgeoisie.

[17] This refers to the situation created by the opportunist leadership of the Central Committee of the Party in the first half of 1927.

WIN THE MASSES IN THEIR MILLIONS FOR THE ANTI-JAPANESE NATIONAL UNITED FRONT

May 7, 1937

Comrades! In the course of the discussions of the last few days you have expressed agreement with my report, "The Tasks of the Chinese Communist Party in the Period of Resistance to Japan"; only a few comrades expressed different views. As these dissenting views were rather significant, I shall discuss them first in my concluding speech before dealing with certain other problems.

THE QUESTION OF PEACE

For nearly two years our Party has fought for internal peace. After the Third Plenary Session of the Kuomintang Central Executive Committee, we declared that peace had been attained, that the stage of "fighting for peace" was over, and that the new task was to "consolidate the peace". We also pointed out that this new task was linked with "fighting for democracy", *i.e.*, consolidating the peace by fighting for democracy. However, some comrades argue that this view of ours is untenable. It follows that they must either arrive at the opposite view or hover between the two. For they argue, "Japan is retreating[1] and Nanking is wavering more than ever; the contradiction between the two countries is becoming weaker and the contradiction within the country is growing sharper." Naturally, according to this appraisal,

---

This was the concluding speech made by Comrade Mao Tse-tung at the National Conference of the Communist Party of China, held in May 1937.

285

there is no new stage or new task, and the situation has reverted to its old stage or even deteriorated. I think this view incorrect.

In saying that peace has been attained, we do not mean that it is consolidated; on the contrary, we have said that it is not consolidated. Bringing about peace and consolidating it are two different things. History might reverse its course for a while and peace might meet with setbacks because of the existence of Japanese imperialism, traitors and the pro-Japanese group. But the fact is that peace was attained after the Sian Incident and was the product of several factors (Japan's fundamental policy of invasion, the favourable attitude of the Soviet Union and also Britain, the United States and France towards internal peace in China, the pressure of the Chinese people, the Communist Party's peace policy during the Sian Incident and its policy for ending the antagonism between the two regimes, the differentiation within the bourgeoisie, the differentiation within the Kuomintang, and so on); peace cannot be made or unmade by Chiang Kai-shek alone. To unmake it, he would have to fight against many forces and draw closer to the Japanese imperialists and the pro-Japanese group. There is no doubt that the Japanese imperialists and the pro-Japanese group are still endeavouring to prolong civil war in China. That is precisely why peace is not yet consolidated. Such being the case, we have come to the conclusion that, instead of reverting to the old slogans of "end the civil war" and "fight for peace", we should take a step forward and adopt the new slogan of "fight for democracy", for this is the only way to consolidate internal peace and bring the war of resistance against Japan into being. Why do we put forward the three closely related slogans of "consolidate the peace", "fight for democracy", and "carry out armed resistance"? The answer is that we desire to push the wheel of revolution forward and that circumstances allow us to do so. Those who deny the new stage and the new task, who deny that the Kuomintang has "begun to change" and by the same logic also deny the achievements of all the forces that have been struggling for peace during the last year and a half will remain where they were before, without advancing an inch.

Why do these comrades make such an unsound appraisal? Because in weighing up the current situation they start not from fundamentals but from a number of limited and transient phenomena (Sato's diplomacy, the Soochow trial,[2] the suppression of strikes, the eastward transfer of the Northeastern Army,[3] General Yang Hu-cheng's journey abroad,[4] and so on); hence their dismal picture. We say that the Kuomintang has begun to change and we also say that it has not changed completely. It is inconceivable that the Kuomintang's reactionary policy over the past ten years will completely change without new efforts — without more and greater efforts — on our part and on the part of the people. Quite a number of reputedly "Left" people, who often bitterly denounce the Kuomintang and who during the Sian Incident advocated putting Chiang to death and "fighting our way out through Tungkuan",[5] are now astonished when events like the Soochow trial occur immediately after peace is attained, and ask, "Why does Chiang Kai-shek still do such things?" They ought to understand that neither the Communists nor Chiang Kai-shek are gods, nor are they isolated individuals, but members of a party or a class. The Communist Party can push the revolution forward by degrees but cannot clear away all the evils in the country overnight. Chiang Kai-shek and the Kuomintang have begun to change, but the accumulated filth of the past ten years will certainly not be rapidly removed without great effort on the part of the whole people. We maintain that the trend is towards peace, democracy and resistance, but this does not imply that the old evils — civil war, dictatorship and non-resistance — will be swept away without any effort. It is only through struggle and hard work, and over a long period too, that we can eliminate the old evils, the old filth, and prevent setbacks or even reversals in the revolution.

"They are bent on destroying us." Quite true, they are always trying to destroy us. I fully admit the soundness of this appraisal, and indeed one would have to be fast asleep to overlook the point. But the question is whether there has been any change in the way they are trying to destroy us. I think there has been. The change is from war and massacre to reform and deceit, from a tough policy to a soft one, from a military to a political policy. Why has there been such a change? Confronted with Japanese imperialism, the bourgeoisie and the Kuomintang are temporarily forced to seek an ally in the proletariat, just as we are seeking an ally in the bourgeoisie. We should take this as our point of departure in considering the question. Internationally, for a similar reason, the French government has changed from hostility towards the Soviet Union to alliance with it.[6] Our domestic task has changed from a military to a political one. We for our part have no use for plotting or scheming; our aim is to defeat Japanese imperialism in a common effort by uniting with all those members of the bourgeoisie and the Kuomintang who favour resistance.

THE QUESTION OF DEMOCRACY

"To put the emphasis on democracy is wrong, the emphasis should be solely on resistance to Japan. Without direct action against Japan, there can be no movement for democracy. The majority of the people want only resistance to Japan, not democracy, and what is needed is another December 9th Movement."[7]

Let me first put a few questions. Can it be said that what the majority of the people wanted in the previous stage (*i.e.*, from the December 9th Movement of 1935 to the Third Plenary Session of the Kuomintang Central Executive Committee in February 1937) was merely resistance to Japan and not internal peace? Was it wrong to emphasize internal peace then? Was it impossible to have a movement for internal peace without direct action against Japan (the Sian Incident and the Third Plenary Session of the Kuomintang Central Executive Committee took place after the resistance in Suiyuan ended, and today, too, there is as yet nothing equivalent to the Suiyuan resistance or the December 9th Movement)? Everybody knew that in order to resist Japan there had to be internal peace, that without internal peace there could be no resistance to Japan, and that internal peace was a condition for resistance. All the anti-Japanese activities in the previous stage, whether direct or indirect (beginning with the December 9th Movement and ending with the Third Plenary Session of the Kuomintang Central Executive Committee), were centred on the struggle for internal peace which was then the central link, the most essential thing, in the anti-Japanese movement.

Similarly today, in the new stage, democracy is the most essential thing for resistance to Japan, and to work for democracy is to work for resistance to Japan. Resistance and democracy are interdependent, just as are resistance and internal peace, democracy and internal peace. Democracy is the guarantee of resistance, while resistance can provide favourable conditions for developing the movement for democracy.

We hope there may be — and indeed there will be — many direct and indirect struggles against Japan in the new stage, and these will give an impetus to the war of resistance and greatly assist the movement for democracy. But the core and essence of the revolutionary task history has set us is the winning of democracy. Is it, then, wrong to keep stressing democracy? I do not think so.

"Japan is stepping back, Britain and Japan are virtually inclined to strike a balance, and Nanking is wavering more than ever." Ignorance of the laws of historical development has given rise to this needless anxiety. If there were a revolution in Japan and she really withdrew from China, it would help the Chinese revolution and would be just what we want, marking the beginning of the collapse of the world front of aggression. What room for anxiety would there be then? But as a matter of fact, this is not what is happening; Sato's diplomatic moves are preparations for a major war, and a major war confronts us. Britain's policy of wavering can get her nowhere, her clash of interests with Japan making this certain. If Nanking continues to waver for long, it will become the enemy of the whole nation, and its own interests do not allow it to keep on wavering. A temporary retrogression cannot change the general law of history. Hence one should not deny the existence of the new stage or the necessity of setting the task of winning democracy. In any case, moreover, the slogan of democracy is appropriate, because it is obvious to everybody that the Chinese people have far too little democracy, and not too much. Actual events have also shown that to define the new stage, and to set the winning of democracy as our task, is to move a step closer to resistance. Events have moved forward; let us not put the clock back!

"Why do we place so much emphasis on a national assembly?" Because it is something which can affect every aspect of life, because it is the bridge from reactionary dictatorship to democracy, because it is connected with national defence, and because it is a legal institution. To recover eastern Hopei and northern Chahar, to combat smuggling,[8] to oppose "economic collaboration",[9] etc., as many comrades have proposed, is quite correct, but this complements rather than in any way conflicts with the fight for democracy and a national assembly; the essential thing is still the national assembly and freedom for the people.

It is correct and indisputable that the day-to-day struggle against Japan and the people's struggle for a better life must be linked up with the movement for democracy. Nevertheless, the central and essential thing in the present stage is democracy and freedom.

THE QUESTION OF THE FUTURE OF THE REVOLUTION

Some comrades have raised this question, and here I can only give a brief answer.

In the writing of an article the second half can be written only after the first half is finished. Resolute leadership of the democratic revolution is the prerequisite for the victory of socialism. We are fighting for socialism, and in this respect we are different from those who confine themselves to the revolutionary Three People's Principles. It is the great future goal to which our present efforts are directed; if we lose sight of the goal, we cease to be Communists. But equally we cease to be Communists if we relax our efforts of today.

We are exponents of the theory of the transition of the revolution[10] and we are for the transition of the democratic revolution in the direction of socialism. The democratic revolution will develop through several stages, all under the slogan of a democratic republic. The change from the predominance of the bourgeoisie to that of the proletariat is a long process of struggle, of struggle for leadership in which success depends on the work of the Communist Party in raising the level of political consciousness and organization both of the proletariat and of the peasantry and urban petty bourgeoisie.

The staunch ally of the proletariat is the peasantry, and next comes the urban petty bourgeoisie. It is the bourgeoisie that will contend with us for leadership.

To overcome the vacillation of the bourgeoisie and its lack of revolutionary thoroughness we must rely on the strength of the masses and on the correctness of our policy, or otherwise the bourgeoisie will come out on top.

A bloodless transition is what we would like and we should strive for it, but what will happen will depend on the strength of the masses.

We are exponents of the theory of the transition of the revolution, and not of the Trotskyite theory of "permanent revolution".[11] We are for the attainment of socialism by going through all the necessary stages of the democratic republic. We are opposed to tailism, but we are also opposed to adventurism and impetuosity.

To reject the participation of the bourgeoisie in the revolution on the ground that it can only be temporary and to describe the alliance with anti-Japanese sections of the bourgeoisie (in a semi-colonial country) as capitulation is a Trotskyite approach, with which we cannot agree. Today such an alliance is in fact a necessary bridge on the way to socialism.

THE QUESTION OF CADRES

A great revolution requires a great party and many first-rate cadres to guide it. In China, with a population of 450 million, it is impossible to carry through our great revolution, which is unprecedented in history, if the leadership consists of a small, narrow group and if the Party leaders and cadres are petty-minded, short-sighted and incompetent. The Chinese Communist Party has been a large party for a long time and it is still large despite the losses during the period of reaction; it has many good leaders and cadres, but still not enough. Our Party organizations must be extended all over the country and we must purposefully train tens of thousands of cadres and hundreds of first-rate leaders. They must be cadres and leaders versed in Marxism-Leninism, politically far-sighted, competent in work, full of the spirit of self-sacrifice, capable of tackling problems on their own, steadfast in the midst of difficulties and loyal and devoted in serving the nation, the class and the Party. It is on these cadres and leaders that the Party relies for its links with the membership and the masses, and it is by relying on their firm leadership of the masses that the Party can succeed in defeating the enemy. Such cadres and leaders must be free from selfishness, from individualistic heroism, ostentation, sloth, passivity, and sectarian arrogance, and they must be selfless national and class heroes; such are the qualities and the style of work demanded of the members, cadres and leaders of our Party. Such is the spiritual legacy handed down to us by the tens of thousands of members, the thousands of cadres, and the scores of first-rate leaders who have laid down their lives for the cause. Beyond any doubt, we ought to acquire these qualities, do still better in remoulding ourselves and raise ourselves to a higher revolutionary level. But even this is not enough; we must also regard it as our duty to discover many more new cadres and leaders in the Party and the country. Our revolution depends on cadres. As Stalin said, "Cadres decide everything."[12]

THE QUESTION OF DEMOCRACY WITHIN THE PARTY

To attain this aim, inner-Party democracy is essential. If we are to make the Party strong, we must practise democratic centralism to stimulate the initiative of the whole membership. There was more centralism during the period of reaction and civil war. In the new period, centralism should be closely linked with democracy. Let us apply democracy, and so give scope to initiative throughout the Party. Let us give scope to the initiative of the whole Party membership, and so train new cadres in great numbers, eliminate the remnants of sectarianism, and unite the whole Party as solidly as steel.

UNITY IN THE CONFERENCE AND IN THE WHOLE PARTY

After explanation, the dissenting views on political issues voiced at this conference have given way to agreement, and the earlier difference between the line of the Central Committee and the line of retreat adopted under the leadership of certain comrades, has also been settled;[13] this shows that our Party is very solidly united. This unity provides the most important basis for the present national and democratic revolution, because it is only through the unity of the Communist Party that the unity of the whole class and the whole nation can be achieved, and it is only through the unity of the whole class and the whole nation that the enemy can be defeated and the national and democratic revolution accomplished.

WIN THE MASSES IN THEIR MILLIONS FOR THE ANTI-JAPANESE NATIONAL UNITED FRONT

The aim of our correct political policy and of our solid unity is to win the masses in their millions for the anti-Japanese national united front. The broad masses of the proletariat, the peasantry and the urban petty bourgeoisie need our work of propaganda, agitation and organization. Further efforts on our part are also needed to establish an alliance with those sections of the bourgeoisie which are opposed to Japan. To make the policy of the Party the policy of the masses requires effort, long and persistent effort, unrelenting and strenuous, patient and painstaking effort. Without such effort, we shall achieve nothing. The formation and consolidation of the anti-Japanese national united front, the accomplishment of the task incumbent on it and the establishment of a democratic republic in China are absolutely inseparable from our effort to win over the masses. If we succeed in bringing millions upon millions of the masses under our leadership by such effort, our revolutionary task can be speedily fulfilled. By our exertions we shall surely overthrow Japanese imperialism and attain complete national and social liberation.

NOTES

[1] The Japanese imperialists made temporary conciliatory gestures after the Sian Incident in order to induce the Kuomintang authorities to disrupt the internal peace which was being restored and to break up the anti-Japanese national united front which was taking shape. They arranged for the bogus autonomous government of Inner Mongolia under their control to release two messages, one in December 1936 and another in March 1937, pledging allegiance to the Kuomintang government in Nanking. And the Japanese foreign minister, Sato himself, publicly wooed Chiang Kai-shek, slyly declaring that Japan would improve its relations with China and help China achieve political unification and economic recovery. Furthermore, Japan sent a so-called Economic Study Group, headed by Kenji Kodama, a Japanese financial magnate, ostensibly to help China "complete the organization of a modern state". These were schemes for aggression and were known as "Sato's diplomacy"; they were called a "retreat on the part of Japan" by those people who were deluded by the Japanese imperialist make-believe.

[2] In April 1937, the Kuomintang High Court in Soochow tried Shen Chun-ju and six other leaders of the Resist Japan and Save the Nation Movement who had been arrested in November 1936 in Shanghai. The charge was "endangering the Republic", the usual trumped-up indictment the reactionary Kuomintang authorities used to stigmatize all patriotic movements.

[3] Prior to the Sian Incident, the Northeastern Army was stationed on the border between Shensi and Kansu Provinces and was in direct contact with the Red Army in northern Shensi. Greatly influenced by the Red Army, it subsequently staged the coup in Sian. In March 1937, the Northeastern Army was forced to go east to Honan and Anhwei Provinces, a move taken by the Kuomintang reactionaries to cut it off from contact with the Red Army and at the same time to sow discord in its ranks.

[4] General Yang Hu-cheng was a military leader in China's Northwest who staged the Sian Incident together with Chang Hsueh-liang. Thus the prime movers

in this incident were popularly linked together in the double-barrelled surname "Chang-Yang". When Chiang Kai-shek was released, Chang accompanied him to Nanking but was immediately placed under detention. In April 1937 Yang, too, was ousted from his post by the Kuomintang reactionaries and had to take leave of absence abroad. When the War of Resistance began, Yang returned to China to offer his services, only to be interned by Chiang Kai-shek for the rest of his life. In September 1949, when the People's Liberation Army was driving forward near Chungking, the Kuomintang had him murdered in a concentration camp.

[5] Tungkuan is a strategically important gateway on the borders of Shensi, Honan and Shansi. At the time of the Sian Incident the Kuomintang troops were mainly quartered east of it. Certain reputedly "Left" people in the Party, like Chang Kuo-tao, then urged that the Red Army should "fight its way out through Tungkuan", which meant that the Red Army should mount an offensive against the Kuomintang troops. This proposal ran counter to the Central Committee's policy for a peaceful settlement of the Sian Incident.

[6] For a long time after the October Revolution, the French imperialists pursued a hostile policy towards the Soviet Union. From 1918 to 1920, the French government took an active part in the armed intervention by 14 powers against the Soviet Union and continued its reactionary policy of isolating the Soviet Union even after the intervention failed. It was not until May 1935 that, under the influence of the Soviet Union's peace policy among the French people and because of the German fascist menace, France concluded a treaty of mutual assistance with the Soviet Union, though her reactionary government failed to observe it.

[7] The students' patriotic demonstration in Peking on December 9, 1935, led by the Chinese Communist Party. The movement called for the cessation of civil war and armed resistance to Japan and won nation-wide support.

[8] The smuggling of Japanese goods into China.

[9] This refers to the self-styled Sino-Japanese economic collaboration.

[10] See Karl Marx and Frederick Engels, *Manifesto of the Communist Party*, Part IV; V. I. Lenin, *Two Tactics of Social-Democracy in the Democratic Revolution*, Part XII and Part XIII; *History of the Communist Party of the Soviet Union (Bolsheviks), Short Course*, Chapter 3, Section 3.

[11] See J. V. Stalin, "The Foundations of Leninism", Part III; "The October Revolution and the Tactics of the Russian Communists", Part II; "Concerning Questions of Leninism", Part III.

[12] See J. V. Stalin, "Address Delivered in the Kremlin Palace to the Graduates from the Red Army Academies" in May 1935, in which he said: ". . . of all the valuable capital the world possesses, the most valuable and most decisive is people, cadres. It must be realized that under our present conditions 'cadres decide everything.' "

[13] This difference was between the line of the Party's Central Committee and Chang Kuo-tao's line of retreat in 1935-36. See "On Tactics Against Japanese Imperialism", Note 22, pp. 175-76 of this volume. In stating that "the earlier difference . . . has . . . been settled", Comrade Mao Tse-tung was referring to the fact that the Fourth Front Army of the Red Army had joined forces with the Central Red Army. Chang Kuo-tao's subsequent open betrayal of the Party and his degeneration into a counter-revolutionary was the act of an individual traitor and no longer a question of differences over Party line.

ON PRACTICE

On the Relation Between Knowledge and Practice, Between Knowing and Doing

July 1937

Before Marx, materialism examined the problem of knowledge apart from the social nature of man and apart from his historical development, and was therefore incapable of understanding the dependence of knowledge on social practice, that is, the dependence of knowledge on production and the class struggle.

Above all, Marxists regard man's activity in production as the most fundamental practical activity, the determinant of all his other activities. Man's knowledge depends mainly on his activity in material production, through which he comes gradually to understand the phenomena, the properties and the laws of nature, and the relations between himself and nature; and through his activity in production he also gradually comes to understand, in varying degrees, certain relations that exist between man and man. None of this knowledge can be acquired apart from activity in production. In a classless society every person, as a member of society, joins in common effort with the other members, enters into definite relations of production with them and engages in production to meet man's material needs. In all class societies, the members of the different social classes also enter, in different ways, into definite relations of production and

There used to be a number of comrades in our Party who were dogmatists and who for a long period rejected the experience of the Chinese revolution, denying the truth that "Marxism is not a dogma but a guide to action" and overawing people with words and phrases from Marxist works, torn out of context. There were also a number of comrades who were empiricists and who for a long period restricted themselves to their own fragmentary experience and did not understand the importance of theory for revolutionary practice or see the revolution as a whole, but worked blindly though industriously. The erroneous ideas of these two types of comrades, and particularly of the dogmatists, caused enormous losses to the engage in production to meet their material needs. This is the primary source from which human knowledge develops.

Man's social practice is not confined to activity in production, but takes many other forms — class struggle, political life, scientific and artistic pursuits; in short, as a social being, man participates in all spheres of the practical life of society. Thus man, in varying degrees, comes to know the different relations between man and man, not only through his material life but also through his political and cultural life (both of which are intimately bound up with material life). Of these other types of social practice, class struggle in particular, in all its various forms, exerts a profound influence on the development of man's knowledge. In class society everyone lives as a member of a particular class, and every kind of thinking, without exception, is stamped with the brand of a class.

Marxists hold that in human society activity in production develops step by step from a lower to a higher level and that consequently man's knowledge, whether of nature or of society, also develops step by step from a lower to a higher level, that is, from the shallower to the deeper, from the one-sided to the many-sided. For a very long period in history, men were necessarily confined to a one-sided understanding of the history of society because, for one thing, the bias of the exploiting classes always distorted history and, for another, the small scale of production limited man's outlook. It was not until the modern proletariat emerged along with immense forces of production (large-scale industry) that man was able to acquire a comprehensive, historical understanding of the development of society and turn this knowledge into a science, the science of Marxism.

Marxists hold that man's social practice alone is the criterion of the truth of his knowledge of the external world. What actually happens is that man's knowledge is verified only when he achieves the anticipated results in the process of social practice (material production, class struggle or scientific experiment). If a man wants to succeed in his work, that is, to achieve the anticipated results,

---

Chinese revolution during 1931-34, and yet the dogmatists, cloaking themselves as Marxists, confused a great many comrades. "On Practice" was written in order to expose the subjectivist errors of dogmatism and empiricism in the Party, and especially the error of dogmatism, from the standpoint of the Marxist theory of knowledge. It was entitled "On Practice" because its stress was on exposing the dogmatist kind of subjectivism, which belittles practice. The ideas contained in this essay were presented by Comrade Mao Tse-tung in a lecture at the Anti-Japanese Military and Political College in Yenan.

he must bring his ideas into correspondence with the laws of the objective external world; if they do not correspond, he will fail in his practice. After he fails, he draws his lessons, corrects his ideas to make them correspond to the laws of the external world, and can thus turn failure into success; this is what is meant by "failure is the mother of success" and "a fall into the pit, a gain in your wit". The dialectical-materialist theory of knowledge places practice in the primary position, holding that human knowledge can in no way be separated from practice and repudiating all the erroneous theories which deny the importance of practice or separate knowledge from practice. Thus Lenin said, *"Practice is higher than (theoretical) knowledge, for it has not only the dignity of universality, but also of immediate actuality."*[1] The Marxist philosophy of dialectical materialism has two outstanding characteristics. One is its class nature: it openly avows that dialectical materialism is in the service of the proletariat. The other is its practicality: it emphasizes the dependence of theory on practice, emphasizes that theory is based on practice and in turn serves practice. The truth of any knowledge or theory is determined not by subjective feelings, but by objective results in social practice. Only social practice can be the criterion of truth. The standpoint of practice is the primary and basic standpoint in the dialectical-materialist theory of knowledge.[2]

But how then does human knowledge arise from practice and in turn serve practice? This will become clear if we look at the process of development of knowledge.

In the process of practice, man at first sees only the phenomenal side, the separate aspects, the external relations of things. For instance, some people from outside come to Yenan on a tour of observation. In the first day or two, they see its topography, streets and houses; they meet many people, attend banquets, evening parties and mass meetings, hear talk of various kinds and read various documents, all these being the phenomena, the separate aspects and the external relations of things. This is called the perceptual stage of cognition, namely, the stage of sense perceptions and impressions. That is, these particular things in Yenan act on the sense organs of the members of the observation group, evoke sense perceptions and give rise in their brains to many impressions together with a rough sketch of the external relations among these impressions: this is the first stage of cognition. At this stage, man cannot as yet form concepts, which are deeper, or draw logical conclusions.

As social practice continues, things that give rise to man's sense perceptions and impressions in the course of his practice are repeated many times; then a sudden change (leap) takes place in the brain in the process of cognition, and concepts are formed. Concepts are no longer the phenomena, the separate aspects and the external relations of things; they grasp the essence, the totality and the internal relations of things. Between concepts and sense perceptions there is not only a quantitative but also a qualitative difference. Proceeding further, by means of judgement and inference one is able to draw logical conclusions. The expression in *San Kuo Yen Yi*,[3] "knit the brows and a stratagem comes to mind", or in everyday language, "let me think it over", refers to man's use of concepts in the brain to form judgements and inferences. This is the second stage of cognition. When the members of the observation group have collected various data and, what is more, have "thought them over", they are able to arrive at the judgement that "the Communist Party's policy of the National United Front Against Japan is thorough, sincere and genuine". Having made this judgement, they can, if they too are genuine about uniting to save the nation, go a step further and draw the following conclusion, "The National United Front Against Japan can succeed." This stage of conception, judgement and inference is the more important stage in the entire process of knowing a thing; it is the stage of rational knowledge. The real task of knowing is, through perception, to arrive at thought, to arrive step by step at the comprehension of the internal contradictions of objective things, of their laws and of the internal relations between one process and another, that is, to arrive at logical knowledge. To repeat, logical knowledge differs from perceptual knowledge in that perceptual knowledge pertains to the separate aspects, the phenomena and the external relations of things, whereas logical knowledge takes a big stride forward to reach the totality, the essence and the internal relations of things and discloses the inner contradictions in the surrounding world. Therefore, logical knowledge is capable of grasping the development of the surrounding world in its totality, in the internal relations of all its aspects.

This dialectical-materialist theory of the process of development of knowledge, basing itself on practice and proceeding from the shallower to the deeper, was never worked out by anybody before the rise of Marxism. Marxist materialism solved this problem correctly for the first time, pointing out both materialistically and dialectically the deepening movement of cognition, the movement by which man in society progresses from perceptual knowledge to logical knowledge in his complex, constantly recurring practice of production and class struggle. Lenin said, "The abstraction of *matter*, of a *law* of nature, the abstraction of *value*, etc., in short, *all* scientific (correct, serious, not absurd) abstractions reflect nature more deeply, truly and *completely*."[4] Marxism-Leninism holds that each of the two stages in the process of cognition has its own characteristics, with knowledge manifesting itself as perceptual at the lower stage and logical at the higher stage, but that both are stages in an integrated process of cognition. The perceptual and the rational are qualitatively different, but are not divorced from each other; they are unified on the basis of practice. Our practice proves that what is perceived cannot at once be comprehended and that only what is comprehended can be more deeply perceived. Perception only solves the problem of phenomena; theory alone can solve the problem of essence. The solving of both these problems is not separable in the slightest degree from practice. Whoever wants to know a thing has no way of doing so except by coming into contact with it, that is, by living (practising) in its environment. In feudal society it was impossible to know the laws of capitalist society in advance because capitalism had not yet emerged, the relevant practice was lacking. Marxism could be the product only of capitalist society. Marx, in the era of laissez-faire capitalism, could not concretely know certain laws peculiar to the era of imperialism beforehand, because imperialism, the last stage of capitalism, had not yet emerged and the relevant practice was lacking; only Lenin and Stalin could undertake this task. Leaving aside their genius, the reason why Marx, Engels, Lenin and Stalin could work out their theories was mainly that they personally took part in the practice of the class struggle and the scientific experimentation of their time; lacking this condition, no genius could have succeeded. The saying, "without stepping outside his gate the scholar knows all the wide world's affairs", was mere empty talk in past times when technology was undeveloped. Even though this saying can be valid in the present age of developed technology, the people with real personal knowledge are those engaged in practice the wide world over. And it is only when these people have come to "know" through their practice and when their knowledge has reached him through writing and technical media that the "scholar" can indirectly "know all the wide world's affairs". If you want to know a certain thing or a certain class of things directly, you must personally participate in the practical struggle to change reality, to change that thing or class of things, for only thus can you come into contact with them as phenomena; only through personal participation in the practical struggle to change reality can you uncover the essence of that thing or class of things and comprehend them. This is the path to knowledge which every man actually travels, though some people, deliberately distorting matters, argue to the contrary. The most ridiculous person in the world is the "know-all" who picks up a smattering of hearsay knowledge and proclaims himself "the world's Number One authority"; this merely shows that he has not taken a proper measure of himself. Knowledge is a matter of science, and no dishonesty or conceit whatsoever is permissible. What is required is definitely the reverse — honesty and modesty. If you want knowledge, you must take part in the practice of changing reality. If you want to know the taste of a pear, you must change the pear by eating it yourself. If you want to know the structure and properties of the atom, you must make physical and chemical experiments to change the state of the atom. If you want to know the theory and methods of revolution, you must take part in revolution. All genuine knowledge originates in direct experience. But one cannot have direct experience of everything; as a matter of fact, most of our knowledge comes from indirect experience, for example, all knowledge from past times and foreign lands. To our ancestors and to foreigners, such knowledge was — or is — a matter of direct experience, and this knowledge is reliable if in the course of their direct experience the requirement of "scientific abstraction", spoken of by Lenin, was — or is — fulfilled and objective reality scientifically reflected, otherwise it is not reliable. Hence a man's knowledge consists only of two parts, that which comes from direct experience and that which comes from indirect experience. Moreover, what is indirect experience for me is direct experience for other people. Consequently, considered as a whole, knowledge of any kind is inseparable from direct experience. All knowledge originates in perception of the objective external world through man's physical sense organs. Anyone who denies such perception, denies direct experience, or denies personal participation in the practice that changes reality, is not a materialist. That is why the "know-all" is ridiculous. There is an old Chinese saying, "How can you catch tiger cubs without entering the tiger's lair?" This saying holds true for man's practice and it also holds true for the theory of knowledge. There can be no knowledge apart from practice.

To make clear the dialectical-materialist movement of cognition arising on the basis of the practice which changes reality — to make clear the gradually deepening movement of cognition — a few additional concrete examples are given below.

In its knowledge of capitalist society, the proletariat was only in the perceptual stage of cognition in the first period of its practice, the period of machine-smashing and spontaneous struggle; it knew only some of the aspects and the external relations of the phenomena of capitalism. The proletariat was then still a "class-in-itself". But when it reached the second period of its practice, the period of conscious and organized economic and political struggles, the proletariat was able to comprehend the essence of capitalist society, the relations of exploitation between social classes and its own historical task; and it was able to do so because of its own practice and because of its experience of prolonged struggle, which Marx and Engels scientifically summed up in all its variety to create the theory of Marxism for the education of the proletariat. It was then that the proletariat became a "class-for-itself".

Similarly with the Chinese people's knowledge of imperialism. The first stage was one of superficial, perceptual knowledge, as shown in the indiscriminate anti-foreign struggles of the Movement of the Taiping Heavenly Kingdom, the Yi Ho Tuan Movement, and so on. It was only in the second stage that the Chinese people reached the stage of rational knowledge, saw the internal and external contradictions of imperialism and saw the essential truth that imperialism had allied itself with China's comprador and feudal classes to oppress and exploit the great masses of the Chinese people. This knowledge began about the time of the May 4th Movement of 1919.

Next, let us consider war. If those who lead a war lack experience of war, then at the initial stage they will not understand the profound laws pertaining to the directing of a specific war (such as our Agrarian Revolutionary War of the past decade). At the initial stage they will merely experience a good deal of fighting and, what is more, suffer many defeats. But this experience (the experience of battles won and especially of battles lost) enables them to comprehend the inner thread of the whole war, namely, the laws of that specific war, to understand its strategy and tactics, and consequently to direct the war with confidence. If, at such a moment, the command is turned over to an inexperienced person, then he too will have to suffer a number of defeats (gain experience) before he can comprehend the true laws of the war.

"I am not sure I can handle it." We often hear this remark when a comrade hesitates to accept an assignment. Why is he unsure of himself? Because he has no systematic understanding of the content and circumstances of the assignment, or because he has had little or no contact with such work, and so the laws governing it are beyond him. After a detailed analysis of the nature and circumstances of the assignment, he will feel more sure of himself and do it willingly. If he spends some time at the job and gains experience and if he is a person who is willing to look into matters with an open mind and not one who approaches problems subjectively, one-sidedly and super-ficially, then he can draw conclusions for himself as to how to go about the job and do it with much more courage. Only those who are subjective, one-sided and superficial in their approach to problems will smugly issue orders or directives the moment they arrive on the scene, without considering the circumstances, without viewing things in their totality (their history and their present state as a whole) and without getting to the essence of things (their nature and the internal relations between one thing and another). Such people are bound to trip and fall.

Thus it can be seen that the first step in the process of cognition is contact with the objects of the external world; this belongs to the stage of perception. The second step is to synthesize the data of per-ception by arranging and reconstructing them; this belongs to the stage of conception, judgement and inference. It is only when the data of perception are very rich (not fragmentary) and correspond to reality (are not illusory) that they can be the basis for forming correct concepts and theories.

Here two important points must be emphasized. The first, which has been stated before but should be repeated here, is the dependence of rational knowledge upon perceptual knowledge. Anyone who thinks that rational knowledge need not be derived from perceptual knowl-edge is an idealist. In the history of philosophy there is the "rationalist" school that admits the reality only of reason and not of experience, believing that reason alone is reliable while perceptual experience is not; this school errs by turning things upside down. The rational is reliable precisely because it has its source in sense perceptions, otherwise it would be like water without a source, a tree without roots, subjective, self-engendered and unreliable. As to the sequence in the process of cognition, perceptual experience comes first; we stress the significance of social practice in the process of cognition precisely because social practice alone can give rise to human knowledge and it alone can start man on the acquisition of perceptual experience from the objective world. For a person who shuts his eyes, stops his ears and totally cuts himself off from the objective world there can be no such thing as knowledge. Knowledge begins with experience — this is the materialism of the theory of knowledge.

The second point is that knowledge needs to be deepened, that the perceptual stage of knowledge needs to be developed to the rational stage — this is the dialectics of the theory of knowledge.[5] To think that knowledge can stop at the lower, perceptual stage and that perceptual knowledge alone is reliable while rational knowledge is not, would be to repeat the historical error of "empiricism". This theory errs in failing to understand that, although the data of perception reflect certain realities in the objective world (I am not speaking here of idealist empiricism which confines experience to so-called introspection), they are merely one-sided and superficial, reflecting things incompletely and not reflecting their essence. Fully to reflect a thing in its totality, to reflect its essence, to reflect its inherent laws, it is necessary through the exercise of thought to reconstruct the rich data of sense perception, discarding the dross and selecting the essential, eliminating the false and retaining the true, proceeding from the one to the other and from the outside to the inside, in order to form a system of concepts and theories — it is necessary to make a leap from perceptual to rational knowledge. Such reconstructed knowledge is not more empty or more unreliable; on the contrary, whatever has been scientifically reconstructed in the process of cognition, on the basis of practice, reflects objective reality, as Lenin said, more deeply, more truly, more fully. As against this, vulgar "practical men" respect experience but despise theory, and therefore cannot have a comprehensive view of an entire objective process, lack clear direction and long-range perspective, and are complacent over occasional successes and glimpses of the truth. If such persons direct a revolution, they will lead it up a blind alley.

Rational knowledge depends upon perceptual knowledge and perceptual knowledge remains to be developed into rational knowledge — this is the dialectical-materialist theory of knowledge. In philosophy, neither "rationalism" nor "empiricism" understands the historical or the dialectical nature of knowledge, and although each of these schools contains one aspect of the truth (here I am referring to materialist, not to idealist, rationalism and empiricism), both are wrong on the theory of knowledge as a whole. The dialectical-materialist movement of knowledge from the perceptual to the rational holds true for a minor process of cognition (for instance, knowing a single thing or task) as well as for a major process of cognition (for instance, knowing a whole society or a revolution).

But the movement of knowledge does not end here. If the dialectical-materialist movement of knowledge were to stop at rational knowledge, only half the problem would be dealt with. And as far as Marxist philosophy is concerned, only the less important half at that. Marxist philosophy holds that the most important problem does not lie in understanding the laws of the objective world and thus being able to explain it, but in applying the knowledge of these laws actively to change the world. From the Marxist viewpoint, theory is important, and its importance is fully expressed in Lenin's statement, "Without revolutionary theory there can be no revolutionary movement."[6] But Marxism emphasizes the importance of theory precisely and only because it can guide action. If we have a correct theory but merely prate about it, pigeonhole it and do not put it into practice, then that theory, however good, is of no significance. Knowledge begins with practice, and theoretical knowledge is acquired through practice and must then return to practice. The active function of knowledge manifests itself not only in the active leap from perceptual to rational knowledge, but — and this is more important — it must manifest itself in the leap from rational knowledge to revolutionary practice. The knowledge which grasps the laws of the world, must be redirected to the practice of changing the world, must be applied anew in the practice of production, in the practice of revolutionary class struggle and revolutionary national struggle and in the practice of scientific experiment. This is the process of testing and developing theory, the continuation of the whole process of cognition. The problem of whether theory corresponds to objective reality is not, and cannot be, completely solved in the movement of knowledge from the perceptual to the rational, mentioned above. The only way to solve this problem completely is to redirect rational knowledge to social practice, apply theory to practice and see whether it can achieve the objectives one has in mind. Many theories of natural science are held to be true not only because they were so considered when natural scientists originated them, but because they have been verified in subsequent scientific practice. Similarly, Marxism-Leninism is held to be true not only because it was so considered when it was scientifically formulated by Marx, Engels, Lenin and Stalin but because it has been verified in the subsequent practice of revolutionary class struggle and revolutionary national struggle. Dialectical materialism is universally true because it is impossible for anyone to escape from its domain in his practice. The history of human knowledge tells us that the truth of many theories is incomplete and that this incompleteness is remedied through the test of practice. Many theories are erroneous and it is through the test of practice that their errors are corrected. That is why practice is the criterion of truth and why "the standpoint of life, of practice, should be first and fundamental in the theory of knowledge".[7] Stalin has well said, "Theory becomes purposeless if it is not connected with revolutionary practice, just as practice gropes in the dark if its path is not illumined by revolutionary theory."[8]

When we get to this point, is the movement of knowledge completed? Our answer is: it is and yet it is not. When men in society throw themselves into the practice of changing a certain objective process (whether natural or social) at a certain stage of its development, they can, as a result of the reflection of the objective process in their brains and the exercise of their subjective activity, advance their knowledge from the perceptual to the rational, and create ideas, theories, plans or programmes which correspond in general to the laws of that objective process. They then apply these ideas, theories, plans or programmes in practice in the same objective process. And if they can realize the aims they have in mind, that is, if in that same process of practice they can translate, or on the whole translate, those previously formulated ideas, theories, plans or programmes into fact, then the movement of knowledge may be considered completed with regard to this particular process. In the process of changing nature, take for example the fulfilment of an engineering plan, the verification of a scientific hypothesis, the manufacture of an implement or the reaping of a crop; or in the process of changing society, take for example the victory of a strike, victory in a war or the fulfilment of an educational plan. All these may be considered the realization of aims one has in mind. But generally speaking, whether in the practice of changing nature or of changing society, men's original ideas, theories, plans or programmes are seldom realized without any alteration.

This is because people engaged in changing reality are usually subject to numerous limitations; they are limited not only by existing scientific and technological conditions but also by the development of the objective process itself and the degree to which this process has become manifest (the aspects and the essence of the objective process have not yet been fully revealed). In such a situation, ideas, theories, plans or programmes are usually altered partially and sometimes even wholly, because of the discovery of unforeseen circumstances in the course of practice. That is to say, it does happen that the original ideas, theories, plans or programmes fail to correspond with reality either in whole or in part and are wholly or partially incorrect. In many instances, failures have to be repeated many times before errors in knowledge can be corrected and correspondence with the laws of the objective process achieved, and consequently before the subjective can be transformed into the objective, or in other words, before the anticipated results can be achieved in practice. But when that point is reached, no matter how, the movement of human knowledge regarding a certain objective process at a certain stage of its development may be considered completed.

However, so far as the progression of the process is concerned, the movement of human knowledge is not completed. Every process, whether in the realm of nature or of society, progresses and develops by reason of its internal contradiction and struggle, and the movement of human knowledge should also progress and develop along with it. As far as social movements are concerned, true revolutionary leaders must not only be good at correcting their ideas, theories, plans or programmes when errors are discovered, as has been indicated above; but when a certain objective process has already progressed and changed from one stage of development to another, they must also be good at making themselves and all their fellow-revolutionaries progress and change in their subjective knowledge along with it, that is to say, they must ensure that the proposed new revolutionary tasks and new working programmes correspond to the new changes in the situation. In a revolutionary period the situation changes very rapidly; if the knowledge of revolutionaries does not change rapidly in accordance with the changed situation, they will be unable to lead the revolution to victory.

It often happens, however, that thinking lags behind reality; this is because man's cognition is limited by numerous social conditions. We are opposed to die-hards in the revolutionary ranks whose thinking fails to advance with changing objective circumstances and has manifested itself historically as Right opportunism. These people fail to see that the struggle of opposites has already pushed the objective process forward while their knowledge has stopped at the old stage. This is characteristic of the thinking of all die-hards. Their thinking is divorced from social practice, and they cannot march ahead to guide the chariot of society; they simply trail behind, grumbling that it goes too fast and trying to drag it back or turn it in the opposite direction.

We are also opposed to "Left" phrase-mongering. The thinking of "Leftists" outstrips a given stage of development of the objective process; some regard their fantasies as truth, while others strain to realize in the present an ideal which can only be realized in the future. They alienate themselves from the current practice of the majority of the people and from the realities of the day, and show themselves adventurist in their actions.

Idealism and mechanical materialism, opportunism and adventurism, are all characterized by the breach between the subjective and the objective, by the separation of knowledge from practice. The Marxist-Leninist theory of knowledge, characterized as it is by scientific social practice, cannot but resolutely oppose these wrong ideologies. Marxists recognize that in the absolute and general process of development of the universe, the development of each particular process is relative, and that hence, in the endless flow of absolute truth, man's knowledge of a particular process at any given stage of development is only relative truth. The sum total of innumerable relative truths constitutes absolute truth.[9] The development of an objective process is full of contradictions and struggles, and so is the development of the movement of human knowledge. All the dialectical movements of the objective world can sooner or later be reflected in human knowledge. In social practice, the process of coming into being, developing and passing away is infinite, and so is the process of coming into being, developing and passing away in human knowledge. As man's practice which changes objective reality in accordance with given ideas, theories, plans or programmes, advances further and further, his knowledge of objective reality likewise becomes deeper and deeper. The movement of change in the world of objective reality is never-ending and so is man's cognition of truth through practice. Marxism-Leninism has in no way exhausted truth but ceaselessly opens up roads to the knowledge of truth in the course of practice. Our conclusion is the concrete, historical unity of the subjective and the objective, of theory and practice, of knowing and doing, and we are opposed to all erroneous ideologies, whether "Left" or Right, which depart from concrete history.

In the present epoch of the development of society, the responsibility of correctly knowing and changing the world has been placed by history upon the shoulders of the proletariat and its party. This process, the practice of changing the world, which is determined in accordance with scientific knowledge, has already reached a historic moment in the world and in China, a great moment unprecedented in human history, that is, the moment for completely banishing darkness from the world and from China and for changing the world into a world of light such as never previously existed. The struggle of the proletariat and the revolutionary people to change the world comprises the fulfilment of the following tasks: to change the objective world and, at the same time, their own subjective world — to change their cognitive ability and change the relations between the subjective and the objective world. Such a change has already come about in one part of the globe, in the Soviet Union. There the people are pushing forward this process of change. The people of China and the rest of the world either are going through, or will go through, such a process. And the objective world which is to be changed also includes all the opponents of change, who, in order to be changed, must go through a stage of compulsion before they can enter the stage of voluntary, conscious change. The epoch of world communism will be reached when all mankind voluntarily and consciously changes itself and the world.

Discover the truth through practice, and again through practice verify and develop the truth. Start from perceptual knowledge and actively develop it into rational knowledge; then start from rational knowledge and actively guide revolutionary practice to change both the subjective and the objective world. Practice, knowledge, again practice, and again knowledge. This form repeats itself in endless cycles, and with each cycle the content of practice and knowledge rises to a higher level. Such is the whole of the dialectical-materialist theory of knowledge, and such is the dialectical-materialist theory of the unity of knowing and doing.

NOTES

[1] V. I. Lenin, "Conspectus of Hegel's *The Science of Logic*", *Collected Works*, Russ. ed., Moscow, 1958, Vol. XXXVIII, p. 205.

[2] See Karl Marx, "Theses on Feuerbach", Karl Marx and Frederick Engels, *Selected Works*, in two volumes, Eng. ed., FLPH, Moscow, 1958, Vol. II, p. 403, and V. I. Lenin, *Materialism and Empirio-Criticism*, Eng. ed., FLPH, Moscow, 1952, pp. 136-42.

[3] *San Kuo Yen Yi (Tales of the Three Kingdoms)* is a famous Chinese historical novel by Lo Kuan-chung (late 14th and early 15th century).

[4] V. I. Lenin, "Conspectus of Hegel's *The Science of Logic*", *Collected Works*, Russ. ed., Moscow, 1958, Vol. XXXVIII, p. 161.

[5] "In order to understand, it is necessary empirically to begin understanding, study, to rise from empiricism to the universal." (*Ibid.*, p. 197.)

[6] V. I. Lenin, "What Is to Be Done?", *Collected Works*, Eng. ed., FLPH, Moscow, 1961, Vol. V, p. 369.

[7] V. I. Lenin, *Materialism and Empirio-Criticism*, Eng. ed., FLPH, Moscow, 1952, p. 141.

[8] J. V. Stalin, "The Foundations of Leninism", *Problems of Leninism,* Eng. ed., FLPH, Moscow, 1954, p. 31.

[9] See V. I. Lenin, *Materialism and Empirio-Criticism*, Eng. ed., FLPH, Moscow, 1952, pp. 129-36.

ON CONTRADICTION

August 1937

The law of contradiction in things, that is, the law of the unity of opposites, is the basic law of materialist dialectics. Lenin said, "Dialectics in the proper sense is the study of contradiction *in the very essence of objects*."[1] Lenin often called this law the essence of dialectics; he also called it the kernel of dialectics.[2] In studying this law, therefore, we cannot but touch upon a variety of questions, upon a number of philosophical problems. If we can become clear on all these problems, we shall arrive at a fundamental understanding of materialist dialectics. The problems are: the two world outlooks, the universality of contradiction, the particularity of contradiction, the principal contradiction and the principal aspect of a contradiction, the identity and struggle of the aspects of a contradiction, and the place of antagonism in contradiction.

The criticism to which the idealism of the Deborin school has been subjected in Soviet philosophical circles in recent years has aroused great interest among us. Deborin's idealism has exerted a very bad influence in the Chinese Communist Party, and it cannot be said that the dogmatist thinking in our Party is unrelated to the approach of that school. Our present study of philosophy should therefore have the eradication of dogmatist thinking as its main objective.

I. THE TWO WORLD OUTLOOKS

Throughout the history of human knowledge, there have been two conceptions concerning the law of development of the universe, the

This essay on philosophy was written by Comrade Mao Tse-tung after his essay "On Practice" and with the same object of overcoming the serious error of dogmatist thinking to be found in the Party at the time. Originally delivered as lectures at the Anti-Japanese Military and Political College in Yenan, it was revised by the author on its inclusion in his *Selected Works*.

metaphysical conception and the dialectical conception, which form two opposing world outlooks. Lenin said:

> The two basic (or two possible? or two historically observable?) conceptions of development (evolution) are: development as decrease and increase, as repetition, *and* development as a unity of opposites (the division of a unity into mutually exclusive opposites and their reciprocal relation).[3]

Here Lenin was referring to these two different world outlooks.

In China another name for metaphysics is *hsuan-hsueh*. For a long period in history whether in China or in Europe, this way of thinking, which is part and parcel of the idealist world outlook, occupied a dominant position in human thought. In Europe, the materialism of the bourgeoisie in its early days was also metaphysical. As the social economy of many European countries advanced to the stage of highly developed capitalism, as the forces of production, the class struggle and the sciences developed to a level unprecedented in history, and as the industrial proletariat became the greatest motive force in historical development, there arose the Marxist world outlook of materialist dialectics. Then, in addition to open and barefaced reactionary idealism, vulgar evolutionism emerged among the bourgeoisie to oppose materialist dialectics.

The metaphysical or vulgar evolutionist world outlook sees things as isolated, static and one-sided. It regards all things in the universe, their forms and their species, as eternally isolated from one another and immutable. Such change as there is can only be an increase or decrease in quantity or a change of place. Moreover, the cause of such an increase or decrease or change of place is not inside things but outside them, that is, the motive force is external. Metaphysicians hold that all the different kinds of things in the universe and all their characteristics have been the same ever since they first came into being. All subsequent changes have simply been increases or decreases in quantity. They contend that a thing can only keep on repeating itself as the same kind of thing and cannot change into anything different. In their opinion, capitalist exploitation, capitalist competition, the individualist ideology of capitalist society, and so on, can all be found in ancient slave society, or even in primitive society, and will exist for ever unchanged. They ascribe the causes of social development to factors external to society, such as geography and climate. They search in an over-simplified way outside a thing for the causes of its development, and they deny the theory of materialist dialectics which holds that development arises from the contradictions inside a thing. Consequently they can explain neither the qualitative diversity of things, nor the phenomenon of one quality changing into another. In Europe, this mode of thinking existed as mechanical materialism in the 17th and 18th centuries and as vulgar evolutionism at the end of the 19th and the beginning of the 20th centuries. In China, there was the metaphysical thinking exemplified in the saying "Heaven changeth not, likewise the Tao changeth not",[4] and it was supported by the decadent feudal ruling classes for a long time. Mechanical materialism and vulgar evolutionism, which were imported from Europe in the last hundred years, are supported by the bourgeoisie.

As opposed to the metaphysical world outlook, the world outlook of materialist dialectics holds that in order to understand the development of a thing we should study it internally and in its relations with other things; in other words, the development of things should be seen as their internal and necessary self-movement, while each thing in its movement is interrelated with and interacts on the things around it. The fundamental cause of the development of a thing is not external but internal; it lies in the contradictoriness within the thing. There is internal contradiction in every single thing, hence its motion and development. Contradictoriness within a thing is the fundamental cause of its development, while its interrelations and interactions with other things are secondary causes. Thus materialist dialectics effectively combats the theory of external causes, or of an external motive force, advanced by metaphysical mechanical materialism and vulgar evolutionism. It is evident that purely external causes can only give rise to mechanical motion, that is, to changes in scale or quantity, but cannot explain why things differ qualitatively in thousands of ways and why one thing changes into another. As a matter of fact, even mechanical motion under external force occurs through the internal contradictoriness of things. Simple growth in plants and animals, their quantitative development, is likewise chiefly the result of their internal contradictions. Similarly, social development is due chiefly not to external but to internal causes. Countries with almost the same geographical and climatic conditions display great diversity and unevenness in their development. Moreover, great social changes may take place in one and the same country although its geography and climate remain unchanged. Imperialist Russia changed into the socialist Soviet Union, and feudal Japan, which had locked its doors against the world, changed into imperialist Japan, although no change occurred in the geography and climate of either country. Long dominated by feudalism, China has undergone great changes in the last hundred years and is now changing in the direction of a new China, liberated and free, and yet no change has occurred in her geography and climate. Changes do take place in the geography and climate of the earth as a whole and in every part of it, but they are insignificant when compared with changes in society; geographical and climatic changes manifest themselves in terms of tens of thousands of years, while social changes manifest themselves in thousands, hundreds or tens of years, and even in a few years or months in times of revolution. According to materialist dialectics, changes in nature are due chiefly to the development of the internal contradictions in nature. Changes in society are due chiefly to the development of the internal contradictions in society, that is, the contradiction between the productive forces and the relations of production, the contradiction between classes and the contradiction between the old and the new; it is the development of these contradictions that pushes society forward and gives the impetus for the supersession of the old society by the new. Does materialist dialectics exclude external causes? Not at all. It holds that external causes are the condition of change and internal causes are the basis of change, and that external causes become operative through internal causes. In a suitable temperature an egg changes into a chicken, but no temperature can change a stone into a chicken, because each has a different basis. There is constant interaction between the peoples of different countries. In the era of capitalism, and especially in the era of imperialism and proletarian revolution, the interaction and mutual impact of different countries in the political, economic and cultural spheres are extremely great. The October Socialist Revolution ushered in a new epoch in world history as well as in Russian history. It exerted influence on internal changes in the other countries in the world and, similarly and in a particularly profound way, on internal changes in China. These changes, however, were effected through the inner laws of development of these countries, China included. In battle, one army is victorious and the other is defeated; both the victory and the defeat are determined by internal causes. The one is victorious either because it is strong or because of its competent generalship, the other is vanquished either because it is weak or because of its incompetent generalship; it is through internal causes that external causes become operative. In China in 1927, the defeat of the proletariat by the big bourgeoisie came about through the opportunism then to be found within the Chinese proletariat itself (inside the Chinese Communist Party). When we liquidated this opportunism, the Chinese revolution resumed its advance. Later, the Chinese revolution again suffered severe setbacks at the hands of the enemy, because adventurism had risen within our Party. When we liquidated this adventurism, our cause advanced once again. Thus it can be seen that to lead the revolution to victory, a political party must depend on the correctness of its own political line and the solidity of its own organization.

The dialectical world outlook emerged in ancient times both in China and in Europe. Ancient dialectics, however, had a somewhat spontaneous and naive character; in the social and historical conditions then prevailing, it was not yet able to form a theoretical system, hence it could not fully explain the world and was supplanted by metaphysics. The famous German philosopher Hegel, who lived in the late 18th and early 19th centuries, made most important contributions to dialectics, but his dialectics was idealist. It was not until Marx and Engels, the great protagonists of the proletarian movement, had synthesized the positive achievements in the history of human knowledge and, in particular, critically absorbed the rational elements of Hegelian dialectics and created the great theory of dialectical and historical materialism that an unprecedented revolution occurred in the history of human knowledge. This theory was further developed by Lenin and Stalin. As soon as it spread to China, it wrought tremendous changes in the world of Chinese thought.

This dialectical world outlook teaches us primarily how to observe and analyse the movement of opposites in different things and, on the basis of such analysis, to indicate the methods for resolving contradictions. It is therefore most important for us to understand the law of contradiction in things in a concrete way.

II. THE UNIVERSALITY OF CONTRADICTION

For convenience of exposition, I shall deal first with the universality of contradiction and then proceed to the particularity of contradiction. The reason is that the universality of contradiction can be explained more briefly, for it has been widely recognized ever since

the materialist-dialectical world outlook was discovered and materialist dialectics applied with outstanding success to analysing many
aspects of human history and natural history and to changing many
aspects of society and nature (as in the Soviet Union) by the great
creators and continuers of Marxism — Marx, Engels, Lenin and
Stalin; whereas the particularity of contradiction is still not clearly
understood by many comrades, and especially by the dogmatists.
They do not understand that it is precisely in the particularity of
contradiction that the universality of contradiction resides. Nor do
they understand how important is the study of the particularity of
contradiction in the concrete things confronting us for guiding the
course of revolutionary practice. Therefore, it is necessary to stress the
study of the particularity of contradiction and to explain it at adequate
length. For this reason, in our analysis of the law of contradiction in
things, we shall first analyse the universality of contradiction, then
place special stress on analysing the particularity of contradiction, and
finally return to the universality of contradiction.

The universality or absoluteness of contradiction has a twofold
meaning. One is that contradiction exists in the process of development of all things, and the other is that in the process of development
of each thing a movement of opposites exists from beginning to end.

Engels said, "Motion itself is a contradiction."[5] Lenin defined
the law of the unity of opposites as "the recognition (discovery) of
the contradictory, *mutually exclusive*, opposite tendencies in *all*
phenomena and processes of nature (*including* mind and society)".[6]
Are these ideas correct? Yes, they are. The interdependence of the
contradictory aspects present in all things and the struggle between
these aspects determine the life of all things and push their development forward. There is nothing that does not contain contradiction;
without contradiction nothing would exist.

Contradiction is the basis of the simple forms of motion (for
instance, mechanical motion) and still more so of the complex forms
of motion.

Engels explained the universality of contradiction as follows:

> If simple mechanical change of place contains a contradiction,
> this is even more true of the higher forms of motion of matter, and
> especially of organic life and its development. . . . life consists
> precisely and primarily in this — that a being is at each moment
> itself and yet something else. Life is therefore also a contradiction

which is present in things and processes themselves, and which constantly originates and resolves itself; and as soon as the contradiction ceases, life, too, comes to an end, and death steps in. We likewise saw that also in the sphere of thought we could not escape contradictions, and that for example the contradiction between man's inherently unlimited capacity for knowledge and its actual presence only in men who are externally limited and possess limited cognition finds its solution in what is — at least practically, for us — an endless succession of generations, in infinite progress.

. . . one of the basic principles of higher mathematics is the contradiction that in certain circumstances straight lines and curves may be the same. . . .

But even lower mathematics teems with contradictions.[7]

Lenin illustrated the universality of contradiction as follows:

In mathematics: + and —. Differential and integral.
In mechanics: action and reaction.
In physics: positive and negative electricity.
In chemistry: the combination and dissociation of atoms.
In social science: the class struggle.[8]

In war, offence and defence, advance and retreat, victory and defeat are all mutually contradictory phenomena. One cannot exist without the other. The two aspects are at once in conflict and in interdependence, and this constitutes the totality of a war, pushes its development forward and solves its problems.

Every difference in men's concepts should be regarded as reflecting an objective contradiction. Objective contradictions are reflected in subjective thinking, and this process constitutes the contradictory movement of concepts, pushes forward the development of thought, and ceaselessly solves problems in man's thinking.

Opposition and struggle between ideas of different kinds constantly occur within the Party; this is a reflection within the Party of contradictions between classes and between the new and the old in society. If there were no contradictions in the Party and no ideological struggles to resolve them, the Party's life would come to an end.

Thus it is already clear that contradiction exists universally and in all processes, whether in the simple or in the complex forms of motion, whether in objective phenomena or ideological phenomena. But does contradiction also exist at the initial stage of each process?

Is there a movement of opposites from beginning to end in the process of development of every single thing?

As can be seen from the articles written by Soviet philosophers criticizing it, the Deborin school maintains that contradiction appears not at the inception of a process but only when it has developed to a certain stage. If this were the case, then the cause of the development of the process before that stage would be external and not internal. Deborin thus reverts to the metaphysical theories of external causality and of mechanism. Applying this view in the analysis of concrete problems, the Deborin school sees only differences but not contradictions between the kulaks and the peasants in general under existing conditions in the Soviet Union, thus entirely agreeing with Bukharin. In analysing the French Revolution, it holds that before the Revolution there were likewise only differences but not contradictions within the Third Estate, which was composed of the workers, the peasants and the bourgeoisie. These views of the Deborin school are anti-Marxist. This school does not understand that each and every difference already contains contradiction and that difference itself is contradiction. Labour and capital have been in contradiction ever since the two classes came into being, only at first the contradiction had not yet become intense. Even under the social conditions existing in the Soviet Union, there is a difference between workers and peasants and this very difference is a contradiction, although, unlike the contradiction between labour and capital, it will not become intensified into antagonism or assume the form of class struggle; the workers and the peasants have established a firm alliance in the course of socialist construction and are gradually resolving this contradiction in the course of the advance from socialism to communism. The question is one of different kinds of contradiction, not of the presence or absence of contradiction. Contradiction is universal and absolute, it is present in the process of development of all things and permeates every process from beginning to end.

What is meant by the emergence of a new process? The old unity with its constituent opposites yields to a new unity with its constituent opposites, whereupon a new process emerges to replace the old. The old process ends and the new one begins. The new process contains new contradictions and begins its own history of the development of contradictions.

As Lenin pointed out, Marx in his *Capital* gave a model analysis of this movement of opposites which runs through the process of development of things from beginning to end. This is the method that must be employed in studying the development of all things. Lenin, too, employed this method correctly and adhered to it in all his writings.

In his *Capital*, Marx first analyses the simplest, most ordinary and fundamental, most common and everyday *relation* of bourgeois (commodity) society, a relation encountered billions of times, viz. the exchange of commodities. In this very simple phenomenon (in this "cell" of bourgeois society) analysis reveals *all* the contradictions (or the germs of *all* the contradictions) of modern society. The subsequent exposition shows us the development (*both* growth *and* movement) of these contradictions and of this society in the Σ [summation] of its individual parts, from its beginning to its end.

Lenin added, "Such must also be the method of exposition (or study) of dialectics in general."[9]

Chinese Communists must learn this method; only then will they be able correctly to analyse the history and the present state of the Chinese revolution and infer its future.

III. THE PARTICULARITY OF CONTRADICTION

Contradiction is present in the process of development of all things; it permeates the process of development of each thing from beginning to end. This is the universality and absoluteness of contradiction which we have discussed above. Now let us discuss the particularity and relativity of contradiction.

This problem should be studied on several levels.

First, the contradiction in each form of motion of matter has its particularity. Man's knowledge of matter is knowledge of its forms of motion, because there is nothing in this world except matter in motion and this motion must assume certain forms. In considering each form of motion of matter, we must observe the points which it has in common with other forms of motion. But what is especially important and necessary, constituting as it does the foundation of our knowledge of a thing, is to observe what is particular to this form of motion of matter, namely, to observe the qualitative difference

between this form of motion and other forms. Only when we have
done so can we distinguish between things. Every form of motion
contains within itself its own particular contradiction. This particular
contradiction constitutes the particular essence which distinguishes
one thing from another. It is the internal cause or, as it may be called,
the basis for the immense variety of things in the world. There are
many forms of motion in nature, mechanical motion, sound, light,
heat, electricity, dissociation, combination, and so on. All these forms
are interdependent, but in its essence each is different from the others.
The particular essence of each form of motion is determined by its
own particular contradiction. This holds true not only for nature but
also for social and ideological phenomena. Every form of society,
every form of ideology, has its own particular contradiction and
particular essence.

The sciences are differentiated precisely on the basis of the particular contradictions inherent in their respective objects of study.
Thus the contradiction peculiar to a certain field of phenomena
constitutes the object of study for a specific branch of science. For
example, positive and negative numbers in mathematics; action and
reaction in mechanics; positive and negative electricity in physics;
dissociation and combination in chemistry; forces of production and
relations of production, classes and class struggle, in social science;
offence and defence in military science; idealism and materialism,
the metaphysical outlook and the dialectical outlook, in philosophy;
and so on — all these are the objects of study of different branches
of science precisely because each branch has its own particular contradiction and particular essence. Of course, unless we understand
the universality of contradiction, we have no way of discovering the
universal cause or universal basis for the movement or development
of things; however, unless we study the particularity of contradiction,
we have no way of determining the particular essence of a thing which
differentiates it from other things, no way of discovering the particular
cause or particular basis for the movement or development of a thing,
and no way of distinguishing one thing from another or of demarcating
the fields of science.

As regards the sequence in the movement of man's knowledge,
there is always a gradual growth from the knowledge of individual
and particular things to the knowledge of things in general. Only
after man knows the particular essence of many different things can
he proceed to generalization and know the common essence of things.

When man attains the knowledge of this common essence, he uses it as a guide and proceeds to study various concrete things which have not yet been studied, or studied thoroughly, and to discover the particular essence of each; only thus is he able to supplement, enrich and develop his knowledge of their common essence and prevent such knowledge from withering or petrifying. These are the two processes of cognition: one, from the particular to the general, and the other, from the general to the particular. Thus cognition always moves in cycles and (so long as scientific method is strictly adhered to) each cycle advances human knowledge a step higher and so makes it more and more profound. Where our dogmatists err on this question is that, on the one hand, they do not understand that we have to study the particularity of contradiction and know the particular essence of individual things before we can adequately know the universality of contradiction and the common essence of things, and that, on the other hand, they do not understand that after knowing the common essence of things, we must go further and study the concrete things that have not yet been thoroughly studied or have only just emerged. Our dogmatists are lazy-bones. They refuse to undertake any painstaking study of concrete things, they regard general truths as emerging out of the void, they turn them into purely abstract unfathomable formulas, and thereby completely deny and reverse the normal sequence by which man comes to know truth. Nor do they understand the interconnection of the two processes in cognition — from the particular to the general and then from the general to the particular. They understand nothing of the Marxist theory of knowledge.

It is necessary not only to study the particular contradiction and the essence determined thereby of every great system of the forms of motion of matter, but also to study the particular contradiction and the essence of each process in the long course of development of each form of motion of matter. In every form of motion, each process of development which is real (and not imaginary) is qualitatively different. Our study must emphasize and start from this point.

Qualitatively different contradictions can only be resolved by qualitatively different methods. For instance, the contradiction between the proletariat and the bourgeoisie is resolved by the method of socialist revolution; the contradiction between the great masses of the people and the feudal system is resolved by the method of democratic revolution; the contradiction between the colonies and imperialism is resolved by the method of national revolutionary war; the contradiction between the working class and the peasant class in socialist society is resolved by the method of collectivization and mechanization in agriculture; contradiction within the Communist Party is resolved by the method of criticism and self-criticism; the contradiction between society and nature is resolved by the method of developing the productive forces. Processes change, old processes and old contradictions disappear, new processes and new contradictions emerge, and the methods of resolving contradictions differ accordingly. In Russia, there was a fundamental difference between the contradiction resolved by the February Revolution and the contradiction resolved by the October Revolution, as well as between the methods used to resolve them. The principle of using different methods to resolve different contradictions is one which Marxist-Leninists must strictly observe. The dogmatists do not observe this principle; they do not understand that conditions differ in different kinds of revolution and so do not understand that different methods should be used to resolve different contradictions; on the contrary, they invariably adopt what they imagine to be an unalterable formula and arbitrarily apply it everywhere, which only causes setbacks to the revolution or makes a sorry mess of what was originally well done.

In order to reveal the particularity of the contradictions in any process in the development of a thing, in their totality or interconnections, that is, in order to reveal the essence of the process, it is necessary to reveal the particularity of the two aspects of each of the contradictions in that process; otherwise it will be impossible to discover the essence of the process. This likewise requires the utmost attention in our study.

There are many contradictions in the course of development of any major thing. For instance, in the course of China's bourgeois-democratic revolution, where the conditions are exceedingly complex, there exist the contradiction between all the oppressed classes in Chinese society and imperialism, the contradiction between the great masses of the people and feudalism, the contradiction between the proletariat and the bourgeoisie, the contradiction between the peasantry and the urban petty bourgeoisie on the one hand and the bourgeoisie on the other, the contradiction between the various reactionary ruling groups, and so on. These contradictions cannot be treated in the same way since each has its own particularity; moreover, the two aspects of each contradiction cannot be treated in the same way since each aspect has its own characteristics. We who are engaged in the Chinese revolution should not only understand the particularity of these contradictions in their totality, that is, in their interconnections, but should also study the two aspects of each contradiction as the only means of understanding the totality. When we speak of understanding each aspect of a contradiction, we mean understanding what specific position each aspect occupies, what concrete forms it assumes in its interdependence and in its contradiction with its opposite, and what concrete methods are employed in the struggle with its opposite, when the two are both interdependent and in contradiction, and also after the interdependence breaks down. It is of great importance to study these problems. Lenin meant just this when he said that the most essential thing in Marxism, the living soul of Marxism, is the concrete analysis of concrete conditions.[10] Our dogmatists have violated Lenin's teachings; they never use their brains to analyse anything concretely, and in their writings and speeches they always use stereotypes devoid of content, thereby creating a very bad style of work in our Party.

In studying a problem, we must shun subjectivity, one-sidedness and superficiality. To be subjective means not to look at problems objectively, that is, not to use the materialist viewpoint in looking at problems. I have discussed this in my essay "On Practice". To be one-sided means not to look at problems all-sidedly, for example, to understand only China but not Japan, only the Communist Party but not the Kuomintang, only the proletariat but not the bourgeoisie, only the peasants but not the landlords, only the favourable conditions but not the difficult ones, only the past but not the future, only individual parts but not the whole, only the defects but not the achievements, only the plaintiff's case but not the defendant's, only underground revolutionary work but not open revolutionary work, and so on. In a word, it means not to understand the characteristics of both aspects of a contradiction. This is what we mean by looking at a problem one-sidedly. Or it may be called seeing the part but not the whole, seeing the trees but not the forest. That way it is impossible to find the method for resolving a contradiction, it is impossible to accomplish the tasks of the revolution, to carry out assignments well or to develop inner-Party ideological struggle correctly. When Sun Wu Tzu said in discussing military science, "Know the enemy and know yourself, and you can fight a hundred battles with no danger of defeat",[11] he was referring to the two sides in a battle. Wei Cheng[12]

of the Tang Dynasty also understood the error of one-sidedness when
he said, "Listen to both sides and you will be enlightened, heed only
one side and you will be benighted." But our comrades often look
at problems one-sidedly, and so they often run into snags. In the
novel *Shui Hu Chuan*, Sung Chiang thrice attacked Chu Village.[13]
Twice he was defeated because he was ignorant of the local conditions and used the wrong method. Later he changed his method;
first he investigated the situation, and he familiarized himself with
the maze of roads, then he broke up the alliance between the Li, Hu
and Chu Villages and sent his men in disguise into the enemy camp
to lie in wait, using a stratagem similar to that of the Trojan Horse
in the foreign story. And on the third occasion he won. There are
many examples of materialist dialectics in *Shui Hu Chuan*, of which
the episode of the three attacks on Chu Village is one of the best.
Lenin said:

> . . . in order really to know an object we must embrace, study,
> all its sides, all connections and "mediations". We shall never
> achieve this completely, but the demand for all-sidedness is a
> safeguard against mistakes and rigidity.[14]

We should remember his words. To be superficial means to consider
neither the characteristics of a contradiction in its totality nor the
characteristics of each of its aspects; it means to deny the necessity
for probing deeply into a thing and minutely studying the characteristics of its contradiction, but instead merely to look from afar and,
after glimpsing the rough outline, immediately to try to resolve the
contradiction (to answer a question, settle a dispute, handle work, or
direct a military operation). This way of doing things is bound to
lead to trouble. The reason the dogmatist and empiricist comrades
in China have made mistakes lies precisely in their subjectivist, one-
sided and superficial way of looking at things. To be one-sided and
superficial is at the same time to be subjective. For all objective things
are actually interconnected and are governed by inner laws, but
instead of undertaking the task of reflecting things as they really
are some people only look at things one-sidedly or superficially and
who know neither their interconnections nor their inner laws, and
so their method is subjectivist.

Not only does the whole process of the movement of opposites
in the development of a thing, both in their interconnections and in

each of the aspects, have particular features to which we must give attention, but each stage in the process has its particular features to which we must give attention too.

The fundamental contradiction in the process of development of a thing and the essence of the process determined by this fundamental contradiction will not disappear until the process is completed; but in a lengthy process the conditions usually differ at each stage. The reason is that, although the nature of the fundamental contradiction in the process of development of a thing and the essence of the process remain unchanged, the fundamental contradiction becomes more and more intensified as it passes from one stage to another in the lengthy process. In addition, among the numerous major and minor contradictions which are determined or influenced by the fundamental contradiction, some become intensified, some are temporarily or partially resolved or mitigated, and some new ones emerge; hence the process is marked by stages. If people do not pay attention to the stages in the process of development of a thing, they cannot deal with its contradictions properly.

For instance, when the capitalism of the era of free competition developed into imperialism, there was no change in the class nature of the two classes in fundamental contradiction, namely, the proletariat and the bourgeoisie, or in the capitalist essence of society; however, the contradiction between these two classes became intensified, the contradiction between monopoly and non-monopoly capital emerged, the contradiction between the colonial powers and the colonies became intensified, the contradiction among the capitalist countries resulting from their uneven development manifested itself with particular sharpness, and thus there arose the special stage of capitalism, the stage of imperialism. Leninism is the Marxism of the era of imperialism and proletarian revolution precisely because Lenin and Stalin have correctly explained these contradictions and correctly formulated the theory and tactics of the proletarian revolution for their resolution.

Take the process of China's bourgeois-democratic revolution, which began with the Revolution of 1911; it, too, has several distinct stages. In particular, the revolution in its period of bourgeois leadership and the revolution in its period of proletarian leadership represent two vastly different historical stages. In other words, proletarian leadership has fundamentally changed the whole face of the revolution, has brought about a new alignment of classes, given rise to a tremendous upsurge in the peasant revolution, imparted thoroughness to the revolution against imperialism and feudalism, created the possibility of the transition from the democratic revolution to the socialist revolution, and so on. None of these was possible in the period when the revolution was under bourgeois leadership. Although no change has taken place in the nature of the fundamental contradiction in the process as a whole, *i.e.*, in the anti-imperialist, anti-feudal, democratic-revolutionary nature of the process (the opposite of which is its semi-colonial and semi-feudal nature), nonetheless this process has passed through several stages of development in the course of more than twenty years; during this time many great events have taken place — the failure of the Revolution of 1911 and the establishment of the regime of the Northern warlords, the formation of the first national united front and the revolution of 1924-27, the break-up of the united front and the desertion of the bourgeoisie to the side of the counter-revolution, the wars among the new warlords, the Agrarian Revolutionary War, the establishment of the second national united front and the War of Resistance Against Japan. These stages are marked by particular features such as the intensification of certain contradictions (*e.g.*, the Agrarian Revolutionary War and the Japanese invasion of the four northeastern provinces), the partial or temporary resolution of other contradictions (*e.g.*, the destruction of the Northern warlords and our confiscation of the land of the landlords), and the emergence of yet other contradictions (*e.g.*, the conflicts among the new warlords, and the landlords' recapture of the land after the loss of our revolutionary base areas in the south).

In studying the particularities of the contradictions at each stage in the process of development of a thing, we must not only observe them in their interconnections or their totality, we must also examine the two aspects of each contradiction.

For instance, consider the Kuomintang and the Communist Party. Take one aspect, the Kuomintang. In the period of the first united front, the Kuomintang carried out Sun Yat-sen's Three Great Policies of alliance with Russia, co-operation with the Communist Party, and assistance to the peasants and workers; hence it was revolutionary and vigorous, it was an alliance of various classes for the democratic revolution. After 1927, however, the Kuomintang changed into its opposite and became a reactionary bloc of the landlords and big bourgeoisie. After the Sian Incident in December 1936, it began another change in the direction of ending the civil war and co-operating with the Communist Party for joint opposition to Japanese imperialism. Such have been the particular features of the Kuomintang in the three stages. Of course, these features have arisen from a variety of causes. Now take the other aspect, the Chinese Communist Party. In the period of the first united front, the Chinese Communist Party was in its infancy; it courageously led the revolution of 1924-27 but revealed its immaturity in its understanding of the character, the tasks and the methods of the revolution, and consequently it became possible for Chen Tu-hsiuism, which appeared during the latter part of this revolution, to assert itself and bring about the defeat of the revolution. After 1927, the Communist Party courageously led the Agrarian Revolutionary War and created the revolutionary army and revolutionary base areas; however, it committed adventurist errors which brought about very great losses both to the army and to the base areas. Since 1935 the Party has corrected these errors and has been leading the new united front for resistance to Japan; this great struggle is now developing. At the present stage, the Communist Party is a Party that has gone through the test of two revolutions and acquired a wealth of experience. Such have been the particular features of the Chinese Communist Party in the three stages. These features, too, have arisen from a variety of causes. Without studying both these sets of features we cannot understand the particular relations between the two parties during the various stages of their development, namely, the establishment of a united front, the break-up of the united front, and the establishment of another united front. What is even more fundamental for the study of the particular features of the two parties is the examination of the class basis of the two parties and the resultant contradictions which have arisen between each party and other forces at different periods. For instance, in the period of its first co-operation with the Communist Party, the Kuomintang stood in contradiction to foreign imperialism and was therefore anti-imperialist; on the other hand, it stood in contradiction to the great masses of the people within the country — although in words it promised many benefits to the working people, in fact it gave them little or nothing. In the period when it carried on the anti-Communist war, the Kuomintang collaborated with imperialism and feudalism against the great masses of the people and wiped out all the gains they had won in the revolution, and thereby intensified its contradictions with them. In the present period of the anti-Japanese war, the Kuomintang stands in contradiction to Japanese imperialism and wants co-operation with the Communist Party, without however relaxing its struggle against the Communist Party and the people or its oppression of them. As for the Communist Party, it has always, in every period, stood with the great masses of the people against imperialism and feudalism, but in the present period of the anti-Japanese war, it has adopted a moderate policy towards the Kuomintang and the domestic feudal forces because the Kuomintang has expressed itself in favour of resisting Japan. The above circumstances have resulted now in alliance between the two parties and now in struggle between them, and even during the periods of alliance there has been a complicated state of simultaneous alliance and struggle. If we do not study the particular features of both aspects of the contradiction, we shall fail to understand not only the relations of each party with the other forces, but also the relations between the two parties.

It can thus be seen that in studying the particularity of any kind of contradiction — the contradiction in each form of motion of matter, the contradiction in each of its processes of development, the two aspects of the contradiction in each process, the contradiction at each stage of a process, and the two aspects of the contradiction at each stage — in studying the particularity of all these contradictions, we must not be subjective and arbitrary but must analyse it concretely. Without concrete analysis there can be no knowledge of the particularity of any contradiction. We must always remember Lenin's words, the concrete analysis of concrete conditions.

Marx and Engels were the first to provide us with excellent models of such concrete analysis.

When Marx and Engels applied the law of contradiction in things to the study of the socio-historical process, they discovered the contradiction between the productive forces and the relations of production, they discovered the contradiction between the exploiting and exploited classes and also the resultant contradiction between the economic base and its superstructure (politics, ideology, etc.), and they discovered how these contradictions inevitably lead to different kinds of social revolution in different kinds of class society.

When Marx applied this law to the study of the economic structure of capitalist society, he discovered that the basic contradiction of this society is the contradiction between the social character of production and the private character of ownership. This contradiction manifests itself in the contradiction between the organized character of production in individual enterprises and the anarchic character of production in society as a whole. In terms of class relations, it manifests itself in the contradiction between the bourgeoisie and the proletariat.

Because the range of things is vast and there is no limit to their development, what is universal in one context becomes particular in another. Conversely, what is particular in one context becomes universal in another. The contradiction in the capitalist system between the social character of production and the private ownership of the means of production is common to all countries where capitalism exists and develops; as far as capitalism is concerned, this constitutes the universality of contradiction. But this contradiction of capitalism belongs only to a certain historical stage in the general development of class society; as far as the contradiction between the productive forces and the relations of production in class society as a whole is concerned, it constitutes the particularity of contradiction. However, in the course of dissecting the particularity of all these contradictions in capitalist society, Marx gave a still more profound, more adequate and more complete elucidation of the universality of the contradiction between the productive forces and the relations of production in class society in general.

Since the particular is united with the universal and since the universality as well as the particularity of contradiction is inherent in everything, universality residing in particularity, we should, when studying an object, try to discover both the particular and the universal and their interconnection, to discover both particularity and universality and also their interconnection within the object itself, and to discover the interconnections of this object with the many objects outside it. When Stalin explained the historical roots of Leninism in his famous work, *The Foundations of Leninism*, he analysed the international situation in which Leninism arose, analysed those contradictions of capitalism which reached their culmination under imperialism, and showed how these contradictions made proletarian revolution a matter for immediate action and created favourable conditions for a direct onslaught on capitalism. What is more, he analysed the reasons why Russia became the cradle of Leninism, why tsarist Russia became the focus of all the contradictions of imperialism, and why it was possible for the Russian proletariat to become the vanguard of the international revolutionary proletariat. Thus, Stalin analysed the universality of contradiction in imperialism, showing why Leninism is the Marxism of the era of imperialism and proletarian revolution, and at the same time analysed the particularity of tsarist Russian imperialism within this general contradiction, showing why Russia became the birthplace of the theory and tactics of proletarian revolution and how the universality of contradiction is contained in this particularity. Stalin's analysis provides us with a model for understanding the particularity and the universality of contradiction and their interconnection.

On the question of using dialectics in the study of objective phenomena, Marx and Engels, and likewise Lenin and Stalin, always enjoin people not to be in any way subjective and arbitrary but, from the concrete conditions in the actual objective movement of these phenomena, to discover their concrete contradictions, the concrete position of each aspect of every contradiction and the concrete interrelations of the contradictions. Our dogmatists do not have this attitude in study and therefore can never get anything right. We must take warning from their failure and learn to acquire this attitude, which is the only correct one in study.

The relationship between the universality and the particularity of contradiction is the relationship between the general character and the individual character of contradiction. By the former we mean that contradiction exists in and runs through all processes from beginning to end; motion, things, processes, thinking — all are contradictions. To deny contradiction is to deny everything. This is a universal truth for all times and all countries, which admits of no exception. Hence the general character, the absoluteness of contradiction. But this general character is contained in every individual character; without individual character there can be no general character. If all individual character were removed, what general character would remain? It is because each contradiction is particular that individual character arises. All individual character exists conditionally and temporarily, and hence is relative.

This truth concerning general and individual character, concerning absoluteness and relativity, is the quintessence of the problem of contradiction in things; failure to understand it is tantamount to abandoning dialectics.

IV. THE PRINCIPAL CONTRADICTION AND THE PRINCIPAL ASPECT OF A CONTRADICTION

There are still two points in the problem of the particularity of contradiction which must be singled out for analysis, namely, the principal contradiction and the principal aspect of a contradiction.

There are many contradictions in the process of development of a complex thing, and one of them is necessarily the principal contradiction whose existence and development determine or influence the existence and development of the other contradictions.

For instance, in capitalist society the two forces in contradiction, the proletariat and the bourgeoisie, form the principal contradiction. The other contradictions, such as those between the remnant feudal class and the bourgeoisie, between the peasant petty bourgeoisie and the bourgeoisie, between the proletariat and the peasant petty bourgeoisie, between the non-monopoly capitalists and the monopoly capitalists, between bourgeois democracy and bourgeois fascism, among the capitalist countries and between imperialism and the colonies, are all determined or influenced by this principal contradiction.

In a semi-colonial country such as China, the relationship between the principal contradiction and the non-principal contradictions presents a complicated picture.

When imperialism launches a war of aggression against such a country, all its various classes, except for some traitors, can temporarily unite in a national war against imperialism. At such a time, the contradiction between imperialism and the country concerned becomes the principal contradiction, while all the contradictions among the various classes within the country (including what was the principal contradiction, between the feudal system and the great masses of the people) are temporarily relegated to a secondary and subordinate position. So it was in China in the Opium War of 1840, the Sino-Japanese War of 1894 and the Yi Ho Tuan War of 1900, and so it is now in the present Sino-Japanese War.

But in another situation, the contradictions change position. When imperialism carries on its oppression not by war, but by milder means — political, economic and cultural — the ruling classes in semi-colonial countries capitulate to imperialism, and the two form an alliance for the joint oppression of the masses of the people. At such a time, the masses often resort to civil war against the alliance of imperialism and the feudal classes, while imperialism often employs indirect methods rather than direct action in helping the reactionaries in the semi-colonial countries to oppress the people, and thus the internal contradictions become particularly sharp. This is what happened in China in the Revolutionary War of 1911, the Revolutionary War of 1924-27, and the ten years of Agrarian Revolutionary War after 1927. Wars among the various reactionary ruling groups in the semi-colonial countries, e.g., the wars among the warlords in China, fall into the same category.

When a revolutionary civil war develops to the point of threatening the very existence of imperialism and its running dogs, the domestic reactionaries, imperialism often adopts other methods in order to maintain its rule; it either tries to split the revolutionary front from within or sends armed forces to help the domestic reactionaries directly. At such a time, foreign imperialism and domestic reaction stand quite openly at one pole while the masses of the people stand at the other pole, thus forming the principal contradiction which determines or influences the development of the other contradictions. The assistance given by various capitalist countries to the Russian reactionaries after the October Revolution is an example of armed intervention. Chiang Kai-shek's betrayal in 1927 is an example of splitting the revolutionary front.

But whatever happens, there is no doubt at all that at every stage in the development of a process, there is only one principal contradiction which plays the leading role.

Hence, if in any process there are a number of contradictions, one of them must be the principal contradiction playing the leading and decisive role, while the rest occupy a secondary and subordinate position. Therefore, in studying any complex process in which there are two or more contradictions, we must devote every effort to finding its principal contradiction. Once this principal contradiction is grasped, all problems can be readily solved. This is the method Marx taught us in his study of capitalist society. Likewise Lenin and Stalin taught us this method when they studied imperialism and the general crisis of capitalism and when they studied the Soviet economy. There are thousands of scholars and men of action who do not understand it, and the result is that, lost in a fog, they are unable to get to the heart of a problem and naturally cannot find a way to resolve its contradictions.

As we have said, one must not treat all the contradictions in a process as being equal but must distinguish between the principal and the secondary contradictions, and pay special attention to grasping the principal one. But, in any given contradiction, whether principal or secondary, should the two contradictory aspects be treated as equal? Again, no. In any contradiction the development of the contradictory aspects is uneven. Sometimes they seem to be in equilibrium, which is however only temporary and relative, while unevenness is basic. Of the two contradictory aspects, one must be principal and the other secondary. The principal aspect is the one playing the leading role in the contradiction. The nature of a thing is determined mainly by the principal aspect of a contradiction, the aspect which has gained the dominant position.

But this situation is not static; the principal and the non-principal aspects of a contradiction transform themselves into each other and the nature of the thing changes accordingly. In a given process or at a given stage in the development of a contradiction, A is the principal aspect and B is the non-principal aspect; at another stage or in another process the roles are reversed — a change determined by the extent of the increase or decrease in the force of each aspect in its struggle against the other in the course of the development of a thing.

We often speak of "the new superseding the old". The supersession of the old by the new is a general, eternal and inviolable law of the universe. The transformation of one thing into another, through leaps of different forms in accordance with its essence and external conditions — this is the process of the new superseding the old. In each thing there is contradiction between its new and its old aspects, and this gives rise to a series of struggles with many twists and turns. As a result of these struggles, the new aspect changes from being minor to being major and rises to predominance, while the old aspect changes from being major to being minor and gradually dies out. And the moment the new aspect gains dominance over the old, the old thing changes qualitatively into a new thing. It can thus be seen that the nature of a thing is mainly determined by the principal aspect of the contradiction, the aspect which has gained predominance. When the principal aspect which has gained predominance changes, the nature of a thing changes accordingly.

In capitalist society, capitalism has changed its position from being a subordinate force in the old feudal era to being the dominant force, and the nature of society has accordingly changed from feudal

to capitalist. In the new, capitalist era, the feudal forces changed from
their former dominant position to a subordinate one, gradually dying
out. Such was the case, for example, in Britain and France. With the
development of the productive forces, the bourgeoisie changes from
being a new class playing a progressive role to being an old class
playing a reactionary role, until it is finally overthrown by the proletariat and becomes a class deprived of privately owned means of
production and stripped of power, when it, too, gradually dies out.
The proletariat, which is much more numerous than the bourgeoisie
and grows simultaneously with it but under its rule, is a new force
which, initially subordinate to the bourgeoisie, gradually gains strength,
becomes an independent class playing the leading role in history,
and finally seizes political power and becomes the ruling class. Thereupon the nature of society changes and the old capitalist society becomes the new socialist society. This is the path already taken by the
Soviet Union, a path that all other countries will inevitably take.

Look at China, for instance. Imperialism occupies the principal
position in the contradiction in which China has been reduced to a
semi-colony, it oppresses the Chinese people, and China has been
changed from an independent country into a semi-colonial one. But
this state of affairs will inevitably change; in the struggle between
the two sides, the power of the Chinese people which is growing under
the leadership of the proletariat will inevitably change China from a
semi-colony into an independent country, whereas imperialism will be
overthrown and old China will inevitably change into New China.

The change of old China into New China also involves a change
in the relation between the old feudal forces and the new popular
forces within the country. The old feudal landlord class will be
overthrown, and from being the ruler it will change into being the
ruled; and this class, too, will gradually die out. From being the
ruled the people, led by the proletariat, will become the rulers.
Thereupon, the nature of Chinese society will change and the old,
semi-colonial and semi-feudal society will change into a new democratic society.

Instances of such reciprocal transformation are found in our past
experience. The Ching Dynasty which ruled China for nearly three
hundred years was overthrown in the Revolution of 1911, and the
revolutionary *Tung Meng Hui* under Sun Yat-sen's leadership was
victorious for a time. In the Revolutionary War of 1924-27, the revolutionary forces of the Communist-Kuomintang alliance in the south

changed from being weak to being strong and won victory in the Northern Expedition, while the Northern warlords who once ruled the roost were overthrown. In 1927, the people's forces led by the Communist Party were greatly reduced numerically under the attacks of Kuomintang reaction, but with the elimination of opportunism within their ranks they gradually grew again. In the revolutionary base areas under Communist leadership, the peasants have been transformed from being the ruled to being the rulers, while the landlords have undergone a reverse transformation. It is always so in the world, the new displacing the old, the old being superseded by the new, the old being eliminated to make way for the new, and the new emerging out of the old.

At certain times in the revolutionary struggle, the difficulties outweigh the favourable conditions and so constitute the principal aspect of the contradiction and the favourable conditions constitute the secondary aspect. But through their efforts the revolutionaries can overcome the difficulties step by step and open up a favourable new situation; thus a difficult situation yields place to a favourable one. This is what happened after the failure of the revolution in China in 1927 and during the Long March of the Chinese Red Army. In the present Sino-Japanese War, China is again in a difficult position, but we can change this and fundamentally transform the situation as between China and Japan. Conversely, favourable conditions can be transformed into difficulty if the revolutionaries make mistakes. Thus the victory of the revolution of 1924-27 turned into defeat. The revolutionary base areas which grew up in the southern provinces after 1927 had all suffered defeat by 1934.

When we engage in study, the same holds good for the contradiction in the passage from ignorance to knowledge. At the very beginning of our study of Marxism, our ignorance of or scanty acquaintance with Marxism stands in contradiction to knowledge of Marxism. But by assiduous study, ignorance can be transformed into knowledge, scanty knowledge into substantial knowledge, and blindness in the application of Marxism into mastery of its application.

Some people think that this is not true of certain contradictions. For instance, in the contradiction between the productive forces and the relations of production, the productive forces are the principal aspect; in the contradiction between theory and practice, practice is the principal aspect; in the contradiction between the economic base and the superstructure, the economic base is the principal aspect;

and there is no change in their respective positions. This is the mechanical materialist conception, not the dialectical materialist conception. True, the productive forces, practice and the economic base generally play the principal and decisive role; whoever denies this is not a materialist. But it must also be admitted that in certain conditions, such aspects as the relations of production, theory and the superstructure in turn manifest themselves in the principal and decisive role. When it is impossible for the productive forces to develop without a change in the relations of production, then the change in the relations of production plays the principal and decisive role. The creation and advocacy of revolutionary theory plays the principal and decisive role in those times of which Lenin said, "Without revolutionary theory there can be no revolutionary movement."[15] When a task, no matter which, has to be performed, but there is as yet no guiding line, method, plan or policy, the principal and decisive thing is to decide on a guiding line, method, plan or policy. When the superstructure (politics, culture, etc.) obstructs the development of the economic base, political and cultural changes become principal and decisive. Are we going against materialism when we say this? No. The reason is that while we recognize that in the general development of history the material determines the mental and social being determines social consciousness, we also — and indeed must — recognize the reaction of mental on material things, of social consciousness on social being and of the superstructure on the economic base. This does not go against materialism; on the contrary, it avoids mechanical materialism and firmly upholds dialectical materialism.

In studying the particularity of contradiction, unless we examine these two facets — the principal and the non-principal contradictions in a process, and the principal and the non-principal aspects of a contradiction — that is, unless we examine the distinctive character of these two facets of contradiction, we shall get bogged down in abstractions, be unable to understand contradiction concretely and consequently be unable to find the correct method of resolving it. The distinctive character or particularity of these two facets of contradiction represents the unevenness of the forces that are in contradiction. Nothing in this world develops absolutely evenly; we must oppose the theory of even development or the theory of equilibrium. Moreover, it is these concrete features of a contradiction and the changes in the principal and non-principal aspects of a contradiction in the course of its development that manifest the force of the new superseding the old. The study of the various states of unevenness in contradictions, of the principal and non-principal contradictions and of the principal and the non-principal aspects of a contradiction constitutes an essential method by which a revolutionary political party correctly determines its strategic and tactical policies both in political and in military affairs. All Communists must give it attention.

V. THE IDENTITY AND STRUGGLE OF THE ASPECTS OF A CONTRADICTION

When we understand the universality and the particularity of contradiction, we must proceed to study the problem of the identity and struggle of the aspects of a contradiction.

Identity, unity, coincidence, interpenetration, interpermeation, interdependence (or mutual dependence for existence), interconnection or mutual co-operation — all these different terms mean the same thing and refer to the following two points: first, the existence of each of the two aspects of a contradiction in the process of the development of a thing presupposes the existence of the other aspect, and both aspects coexist in a single entity; second, in given conditions, each of the two contradictory aspects transforms itself into its opposite. This is the meaning of identity.

Lenin said:

> *Dialectics* is the teaching which shows how *opposites* can be and how they happen to be (how they become) *identical* — under what conditions they are identical, transforming themselves into one another, — why the human mind should take these opposites not as dead, rigid, but as living, conditional, mobile, transforming themselves into one another.[16]

What does this passage mean?

The contradictory aspects in every process exclude each other, struggle with each other and are in opposition to each other. Without exception, they are contained in the process of development of all things and in all human thought. A simple process contains only a single pair of opposites, while a complex process contains more. And in turn, the pairs of opposites are in contradiction to one another.

That is how all things in the objective world and all human thought
are constituted and how they are set in motion.

This being so, there is an utter lack of identity or unity. How then
can one speak of identity or unity?

The fact is that no contradictory aspect can exist in isolation.
Without its opposite aspect, each loses the condition for its existence.
Just think, can any one contradictory aspect of a thing or of a concept
in the human mind exist independently? Without life, there would
be no death; without death, there would be no life. Without "above",
there would be no "below"; without "below", there would be no
"above". Without misfortune, there would be no good fortune; without good fortune, there would be no misfortune. Without facility,
there would be no difficulty; without difficulty, there would be no
facility. Without landlords, there would be no tenant-peasants; without tenant-peasants, there would be no landlords. Without the bourgeoisie, there would be no proletariat; without the proletariat, there
would be no bourgeoisie. Without imperialist oppression of nations,
there would be no colonies or semi-colonies; without colonies or semi-
colonies, there would be no imperialist oppression of nations. It is
so with all opposites; in given conditions, on the one hand they are
opposed to each other, and on the other they are interconnected,
interpenetrating, interpermeating and interdependent, and this character is described as identity. In given conditions, all contradictory
aspects possess the character of non-identity and hence are described
as being in contradiction. But they also possess the character of identity
and hence are interconnected. This is what Lenin means when he
says that dialectics studies "how *opposites* can be . . . *identical*".
How then can they be identical? Because each is the condition for the
other's existence. This is the first meaning of identity.

But is it enough to say merely that each of the contradictory aspects
is the condition for the other's existence, that there is identity between
them and that consequently they can coexist in a single entity? No,
it is not. The matter does not end with their dependence on each
other for their existence; what is more important is their transformation into each other. That is to say, in given conditions, each of the
contradictory aspects within a thing transforms itself into its opposite,
changes its position to that of its opposite. This is the second meaning
of the identity of contradiction.

Why is there identity here, too? You see, by means of revolution
the proletariat, at one time the ruled, is transformed into the ruler,

while the bourgeoisie, the erstwhile ruler, is transformed into the ruled and changes its position to that originally occupied by its opposite. This has already taken place in the Soviet Union, as it will take place throughout the world. If there were no interconnection and identity of opposites in given conditions, how could such a change take place?

The Kuomintang, which played a certain positive role at a certain stage in modern Chinese history, became a counter-revolutionary party after 1927 because of its inherent class nature and because of imperialist blandishments (these being the conditions); but it has been compelled to agree to resist Japan because of the sharpening of the contradiction between China and Japan and because of the Communist Party's policy of the united front (these being the conditions). Things in contradiction change into one another, and herein lies a definite identity.

Our agrarian revolution has been a process in which the landlord class owning the land is transformed into a class that has lost its land, while the peasants who once lost their land are transformed into small holders who have acquired land, and it will be such a process once again. In given conditions having and not having, acquiring and losing, are interconnected; there is identity of the two sides. Under socialism, private peasant ownership is transformed into the public ownership of socialist agriculture; this has already taken place in the Soviet Union, as it will take place everywhere else. There is a bridge leading from private property to public property, which in philosophy is called identity, or transformation into each other, or interpenetration.

To consolidate the dictatorship of the proletariat or the dictatorship of the people is in fact to prepare the conditions for abolishing this dictatorship and advancing to the higher stage when all state systems are eliminated. To establish and build the Communist Party is in fact to prepare the conditions for the elimination of the Communist Party and all political parties. To build a revolutionary army under the leadership of the Communist Party and to carry on revolutionary war is in fact to prepare the conditions for the permanent elimination of war. These opposites are at the same time complementary.

War and peace, as everybody knows, transform themselves into each other. War is transformed into peace; for instance, the First World War was transformed into the post-war peace, and the civil war in China has now stopped, giving place to internal peace. Peace is transformed into war; for instance, the Kuomintang-Communist co-operation was transformed into war in 1927, and today's situation of world peace may be transformed into a second world war. Why is this so? Because in class society such contradictory things as war and peace have an identity in given conditions.

All contradictory things are interconnected; not only do they coexist in a single entity in given conditions, but in other given conditions, they also transform themselves into each other. This is the full meaning of the identity of opposites. This is what Lenin meant when he discussed "how they happen to be (how they become) *identical* — under what conditions they are identical, transforming themselves into one another".

Why is it that "the human mind should take these opposites not as dead, rigid, but as living, conditional, mobile, transforming themselves into one another"? Because that is just how things are in objective reality. The fact is that the unity or identity of opposites in objective things is not dead or rigid, but is living, conditional, mobile, temporary and relative; in given conditions, every contradictory aspect transforms itself into its opposite. Reflected in man's thinking, this becomes the Marxist world outlook of materialist dialectics. It is only the reactionary ruling classes of the past and present and the metaphysicians in their service who regard opposites not as living, conditional, mobile and transforming themselves into one another, but as dead and rigid, and they propagate this fallacy everywhere to delude the masses of the people, thus seeking to perpetuate their rule. The task of Communists is to expose the fallacies of the reactionaries and metaphysicians, to propagate the dialectics inherent in things, and so accelerate the transformation of things and achieve the goal of revolution.

In speaking of the identity of opposites in given conditions, what we are referring to is real and concrete opposites and the real and concrete transformations of opposites into one another. There are innumerable transformations in mythology, for instance, Kua Fu's race with the sun in *Shan Hai Ching*,[17] Yi's shooting down of nine suns in *Huai Nan Tzu*,[18] the Monkey King's seventy-two metamorphoses in *Hsi Yu Chi*,[19] the numerous episodes of ghosts and foxes metamorphosed into human beings in the *Strange Tales of Liao Chai*,[20] etc. But these legendary transformations of opposites are not concrete changes reflecting concrete contradictions. They are naive, imaginary, subjectively conceived transformations conjured up in men's minds by innumerable real and complex transformations of opposites into one another. Marx said, "All mythology masters and dominates and shapes the forces of nature in and through the imagination; hence it disappears as soon as man gains mastery over the forces of nature."[21] The myriads of changes in mythology (and also in nursery tales) delight people because they imaginatively picture man's conquest of the forces of nature, and the best myths possess "eternal charm", as Marx put it; but myths are not built out of the concrete contradictions existing in given conditions and therefore are not a scientific reflection of reality. That is to say, in myths or nursery tales the aspects constituting a contradiction have only an imaginary identity, not a concrete identity. The scientific reflection of the identity in real transformations is Marxist dialectics.

Why can an egg but not a stone be transformed into a chicken? Why is there identity between war and peace and none between war and a stone? Why can human beings give birth only to human beings and not to anything else? The sole reason is that the identity of opposites exists only in necessary given conditions. Without these necessary given conditions there can be no identity whatsoever.

Why is it that in Russia in 1917 the bourgeois-democratic February Revolution was directly linked with the proletarian socialist October Revolution, while in France the bourgeois revolution was not directly linked with a socialist revolution and the Paris Commune of 1871 ended in failure? Why is it, on the other hand, that the nomadic system of Mongolia and Central Asia has been directly linked with socialism? Why is it that the Chinese revolution can avoid a capitalist future and be directly linked with socialism without taking the old historical road of the Western countries, without passing through a period of bourgeois dictatorship? The sole reason is the concrete conditions of the time. When certain necessary conditions are present, certain contradictions arise in the process of development of things and, moreover, the opposites contained in them are interdependent and become transformed into one another; otherwise none of this would be possible.

Such is the problem of identity. What then is struggle? And what is the relation between identity and struggle?

Lenin said:

> The unity (coincidence, identity, equal action) of opposites is conditional, temporary, transitory, relative. The struggle of

mutually exclusive opposites is absolute, just as development and
motion are absolute.[22]

What does this passage mean?

All processes have a beginning and an end, all processes transform
themselves into their opposites. The constancy of all processes is relative, but the mutability manifested in the transformation of one
process into another is absolute.

There are two states of motion in all things, that of relative rest
and that of conspicuous change. Both are caused by the struggle
between the two contradictory elements contained in a thing. When
the thing is in the first state of motion, it is undergoing only quantitative and not qualitative change and consequently presents the out-
ward appearance of being at rest. When the thing is in the second
state of motion, the quantitative change of the first state has already
reached a culminating point and gives rise to the dissolution of the
thing as an entity and thereupon a qualitative change ensues, hence
the appearance of a conspicuous change. Such unity, solidarity,
combination, harmony, balance, stalemate, deadlock, rest, constancy,
equilibrium, solidity, attraction, etc., as we see in daily life, are all
the appearances of things in the state of quantitative change. On the
other hand, the dissolution of unity, that is, the destruction of this
solidarity, combination, harmony, balance, stalemate, deadlock, rest,
constancy, equilibrium, solidity and attraction, and the change of
each into its opposite are all the appearances of things in the state
of qualitative change, the transformation of one process into another.
Things are constantly transforming themselves from the first into
the second state of motion; the struggle of opposites goes on in both
states but the contradiction is resolved through the second state.
That is why we say that the unity of opposites is conditional, temporary and relative, while the struggle of mutually exclusive opposites
is absolute.

When we said above that two opposite things can coexist in a
single entity and can transform themselves into each other because
there is identity between them, we were speaking of conditionality,
that is to say, in given conditions two contradictory things can be
united and can transform themselves into each other, but in the absence
of these conditions, they cannot constitute a contradiction, cannot
coexist in the same entity and cannot transform themselves into one
another. It is because the identity of opposites obtains only in given

conditions that we have said identity is conditional and relative. We may add that the struggle between opposites permeates a process from beginning to end and makes one process transform itself into another, that it is ubiquitous, and that struggle is therefore unconditional and absolute.

The combination of conditional, relative identity and unconditional, absolute struggle constitutes the movement of opposites in all things.

We Chinese often say, "Things that oppose each other also complement each other."[23] That is, things opposed to each other have identity. This saying is dialectical and contrary to metaphysics. "Oppose each other" refers to the mutual exclusion or the struggle of two contradictory aspects. "Complement each other" means that in given conditions the two contradictory aspects unite and achieve identity. Yet struggle is inherent in identity and without struggle there can be no identity.

In identity there is struggle, in particularity there is universality, and in individuality there is generality. To quote Lenin, ". . . there *is* an absolute *in* the relative."[24]

VI. THE PLACE OF ANTAGONISM IN CONTRADICTION

The question of the struggle of opposites includes the question of what is antagonism. Our answer is that antagonism is one form, but not the only form, of the struggle of opposites.

In human history, antagonism between classes exists as a particular manifestation of the struggle of opposites. Consider the contradiction between the exploiting and the exploited classes. Such contradictory classes coexist for a long time in the same society, be it slave society, feudal society or capitalist society, and they struggle with each other; but it is not until the contradiction between the two classes develops to a certain stage that it assumes the form of open antagonism and develops into revolution. The same holds for the transformation of peace into war in class society.

Before it explodes, a bomb is a single entity in which opposites coexist in given conditions. The explosion takes place only when a new condition, ignition, is present. An analogous situation arises in all those natural phenomena which finally assume the form of open conflict to resolve old contradictions and produce new things.

It is highly important to grasp this fact. It enables us to understand that revolutions and revolutionary wars are inevitable in class
society and that without them, it is impossible to accomplish any
leap in social development and to overthrow the reactionary ruling
classes and therefore impossible for the people to win political power.
Communists must expose the deceitful propaganda of the reactionaries, such as the assertion that social revolution is unnecessary and
impossible. They must firmly uphold the Marxist-Leninist theory of
social revolution and enable the people to understand that social
revolution is not only entirely necessary but also entirely practicable,
and that the whole history of mankind and the triumph of the Soviet
Union have confirmed this scientific truth.

However, we must make a concrete study of the circumstances
of each specific struggle of opposites and should not arbitrarily apply
the formula discussed above to everything. Contradiction and struggle are universal and absolute, but the methods of resolving contradictions, that is, the forms of struggle, differ according to the
differences in the nature of the contradictions. Some contradictions
are characterized by open antagonism, others are not. In accordance with the concrete development of things, some contradictions
which were originally non-antagonistic develop into antagonistic ones,
while others which were originally antagonistic develop into non-
antagonistic ones.

As already mentioned, so long as classes exist, contradictions
between correct and incorrect ideas in the Communist Party are
reflections within the Party of class contradictions. At first, with
regard to certain issues, such contradictions may not manifest themselves as antagonistic. But with the development of the class struggle,
they may grow and become antagonistic. The history of the Communist Party of the Soviet Union shows us that the contradictions
between the correct thinking of Lenin and Stalin and the fallacious
thinking of Trotsky, Bukharin and others did not at first manifest
themselves in an antagonistic form, but that later they did develop
into antagonism. There are similar cases in the history of the Chinese
Communist Party. At first the contradictions between the correct
thinking of many of our Party comrades and the fallacious thinking
of Chen Tu-hsiu, Chang Kuo-tao and others also did not manifest
themselves in an antagonistic form, but later they did develop into
antagonism. At present the contradiction between correct and incorrect thinking in our Party does not manifest itself in an antago-

nistic form, and if comrades who have committed mistakes can correct them, it will not develop into antagonism. Therefore, the Party must on the one hand wage a serious struggle against erroneous thinking, and on the other give the comrades who have committed errors ample opportunity to wake up. This being the case, excessive struggle is obviously inappropriate. But if the people who have committed errors persist in them and aggravate them, there is the possibility that this contradiction will develop into antagonism.

Economically, the contradiction between town and country is an extremely antagonistic one both in capitalist society, where under the rule of the bourgeoisie the towns ruthlessly plunder the countryside, and in the Kuomintang areas in China, where under the rule of foreign imperialism and the Chinese big comprador bourgeoisie the towns most rapaciously plunder the countryside. But in a socialist country and in our revolutionary base areas, this antagonistic contradiction has changed into one that is non-antagonistic; and when communist society is reached it will be abolished.

Lenin said, "Antagonism and contradiction are not at all one and the same. Under socialism, the first will disappear, the second will remain."[25] That is to say, antagonism is one form, but not the only form, of the struggle of opposites; the formula of antagonism cannot be arbitrarily applied everywhere.

VII. CONCLUSION

We may now say a few words to sum up. The law of contradiction in things, that is, the law of the unity of opposites, is the fundamental law of nature and of society and therefore also the fundamental law of thought. It stands opposed to the metaphysical world outlook. It represents a great revolution in the history of human knowledge. According to dialectical materialism, contradiction is present in all processes of objectively existing things and of subjective thought and permeates all these processes from beginning to end; this is the universality and absoluteness of contradiction. Each contradiction and each of its aspects have their respective characteristics; this is the particularity and relativity of contradiction. In given conditions, opposites possess identity, and consequently can coexist in a single entity and can transform themselves into each other; this again is the particularity and relativity of contradiction. But the struggle of opposites is ceaseless, it goes on both when the opposites are coexisting and when they are transforming themselves into each other, and becomes especially conspicuous when they are transforming themselves into one another; this again is the universality and absoluteness of contradiction. In studying the particularity and relativity of contradiction, we must give attention to the distinction between the principal contradiction and the non-principal contradictions and to the distinction between the principal aspect and the non-principal aspect of a contradiction; in studying the universality of contradiction and the struggle of opposites in contradiction, we must give attention to the distinction between the different forms of struggle. Otherwise we shall make mistakes. If, through study, we achieve a real understanding of the essentials explained above, we shall be able to demolish dogmatist ideas which are contrary to the basic principles of Marxism-Leninism and detrimental to our revolutionary cause, and our comrades with practical experience will be able to organize their experience into principles and avoid repeating empiricist errors. These are a few simple conclusions from our study of the law of contradiction.

NOTES

[1] V. I. Lenin, "Conspectus of Hegel's *Lectures on the History of Philosophy*", *Collected Works*, Russ. ed., Moscow, 1958, Vol. XXXVIII, p. 249.

[2] In his essay "On the Question of Dialectics", Lenin said, "The splitting in two of a single whole and the cognition of its contradictory parts (see the quotation from Philo on Heraclitus at the beginning of Section 3 'On Cognition' in Lassalle's book on Heraclitus) is the *essence* (one of the 'essentials', one of the principal, if not the principal, characteristics or features) of dialectics." (*Collected Works*, Russ. ed., Moscow, 1958, Vol. XXXVIII, p. 357.) In his "Conspectus of Hegel's *The Science of Logic*", he said, "In brief, dialectics can be defined as the doctrine of the unity of opposites. This grasps the kernel of dialectics, but it requires explanations and development." (*Ibid.*, p. 215.)

[3] V. I. Lenin, "On the Question of Dialectics", *Collected Works*, Russ. ed., Moscow, 1958, Vol. XXXVIII, p. 358.

[4] A saying of Tung Chung-shu (179-104 B.C.), a well-known exponent of Confucianism in the Han Dynasty.

[5] Frederick Engels, "Dialectics. Quantity and Quality", *Anti-Dühring*, Eng. ed., FLPH, Moscow, 1959, p. 166.

[6] V. I. Lenin, "On the Question of Dialectics", *Collected Works*, Russ. ed., Moscow, 1958, Vol. XXXVIII, pp. 357-58.

[7] Frederick Engels, *op. cit.*, pp. 166-67.

[8] V. I. Lenin, "On the Question of Dialectics", *Collected Works*, Russ. ed., Moscow, 1958, Vol. XXXVIII, p. 357.

[9] *Ibid.*, pp. 358-59.

[10] See "Problems of Strategy in China's Revolutionary War", Note 10, p. 251 of this volume.

[11] See *ibid.*, Note 2, p. 249 of this volume.

[12] Wei Cheng (A.D. 580-643) was a statesman and historian of the Tang Dynasty.

[13] *Shui Hu Chuan (Heroes of the Marshes)*, a famous 14th century Chinese novel, describes a peasant war towards the end of the Northern Sung Dynasty. Chu Village was in the vicinity of Liangshanpo, where Sung Chiang, leader of the peasant uprising and hero of the novel, established his base. Chu Chao-feng, the head of this village, was a despotic landlord.

[14] V. I. Lenin, "Once Again on the Trade Unions, the Present Situation and the Mistakes of Trotsky and Bukharin", *Selected Works*, Eng. ed., International Publishers, New York, 1943, Vol. IX, p. 66.

[15] V. I. Lenin, "What Is to Be Done?", *Collected Works*, Eng. ed., FLPH, Moscow, 1961, Vol. V, p. 369.

[16] V. I. Lenin, "Conspectus of Hegel's *The Science of Logic*", *Collected Works*, Russ. ed., Moscow, 1958, Vol. XXXVIII, pp. 97-98.

[17] *Shan Hai Ching (Book of Mountains and Seas)* was written in the era of the Warring States (403-221 B.C.). In one of its fables Kua Fu, a superman, pursued and overtook the sun. But he died of thirst, whereupon his staff was transformed into the forest of Teng.

[18] Yi is one of the legendary heroes of ancient China, famous for his archery. According to a legend in *Huai Nan Tzu*, compiled in the 2nd century B.C., there were ten suns in the sky in the days of Emperor Yao. To put an end to the damage to vegetation caused by these scorching suns, Emperor Yao ordered Yi to shoot them down. In another legend recorded by Wang Yi (2nd century A.D.), the archer is said to have shot down nine of the ten suns.

[19] *Hsi Yu Chi (Pilgrimage to the West)* is a 16th century novel, the hero of which is the monkey god Sun Wu-kung. He could miraculously change at will into seventy-two different shapes, such as a bird, a tree and a stone.

[20] The *Strange Tales of Liao Chai*, written by Pu Sung-ling in the 17th century, is a well-known collection of 431 tales, mostly about ghosts and fox spirits.

[21] Karl Marx, "Introduction to the Critique of Political Economy", *A Contribution to the Critique of Political Economy*, Eng. ed., Chicago, 1904, pp. 310-11.

[22] V. I. Lenin, "On the Question of Dialectics", *Collected Works*, Russ. ed., Moscow, 1958, Vol. XXXVIII, p. 358.

[23] The saying "Things that oppose each other also complement each other" first appeared in the *History of the Earlier Han Dynasty* by Pan Ku, a celebrated historian in the 1st century A.D. It has long been a popular saying.

[24] V. I. Lenin, "On the Question of Dialectics", *Collected Works*, Russ. ed., Moscow, 1958, Vol. XXXVIII, p. 358.

[25] V. I. Lenin, "Remarks on N. I. Bukharin's *Economics of the Transitional Period*", *Selected Works*, Russ. ed., Moscow-Leningrad, 1931, Vol. XI, p. 357.

毛 泽 东 选 集

第 一 卷

*

外文出版社出版（北京）

一九六五年第一版

一九六七年第二次印刷

编号：（英）1050—289